DO IT YOURSELF

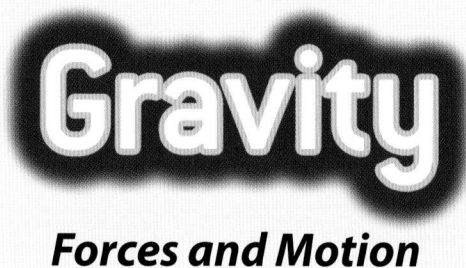

Gravity

Forces and Motion

Rachel Lynette

Heinemann Library

Chicago, Illinois

© 2008 Heinemann Library
a division of Pearson Inc.
Chicago, Illinois

Customer Service 888-454-2279

Visit our website at www.heinemannraintree.com

Designed by Richard Parker and Tinstar Design Ltd, www.tinstar.co.uk

Printed and bound in China by Leo Paper Group.

12 11 10 09 08
10 9 8 7 6 5 4 3 2 1

Library of Congress Cataloging-in-Publication Data
Lynette, Rachel.
  Gravity : forces and motion / Rachel Lynette.
    p. cm. -- (Do it yourself science)
  Includes bibliographical references and index.
  ISBN 978-1-4329-1096-9 (hbk) -- ISBN 978-1-4329-1112-6 (pbk) 1. Rotational motion--Juvenile
literature. 2. Force and energy--Juvenile literature. 3. Gravity--Juvenile literature. I. Title.
  QC133.5.L96 2008
  531'.14078--dc22
                    2007050747

Acknowledgments
The publishers would like to thank the following for permission to reproduce photographs:
©Alamy pp. **9** (Oleksiy Maksymenko), **10** (Leslie Garland Picture Library), **12** (Shenval),
15 (imagebroker), **17** (Davo Blair), **21** (David R. Frazier Photolibrary, Inc.), **40** (Brand X/Jupiterimages)
43 (I love images); ©Alan Bean p. **7**; ©Bridgeman Art Library p. **13** (Bibliotheque des Arts Decoratifs,
Paris, France/ Archives Charmet); ©Comstock Images p. **41**; ©Corbis pp. **11** (David Brooks),
19 (Eye Ubiquitous/ Nick Wiseman), **29** (zefa/Ruediger Knobloch/A.B.), **35** (Kevin Fleming),
37 (zefa/Ole Graf), **39** (Galen Rowell), **25** Corbis Royalty Free; ©Getty Images pp. **4** (Philip Lee
Harvey), **20** (Time & Life Pictures), **24** (Chad Baker), **30** (David Madison), **31** (Peter Gridley); ©NASA
pp. **5**, **42**; ©Vilac p. **23**.

Cover photograph of male teenager swinging reproduced with permission of ©Corbis/zefa/Ole Graf.

The publishers would like to thank Ann Fullick for her help in the preparation of this book.

4127

Contents

Any words appearing in the text in bold, **like this**, are explained in the glossary.

Drawn Together

When you jump up, why do you come back down instead of just floating away? The answer is an invisible **force** called gravity. Gravity keeps you, and everything else, on Earth. Gravity pulls all **matter** together. Matter is everything that takes up space or can be weighed. This book, you, and even the air are all made of matter. The more matter something has, the more **mass** it has. For example, a bowling ball has more mass than a baseball because it is made of more matter than a baseball.

Gravity will bring this girl back to Earth again.

Because Earth is so massive, it has a great deal of **gravitational force**. That is why everything on Earth stays on Earth—Earth's gravity pulls everything toward itself. The more mass something has, the stronger Earth's gravitational force will be on it. That is why it is harder to pick up a bowling ball than it is to pick up a baseball. The bowling ball has more mass than the baseball, so the gravitational force pulling it toward Earth is stronger.

Beyond Earth

If you could take a bowling ball to the Moon, you would find that it would feel much lighter there than on Earth. That is because the Moon has less mass than Earth, so its gravitational force is also less. If you were on the Moon, you would weigh one-sixth of what you weigh on Earth. That is why astronauts on the Moon can take giant, leaping steps.

If you could take a baseball to Jupiter, it would feel much heavier. That is because Jupiter has more mass than Earth. If you were on Jupiter, you would weigh almost two times what you do on Earth!

Isaac and the apple

In 1666 Sir Isaac Newton saw an apple fall from a tree in his garden. He started thinking about why the apple was drawn to the ground. He soon realized that an invisible force was pulling the apple down. That force was gravity.

There is less gravity on the Moon than on Earth.

Gravity at Work

Steps to follow

The way things fall

For this experiment you will need:

* Several balls and marbles of different sizes and **weights**
* A cookie sheet
* Modeling clay or play dough
* A rolling pin.

1 Roll the clay into a flat rectangle about as big as your cookie sheet. The clay should be about as thick as your thumb.

2 Choose two balls of different weights. Hold them high above the cookie sheet. Which one do you think will hit the clay first? Drop the balls at the same time. Watch to see which ball hits the clay first. Listen for the sound of the balls as they hit the clay.

It's all the same to gravity

Did the heavier ball hit the clay first? No! They hit the clay at exactly the same time. That is because gravity causes things to fall at the same rate, no matter how big or heavy they are. If you could do this experiment with a marble and a bowling ball, they would still hit the clay at exactly the same time!

Look at the dents that the balls left. Which ball left the deeper dent? Even though the balls fall at the same rate, gravity pulls the heavier ball down with greater **force**, so the heavier ball makes a bigger dent in the clay. Try some of the other balls.

Falling objects

Over 400 years ago the famous astronomer Galileo experimented with how things fall. His experiments were very much like the one you just performed except that, according to the legend, he dropped balls off the Leaning Tower of Pisa in Italy!

On the Moon

In 1971 Commander David Scott did an experiment on the Moon. He dropped a hammer and a feather at the same time. On Earth, the feather would fall more slowly because the air would hold it up. Air works against gravity. But there is no air on the Moon, so the two objects hit the Moon's surface at exactly the same time!

Because there is no air on the moon, the hammer and the feather will hit the ground at the same time.

Make a ramp racer

For this experiment you will need:

* A board or stiff piece of cardboard, ideally 2 to 3 feet (60 to 90 cm) long
* A toy car
* Several thick books
* A piece of string
* A stopwatch.

1 Make a stack of books and position the board on the books to make a low ramp. Put the string on the floor about 12 in (30 cm) from the end of the ramp, like a finish line.

2 Let go of your car at the top of the ramp. Use your stopwatch to time how long it takes the car to cross the string from the time you release it.

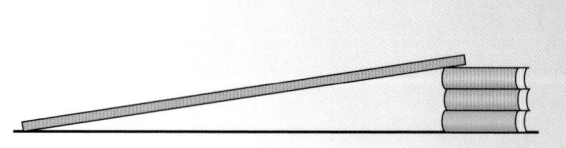

3 Now add more books to make your ramp higher. Run the car down the ramp again and time it. Which ramp made the car go faster?

Higher and faster

Did the higher ramp make the car go faster? Yes! Gravity makes things move faster when they fall farther—or in this case, when they roll farther. When you dropped two balls in the last experiment, they fell the same distance, so they hit the clay at the same time. This time, you changed the distance between the top of the ramp and the floor. The second time you ran the car, the ramp was higher, so the car was farther from the floor. The farther something falls—or rolls—the more gravity increases its speed. This change in speed is called **acceleration**.

The bigger the hill, the faster the sled ride!

Acceleration is the reason that it is more exciting to sled down a big hill than a small one. Imagine starting a sled ride at the top of a tall, steep hill. The ride starts off slowly, but as you continue down the hill, the sled speeds up! It continues to go faster and faster, until the ground levels out at the bottom of the hill and the sled slows down. If you were to sled down a smaller hill, the ride would be over before the sled had time to gather much speed.

Friction

Why did the car in your ramp racer eventually slow down and stop? The answer is **friction**. Friction is caused when the surfaces of objects rub against each other. The car loses some of its **energy** to heat because the wheels touch the ramp and the floor. You can see how friction makes heat if you rub your hands together quickly. In addition, there is also friction from the air. The car moves through the air, and the friction from the air slows it down. Friction from the air is sometimes called **drag**. If you could make your car move with no friction, it would not lose energy and would roll forever—unless something stopped it.

Trucks like this one spread sand on icy roads to increase the friction. This helps to prevent cars sliding.

Experimenting with friction

Try covering your ramp with materials that have different textures. Some things you might want to try include paper towels, wax paper, and a pillowcase. Which of these materials slowed down your car the most? Did you find a texture that helped your car go faster?

Using friction to stay safe

A sled has a smooth bottom so that it will slide easily over the snow for an exciting ride. How do you think a sled would work if the bottom were covered with sandpaper? Sandpaper would increase the friction, making it harder for your sled to move. When it snows, road crews often put sand on the road to add friction, so that cars will not slip. People use chains and snow tires for the same reason. The chains create more friction.

Using air friction

Skydivers use the friction from air to slow down their fall. When a skydiver opens a parachute, the parachute takes up a great deal of space in the air. This increases the amount of air friction (drag) and slows a skydiver's fall. If there were no air in Earth's **atmosphere**, a parachute would not work.

The open parachute causes air friction, slowing down the skydiver's fall.

Roller coasters

Like your ramp racer and a sled, most roller coasters do not have motors. Instead, they rely on gravity to make the ride exciting. Most roller coasters are pulled by chains to the top of a big, steep hill. As the coaster moves down the hill, it accelerates—it gathers more speed. The coaster moves most quickly near the bottom of the hill. This speed, also called **momentum**, propels the roller coaster to the top of the next hill.

The second hill must be smaller than the first hill because the coaster has lost some of its energy due to friction. Friction comes from the coaster touching the tracks and going through the air. As the ride nears the end, the hills get smaller and smaller, until the coaster has lost most of its energy and is moving slowly.

Roller coasters like this one rely on the force of gravity.

Feel the acceleration

One of the reasons why a roller coaster is so exciting is that you feel the acceleration—the change in speed. When something speeds up, it is called positive acceleration. When it slows down, it is called negative acceleration, or deceleration. When you travel in a car on the freeway, you are actually moving much faster than most roller coasters. Riding in a car is not exciting like riding a roller coaster because the change in speed (acceleration) is gradual. Have you ever been in a car when the driver had to slam on the brakes to avoid hitting something? No doubt you felt that sudden negative acceleration!

This is the Promenades Aeriennes, one of the first roller coasters ever built.

The next time you are riding in a car, try closing your eyes. See if you can feel when the car speeds up. What happens to your body? How about when the car slows down? Can you feel any movement when the car is traveling at a steady speed?

The first roller coaster

The first wheeled roller coasters were built in France in 1817.

Center of Gravity

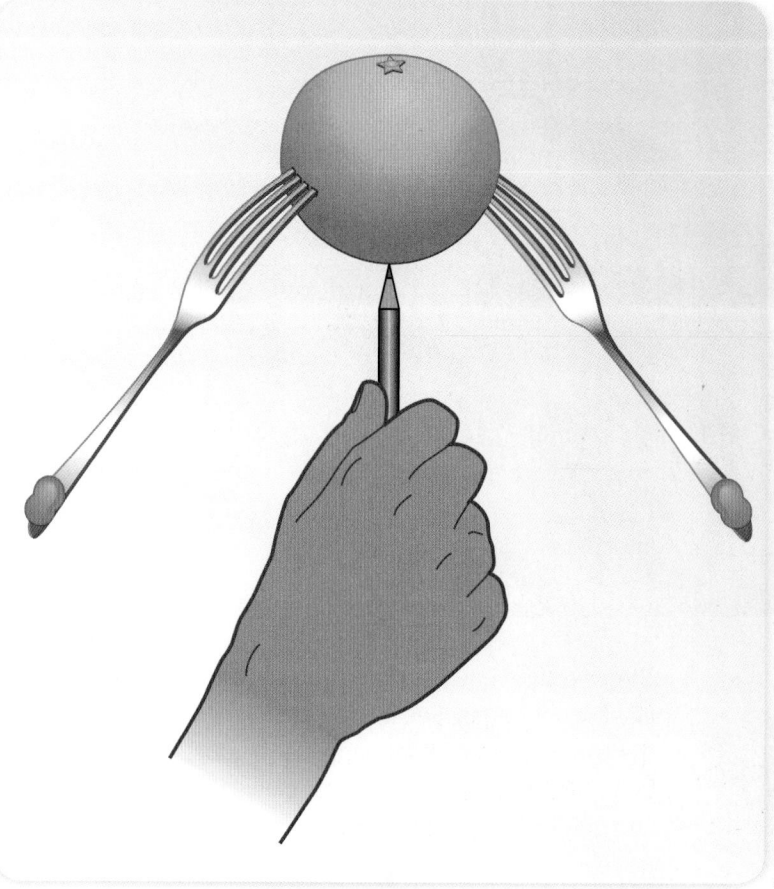

Balancing fruit

For this experiment you will need:

* An orange, lemon, peach, or other fruit
* Two metal forks
* Modeling clay or play dough
* A sharpened pencil.

1 Try to balance the orange on the tip of the pencil. Can you do it?

2 Poke the forks into the sides of the orange so that the handles are pointing down at an angle. The forks should be directly across from each other. Make two identical balls of modeling clay. Stick them to the bottoms of the fork handles.

3 Now try to balance the orange on the tip of the pencil again.

What happened?

The first time you tried to balance the orange on the pencil tip, it fell off. That was because the **center of gravity** was in the middle of the orange. The center of gravity is the heaviest part of an object. Since the center of gravity is the heaviest part of an object, the **gravitational force** pulls the object downward from that point.

When you added the forks and the modeling clay, the center of gravity was no longer in the orange. The heavy modeling clay brought the center of gravity down below the orange. When you balanced the orange on the tip of the pencil, the center of gravity was below the pencil tip, so the orange was pulled downward, making it easy to balance. Try other fruits and vegetables. Also try a large potato. Can you balance it?

The long pole changes this man's center of gravity so he can balance on the wire.

Short versus tall

Height may be great for basketball, but when you are talking about the center of gravity, shortness wins out. People and things that are lower to the ground have a lower center of gravity, making them steadier. That is why race cars are short and flat, rather than tall and skinny. If race cars were shaped like double-decker buses, they would tip over when they were speeding around corners.

Take a bow

You can experiment with your own center of gravity. Stand with your back against a wall. Make sure the backs of your heels are touching the wall. Now try to bend at the waist as if you are bowing. Can you do it? Now try the same bow in the middle of a room.

You were able to bend farther forward when you were in the middle of the room because you were able to adjust your center of gravity to keep it over your legs. But when you had your back to the wall, the wall prevented you from adjusting. This meant, your center of gravity moved forward, making you lose your balance.

The keel on the bottom of this sailboat helps to keep it from tipping over in the water.

Adjusting the center of gravity

Some things, like sailboats, have to be tall. On a sailboat, the tall mast raises the center of gravity, making the whole boat unstable. In order to keep from tipping over, a sailboat must have a heavy **keel** on its bottom. The keel is a large structure that runs lengthwise down the center of the boat. The keel moves the center of gravity under water so that the boat does not tip over.

Fool your friends!

You can fool your friends by putting a heavy rock into the corner of a box. You may want to tape it in place so that it does not roll around. Close the box and then balance the weighted corner on the edge of a table. The rock changes the center of gravity so that the box balances on the edge. Your friends cannot see the rock, so they will think the box is magically balancing on the corner edge of the table.

Time for Gravity

Steps to follow

1 Use the thumbtack to make a tiny hole in the bottom of the plastic container. The hole should be in the center and should be as small as you can make it.

2 Cover the hole with your finger and fill the container about two-thirds full with water.

3 Put the plastic container on top of the jar so that that the water can drip into the jar. Use a stopwatch or clock to time the minutes. Every time a minute passes, use the marker to draw a line showing how high the water is in the jar. Be sure to position yourself so that your eyes are level with the waterline in order to get an accurate measurement.

4 When your clock runs out, empty the jar and fill the top container again with the same amount of water you used the first time. The water should drip at the same rate. Now you can use your water clock as a timer. As the jar fills, look at the marks you made to tell how many minutes have passed.

Make a water clock

For this experiment you will need:

* A large, empty, clear jar like the type peanut butter or mayonnaise comes in. You do not need the lid.
* A disposable plastic container like the type margarine or cottage cheese comes in. You do not need the lid.
* A thumbtack
* A fine-tipped permanent marker
* A stopwatch or a clock with a second hand
* Water.

How does it work?

The **force** that makes this clock work is gravity! Gravity pulls the water from the upper container into the lower one. You probably noticed that the drips got slower as the upper container emptied. That is because as the **weight** of the water in the top container decreases, there is less pressure to push the water through the hole. This will not affect the accuracy of your clock as long as you draw lines after each minute has passed—even if the lines are closer together than they were at the bottom of the jar.

This clock is powered by water and gravity.

Improving your water clock

If you want your clock to measure a longer period of time, try making a smaller hole with a straight pin. You can also use bigger containers and more water. Another fun method for measuring longer periods of time is to use several containers. Smaller containers like the ones yogurt comes in work well. Make a hole in the bottom of each container and tape the containers to a wall, one above another so that the water from one container will drip into the one below. Put the jar under the bottom container. Fill only the top container with water. Since the water must flow through several containers, it will take longer to get to the jar at the bottom.

This ancient water clock helped people keep track of time thousands of years ago.

Ancient clocks

A water clock, named **clepsydra** by the ancient Greeks, is one of the oldest methods of keeping time. Water clocks have been used all over the world for thousands of years. Just like your water clock, these ancient clocks also used gravity to measure time.

Some of the oldest water clocks were simply a stone or pottery bowl with a small hole near the bottom. The inside of the bowl was marked with lines to measure the waterline as the water flowed out of the bowl. Another version consists of a metal bowl with a small hole in the bottom. When placed in a larger container of water, the bowl would fill slowly with water and eventually sink.

You can tell the time on this water clock by counting how many balls are filled with liquid.

Over time, people began to make more elaborate water clocks. But no matter how fancy the clocks became, they still depended on gravity to work. A cord could be tied to a float in the water. As the water level sank, the cord would turn a wheel. The position of the wheel would show the time, not unlike a modern clock. Water clocks were also made to sound bells or gongs using the level or pressure of the water.

Action and Reaction

Make a balloon rocket

For this experiment you will need:

* A balloon
* A piece of thread or smooth string about 5 feet (1.5 m) long
* A drinking straw
* Tape.

1 Put the thread through the straw. The thread should move easily through it. Secure the ends of the thread to walls or furniture so that the thread stretches across at about chest height, like a clothesline. The thread should be tight. Slide the straw near one end.

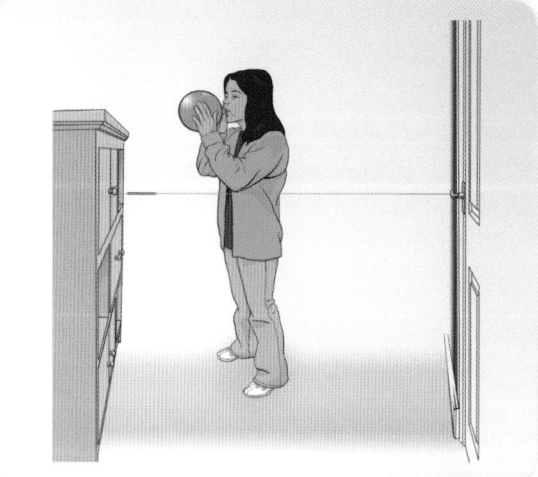

2 Blow up the balloon, but do not knot it. Tape the side of the balloon to the straw keeping hold of the end of the balloon. You may need a friend to help. The balloon should hang under the thread.

3 Let the balloon go!

How does it work?

When you let go of the balloon, the **force** of the air rushing out of the back of the balloon pushed the balloon forward. Forces come in pairs. Whenever there is an **action**, there is an opposite and equal **reaction**. In your balloon rocket, the air rushing out of the balloon was the action and the balloon moving forward was the reaction.

The force of gravity also has an action and a reaction. You can feel the action of Earth's **gravitational force** pulling you down. The opposite reaction is the gravitational force that you exert toward Earth. Even though you cannot feel it, you are pulling Earth toward you!

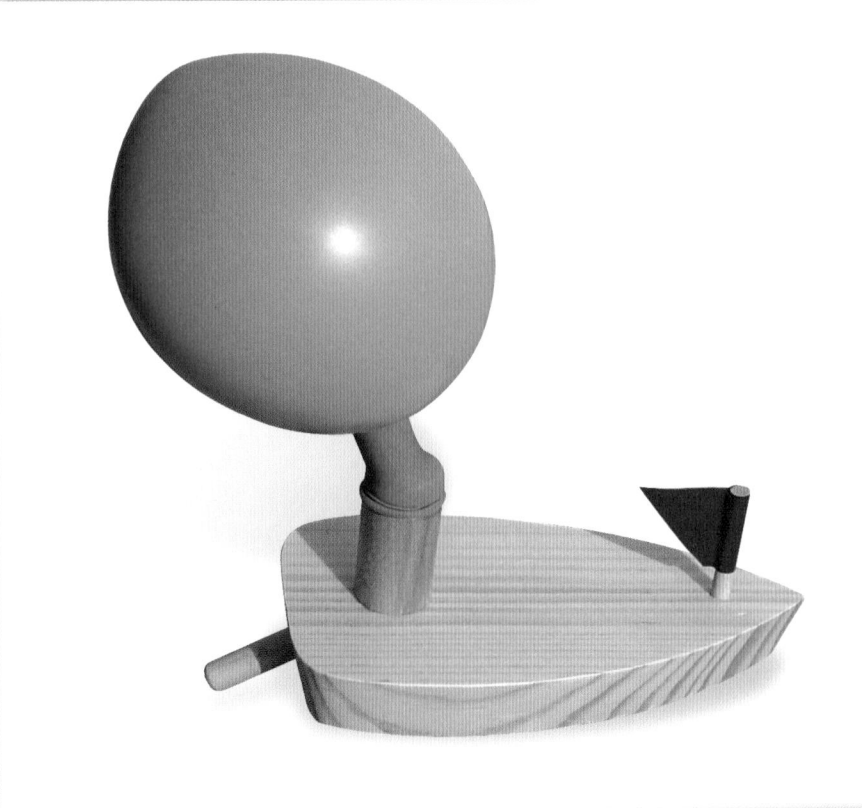

You can use a balloon to make an air-powered boat!

More with your balloon rocket

What can you do to improve your balloon rocket? Do some balloons work better than others? Try different shapes and sizes. What if you add cardboard fins? Try adding another string and having balloon rocket races with a friend.

You can make your balloon into a powerboat by taping it to a Styrofoam tray like the kind meat comes on. Ask an adult to help you float the tray in a lake or pool and watch the force of the air push it across the water.

Energy transfer

Sometimes a moving object will **transfer** its **energy** to another object. You can see this with pool balls or marbles. When a moving pool ball hits a ball that is not moving head-on, the moving ball stops and the ball that was not moving continues on the path that the first ball was traveling. The moving ball has transferred its energy to the stationary ball.

What will happen when the swinging ball hits the line of hanging balls?

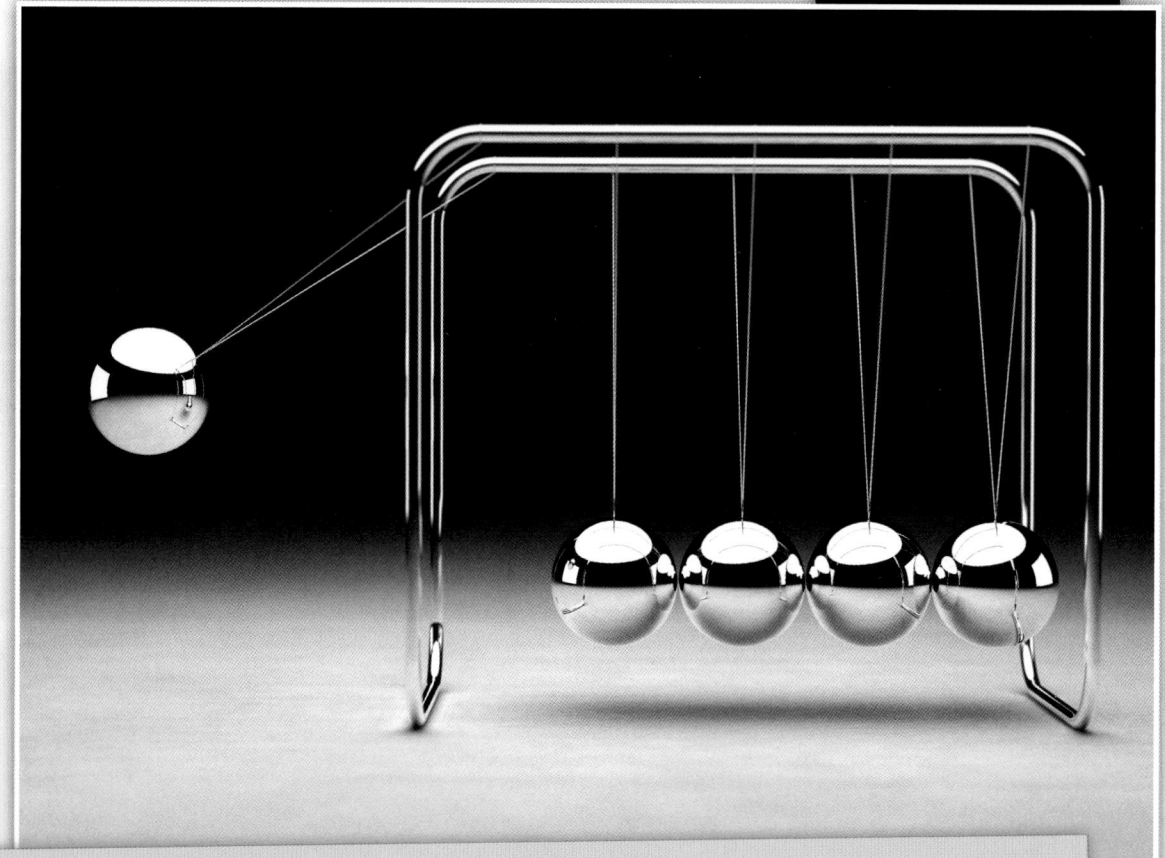

Pushing and pulling

You can experiment with action and reaction with a friend and some roller skates. While both of you are on skates, put your palms together as if you were playing pat-a-cake. Now gently push. If you and your friend weigh about the same amount, you probably both went backward. If you are lighter than your friend, you probably went backward farther. What happens when you try to pull your friend toward you?

Combined forces

Moving objects are usually affected by more than one force. For example, your balloon rocket was propelled forward by the force of the escaping air. But it also had the force of gravity pulling it toward the ground. In addition, **friction** between the straw and the thread, as well as between the rocket and the air, was slowing the balloon down. These forces all affected the balloon in different ways. If you could remove any one of them, the balloon would behave differently.

Whenever there is movement, there is force. When you turn the page of this book, you are applying a force to it. Other forces include **magnetic forces**, **electrical forces**, and forces from materials that stretch such as springs or **elastic**.

The space shuttle uses a great deal of force to break through Earth's atmosphere.

Space shuttle

A space shuttle is not unlike your balloon rocket. It uses huge engines to blast hot gases downward. The force of the gases pushes the shuttle off the ground and through Earth's **atmosphere**. A great deal of force is needed to escape Earth's gravity. A space shuttle uses as much force as 140 jumbo jets!

Make a ring wing glider

For this experiment you will need:

* A drinking straw
* A piece of printer paper
* Scissors
* Tape.

1 Cut a strip of paper that is about ¾ in by 5 in (1.5 by 13 cm). Then cut a longer piece that is about 1 by 8 in (2.5 by 20 cm).

2 Make the strips of paper into loops by taping the ends. You should have two loops, one a little bigger than the other.

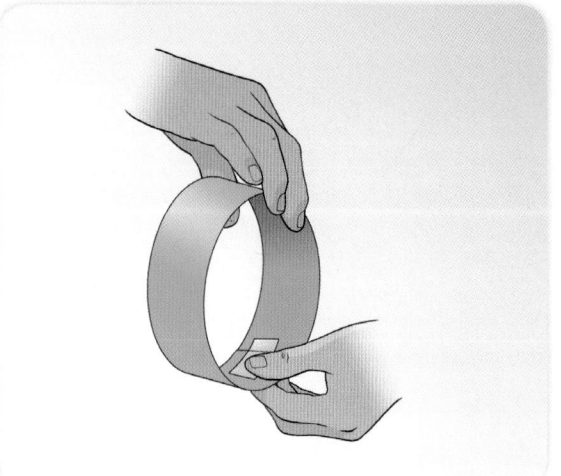

3 Put one end of the straw over the part that you taped inside the bigger loop. Tape the straw to the paper loop. Tape the smaller loop to the other end of the straw.

4 Try your glider by launching it into the air!

Your glider

Your glider is a plane with circle-shaped wings. Just like an **airfoil**, (see diagram below) the ring wings cause the air to move faster over them than under them, giving your glider **lift**!

Experiment with your glider. Try using different sizes of loop. What happens if you make the straw shorter? What if you use three loops?

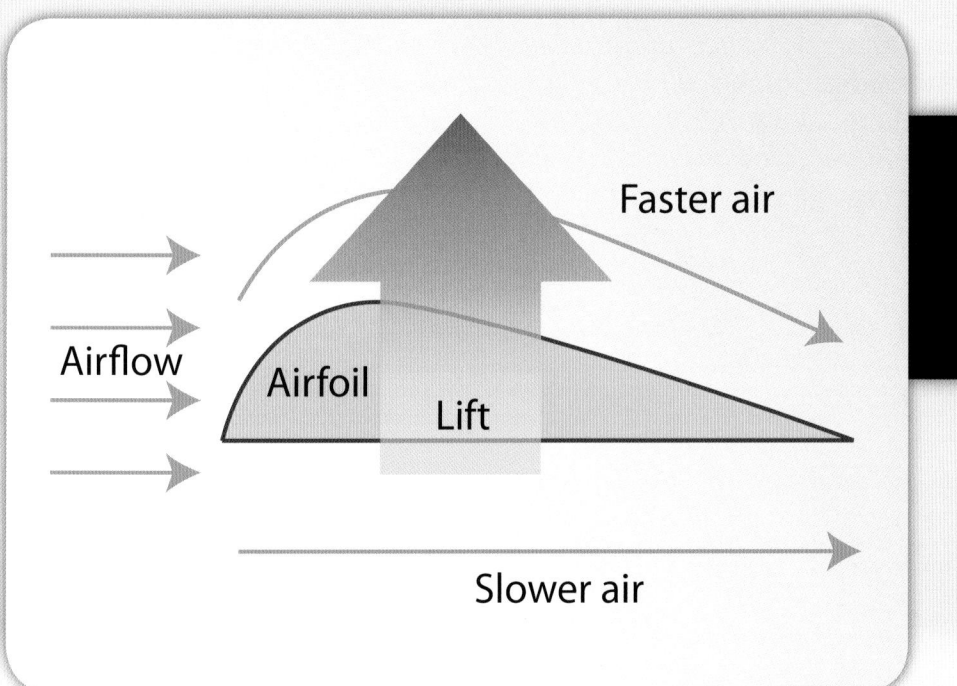

Faster air

Airflow

Airfoil

Lift

Slower air

The curved shape of an airfoil gives it lift.

How airplanes fly

It is hard to believe that a heavy airplane full of hundreds of people can stay in the air. Airplanes have powerful engines, but these are used to propel the plane forward. In order to stay airborne, the plane needs lift. This allows the plane to overcome the force of gravity.

A plane gets most of its lift from the wings. The wings are designed to be curved on top. This shape is called an airfoil. The curved top means the air that goes over the wing must go farther than the air that goes under it. To cover the longer distance, the air on top moves faster. This creates less **air pressure** on top of the wing and more under it. The higher air pressure under the wing pushes it upward, giving it lift.

Round and Round

Steps to follow

1   Tie the cork tightly onto one end of the string.

2   You only need half of the straw, so cut the straw in half. Thread the string through one half of the straw.

3   Tie the key ring or the washers onto the other end of the string. You should now have a 2-foot (60-cm) piece of string with a cork on one end, keys on the other end, and half a straw in the middle.

4   Hold the straw at arm's length so that the keys are hanging down below the straw. The cork should be resting on top of the straw. Move your hand so that the cork starts to swing around in a circle. At first the circle will be very small. But as you increase the speed, the circle will get bigger, using more string. Soon you will notice that the keys are getting closer to the straw. The spinning cork is lifting the heavy keys! If you can swing the cork fast enough, the keys will rise all the way to the bottom of the straw.

Spinning forces

For this experiment you will need:

* A cork
* A ring with several keys on it or several heavy washers
* A 2-foot (60-cm) length of string
* A thick plastic straw like the type you might drink a milkshake through.

What is happening?

How can the light cork lift the heavy keys? As you spun the cork faster, you could feel a **force** pulling the cork outward. At the same time, the string was pulling the cork inward. As you spun the cork faster and faster, the force pulling the cork outward became stronger than gravity! It was so strong that it lifted the heavy keys.

Spinning forces keep this top from falling over.

Don't get wet!

Try this experiment outside. You will need a small plastic bucket with a strong handle and some water. Fill the bucket halfway with water. Stand where you have a lot of room. Start by gently swinging the bucket back and forth in front of you. Swing it faster and higher. Try swinging it up and over your head. If you swing the bucket fast enough, you should be able to spin it all the way around over your head without spilling the water. The spinning force is stronger than gravity! The force caused by spinning the bucket is pushing the water outward, but the bucket is holding it in.

These skaters are using spinning forces to keep from falling.

Spinning forces at the amusement park

Many amusement park rides use spinning forces. The next time you go to the amusement park, look for all the rides that spin round and round. Some of these rides rely on the force created by spinning to keep you from flying out of the ride. When you go on these kinds of rides, you will feel the force pushing you to the seat or wall of the ride.

You can feel this kind of force on a roller coaster with every curve. Some roller coasters also have loops in the tracks. The coaster has a great deal of **momentum** when it travels around these loops. Just like the experiment with the water in the bucket, the forces pushing the coaster outward keep the coaster on the tracks and you in your seat!

The strong cables on each swing keep these people from being thrown by the spinning forces of the ride.

Spinning eggs

You can use spinning force to tell whether or not an egg has been hard-boiled. Lay the egg on its side and give it a gentle spin. An egg that has not been hard-boiled is liquid inside. The shifting liquid keeps the egg from spinning. The inside of a hard-boiled egg is solid, making it possible for it to spin much longer and faster than an egg that has not been hard-boiled.

Get Some Leverage

Steps to follow

1 Cut off the top and most of one side of the milk carton. Leave about 1 ½ in (4 cm) at the bottom of the side that is mostly cut away. Your milk carton should be open at the top, with three tall sides and one short one.

2 Use a hole punch to make a hole in one of the upper corners of the milk carton that is closest to the side that has been cut away. Make another hole in the corner directly across from the first hole. Put a pencil through the holes so that it stretches across the opening of the milk carton like a bridge.

3 Use the other pencil to poke a hole in the center of the short side of the front of the carton. Thread a rubber band through the hole and then secure it to the outside of the carton by putting a toothpick through the loop.

Make a catapult

For this experiment you will need:

* A small, empty milk carton
* Scissors
* A hole punch
* Two pencils
* A toothpick
* A rubber band
* A plastic spoon
* Mini marshmallows or cotton balls.

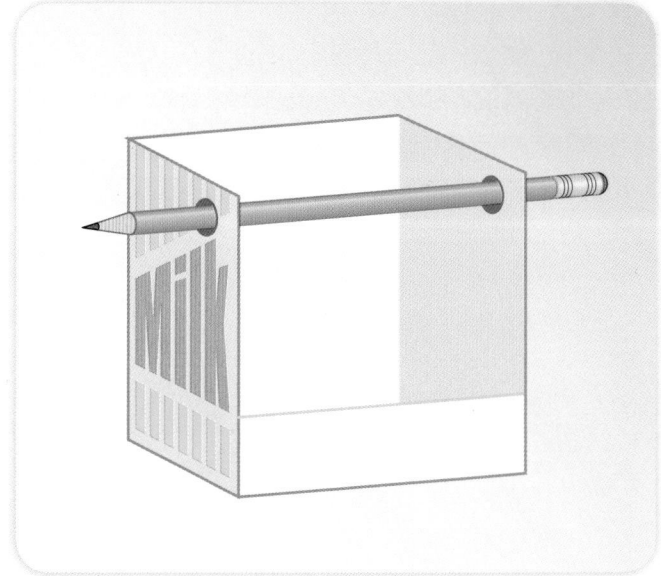

4 Lean the handle of the spoon over the pencil. The bowl part of the spoon should be touching the table. Hold the bowl part of the spoon down while you loop the free end of the rubber band under the pencil and over the end of the spoon handle. The rubber band should be tight. If it is loose, try a shorter rubber band.

5 Load the spoon with a mini marshmallow or another small, soft item. Let the spoon go and watch the marshmallow fly!

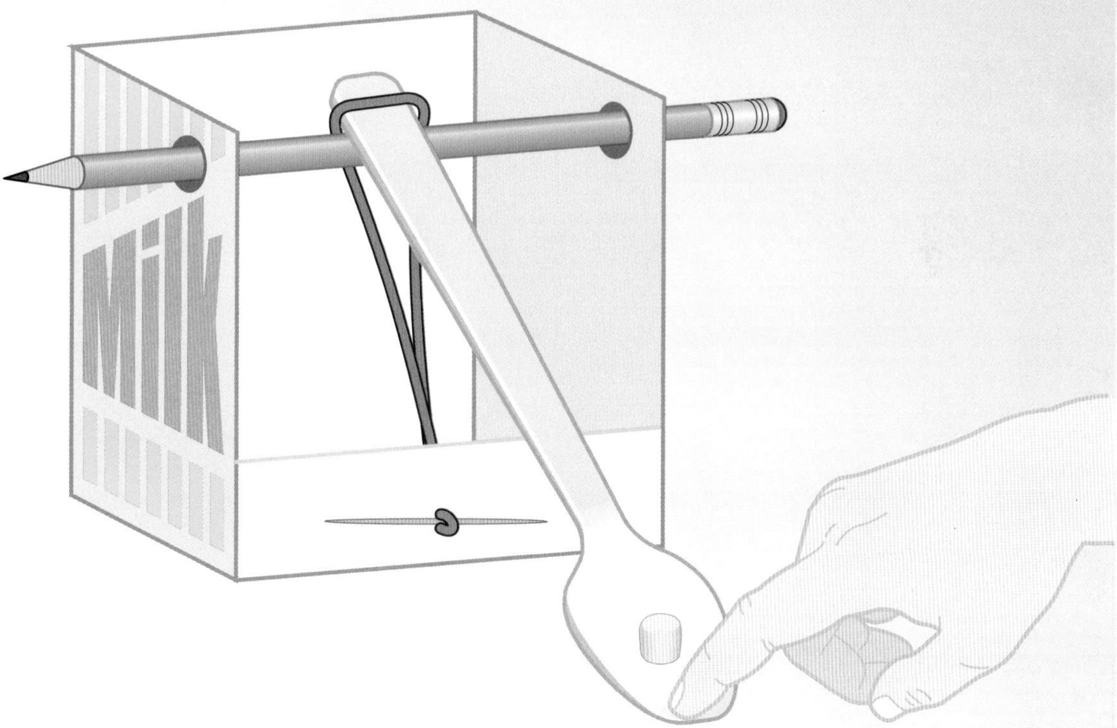

How does it work?

This **catapult** works because the spoon is a **lever**. A lever is a board or rod that rests on a pivot point called a **fulcrum**. Levers are often used to overcome gravity to lift a heavy **load**. In your catapult, the lever is being used to fling an object rather than to lift something. The pencil is the fulcrum. The stored **energy** in the rubber band is the **force** that moves the lever to fling the marshmallow.

Catapulting airplanes

Since **aircraft carriers** have a short runway, they use a catapult-type device to give an extra push to airplanes that are taking off. The catapult is located under the deck and is powered by steam. Operating the catapult requires perfect timing. Even a small mistake could send a pilot and his plane into the ocean.

Can you improve your catapult? Try moving the pencil. What if you use a longer spoon? Will different rubber bands make the marshmallow fly farther? How about using two rubber bands?

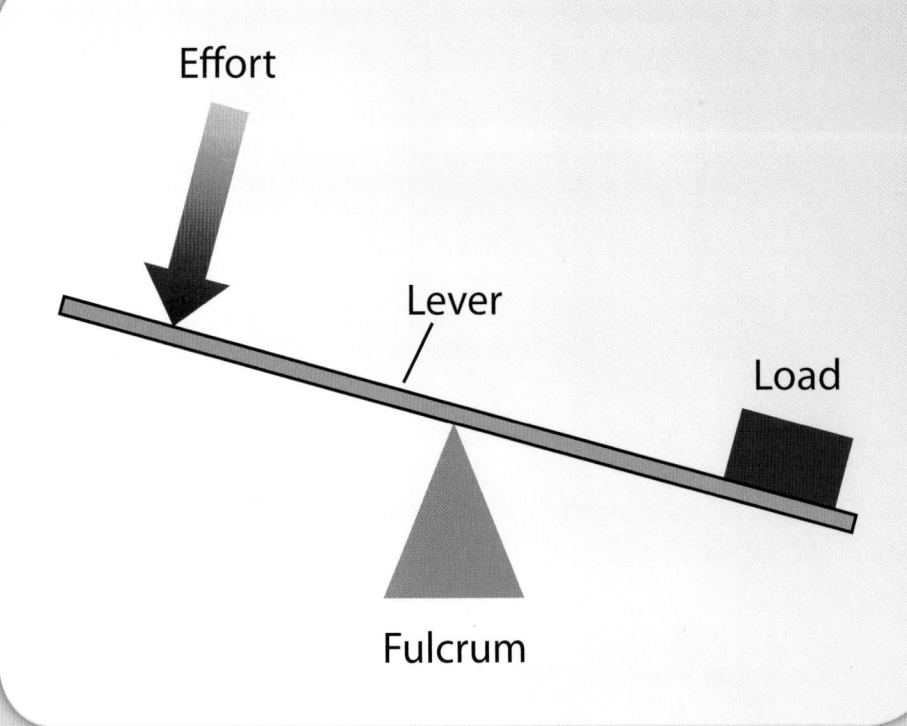

Effort

Lever

Load

Fulcrum

A lever can be used to lift a heavy load.

Pumpkin chucking

In some parts of the United States, annual pumpkin-flinging contests are held, in which participants construct catapults to hurl pumpkins.

Catapults in the Middle Ages

Europeans began using catapults in the 1200s. At that time, catapults were the most powerful weapons available. Large catapults that could hurl up to 300 lbs (136 kg) were used to destroy castle walls. Catapults were also used to hurl things over castle walls. Armies used catapults to hurl a variety of unpleasant things including spears, burning wood, beehives, spoiled food, manure, diseased cattle, and even dead bodies, which spread deadly diseases such as **bubonic plague**. If a spy were caught behind enemy lines, he might find himself being hurled back to his people in a catapult! Armies stopped using catapults in the 1300s, when cannons powered by gunpowder became the most powerful weapon.

Making levers work for you

A lever allows you to overcome gravity by using less force to do work. You can experiment with levers by using a strong ruler, a small wooden block, and a book. The ruler is the lever, the block is the fulcrum, and the book is the load. Put the ruler on top of the block so the block is under the 2-in (5-cm) mark. Then slide the other end of the ruler under a book. The ruler should be at an angle, like a ramp. Push down on the end of the ruler near the block. Is it hard or easy to lift the book? Now move the block so it is only a few inches from the book. Push down on the end of the ruler again. Is it easier this time? The closer the fulcrum is to the load, the less force is needed.

Historians believe that ancient Egyptians may have used levers to lift the heavy blocks of stones that they used to build the pyramids.

Levers in life

Levers are handy things to have around. A lot of everyday items are actually made from levers. A wheelbarrow is a kind of lever. The handles and the bin are the lever, and the wheel is the fulcrum. A pair of scissors is made of two levers. Each blade, along with the handle, is a lever. The fulcrum is the place where the blades cross. Tweezers are also made from two levers. The fulcrum is where the two parts of the tweezers are connected.

A fun example of a lever is a playground seesaw. The next time you are on a seesaw, try some experiments. What happens when you move closer to the fulcrum at the center? Can you find a way to lift someone who is much heavier than you are?

A seesaw is a actually a large lever!

Pulleys at Work

Steps to follow

1 Put the wire through the spool. Ask an adult to help bend the wire into a triangle shape with a hook at the bottom. It will look a bit like a small hanger. This will be your **pulley**.

2 Put the washers on the hook. They will be your **load**.

3 Move two chairs several feet apart, back to back. Put the broomstick on the top of the chair backs so that it is like a bridge between them. You may want to tape the stick to the chairs to secure it.

4 Tie one end of the string to the broomstick. Loop the string through your pulley so that the spool sits on top of the string and the washers dangle under it. Pull the string up to lift the load. The load should feel lighter than if you lifted it without the pulley. If you loop the string over the broomstick, you can move the load by pulling down on the string rather than pulling up on it.

Lift a load

For this experiment you will need:

* A spool
* A piece of strong (but bendable) wire
* Large washers or other weights
* A broomstick or other sturdy stick
* Two chairs
* String
* Tape.

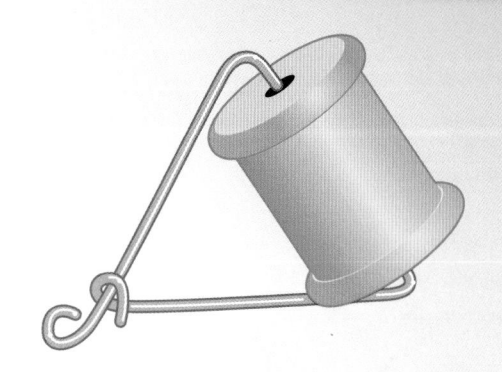

Warning: Adult help may be needed for this experiment.

38

How does it work?

Objects are heavy to lift because gravity is pulling them toward Earth. Like **levers**, pulleys can be used to reduce the amount of **force** needed to lift something. A pulley is a wheel with a groove for a rope or cable. A pulley works by distributing the load. When you used the pulley, the string was doubled up around the pulley. With the doubled string, the load is shared between the two parts of the string, making it easier for you to lift. Heavy objects can be lifted using several pulleys. The more pulleys and rope that are added, the more the weight of the load is distributed.

Pulleys make it easier to lift this truck by distributing its weight.

Making life easier with simple machines

Levers and pulleys are two of the six types of **simple machine**. Simple machines require only one force to work. Often, as in the case of levers and pulleys, simple machines make it easier to overcome the force of gravity by making it easier to lift a load.

An **inclined plane** (ramp) is another simple machine that can make it easier to overcome the force of gravity. One way to move a heavy load to a high place is to push it up a ramp. That is why trucks often have ramps for loading cargo.

A ramp makes it easier to bring a heavy load to a high place.

A **wedge** is another type of simple machine. A wedge looks a lot like an inclined plane because it has a slanted surface. A wedge can stop the force of gravity by keeping something in place. For example, a wedge can be put in front of the wheel of a car to keep it from rolling down a hill. A wedge is often used for separating one thing from another.

A screw is really just an inclined plane that has been wrapped around a shaft in a spiral. Screws are simple machines that are used to hold things together. The base of a lightbulb is an example of a screw.

The sixth kind of simple machine is a **wheel and axle**. Wheels and axles make it easier to move a load. It is easier to move a heavy object in a wagon than by pushing or carrying it. Sometimes gravity is used as the force pushing wheels and axles, like when you go down a hill on a scooter.

A bicycle contains several simple machines. How many can you see?

Compound machines

A **compound machine** is a combination of two or more simple machines. A bicycle is an example of a compound machine. There are several wheels and axles on a bike, including the wheels themselves and the gears. The edges of the gears are actually tiny wedges. The brake handles and gearshifts are levers. Look around—how many simple machines do you see?

Gravity Then and Now

Thousands of years ago, people did not know what gravity was. They did not know why objects fell to the ground when they were dropped, or that things felt heavy because of gravity. Even though they did not know what it was, they found clever ways to work against the **force** of gravity. All six of the **simple machines** were invented long ago. Without these simple inventions, moving heavy objects over long distances and constructing even a small building would have been very difficult. Building a large structure such as England's Stonehenge or the Great Wall of China would have been impossible. Today, we still use these simple machines every day. But we have also learned to use forces to do things that ancient people could never have dreamed of.

Gravity holds the stars together!

Gravity and stars

Sir Isaac Newton figured out that Earth orbits the Sun because of gravity, but he did not know that gravity holds our Sun, as well as every other star in the universe, together! The gases that make up a star are held together by its own gravity. At the end of a star's life, the pressure from the gases gets weaker. Then the force of gravity causes the star to collapse into itself.

Gravity in sports

Gravity plays an important role in almost every sport. Athletes must consider how gravity will affect their bodies and their equipment. For example, high divers must know how to deal with the rapid **acceleration** of their bodies falling through the air, so that they will not get hurt when they hit the water. Other forces, such as air **friction** and the force from the muscles in the body, also come into play. Gravity affects not only athletes' bodies but also the balls that they throw or hit, how fast they can run, and how high they can jump. The next time you are playing your favorite sport, think about the role that gravity is playing!

Divers must take forces such as gravity into consideration.

Glossary

acceleration change in the speed or direction of an object. When you ride your bike down a hill, you feel the acceleration as you go faster and faster.

action movement. Every move you make is an action.

aircraft carrier large ship that carries airplanes and has a runway on the deck. Landings and takeoffs are riskier on an aircraft carrier because the runway is much shorter than at an airport.

airfoil shape of a wing that has a curved upper surface to give it lift. Birds have airfoil-shaped wings to help them fly.

air pressure force of air. An airplane can fly because the air pressure is different over the wing than it is under the wing.

atmosphere mix of gases that surrounds Earth. Gravity keeps our atmosphere close to Earth.

bubonic plague contagious, usually fatal illness that killed nearly half the population of Europe in the Middle Ages. Armies in the Middle Ages spread bubonic plague by using catapults to hurl infected bodies into castles.

catapult large war machine that was used in the Middle Ages to hurl heavy objects at the enemy. You can make a homemade catapult and hurl objects at a target.

center of gravity heaviest part of an object. If you are using a skateboard, you can lower your center of gravity by bending down.

clepsydras clock that tells the time using gravity and water

compound machine combination of two or more simple machines

drag friction or resistance caused by air or water. You can decrease the drag on a model race car by giving it a curved top.

elastic object that stretches and changes shape when a force is applied to it, but then returns to its original shape when the force is no longer there

electrical force force that comes from electricity. A forklift uses electrical force to lift a heavy load.

energy force it takes to move an object. You use energy just by turning the page of this book.

force ability to make something move or do something

friction resistance that slows a moving object when it makes contact with another object. You can slide across the floor in your socks because socks have less friction than shoes.

fulcrum point at which a lever pivots. You can change how a lever works by moving the fulcrum.

gravitational force force that draws all matter together—specifically, the force that keeps matter on Earth. Astronauts can float in space because without Earth, there is no strong gravitational force.

inclined plane angled surface that makes it easier to lift a load. You can make an inclined plane from snow.

keel structure that spans the underside length of a boat, often extending into the water to increase stability. If you make a boat that tips over, you can add a keel to the bottom to keep it upright.

lever stiff board or rod that uses a pivot to decrease the amount of force needed to do work. When you use a hammer to pull out a nail, you are using a lever.

lift upward force produced by the shape of a wing as it travels through the air. You can make a model airplane fly higher by shaping the wings to give it lift.

load something that must be lifted or carried. You can carry more dirt with a wheelbarrow than you can with a bucket because the wheelbarrow lightens the load.

magnetic force force that comes from magnets. Magnets stick to a refrigerator because magnetic force is stronger than gravity.

mass measurement of how heavy something is. The more mass something has, the stronger its gravitational force is.

matter anything that has weight and takes up space. Everything you see, including yourself, is made from matter.

momentum tendency for an object in motion to keep moving. You can rest your legs and coast on a bicycle because your bike has momentum.

pulley grooved wheel with a rope or cable that allows loads to be lifted more easily. You can use a pulley to move heavy things up to a tree house.

reaction action, or movement, that occurs in response to another action. If you push on a shopping cart, the reaction will be that the cart moves.

simple machine one of six devices that require only one force to make work easier. You can use building sets to make all six simple machines.

transfer move from one place to another. When you ride bumper cars, you can transfer the energy from your car to someone else's by bumping into it.

wedge solid block that is thick on one end and thin on the other; it can be used to separate things or to keep them from moving. A block can be used as a wedge to keep a door open.

weight gravitational force on an object. If there were no gravity, you would not have any weight.

wheel and axle disc or ring that revolves around a shaft through its center; it can be used for transporting or lifting loads. You can make wheels and axles from plastic yogurt lids and toothpicks.

Find Out More

Books

Gurstelle, William. *The Art of the Catapult*. Chicago: Chicago Review, 2004.

Gives instructions on how to build ten working catapults.

Hopwood, James. *Cool Gravity Activities: Fun Science Projects About Balance* (*Cool Science*). Edina, Minn.: Checkerboard, 2007.

Bright and colorful book with lots of experiments about gravity.

Krull, Kathleen. *Isaac Newton* (*Giants of Science*). New York: Viking Juvenile, 2006.

Lively, humorous biography of the man who devoted his life to studying gravity.

Parker, Steve. *Forces and Motion* (*Science View*). New York: Chelsea House, 2005.

Information and projects about forces and motion.

Websites

Exploratorium: Science Snacks About Mechanics

www.exploratorium.edu/snacks/iconmechanics.html

A collection of science experiments from San Francisco's Exploratorium science museum. Includes pictures, step-by-step instructions, and background information.

Motion and Forces

www.learningscience.org/psc2bmotionforces.htm

A collection of links to interactive sites that let you explore forces and motions online. Among other things, you can virtually experiment with a ramp and a truck or drop balls from the Leaning Tower of Pisa.

Organizations

The American Association for the Advancement of Science (AAAS)

1200 New York Avenue NW
Washington, D.C. 20005
(202) 326-6400

www.aaas.org

An international nonprofit organization dedicated to advancing science around the world.

Places to visit

Oregon Museum of Science and Industry

1945 SE Water Avenue
Portland, Ore. 97214-3354
(503) 797-OMSI (6674)

www.omsi.edu

Large interactive science museum that features a "Turbine Hall" with many exhibits about the physical sciences, including gravity, forces, and motion.

The Franklin Institute Science Museum

222 North 20th Street
Philadelphia, Pa. 19103
(215) 448-1200

www2.fi.edu

Science museum with many exhibits, including "Sir Isaac's Loft," which focuses on forces and motion.

Index

THE NORTH LIGHT
HANDBOOK OF
ARTISTS'
MATERIALS

THE NORTH LIGHT HANDBOOK OF
ARTISTS'

MATERIALS

IAN HEBBLEWHITE

NORTH LIGHT

Cincinnati, Ohio

A QUARTO BOOK

Published in North America by
North Light, an imprint of Writer's Digest Books
9933 Alliance Road
Cincinnati, Ohio 45242

First published 1986
© Quarto Publishing Limited 1986

ISBN 0-89134-176-5

This book was designed and produced by
Quarto Publishing Limited
The Old Brewery
6 Blundell Street
London N7 9BH

Senior Editors Polly Powell, Sandy Shepherd
Art Editor Marnie Searchwell

Designer Michelle Stamp
Design Assistant Gill Elsbury

Photography Paul Forrester
Illustrations Mick Hill, Andrew Popkiewicz, Ian Sidaway

Paste up Patrizio Semproni, Dave Evans, Elly King, Paul Swain

Art Director Pete Laws
Editorial Director Jim Miles

The publishers would like to take this opportunity to thank Carole
Antoniou, Teresa Armstrong, Jack Buchan, Marilla Clements, Ursula
Dawson, Ian Denison, Paul Gardner, Rachel Huckstep, Diedre McGarry
and Eleanor van Zandt.

Typeset in Great Britain by QV Typesetting, London
Manufactured in Hong Kong by Regent Publishing Services Limited
Printed in Hong Kong by Leefung Asco Printers Limited

CONTENTS

BRUSHES AND PAINTING EQUIPMENT · 43

Brushes • Palette and painting knives • Palettes • Miscellaneous equipment

COLOR AND MEDIA · 66

Paints and pigments • Painting sets • Inks • Soft pastels, oil pastels and oil painting sticks •
Colored pencils • Crayons • Mediums, additives and fixatives

FOREWORD

Today, a vast increase in leisure time is causing many people to look around for something more satisfying to do than just sitting in front of the television set. More and more people are taking up painting and drawing as a pursuit that can be equally rewarding at both amateur and professional levels. Retailers of artists' materials are therefore benefitting more than ever before from an influx of enthusiastic artists seeking the wherewithal to paint. They may be asked a multitude of questions about materials; how to use them, what they are for, and why is one product better than another. Retailers or their assistants, however experienced they may be, are sometimes hard put to answer these questions. It is the intention of this book to answer such questions so that you, the artist, can make the best possible choice when buying artists' materials.

My thanks are due to so many people; it is possible that I may have inadvertently omitted one or two — I trust that I may beg their forgiveness. Many thanks to D G Evans, David Varley and Dr Tordoff of the Society of Dyers and Colourists, Stuart Welch and David Brown of Atlantis Paper Co Ltd, Michael Harding, Michael Venus of Handover Brushes Ltd, Robert Burt of R K Burt & Co Ltd, Andrew Farmer of E Ploton Ltd, Keith Lockwood of Langford & Hill, Richard Turpin of Chelsea Art Stores, Eric Pond of Jakar International Ltd, Jas Campbell of Green & Stone, Philip Poole Ltd, Peter Comley of APT, José M Parramon, Donald Jackson, Tom Barnard, Basil Oakley and John Wright of E S Perry Ltd (Osmiroid), David Ford of Automatic Lettering Pen Co, Bruce Mitchell of Hampton Hill Gallery, Ron Ranson, Patrick Fitzgerald-Moore, Kevin Kember and Jean-François Paris. Last but not least, thanks to my lovely wife Wendy for her encouragement and for all those endless cups of tea she made for me while I wrote this book.

The publishers would also like to add their thanks to Berol (UK) Ltd, Chartpak Ltd, Ian Biggs and Merlin Leulier of Conté (UK) Ltd, Rita Perry of L Cornelissen & Son, Colyer Graphics, James Stock and Denise Bungey of Daler-Rowney Ltd, Faber-Castell (UK) Ltd, Falkiner Fine Paper, Alan Hebdon, Chris Court and Viv Arthur of Frisk Products Ltd, Geliot Whitman Ltd, Maimeri Ltd, Dorothy Wood of Paintworks, Paperpoint, W H Peel & Co Ltd, Andrew Alexander of Platignum PLC, Premier Brush Co, Quillcraft, Rexel Ltd, Rotring (UK) Ltd, Russell & Chapple, Ian Haynes of Smith & Partners Group, Staedtler (UK) Ltd, Jonathan Stephenson of J P Stephenson, Straker Ltd, David White of Wheatsheaf Graphics and Winsor & Newton Ltd. A special thanks is owed to Chris Turner and all at Langford & Hill.

INTRODUCTION

Artists have far greater control of their work the more they prepare their own paints, supports and grounds. In practical terms, however, there are drawbacks: modern professional artists can rarely afford to have apprentices to grind their colors for them or prepare canvases, and they may not have time to do so themselves. Amateur artists may not have sufficient knowledge to carry out the basic preparation of their materials.

Forced to buy ready-prepared materials, artists face a big problem in that the quality of some ready-made materials on sale today is poor. Recently, for example, a world-famous art gallery did comparative tests on internationally known brands of oil paints. It found that, of all the brands tested, a well-known brand available on virtually every continent had the most destructive effect on supports, due to its high content of drying oils. However, it is heartening to know that some manufacturers are acutely aware of the deterioration in the quality of their products and are attempting to rectify it. There are also some manufacturers who have always maintained high standards and continue to do so today.

It is essential, therefore, that artists know what materials are available ready-prepared, what their qualities are, whether they are suitable for the artist's purpose, and what manufacturers they are available from, and it is for this reason that this book has been produced. Artists concerned about the permanence and quality of their work should consult, in addition, not only the pigmentation data and other information from manufacturers' literature, but also the standard professional works on artists' materials such as Max Doerner's *The Materials of the Artist*, Ralph Mayer's *Artists' Handbook of Techniques and Materials*, or, more popularly, Hilaire Hiler's *Artist's Pocket Book*.

Artists' Materials is divided up into five sections; supports, studio furniture and equipment, drawing and calligraphy instruments, brushes and painting equipment, and colour and media. As well as introductory text on all artists' materials, detailed charts and lists outline many materials and who manufactures them. Keys on how to use the charts are also included. At the back of the book you will find a measurement conversion table and a list of names and addresses of all the manufacturers and distributors mentioned in this book.

SUPPORTS

Canvases · Metal · Ivory ·
Wood · Masonite · Paper ·
Boards · Pads · Blocks

Choosing the right surface on which to work and treating the material correctly may contribute to the permanence of your drawing or painting. For the best results, paper and board should be acid-free and canvases should ideally be prepared at home. However, careful selection should not stop you from experimenting with the more unusual materials. You may be surprised at the selection available — anything from papyrus to finest ivory.

CANVASES

Canvas fabric is made from a variety of materials. Ramie is a bast fiber which makes superb canvases, but is hard to find. Linen is woven from flax and is by far the best of all the commonly available fabrics, in terms both of strength and resistance to decay. Egyptian mummies were wrapped in linen that has survived to this day. Similarly, the Shroud of Turin is nearly 2000 years old and is in remarkably good condition, given that it was not originally treated by a trained conservationist.

Cotton is a seed-hair fiber and is the most popular canvas material. It is inferior to linen in strength, longevity and appearance, but it is far cheaper to buy. Jute is another bast fiber, but is vastly inferior to linen. It is usually chosen by artists for its very coarse texture. It is unsuitable for permanent work, since it becomes brittle, loses its elasticity and becomes lifeless in a relatively short time.

Canvases are also manufactured from synthetic materials. Polypropylene, nylon and polyester are used for canvases but are generally unsatisfactory because they have poor paint adhesion. Of the three filaments, polyester is most responsive to surface treatments to improve adhesion. Lefranc and Bourgeois' Polytoile is a prepared canvas which has dimensional stability, is relatively unaffected by humidity, is resistant to ultra-violet light degeneration and adaptable to painting in most media.

Although canvas can be bought ready-prepared, it is worthwhile taking the trouble to prepare a canvas yourself because you have far greater control of the finished product. The canvas should always be stretched first. Whether preparing with an oil ground (suitable only for oil painting) or with an acrylic ground (suitable for oils and acrylics) it is wise to use a size of neutral pH such as rabbit-skin size. An alternative is a transparent acrylic size. Both of these sizes will isolate the cloth from the acids in the oil paints and furnish a good surface for the adhesion of the primer. Lead carbonate in linseed oil, such as Winsor and Newton's Foundation White, is an ideal primer because it retains its flexibility, whereas zinc oxide and titanium dioxide, although much brighter whites, are more brittle when dry and are susceptible to cracking. Even so, a little titanium dioxide can be added to a primer to offset the yellowing tendency of the linseed oil. Although more flexible, acrylic priming is less satisfactory for oil painting because it does not impart the same finish and refined appearance compared to oil ground.

Stretchers — the wooden frames to which the canvas is attached — can be bought in many sizes from art materials shops. Buy stretchers with small wedges of wood which fit into the corners of the frame so that the canvas can be tightened or slackened as needed.

Pre-stretched canvases can be bought in a wide variety of sizes, finishes and qualities, but it is not always easy to find out the exact specifications of the priming and the sizing. Many canvases are primed two or three times, which is not always desirable because the canvas becomes more inflexible and may crack. Watch out for cracking on the edges when buying prepared canvas to stretch yourself.

Canvas boards are adequate and cheap but are unsuitable for permanent work. They come in a variety of textures and grains with priming suitable for oil or acrylic paints. Manufacturers of canvas boards include Grumbacher, Maimeri and Tara Materials (Fredrix).

List on pp11-15
Photograph on p13

RIGID SUPPORTS

Rigid supports are best suited to oil, acrylic or tempera although ivory can be used for watercolor.

Metal and ivory

Generally, the use of metal supports is not recommended for beginners because it is difficult to get paint to adhere to a metallic surface. In the past, copper was traditionally used for miniature work, particularly by the Dutch. Today, stainless steel has many advantages over copper, including greater rigidity and strength. Any metal support will need careful preparation to take oil paint: the surface should be abraded to give it some tooth and it should be primed. Metal that is susceptible to rust should be rustproofed before priming.

Ivory panels suitable for painting on are relatively hard to find. J P Stephenson offer African elephant ivory in $2\frac{1}{2} \times 2$in pieces. It is finished for watercolor and its translucent surface is particularly appropriate for delicate portrait miniatures.

Wood and masonite

Wood panels are most suited to traditional tempera, a medium that requires a rigid support. They may be used for oil painting but are heavy and inflexible for this medium. Plain wood supports include mahogany and oak, but these are expensive and tend to warp.

It is possible to buy ready-prepared wood panels in a variety of tinted finishes and in cheaper, sketching forms, such as those offered by J P Stephenson.

Plywood is both cheap and readily available. It should be at least 5 ply and about $\frac{3}{4}$in thick. It will also need bracing with $2\frac{1}{2} \times 1$in timber on the back if it is to be used in very large sizes where there is a possibility of flexing or warping. It should be prepared with a true gesso ground consisting of an animal glue, such as rabbit-skin or gelatine, and an inert pigment, such as one of the calcium carbonates (eg whiting, marble dust or precipitated chalk).

Masonite (also called hardboard) is a

popular rigid support but is best confined to sketches and trials for work executed on canvas. Although it seems to have no severe deterioration problems, it should be remembered that this support has not been in use for an extended period. Sizing, such as a paraffin compound, is added to artists' masonite, which confers high moisture resistance to it. However, it still retains its natural lignins, which may jeopardize its permanence if exposed to high humidity for any length of time. It can be painted on either the smooth or the rough side, but the smooth side will need to be roughened in order to give a key to the ground.

 Photograph on p13

PAPER, BOARDS AND PADS

Many types of paper can be bought not only in loose sheets but also in pads or attached to boards. When buying a board, always remember that acid in the substrate can permeate through to the paper surface. Select either a board with an alkaline buffering or one which is constructed from an acid-free substrate using a starch-based or acid-free adhesive. The newly developed ethylene vinyl acetate (EVA) is a synthetic adhesive containing no plasticizers, which is used by Atlantis in their Museum and Conservation boards.

Cartridge paper derives its name from its original use — to hold a small charge of powder in a firearm. It is most suitable for pencil drawings and, if it has sufficient tooth, can be used for charcoal. Acid-free cartridge is recommended for permanence. It is most commonly available in pads but is also readily obtainable in loose sheets. Hard-surfaced papers, such as those used on CS10 boards made by Frisk, are useful where a very smooth, dense surface is required.

Vellum is a fine parchment ideal for calligraphy. You can buy skins of vellum paper, which works out cheaper than buying pieces, although if you are working in miniature, scraps are sufficient. The hair side is preferable to the flesh side for working on.

Oil painting paper is available loose, in pads or mounted on boards. It is useful for rough work, such as color notes, but should not be used for serious work. For amateurs intent on working up their techniques, it is an inexpensive and useful alternative to canvas. However, as soon as technique warrants it, you should progress to canvas.

Ingres paper comes in a range of colors and sometimes in more than one weight. It is recommended for use with pastels, conté crayons or pencils because of its rough surface. Fixed to a board, it makes attractively textured mounting board.

Watercolor paper is available loose, in pads or laminated onto boards. Surface finishes vary from Rough, Not (or cold pressed) which is less rough, to Hot-Pressed (HP), which is smooth. Today, it is hard to find a watercolor paper which is not acid-free. It is possible to find watercolor papers made with 100 percent linen rags: several of the small French manufacturers make a pure linen paper, and it may be worthwhile checking with a good art shop to see if they stock this. Some very good papers are made with mixed rag and fiber. Handmade paper is increasingly popular for printing and for watercolor. If you are prepared to be adventurous, Egyptian handmade papyrus is obtainable from Sennelier.

Blotting paper is basically unsized paper, and it is always useful to the watercolorist and to the calligrapher. White is best for fine art. Tracing and graph paper are extremely useful for planning a layout and are almost essential in calligraphic work. Sheets of tracing paper with individual drawings on each can be overlaid to work out composition and layout. Layout paper can also be used for the same purpose, but it is slightly more opaque. All these types of paper should be available not only from an artists' materials shop but also from your local stationers.

 Chart on pp18-22
Photographs on pp16-17 & 22

CANVASES

LINEN

CLAESSENS

TYPE 66
Tight weave, medium weight, primed (O)
Rolls 82in × 10yd

TYPE 13 BELGIAN
Fine, smooth surface, primed (O)
Rolls 82in × 5½ yd

TYPE 29
Rough weave, heavyweight, primed (O)
Rolls 82in × 11yd

TYPE 9
Medium, medium weight, primed (O)
Rolls 82in × 11yd

TYPE 70
Medium, medium weight, primed (O)

TYPE 109
Medium, light weight, double-primed (A)
Rolls 82in × 11yd

TYPE 166
Tight weave, medium weight, double-primed (A)
Rolls 82in × 11yd

TYPE 170
Medium, medium weight, double-primed (A)
Rolls 82in × 11yd

TYPE 707
Fine, smooth surface, medium weight, quadruple-primed (O)
Rolls 82in × 11yd

L CORNELISSEN

BELGIAN NO 3
Medium, unprimed
Rolls 83in (2.1m) wide

BELGIAN NO 1
Fine, unprimed
Rolls 87in (2.2m) wide

BELGIAN NO 1
Fine, primed (O)
Rolls 83in (2.1m) wide

BELGIAN NO 3
Medium, primed
(O and A)
Rolls 83in (2.1m) wide
Stretched in 11 sizes from
10 × 8in to 40 × 60in and
to order

BELGIAN NO 707
Fine, triple-primed (O)
Rolls 83in (2.1m) wide

DALER-ROWNEY

HERSTON
Fine, double-primed
Rolls 42, 84in × 6yd
Stretched in 26 sizes from
12 × 10in to 60 × 40in

LYTCHETT
Medium, double-primed
Rolls 42, 84in × 6yd
Stretched in 26 sizes from
12 × 10in to 60 × 40in

'X' RAW LINEN
unprimed
Rolls 84in × 6yd

QUALITY 'X'
Fine, close weave, double-primed (O)
Rolls 84in × 6yd (213 × 548cm)
Stretched in 25 sizes from
7 × 5in to 48 × 36in

KEY

Quality of grain
Portrait, Superfine, Fine, Smooth, Medium, Rough, Coarse (unless otherwise stated)

Weight of fabric (expressed in)
Ounces per square yard, Grams per square meter

Duck	Popular cotton canvas
Osnaburg	Light cotton of lower quality than duck
Sheeting	Finely woven light cotton canvas
O	Primed for oil
A	Primed for acrylic
(where manufacturers have indicated)	

FREDRIX

RAW LINEN 1042-43
Medium weave, medium weight, unprimed
Rolls 52, 84in × 6yd

RAW LINEN 1044-45
Medium, heavyweight, unprimed
Rolls 120, 144in × 6yd

RAW LINEN 1046
Rough weave, medium weight, unprimed
Rolls 54in × 6yd

RIX SP BELGIAN
Fine, primed (O)
Rolls 45, 92in × 6yd +

RIX DP BELGIAN
Fine, primed (O)
Rolls 45, 92in × 6yd +

ANTWERP SP
Rough, primed (O and A)
Rolls 52, 72, 84in × 6yd

ANTWERP DP
Rough, primed
Rolls 52, 72, 84in × 6yd

PORTRAIT BELGIAN
Smooth surface, primed
Rolls 52in × 6yd

OSTEND SP
Fine, even weave, heavyweight, primed
Rolls 120, 144in × 6yd

BELGIAN 5701-14
Primed
Stretched in 14 sizes from 8 × 10in to 36 × 48in

MURAL LINEN 5060-61
Primed
Stretched 30 × 40in, 36 × 48in

HOLBEIN

NOS 1111-17F, −20F, −60F
Fine, primed
Rolls 115, 140, 200cm × 10m

NOS 1111-1A, −2A, −3A, −5A, 10A
Medium, primed
Rolls 80, 100, 110, 115, 140cm × 10m

NOS 1111-7BA, −8BA
Medium rough, double-primed
Rolls 140cm × 10m

NOS 1111-11B, −50B
Rough, double-primed
Rolls 227cm × 10m

NO 1111-70B/DX
Rough delux, double-primed
Rolls 227cm × 10m

NO 1111-23H
Heavy rough, double-primed
Rolls 140cm × 10m

NO 1111-220F
Fine, double-primed
Rolls 140cm × 10m

NOS 1111-201A, 202A, 203A, 205A, 210A
Medium, double-primed
Rolls 80, 100, 110, 115, 140cm × 10m

NO 1111-208BA
Medium rough, double-primed
Rolls 140cm × 10m

NO 1111-211B
Rough, double-primed
Rolls 140cm × 10m

ITALPLASTIC

2343 LINEN 100%
Unprimed
Rolls 155cm × 10, 15, 25, 50m

2403 LINEN 100%
Rolls 210cm × 10m

LASCAUX

TH NO 280
280gr/m², unprimed
Rolls 300cm × 60m

NO 380
Rough, 380gr/m², primed
Rolls 206cm × 44, 48m

LEFRANC & BOURGEOIS

181
Medium heavy, double-primed (O)
Rolls 1m × 5, 10m
2m × 5, 10m

1515
Smooth, primed (A)
Rolls 2m × 10m

1516
Coarse, primed
Rolls 2m × 10m

LUKAS

NOS 2091-92
Medium fine, primed (O and A)
Rolls 55, 65, 75, 85, 105, 210cm × 10m

NOS 2141-2
Coarse, primed
Rolls 65, 85, 105, 210cm × 10m

NOS 2171
Fine, primed
Rolls 65, 85, 105, 210cm × 10m

NO 2181
Superfine, primed
Rolls 65, 85, 105, 210cm × 10m

NOS 1214-80
Primed
Stretched in 16 sizes from 18 × 24cm to 80 × 100cm

MAIMERI

1613
Primed (O)
Rolls 210cm × 10m

1617
Gesso primed
Rolls 210cm × 10m

1621
Synthetic resin primed
Rolls 150cm × 10m

1750-1-1773-1
Stretched in 13 sizes from 18 × 24cm to 70 × 100cm

MARCUS ART

LINEN AND COTTON
Rolls 140cm × 10m

JM PAILLARD

7/1 NO 1 PORTRAIT
Stretched in 19 sizes from 22 × 16cm to 195 × 130cm

7/2 NO 2 LANDSCAPE
Stretched in 19 sizes from 22 × 14cm to 195 × 114cm

7/3 NO 3 SEASCAPE
Stretched in 19 sizes from 22 × 12cm to 195 × 97cm

E PLOTON

NOS 181, 1515, 1516 FRENCH
Primed (O and A)
Rolls 2m × 10m

NOS 13, 20, 29, 707 BELGIAN
Primed (O)
Rolls 2m 10cm × 10m

NO 120
Primed (A)
Rolls 2.10m × 10m

RUSSELL & CHAPPLE

ARTISTS' LINEN
Superfine, unprimed
Rolls 220cm (87in) wide

ARTISTS' LINEN
Fine, unprimed
Rolls 183cm (72in), 213cm (84in), 274cm (108in), 305cm (120in) wide

12OZ FLAX
Unprimed
Rolls 183cm (72in) wide

12OZ SUPER FLAX
Unprimed
Rolls 213cm (84in) wide

16OZ FLAX
Unprimed
Rolls 183cm (72in) wide

LINEN
Superfine, primed
Rolls 145cm (57in) wide

LINEN
Fine, primed
Rolls 145cm (57in) wide

SCHMINCKE

NO 83701 BELGIAN
Fine, very thick, 260g/m², primed
Rolls 45, 55, 65, 75, 85, 105cm × 10m

NO 83703 BELGIAN
Medium, primed
Rolls 45, 55, 65, 75, 85, 105cm × 10m

NO 83702
Coarse, primed
Rolls 45, 55, 65, 75, 85, 105cm × 10m

NO 8400091
Primed
Stretched in 7 sizes from 24 × 30cm to 60 × 80cm

A SCHUTZMANN/ VIKTORIA

V700 RAW LINEN
Medium, heavyweight, unprimed
Rolls 215cm wide

V500 RAW LINEN
Even texture, heavyweight, unprimed
Rolls 215cm wide

V560 RAW LINEN
Even texture, heavyweight, unprimed
Rolls 320cm wide

V3
Heavyweight, primed (O and A)
Rolls 45, 55, 65, 75, 85, 105, 210cm × 10m

V4
Fine, lightweight, primed (O and A)
Rolls 45, 55, 65, 75, 85, 105, 210cm × 10m

V5
Even texture, heavyweight, primed (O and A)
Rolls 45, 55, 65, 75, 85, 105, 210cm × 10m

V6
Fine weave, portrait, primed (O and A)
Rolls 45, 55, 65, 75, 85, 105, 210cm × 10m

V7
Medium, heavyweight, primed (O and A)
Rolls 45, 55, 65, 75, 85, 105, 210cm × 10m

V10
Fine weave, even texture portrait, primed (O and A)
Rolls 45, 55, 65, 75, 85, 105, 210cm × 10m

ARTISTS' LINEN
Stretched in 20 sizes from 18 × 24cm to 90 × 120cm

F UCHIYAMA & CO

140C ART CANVAS
Primed
Rolls 140cm × 10m

UTRECHT

TYPE 185 SINGLE PLY
Medium, 9oz/yd², unprimed
Rolls 125in × 6, 10, 20yd+

TYPE 144 SINGLE PLY
Medium, 10oz/yd², unprimed
Rolls 84in × 6, 10, 20yd+

TYPE 66J SINGLE PLY
Smooth, 9oz/yd², unprimed
Rolls 54in × 3, 6, 10, 20yd+

KEY

Quality of grain
Portrait, Superfine, Fine, Smooth, Medium, Rough, Coarse (unless otherwise stated)

Weight of fabric (expressed in)
Ounces per square yard, Grams per square meter

Duck	Popular cotton canvas
Osnaburg	Light cotton of lower quality than duck
Sheeting	Finely woven light cotton canvas
O	Primed for oil
A	Primed for acrylic

(where manufacturers have indicated)

UNPRIMED LINEN
FINE

MEDIUM

COARSE

PRIMED LINEN
FINE

MEDIUM

COARSE

UNPRIMED COTTON
LIGHT

MEDIUM

HEAVY

PRIMED COTTON
LIGHT

MEDIUM

HEAVY

UNPRIMED JUTE

PRIMED JUTE

PRIMED SYNTHETIC

MASONITE
(SMOOTH SIDE)

MASONITE
(ROUGH SIDE)

MAHOGANY

OAK

PLYWOOD

COPPER

STAINLESS
STEEL

IVORY

TYPE 73D DOUBLE PLY
Smooth, 10oz/yd^2,
unprimed
Rolls 72in × 3, 6, 10,
20yd+

TYPE 74D DOUBLE PLY
Medium, 14$\frac{1}{2}$oz/yd^2,
unprimed
Rolls 54in × 3, 6, 10,
20yd+

TYPE 76D DOUBLE PLY
Rough, 17oz/yd^2,
unprimed
Rolls 119in × 3, 6, 10,
20yd+

TYPE 79D DOUBLE PLY
Medium-rough, 13oz/yd^2,
unprimed
Rolls 76in × 3, 6, 10,
20yd+

TYPE 215 SINGLE PLY
Medium, 11$\frac{3}{4}$oz/yd^2,
unprimed
Rolls 84in × 6, 20yd+

Type 135 SINGLE PLY
Medium-smooth,
unprimed
Rolls 54in × 6, 20yd+

Type 560
Medium, double-primed
(O and A)
Rolls 54in × 6yd

**HANDMADE OIL
PRIMED LINEN AND
COTTON**
Rolls 6yd

TYPE 950, 990
Medium, primed (O and
A)
Rolls 54, 84in × 6yd

WINSOR AND NEWTON

WINTON
Rough, double-primed
Rolls 27, 36, 42, 54, 84in ×
1-12yd
Stretched in 14 sizes from
12 × 10in (305 ×
254mm) to 48 × 36in
(1219 × 914mm)

HERGA
Fine, double-primed
Rolls 27, 36, 42, 54, 84in ×
1-12yd
Stretched in 14 sizes from
12 × 10in (305 ×
254mm) to 48 × 36in
(1219 × 914mm)

COLOURMAN
Medium, acrylic primed
Rolls 60in × 6yd
Stretched in 12 sizes from
12 × 10in (305 ×
254mm) to 36 × 28in
(914 × 717mm)

COTTON

CLAESSENS

TYPE 2
Open weave, medium
weight, primed (O)
Rolls 82in × 11yd

TYPE 102
Open weave, light weight,
double-primed (A)
Rolls 82in × 11yd

DALER-ROWNEY

LULWORTH
Unbleached, primed
Stretched in 6 sizes from
12 × 10in to 24 × 20in

GRANGE
Medium, primed
Rolls 42, 84in × 6yd
Stretched in 26 sizes from
12 × 10in to 80 × 40in

QUALITY PP
Even texture, double-
primed
Rolls 52, 86in × 6yd
Stretched in 25 sizes from
7 × 5in to 48 × 36in

ROWNEY

'P' PURE COTTON
Unprimed
Rolls 86in wide

QUALITY DOUBLE P
Even texture, double-
primed
Rolls 52in × 6yd
Stretched in 25 sizes from
7 × 5in to 48 × 36in

DURO

NO 2525
Medium, heavyweight,
triple-primed
Rolls 53in × 6yd

NOS 2510-2520
Double-primed
Stretched in 12 sizes from
8 × 10in to 24 × 36in

FREDRIX

RAW COTTON
7oz enamelling duck
Rolls 52in × 3, 6, 30,
100yd
72in × 3, 6, 30, 100yd

RAW COTTON
Heavy 12oz duck, fine
weave
Rolls 54, 72, 84, 96, 120,
144in wide

**WASHINGTON
SQUARE**
Osnaburg, close weave (A)
Rolls 52in × 6yd

TRYON
Duck, heavyweight
Rolls 54in × 6yd

UNIVERSAL
Duck, even texture,
primed
Rolls 52in × 6yd

MOHAWK
Sheeting, even weave,
slight texture, primed
Rolls 45in × 6yd

DALLAS
Even weave, medium
texture, primed
Rolls 60in × 6yd

YANKEE
Strong, medium weight,
primed
Rolls 72in × 6yd

MANHATTAN
Rough osnaburg, irregular
weave, primed
Rolls 40in × 6yd

ULTRASMOOTH
Fine, portrait, primed
Rolls 53in × 6yd

SCARLETT O'HARA
Hand-primed (O)
Rolls 52in × 6yd

STUYVESANT
Sheeting, close weave,
smooth surface, primed
Rolls 40in × 6yd

HUDSON
Chafer duck, medium-
weight, primed
Rolls 42in × 6yd

STANDARD
Even weave, bold surface,
primed
Rolls 40in × 6yd

KNICKERBOCKER
Sheeting, smooth, primed
Rolls 42in × 6yd

ATLANTA
Duck, primed
Rolls 53in × 6yd

DIXIE
Heavy 12oz duck, rough,
primed
Rolls 54, 72, 84, 96, 120,
144in × 6yd

PASTEL VELVET
Smooth
Rolls 40in × 6yd

PASTEL SAND
Rough
Rolls 40in × 6yd

ALABAMA
Chafer duck, pronounced
weave, primed
Rolls 52in × 3, 6, 12, 60yd

CHEROKEE
Cotton/polyflax duck,
smooth, primed
Rolls 52in × 6yd

**5003-5042 STANDARD
COTTON DUCK**
Primed
Stretched in 43 sizes from
3 × 5in to 48 × 48in

**5601-5614 PORTRAIT
ULTRA-SMOOTH DUCK**
Primed
Stretched in 18 sizes from
8 × 10in to 36 × 48in

**5401-5406 OVAL
COTTON**
Primed
Stretched in 4 sizes from
24 × 48in to 36 × 48in

GOLDEN ARTIST
COLORS

7010, 20, 30, 40
Duck, unprimed
Rolls 56in × 4yd 28in
72in × 5yd 10in, 6yd, 7yd
7in
84in × 6yd 18in, 7yd 18in,
8yd 18in
92in × 7yd 18in, 8yd 7in

GRUMBACHER

C60/62
Heavyweight, unprimed
Rolls 52, 72in × 6yd

C1
Fine, lightweight, primed
(O and A)
Rolls 40in × 6yd

C2
Medium, medium-weight,
primed (O and A)
Rolls 42in × 6yd

C3
Medium, heavyweight (O
and A)
Rolls 42in × 6yd

C4
Medium, heavyweight (O)
Rolls 52in × 6yd

625-1/23
Triple-primed
Stretched in 23 sizes from
8 × 10in to 36 × 48in

ITALPLASTIC

2000 F-TYPE O/E
Cotton and rayon
Rolls 160, 210cm × 10,
15, 25, 50m

2001 F-TYPE E/R
Cotton and rayon
Rolls 160, 210cm × 10,
15, 25, 50m

2225 REPS GAL TYPE E/R
Rolls 160cm × 10, 15, 25,
50m

LASCAUX

S6701
Duck, 360g/m^2, unprimed
Rolls 315cm wide

LUKAS

2004
Fine, primed
Rolls 45, 55, 65, 75, 85,
105, 150cm × 20m

SORTE S 1414-1480
Primed
Stretched in 16 sizes from
18 × 24cm to 80 ×
100cm

MAIMERI

2699-2720
Finest cotton
Stretched in 22 sizes from
8 × 10in to 40 × 30in

1610
Dark back, primed (O)
Rolls 210cm × 10m

1611
Light back, primed (O)
Rolls 210cm × 10m

1614
Dark back, gesso primed
Rolls 210cm × 10m

1615
Light back, gesso primed
Rolls 210cm × 10m

1618
Dark mixed cotton,
synthetic resin primed
Rolls 150cm × 20m

1619
Light mixed cotton,
synthetic resin primed
Rolls 150cm × 20m

MARCUS ART

COTTON DUCK 6OZ
Lightweight
Rolls 189cm wide

COTTON DUCK 10OZ
Heavyweight
Rolls 189cm wide

ARTISTS' ACRYLIC
PRIMED CANVAS
(O and A)
Rolls 137cm × 5.5m

STUDENTS' ACRYLIC
PRIMED CANVAS
(O and A)
Rolls 137cm × 5.5m

**RUSSELL AND
CHAPPLE**

NO 1
Duck, unprimed
Rolls 8oz-36in wide
10oz-36, 72in wide
12oz-36, 72, 136in wide
15oz-36, 72in wide

NO 2
Duck, unprimed
Rolls 8oz-58in wide
9oz-96in wide
10oz-36, 72in wide

NO 3
Duck, unprimed
Rolls 9oz-96in wide

COTTON DUCK 9OZ
Unprimed
Stretched 20 × 16in
24 × 18in
30 × 20in

COTTON DUCK 8OZ
Primed
Rolls 34, 58 in wide

SCHMINCKE

NO 83600
Medium, primed
Rolls 45, 55, 65, 75, 85,
105cm × 10m

NO 8400092(B)
Primed
Stretched in 7 sizes from
24 × 30cm to 60 × 80cm

**A SCHUTZMANN/
VIKTORIA**

V1
Medium texture,
lightweight, primed
Rolls 45, 55, 65, 75, 85,
105, 210cm × 10m
Stretched in 20 sizes from
18cm × 24cm to 90cm ×
120cm

UTRECHT

TYPE CD 53
Medium texture, 9oz/yd^2,
unprimed
Rolls 63in × 6, 50, 100yd

TYPE CD 49
Medium texture, 7oz/yd^2,
unprimed
Rolls 72in × 6, 50, 100yd

TYPE CD 10
Medium rough texture,
14$\frac{1}{2}$oz/yd^2, unprimed
Rolls 60, 76, 144in × 6, 50,
100yd

TYPE CD 12
Medium texture, 11$\frac{4}{10}$oz/
yd^2, unprimed
Rolls 60, 72, 84, 120 × 6,
50, 100yd

TYPE 578
Duck, double-primed
Rolls 54, 60, 72in × 6yd

TYPE 800
Duck, primed
Rolls 72in × 6yd

PREPARED COTTON
DUCK
Acrylic gesso primed
Stretched in 6 sizes from
11 × 14in to 24 × 30in

WINSOR AND NEWTON

SCHOOL OF ART
Rough, primed
Rolls 27, 42, 54, 84in ×
1-12yd
Stretched in 18 sizes from
12 × 10in to 36 × 24in

SCHOOL OF ART
Smooth, primed
Rolls 27, 42, 54, 84in ×
1-12yd
Stretched in 18 sizes from
12 × 10in to 36 × 24in

ACRYLIC PRIMED
CANVAS
Smooth
Rolls 52in × 1-12yd
Stretched in 11 sizes from
12 × 10in to 36 × 24in

JUTE

DALER-ROWNEY

WESSEX
Coarse, primed (O and A)
Rolls 42, 84in × 6yd
Stretched in 26 sizes from
12 × 10in to 60 × 40in

FREDRIX

ALEXANDER JUTE SP
Medium rough, primed
Rolls 42, 52, 120in × 6yd

LUKAS

2191-92
Fine weave, primed
Rolls 65, 85, 105, 210cm
× 10m

MAIMERI

1616 HEMP CLOTH
Gesso primed
Rolls 210cm × 10m

**RUSSELL AND
CHAPPLE**

16OZ JUTE AND FLAX
CANVAS
Unprimed
Rolls 72in wide

SYNTHETIC

FREDRIX

RED LION POLYFLAX
Even texture, primed
Rolls 55in × 6yd

AMAZON–
POLYPROPYLENE FIBER
Smooth, primed
Rolls 56in × 6yd

HOLBEIN

NOS 1111-105AF,
−110AF VINYLON
Medium fine, double-primed
Rolls 115, 140cm × 10m

NO 111A VINYLON
Medium, double-primed
Rolls 140cm × 10m

NO 120FF VINYLON/
COTTON
Extremely fine
Rolls 140cm × 10m

ITALPLASTIC

2020 S-TYPE O/R
RAYON
Rolls 150cm × 10, 15, 25,
50m

LUKAS

2024 RAYON
Fine, primed
Rolls 45, 55, 65, 75, 85,
105, 150cm × 10m

**A SCHUTZMANN/
VIKTORIA**

V2 RAYON
Fine weave, even texture,
primed
Rolls 45, 55, 65, 75, 85,
105, 210cm × 10m
Stretched in 20 sizes from
18 × 24cm to 90 ×
120cm

STRETCHER
PIECES

FLAT PIECES

RIDGED PIECES

CORNER WEDGES

WATERCOLOR PAPER

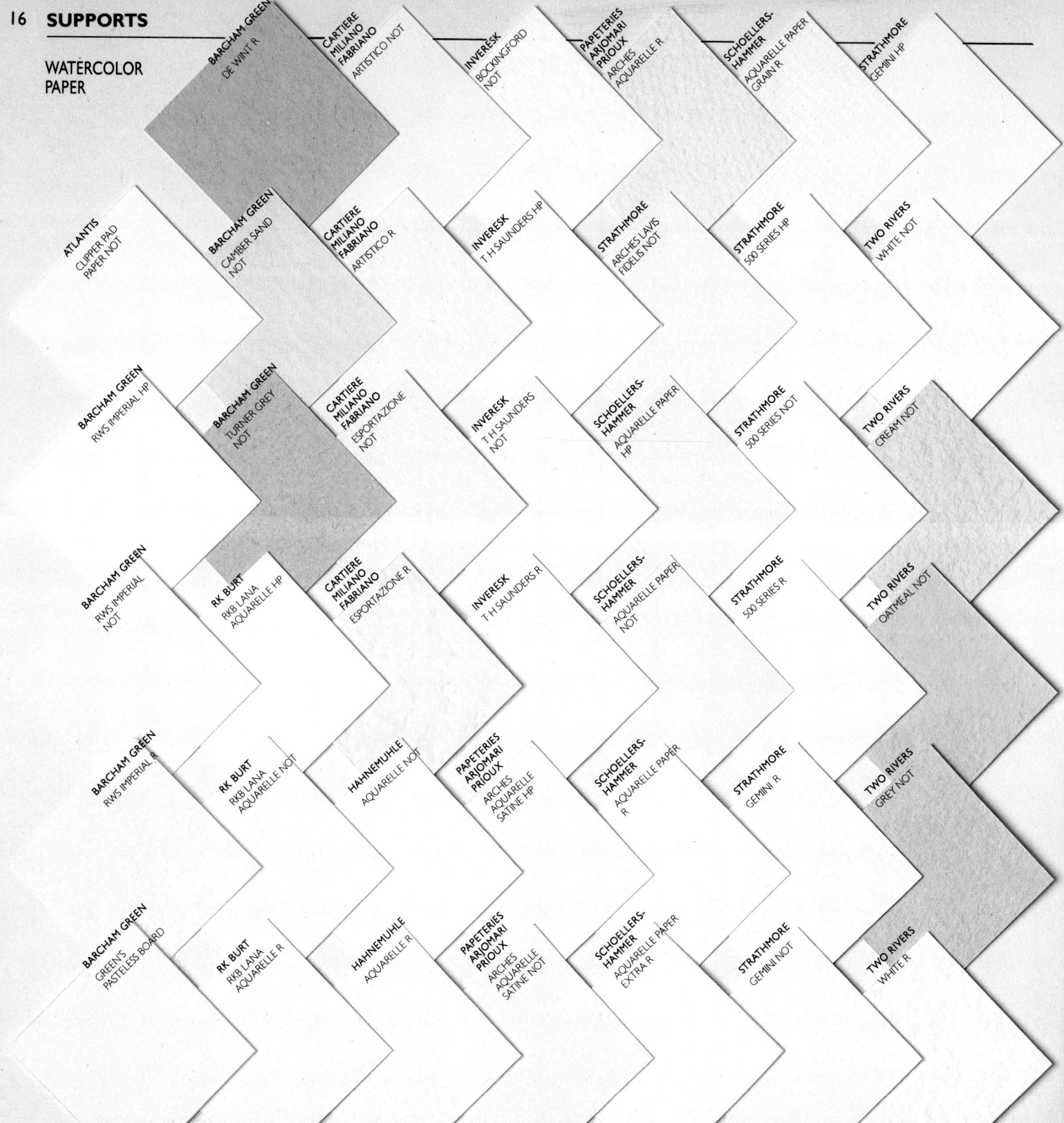

BARCHAM GREEN
DE WINT R.

CARTIERE MILIANO FABRIANO
ARTISTICO NOT

INVERESK
BOCKINGFORD
NOT

PAPETERIES ARJOMARI PRIOUX
ARCHES
AQUARELLE R.

SCHOELLERS-HAMMER
AQUARELLE PAPER
GRAIN R.

STRATHMORE
GEMINI HP

ATLANTIS
CLIPPER PAD
PAPER NOT

BARCHAM GREEN
CAMBER SAND
NOT

CARTIERE MILIANO FABRIANO
ARTISTICO R.

INVERESK
T H SAUNDERS HP

STRATHMORE
ARCHES LAVIS
FIDELIS NOT

STRATHMORE
500 SERIES HP

TWO RIVERS
WHITE NOT

BARCHAM GREEN
RWS IMPERIAL HP

BARCHAM GREEN
TURNER GREY
NOT

CARTIERE MILIANO FABRIANO
ESPORTAZIONE
NOT

INVERESK
T H SAUNDERS
NOT

SCHOELLERS-HAMMER
AQUARELLE PAPER
HP

STRATHMORE
500 SERIES NOT

TWO RIVERS
CREAM NOT

BARCHAM GREEN
RWS IMPERIAL
NOT

RK BURT
RKB LANA
AQUARELLE HP

CARTIERE MILIANO FABRIANO
ESPORTAZIONE R.

INVERESK
T H SAUNDERS R.

SCHOELLERS-HAMMER
AQUARELLE PAPER
NOT

STRATHMORE
500 SERIES R.

TWO RIVERS
OATMEAL NOT

BARCHAM GREEN
RWS IMPERIAL R.

RK BURT
RKB LANA
AQUARELLE NOT

HAHNEMUHLE
AQUARELLE NOT

PAPETERIES ARJOMARI PRIOUX
ARCHES
AQUARELLE
SATINE HP

SCHOELLERS-HAMMER
AQUARELLE PAPER
R.

STRATHMORE
GEMINI R.

TWO RIVERS
GREY NOT

BARCHAM GREEN
GREEN'S
PASTELESS BOARD

RK BURT
RKB LANA
AQUARELLE R.

HAHNEMUHLE
AQUARELLE R.

PAPETERIES ARJOMARI PRIOUX
ARCHES
AQUARELLE
SATINE NOT

SCHOELLERS-HAMMER
AQUARELLE PAPER
EXTRA R.

STRATHMORE
GEMINI NOT

TWO RIVERS
WHITE R.

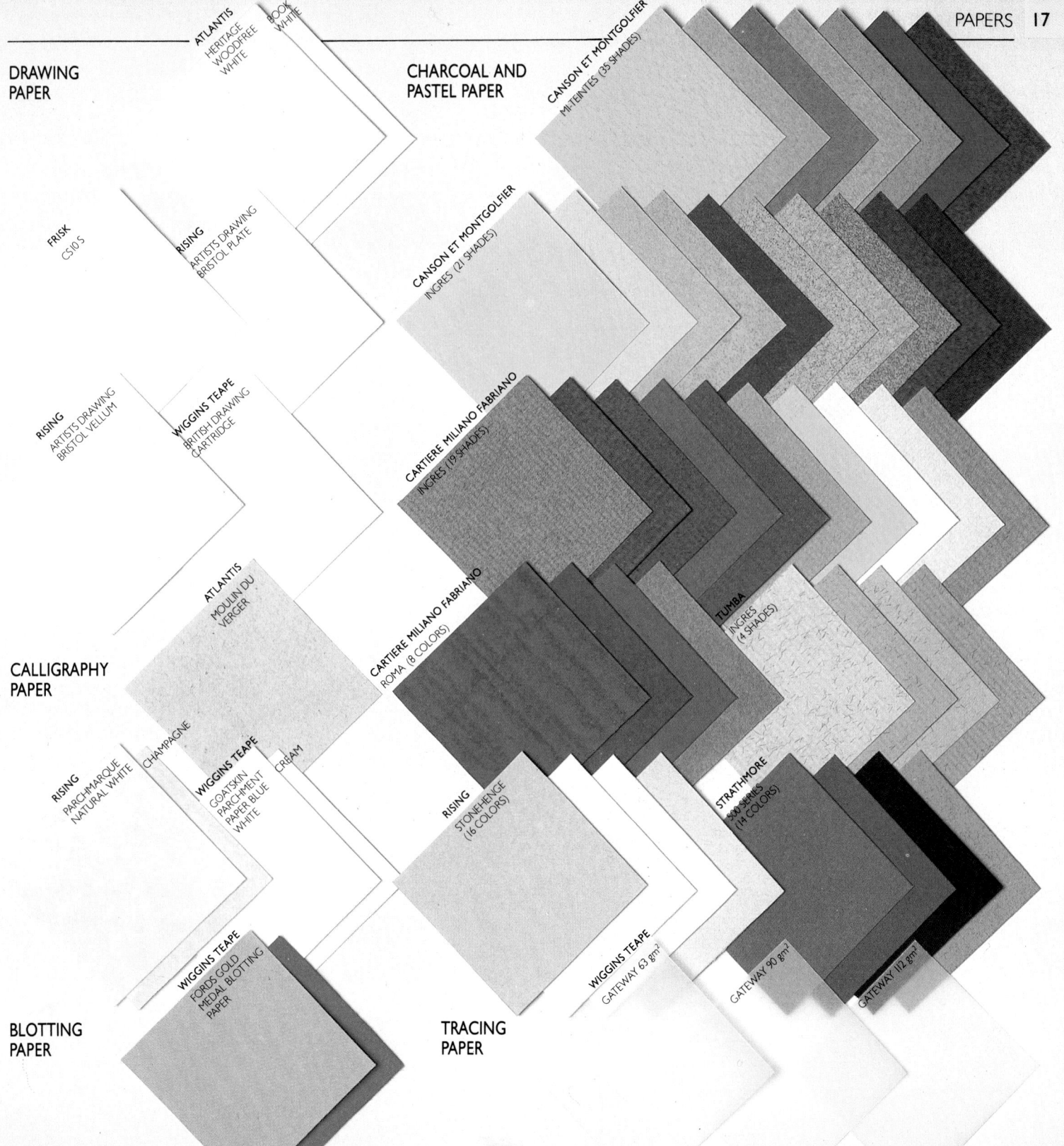

DRAWING
PAPER

CHARCOAL AND
PASTEL PAPER

ATLANTIS
HERITAGE
WOODFREE
WHITE

BOOK
WHITE

CANSON ET MONTGOLFIER
MI-TEINTES (35 SHADES)

FRISK
CS10 S

RISING
ARTISTS DRAWING
BRISTOL PLATE

CANSON ET MONTGOLFIER
INGRES (21 SHADES)

RISING
ARTISTS DRAWING
BRISTOL VELLUM

WIGGINS TEAPE
BRITISH DRAWING
CARTRIDGE

CARTIERE MILIANO FABRIANO
INGRES (19 SHADES)

ATLANTIS
MOULIN DU
VERGER

CARTIERE MILIANO FABRIANO
ROMA (8 COLORS)

TUMBA
INGRES
(4 SHADES)

CALLIGRAPHY
PAPER

RISING
PARCHMARQUE
NATURAL WHITE

CHAMPAGNE

WIGGINS TEAPE
GOATSKIN
PARCHMENT
PAPER BLUE
WHITE

CREAM

RISING
STONEHENGE
(16 COLORS)

STRATHMORE
500 SERIES
(4 COLORS)

WIGGINS TEAPE
FORDS GOLD
MEDAL BLOTTING
PAPER

WIGGINS TEAPE
GATEWAY 63 gm²

GATEWAY 90 gm²

GATEWAY 112 gm²

BLOTTING
PAPER

TRACING
PAPER

PAPERS AND BOARDS

MANUFACTURER/ DISTRIBUTOR	PAPER OR BOARD	TECHNICAL SPECIFICATIONS					USES					
		WEIGHT	SIZE	ROLL	RAG CONTENT	SURFACE	WATER-BASED	PENCIL	PASTEL	PEN	CALLIGRAPHY	OIL
ATLANTIS PAPER CO	Atlantis Drawing and Watercolour (Clipper) Paper	2	1	3	70%	Not	A	B	B	B		
	Heritage Rag Paper	2	3	2	100%	W		B				
	Heritage Woodfree Paper	4	6	1	0	W		B			B	
	Somerset Sized Paper	3	4		100%	HP/Not		B	B			
BARCHAM GREEN	Chatham Vellum Paper	2	1		?	HP/Not	B				A	
	RWS Demy Paper	55 lb	1		0	Not/R	A					
	RWS Imperial Paper	90 lb	1		0	HP/Not/R	A	B	B	B	B	
		140 lb	1		0	HP/Not/R	A	B	B	B	B	
	De Wint Paper (Light brown earth tint)	90 lb	1		100%	R	A	B	B			
	Turner Grey Paper (Grey tint)	90 lb	1		?	Not	A	B	B	B	B	
	Camber Sand Paper (Deep cream tint)	90 lb	1		?	Not	A	B	B	B	B	
	Greens Pasteless Board	300 lb	1		?	HP/Not/R	A	B	B	B	B	
RK BURT	RKB Lana Aquarelle Paper	90 lb	1	1	100%	HP/Not/R	A	B	B	B	B	
		140 lb	1	1	100%	HP/Not/R	A	B	B	B	B	
CANSON ET MONTGOLFIER	Mi-teintes Paper (35 colors)	160 gm²	1		65%	W	B	B	A	B	B	
	Ingres Paper (21 colors)	100 gm²	1		65%	L		B	A	B		
	C à Grain White Paper	125 gm²	1		?	G	B	A	B	B	B	
		180 gm²	1		?	G	B	A	B	B	B	
	Bristol Paper	180 gm²	1		?	S		A		A		
		250 gm²	1		?	S		A		A		
	Croquis Echelle Tracing Paper	70 gm²	1		?	S		A		A		
	Calque Satin Paper	90 gm²	1		?	S		A		A		
	Val Deûme Outline Paper	50 gm²	1		?	S		A		A		
	Vergé Ivoire Paper	140 gm²	1		?	L		A	A	A	A	
CARTIERE MILIANO FABRIANO	Artistico Paper	200 gm²	1		100%	HP/Not/R	A	B	B			
		300 gm²	1		100%	HP/Not/R	A	B	B			
		600 gm²	1		100%	HP/Not/R	A	B	B			
	5 Classico Paper	130 gm²	1		50%	HP/Not	B	A		A	B	
		4	2		50%	HP/Not	B	A	B	A	B	
	Esportazione Paper	3	1		100%	Not/R	A	B	B	B	B	
	Roma Handmade Paper (9 colors)	130 gm²	1		100%	L		B	A			
	Ingres Paper	160 gm²	1		?%	L		B	A	B		
	Murillo Paper	190 gm²	1		15%	Not		B	A	B		

MANUFACTURER/ DISTRIBUTOR	PAPER OR BOARD	TECHNICAL SPECIFICATIONS					USES					
		WEIGHT	SIZE	ROLL	RAG CONTENT	SURFACE	WATER-BASED	PENCIL	PASTEL	PEN	CALLIGRAPHY	OIL
CARTIERE MILIANO FABRIANO	Murillo Paper	260 gm²	1		15%	Not		B	A	B		
		360 gm²	1		15%	Not		B	A	B		
COLUMBIA	1776 Illustration Board	2	4		0	HP	A	A		A	A	
		2	4		0	Not/R	A	A	A	B		
	1812 Illustration Board	2	4		0	HP		B		A		
		2	4		0	Not	A	B	B	B	B	
CRESCENT	Art Poster Board 8 ply (2 colors)	1	1		0	S	A	B		A	A	
	Art Poster Board 14 ply (40 colors)	1	1		0	S	A	B		A	A	
	Art Poster Board White 22 ply	1	1		0	S	A	B		A	A	
	Display Blanks 6 ply (13 colors)	1	1		0	S	A	B		A	A	
	Display Blanks White 8 ply	1	1		0	S	A	B		A	A	
	Display Blanks White 12 ply	1	1		0	S	A	B		A	A	
	Display Blanks White 14 ply	1	1		0	S	A	B		A	A	
	Melton Mounting Board 14 ply (10 colors)	1	2		0		A	B		B		
	Regular Mat Board (125 colors)	1	1		0	S	A	B	B	B		
	Illustration Board (3 types)	2	2		0	Not	A	A	A	A	A	
	Illustration Board	2	3		100%	Not	A	B	B	B	B	
		1	3		0	Li	A	A	A	A	A	
	Charko Board (3 colors)	1	1		0	L		A	A			
	Charko Board (2 types)	2	4		0	HP				A		
	Charko Board	1	2		0	HP				A		
	Line-kote Paper	3	3		0	HP				A		
	Imperial Bristol Board	1	1		0	W		A		A		
	Coloured Drawing Paper (56 colors)	1	1		0		A	B	A	B	B	
	Watercolour Board	1	3		0	HP	A	A		A	A	
		1	3		0	Not/R	A	A	A	B		
DALER-ROWNEY	Oil Painting Board (Oil Paper Surface)	1	19		0	Li/G						A
DRAMANT	Tracing Paper	2	1		0	S		A		A		
FRISK	CSIO Paper	150 gm²	24 × 34 in		?	S		A		A		
	CSIO Board	4	4		?	S		A		B		

KEY

Weight of paper or number of weights available
Content ?% rag present % unknown **0** no rag content **?** content unknown
Surface **HP** Hot-pressed (cold pressed) **R** Rough **Li** Linen **L** Laid **G** Grained **W** Wove or Vellum **M** Mat **S** Smooth
Suitability **Water-based** watercolor, gouache, tempera, acrylic, PVA, vinyl, polymer **A** main use **B** subsidiary use
Size of paper or number of sizes available
Roll number of sizes available

		TECHNICAL SPECIFICATIONS					USES					
MANUFACTURER/ DISTRIBUTOR	PAPER OR BOARD	WEIGHT	SIZE	ROLL	RAG CONTENT	SURFACE	WATER-BASED	PENCIL	PASTEL	PEN	CALLIGRAPHY	OIL
GUARRO	Acuarela Paper				?	HP/Not/R						
	Acuarela Board				?	HP/Not/R	A	B	B	B	B	
HAHNEMUHLE	Aquarelle Paper	I	2		0	Not/R	A	B	B	B	B	
	Ingres Paper (19 colors)	95 gm²	I		?	L		B	A	B	A	
	Bugra Butten Paper (15 colors)	130 gm²	I		?	L		B	A	B	A	
HERGA	Pastel Paper	100 gm²	I		?			B	A			
HOLLINGWORTH	Kent Drawing Paper	160 gm²			100%	HP/Not		A		A		
INVERESK (ST CUTHBERTS MILL)	Inverurie Drawing Cartridge Paper	3	4		0	M		A		A		
	Bockingford Watercolour Paper		22 × 30 in		0	Not	A	B	B	B	B	
	TH Saunders Watercolour Paper	150 gm²	22 × 30 in		100%	HP/Not/R	A	B	B	B	B	
		180 gm²	22 × 30 in		100%	HP/Not/R	A	B	B	B	B	
		285 gm²	22 × 30 in		100%	HP/Not/R	A	B	B	B	B	
		614 gm²	22 × 30 in		100%	Not/R	A	B	B	B	B	
		285 gm²	60 in wide	I	100%	Not	A	B	B	B	B	
KEUFFEL & ESSER	Albanene Tracing Paper	17 lb 20 lb			100%	S		A		A		
	Crystalene Tracing Paper	17 lb 20 lb			100%	S		A		A		
MELRAT	Velásquez Aquarelle Paper	250 gm²			?	HP/Not/R	A	B	B	B	B	
ORAM AND ROBINSON	Fine Pen Board		20 × 30 in		?	S	B	A		A		B
	Academy Line Board	3	3		?	HP	B	A		A		B
	Watercolour Board	I	4		?%	HP/Not/R	A	B	B	B		
	Heavy Watercolour Board	I	2		?	HP/Not/R	A	B	B	B		
	Tracing Paper	I	I		0			A		A		
	Tolmers Wash Paper				?		A	B	B	A		
	Academy Line Paper				?	S	B	A		A		
PAPETERIE ARJOMARI PRIOUX	Arches Aquarelle Paper	185 gm²	22 × 30 in		100%	HP/Not/R	A	B	B	B	B	
		300 gm²	22 × 30 in		100%	HP/Not/R	A	B	B	B	B	
		356 gm²	26 × 40 in		100%	HP/Not/R	A	B	B	B	B	
		640 gm²	22 × 30 in		100%	Not/R	A	B	B	B	B	
		850 gm²	22 × 30 in		100%	Not/R	A	B	B	B	B	
		640 gm²	29 × 41 in		100%	Not/R	A	B	B	B	B	
		640 gm²	40 × 60 in		100%	Not/R	A	B	B	B	B	
		185 gm²	43 in wide	I	100%	Not/R	A	B	B	B	B	
		300 gm²	43 in wide	I	100%	Not/R	A	B	B	B	B	

		TECHNICAL SPECIFICATIONS					USES					
MANUFACTURER/ DISTRIBUTOR	PAPER OR BOARD	WEIGHT	SIZE	ROLL	RAG CONTENT	SURFACE	WATER-BASED	PENCIL	PASTEL	PEN	CALLIGRAPHY	OIL
PAPETERIE ARJOMARI PRIOUX	Arches Lavis Fidelis Paper	220 gm²	3		25%	HP/Not						
		280 gm²		1	25%	HP/Not	B	A	A	A	B	
	Arches MBM Ingres Paper (4 colors)	3			75%	L	B	B	A	B	A	
RISING PAPER	Stonehenge Antique Paper	245 gm²			100%	W		A	A	A		
	Stonehenge High White Paper	320 gm²			100%	W		A	A	A		
	Photolene Bristol Paper				0					A		
	Gallery 25 Paper				25%				A			
	Charcoal Drawing Paper	60 lb			0	L			A			
	Parchmarque Paper (9 colors)				0	W					A	
	Artist's Drawing Bristol Paper	4	1		0	W		B		A		
	Mirage Paper	310 gm²	2		100%	W			A			
	Archival Parchment Paper		2		100%	S		A				
SCHOELLERSHAMMER	Artists' Paper (10 types)	3	2		?%		A	B	A	B	B	
	Aquarelle Paper	2	3		100%	HP/Not/R	A	B	B	B	B	
	Oil Painting Paper (3 types)		2		?							A
	Fine Line Illustration Board	2	18		?	HP/R		A		A		
	Laminated Drawing Board	3	4		0	S		A		A		
	Artists' Board	1	2		?	4		A		A		
	Graficolor Board (16 colors)				?	M		A		A		
	Drawing Paper (3 colors)	4	1		?			A		A		
	Trifoldia Tracing Paper		5		?	S		A		A		
STRATHMORE	400 Series Watercolour Paper	2	2	1	?	Not/R	A	B	B	B		
	500 Series Watercolour Paper	2	1	1	100%	HP/Not/R	A	B	B	B	B	
	Aquarius II Watercolour Paper	80 lb	22 × 30 in		?	R	A	B	B	B		
	Gemini Watercolour Paper	2	22 × 30 in		100%	HP/Not/R	A	B	B	B	B	
		2	27 × 40 in		100%	HP/R	A	B	B	B	B	
	300 Series Drawing Paper	70 lb		1	?	W	B	A		A	B	
	400 Series Drawing Paper	3	1	2	?	M/S	B	A		A	B	
	500 Series Drawing Paper	106 lb	2		100%	M/S	B	A		A	B	
	500 Series Charcoal Paper (14 colors)		64 lb	1	100%	R		A	A			

KEY

Weight of paper or number of weights available

Content ?% rag present % unknown 0 no rag content ? content unknown

Surface HP Hot-pressed Not Not hot-pressed (cold pressed) R Rough Li Linen L Laid G Grained W Wove or Vellum M Mat S Smooth

Water-based watercolor, gouache, tempera, acrylic, PVA, vinyl, polymer A main use B subsidiary use

Suitability

Size of paper or number of sizes available

Roll number of sizes available

MANUFACTURER/ DISTRIBUTOR	PAPER OR BOARD	TECHNICAL SPECIFICATIONS					USES					
		WEIGHT	SIZE	ROLL	RAG CONTENT	SURFACE	WATER-BASED	PENCIL	PASTEL	PEN	CALLIGRAPHY	OIL
STRATHMORE	300 Series Bristol Paper	100 lb	1		?	W	B	A	B	B	B	
	400 Series Bristol Paper	3	1		?	W		A		A		
	500 Series Bristol Paper	4	2	100%		B	A	B	A	B		
	500 Series Illustration Board	2	3		100%		B	A	B	A	B	
TUMBA	Ingres Paper				50%	L	A	B	A	B	B	
TWO RIVERS	Watercolour Paper (14 colors)	350 gm²	2		?%	Not	A	B	A	B	B	
	White Watercolour Paper	510 gm²	1		?%	R	A	B	B	B	B	
UTRECHT	Watercolour Paper	2	2		0	Not	A	B	A	B	B	
	Bristol Board				0		B	A	B	A	B	
	Drawing Paper	70 lb			0			A	B	A		
	Drawing & Charcoal Paper	70 lb			0	L		A	A			
J & R WALKER	Bemboka Handmade Artist's Paper	300 gm²			100%	Not	A	B	B	B		
WIGGINS TEAPE	Gateway Tracing Paper	3	5	2	0	S		A		A		
	Fords Gold Medal Blotting Paper	2	1		25%							
	British Drawing Cartridge Paper	2	2	4	0	M		A		A		

PADS AND BLOCKS

1 TRACING PAPER
2 DRAWING PAPER
3 PASTEL PAPER
4 ACID-FREE RAG PAPER
5 WATERCOLOR BLOCK
6 DRAWING AND WATERCOLOR PAPER
7 LAYOUT AND PRACTICE PAD
8 INGRES PAPER
9 ACRYLIC PAPER PALETTES

STUDIO FURNITURE & EQUIPMENT

Easels · Drawing boards · Lay figures · Miscellaneous equipment

For both the professional and the amateur artist, it is essential to have adequate instruments and equipment. Most important is a firm support on which to put your canvas or drawing board. This may be an easel that you have bought or something that you have made yourself. Similarly, equipment such as cutting instruments and adhesives should be readily available, particularly if you intend to make your own canvases and mounting boards.

EASELS

An easel is a wooden or metal frame that supports the picture as the artist paints or draws. The word easel, interestingly enough, comes from the Latin *asellus* meaning little ass. The French call it *chevalet*, meaning little horse and, certainly, the easel is the work horse of the artist and needs to be sturdy enough to do the work demanded of it. Easels are made in a variety of shapes, sizes and materials, and it is important to choose the right model for your own specific requirements. Many easels can be used for both oil and watercolor painting, but in the latter case you will also need a drawing board.

For outdoor work a box easel or a sketching easel is advisable. It helps if you can buy one with spikes on its feet. Usually the spikes are screw-mounted to swivel through 180°, from a safe position to one which allows you to thrust them into the ground. This provides stability on a breezy day when canvases can make splendid sails. The added weight of the box and its contents give further stability above that of the regular sketching easel. For painting out-of-doors it is also useful to have a lightweight folding stool or a shooting stick if you want to sit down.

The main considerations when buying an easel for indoor painting are space, cost and also media. In a studio, a substantial easel such as a tripod or an all-square style on casters is suitable for oil painting. These come with adjustment systems ranging from pegs and rachets to electric, motor-driven systems. Alternatively you can use a traditional artist's donkey.

However, when painting in a room used for other purposes, storage of the easel is an important consideration. A radial easel is a good choice, particularly one with an incline facility if you wish to use it for watercolor. A sketching easel is an inexpensive alternative but, those who like to sit down to their work might consider a table easel or a bench easel. The latter is available in two forms; one type converts to an ordinary bench, whereas the other can be folded into a small space. Generally, aluminum easels are less expensive than wooden ones, but they are not so sturdy.

 Illustration on pp26-30

DRAWING BOARDS

The drawing board required for fine art work is not necessarily the modern technological wonder found in today's design studios. A simple board will usually suffice. It should be large enough to take a sheet of watercolor, pastel or vellum paper, fixed with gummed tape, thumbtacks or drawing board clips.

It may be as inexpensive as a piece of plywood picked up cheaply at your local lumberyard. However, a good quality square drawing board, preferably with a metal edge, is necessary if you wish to use a T-square on it. The choice of materials is between flooring quality particleboard, plastic-faced particleboard or plywood. A plastic-faced board is more easily wiped clean, but avoid using one if you intend to use thumbtacks.

 Chart on p31

LAY FIGURES

There are very few manufacturers of good lay figures (manikins). Kiu Fong are one of the largest manufacturers and make them in both male and female forms ranging from 25cm (10in) to 90cm (36in) in height. They also make articulated hands. Cornelissens make a magnificent mahogany equine lay figure that is

expensive but an invaluable investment for the painter of equestrian pictures.

 Photograph on p31

STUDIO TOOLS

An abundance of tools in the studio is not vital for the creation of good work but will broaden the possibilities open to you for experimenting.

Cutting equipment

It is always useful for an artist to have a variety of cutting instruments on hand. They may be used to cut paper to size, to cut paper or cloth for collage, montage, découpage, etc, or may be used for cutting a piece of masonite to make an oil painting support.

There are four main types of cutter favored by artists, the most popular of which is the bladed knife such as the Stanley 199 knife. It is also made in a retractable model known as the Stanley 99E. Similar knives are marketed by Rabone Chesterman, Martor, Grifhold and the Good Fly Co. The second type is the snap-off blade cutter said to have been invented by the founder of the Olfa Cutter Co. Although other snap-off blade cutters may match the Olfa Cutter in quality, so far none have bettered it. Equivalents are marketed by Kaicut Edding, Good Fly Co, Martor and Nippon Transfer Paper Co (NT). The third type of cutter, particularly favored for use with very fine work, is the surgical scalpel and blade. This market has been dominated for many years by Swann-Morton on the grounds of price and quality. The most popular handle is the No 3 and the favorite blades are Nos 10a and 11. Manufacturers in this field offer high quality products in most cases because the surgical requirements dictate the quality of the blade. They include Paragon, Gillette, Martor and Stanley. The fourth variety of cutter is the small art or hobby knife, such as the Olfa AKI art knife and the NT D400, D500, and DS800. Excellent ranges are also offered by X-Acto, Kaicut and Lerche.

With scissors, you get what you pay for. Cheap scissors rarely last for any length of time. There are many excellent scissors on the market from Japan, Germany and the UK, particularly those offered by Dahle, Kaicut, Penol, Wilkinson Sword and Richards. The Lerche Graphica range is specifically directed at the art studio, although many of the others are of excellent quality and very useful.

Rotary trimmers such as those from Dahle, Myers or Westwood are ideal for cutting large sheets of paper. However, a large trimmer is fairly expensive, and a sharp knife may be preferred. Martor and NT offer rotary cutters which are extremely easy to use.

A protective cutting mat made from self-healing vinyl is very effective for cutting with knives. They are usually offered in A1, A2, and A3 sizes, and even A0 is occasionally obtainable. They are available in green or translucent, for use with a light-box. Good mats are manufactured by Olfa, Uchida, NT, KDS Hi and Edding.

Rulers, triangles and templates

A metal straight-edge or ruler is useful for drawing and essential for cutting with a knife. Micron offers a range with rubber anti-slip backs; Pickett, Fairgate and Gaebel all offer them with anti-skid cork backs. The Gaebel range of rulers is particularly extensive, but excellent ranges are also offered by four British companies; Rabone Chesterman, Mann, Hellerman and Fisco. Wooden and plastic rulers range from the cheap wooden scholastic rulers to the expensive, raised-edge Lucite rulers with engraved gradations. Opaque, gradated plastic rulers are usually more expensive, but a transparent ruler is preferable if you want to see the paper underneath.

It is useful to have a few right-angled triangles and templates, particularly if you are painting pictures of houses or objects with straight edges, right-angles or regular curves. An adjustable triangle, or a pair of 45° and 60° triangles, some French curves and the invaluable Flexicurve made by Unique Instruments are handy tools. The latter is designed to assist the drawing of regular or irregular curves and is constructed of a vinyl outer casing enclosing a core of lead, with regulating strips of spring steel on each side. The thicker of the two available types forms curves as small as 1in radius, whereas the thinner model forms curves as small as $\frac{5}{8}$in radius. They are available in a range of standard and metric sizes from 8-39in.

Staple guns and canvas pliers

A staple gun makes a very efficient alternative to hammer and nails when stretching a canvas. The main advantages are speed — one squeeze and the staple is in — and the fact that it can be used with one hand, leaving the other hand free.

A heavy duty staple gun like the Rexel Titan should last forever. A lighter model, such as the Rexel 2000, will not last as long but it costs a third of the price. Electric staple guns have recently become available, and are particularly useful for those with arthritic hands.

Canvas pliers are used to pull the canvas tight over the stretcher before inserting the staples. When buying one, look for a well-fitting fulcrum and teeth on each side of the jaws that mesh properly into each other.

Adhesives

There are several tapes that are useful around the studio. Perhaps the most useful is an invisible mending tape, such as Scotch Magic Tape, which has a mat surface, will not reproduce when photocopied and can be written or painted over. Double-sided tape is useful when you want to avoid tube or jar adhesive.

Drafting tape is designed to hold artwork in place and has a low-tack, easy release adhesive that will not damage the paper when removed. Masking tape, however, should be used with some circumspection, since it has certain disadvantages: it embrittles in time and the adhesive becomes more effective the longer it is left in place.

Some companies offer masking tape with standard tack or low-tack adhesive strengths — choose the low-tack or remove the tape from the artwork as soon as possible. Thick, gummed paper should be used to fasten wet watercolor paper to board.

Rubber gum is a traditional adhesive that is cheap and easy to use, although spray adhesives are increasingly popular. Latex glue is effective at bonding fabrics.

Erasers and sharpeners

Soft vinyl erasers are more efficient than India rubber erasers at removing pencil marks. A typical example is the Staedtler Mars 526-50 eraser, which is available in several sizes. Faber-Castell's TK Plast, Colonel Y72 and Factis P24 are among many others. However, the traditionalist who prefers the genuine soft India rubber, can choose from the Rowney QED, the TK Extra, Colonel Y27, the Velos Evergreen and many more.

Different types of eraser are recommended for the removal of pastel and charcoal. They are the bread eraser like the Factis S20 or the Faber-Castell Magic Rub, the gum eraser like the Rowney Art Cleaner or the Faber-Castell Artgum, and the kneadable putty eraser obtainable from Winsor and Newton, Rowney, Faber-Castell, Conté and several other companies.

Manual and electric desk sharpeners, although quick to use, are less controllable than a pocket version. The plastic pocket sharpener and the container sharpener have their adherents, but the type that does the best sharpening and is most controllable is the metal sharpener. It is as well to have the two-hole variety, since this enables you to sharpen thicker types of pencil.

If possible, buy a sharpener for which you can buy spare blades, such as those made by Dux. Good models are also offered by manufacturers including Faber-Castell, Kum-Onit and Möbius and Ruppert.

 Photograph on p32

EASELS

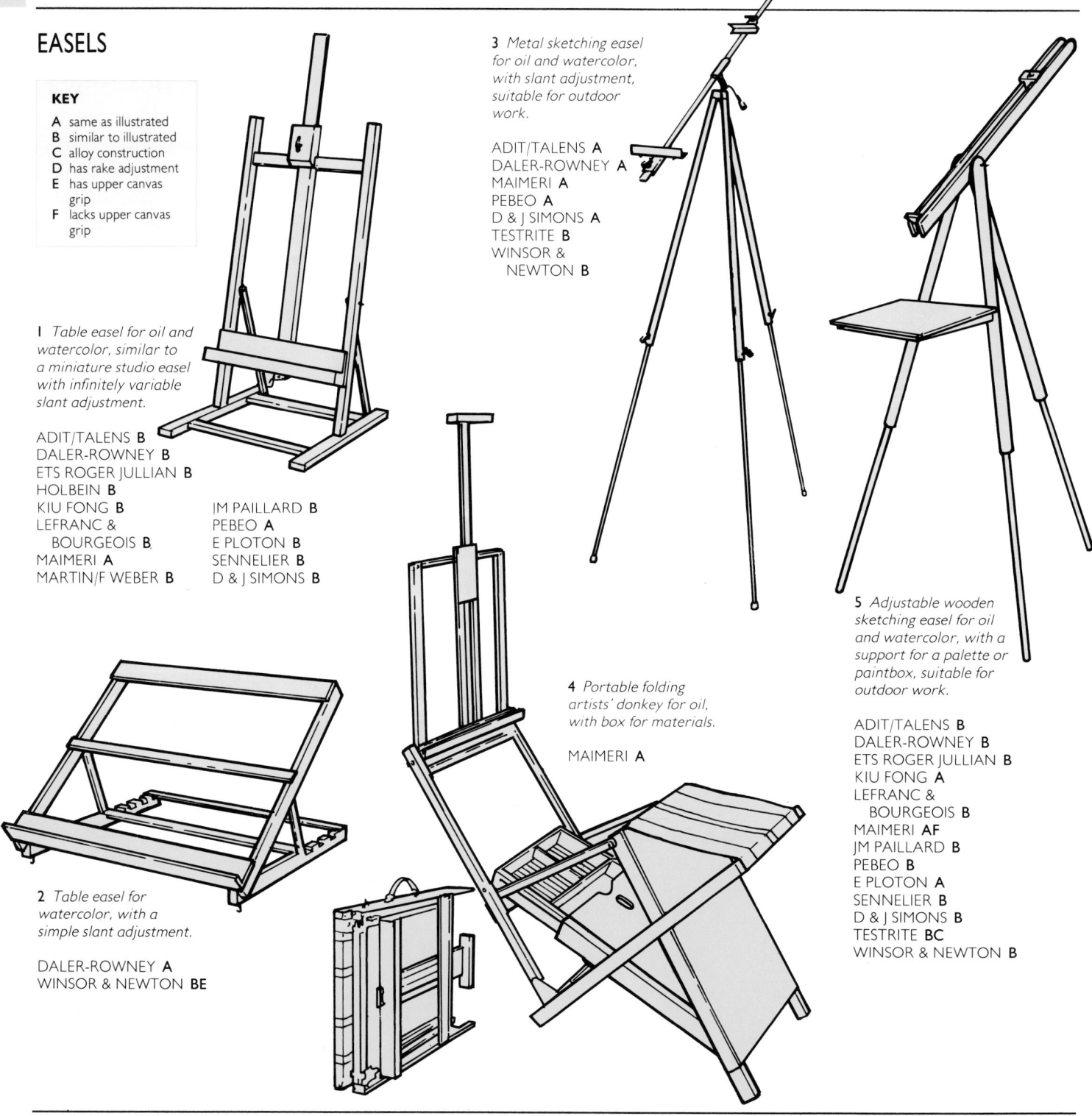

KEY
A same as illustrated
B similar to illustrated
C alloy construction
D has rake adjustment
E has upper canvas grip
F lacks upper canvas grip

I *Table easel for oil and watercolor, similar to a miniature studio easel with infinitely variable slant adjustment.*

ADIT/TALENS **B**
DALER-ROWNEY **B**
ETS ROGER JULLIAN **B**
HOLBEIN **B**
KIU FONG **B**
LEFRANC & BOURGEOIS **B**
MAIMERI **A**
MARTIN/F WEBER **B**

JM PAILLARD **B**
PEBEO **A**
E PLOTON **B**
SENNELIER **B**
D & J SIMONS **B**

2 *Table easel for watercolor, with a simple slant adjustment.*

DALER-ROWNEY **A**
WINSOR & NEWTON **BE**

3 *Metal sketching easel for oil and watercolor, with slant adjustment, suitable for outdoor work.*

ADIT/TALENS **A**
DALER-ROWNEY **A**
MAIMERI **A**
PEBEO **A**
D & J SIMONS **A**
TESTRITE **B**
WINSOR & NEWTON **B**

4 *Portable folding artists' donkey for oil, with box for materials.*

MAIMERI **A**

5 *Adjustable wooden sketching easel for oil and watercolor, with a support for a palette or paintbox, suitable for outdoor work.*

ADIT/TALENS **B**
DALER-ROWNEY **B**
ETS ROGER JULLIAN **B**
KIU FONG **A**
LEFRANC & BOURGEOIS **B**
MAIMERI **AF**
JM PAILLARD **B**
PEBEO **B**
E PLOTON **A**
SENNELIER **B**
D & J SIMONS **B**
TESTRITE **BC**
WINSOR & NEWTON **B**

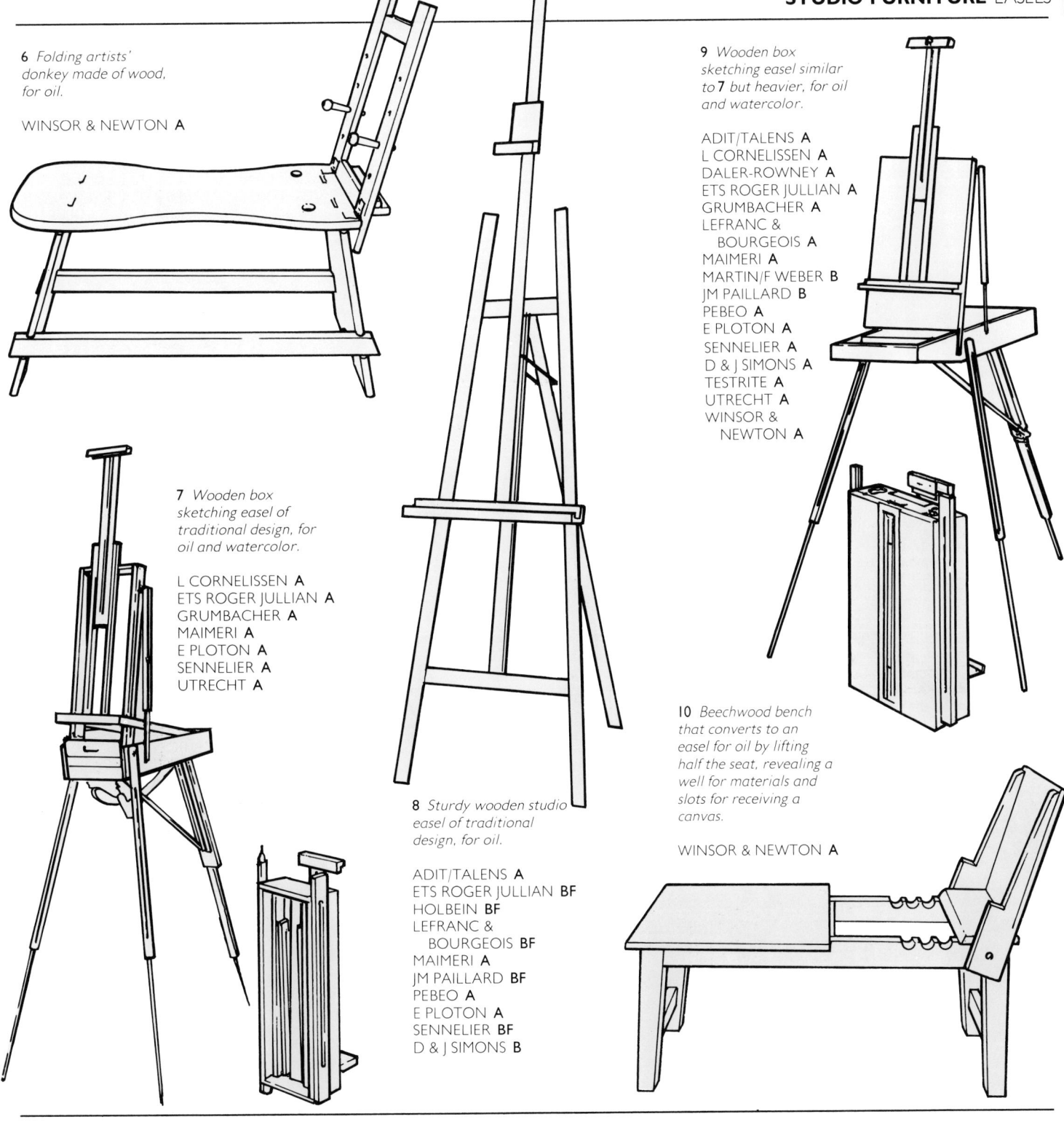

6 *Folding artists' donkey made of wood, for oil.*

WINSOR & NEWTON **A**

7 *Wooden box sketching easel of traditional design, for oil and watercolor.*

L CORNELISSEN **A**
ETS ROGER JULLIAN **A**
GRUMBACHER **A**
MAIMERI **A**
E PLOTON **A**
SENNELIER **A**
UTRECHT **A**

8 *Sturdy wooden studio easel of traditional design, for oil.*

ADIT/TALENS **A**
ETS ROGER JULLIAN **BF**
HOLBEIN **BF**
LEFRANC &
  BOURGEOIS **BF**
MAIMERI **A**
JM PAILLARD **BF**
PEBEO **A**
E PLOTON **A**
SENNELIER **BF**
D & J SIMONS **B**

9 *Wooden box sketching easel similar to* **7** *but heavier, for oil and watercolor.*

ADIT/TALENS **A**
L CORNELISSEN **A**
DALER-ROWNEY **A**
ETS ROGER JULLIAN **A**
GRUMBACHER **A**
LEFRANC &
  BOURGEOIS **A**
MAIMERI **A**
MARTIN/F WEBER **B**
JM PAILLARD **B**
PEBEO **A**
E PLOTON **A**
SENNELIER **A**
D & J SIMONS **A**
TESTRITE **A**
UTRECHT **A**
WINSOR &
  NEWTON **A**

10 *Beechwood bench that converts to an easel for oil by lifting half the seat, revealing a well for materials and slots for receiving a canvas.*

WINSOR & NEWTON **A**

KEY

A same as illustrated
B similar to illustrated
C alloy construction
D has rake adjustment
E has upper canvas grip
F lacks upper canvas grip

13 *Rigid radial easel in metal and adjustable for rake and height, for oil.*

MAIMERI **A**
TESTRITE **B**

14 *Studio easel for oil, adjustable for height but not for rake. It has a strong fanlight catch and is available with or without wheels.*

ADIT/TALENS **BD**
DALER-ROWNEY **BD**
ETS ROGER JULLIAN **B**
GRUMBACHER **BD**
HOLBEIN **BD**
PEBEO **BD**
E PLOTON **BD**
SENNELIER **B**
D & J SIMONS **BD**
UTRECHT **BD**
WINSOR & NEWTON **B**

11 *Radial studio easel for oil, with folding legs. Some models have a central joint, enabling them to be tilted for watercolor.*

DALER-ROWNEY **A**
LUDWIG **B**
RABAN NOAKES **B**
TESTRITE **BC**
UTRECHT **BC**
WINSOR & NEWTON **A**

12 *Bench easel for oil, with folding legs and an adjustable stand capable of holding a canvas up to 20in.*

WINSOR & NEWTON **A**

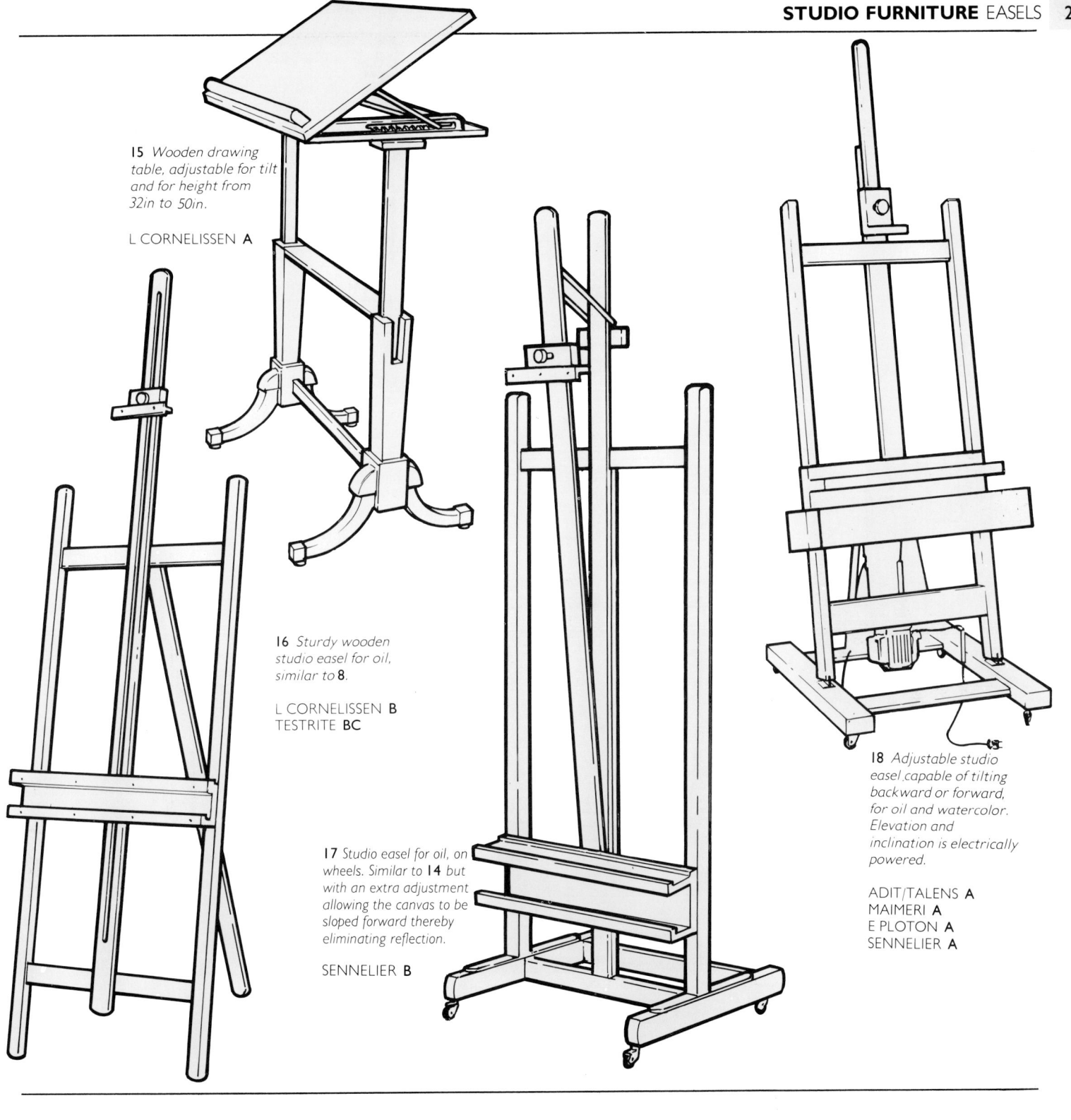

15 *Wooden drawing table, adjustable for tilt and for height from 32in to 50in.*

L CORNELISSEN **A**

16 *Sturdy wooden studio easel for oil, similar to* **8**.

L CORNELISSEN **B**
TESTRITE **BC**

17 *Studio easel for oil, on wheels. Similar to* **14** *but with an extra adjustment allowing the canvas to be sloped forward thereby eliminating reflection.*

SENNELIER **B**

18 *Adjustable studio easel, capable of tilting backward or forward, for oil and watercolor. Elevation and inclination is electrically powered.*

ADIT/TALENS **A**
MAIMERI **A**
E PLOTON **A**
SENNELIER **A**

20 *Metal studio easel with drawing board, adjustable for height, for oil and watercolor.*

MAIMERI **A**
TESTRITE **B**

22 *Chromed steel tube for oil extending from floor to ceiling, minimum height 9ft 3in to maximum height 12ft 9½in. Fitments to hold canvas, a display shelf and a lamp.*

MAIMERI **A**

21 *Adjustable studio easel for oil and watercolor, similar to* **18** *but adjustment is manual.*

ADIT/TALENS **A**
DALER-ROWNEY **A**
L CORNELISSEN **A**
LEFRANC &
     BOURGEOIS **A**
MAIMERI **A**
E PLOTON **A**
SENNELIER **B**

19 *Adjustable studio easel equipped with a drawing board, for oil and watercolor.*

L CORNELISSEN **A**
HOLBEIN **B**

DRAWING BOARDS

TYPE	APPROXIMATE SIZES	ALVIN	BLUNDELL HARLING	HELIX	HELLERMAN
Chipboard	19 × 26 in A2			•	
Plywood	13 × 19 in A3	•			
	14 × 20 in A3				•
	17 × 22 in	•			
	19 × 25 in A2	•			
	19 × 26 in A2			•	
	26 × 36 in A1			•	
White-faced	16 × 21 in	•			
	18 × 24 in	•			
	18½ × 25½ in A2		•		
	19 × 26 in A2			•	•
	20 × 26 in A2	•			
	23 × 31 in	•			
	24 × 36 in	•			
	25½ × 36½ in A1		•		
	26 × 36 in A1			•	•
	25½ × 43½ in		•		
	27½ × 47½ in		•		
	31 × 42 in	•			
	32 × 42 in		•		
	36 × 48 in	•			
	36½ × 50 in AO		•		
	36½ × 54 in		•		
	36½ × 59 in		•		
	40 × 50 in AO				•
	37½ × 60 in	•			
	37½ × 72 in	•			

LAY FIGURES

Most spectacular of lay figures on the market is the equestrian figure with an adjustable neck. Manikin figures are more commonly available in a number of heights, and articulated hands can be bought in a lefthand and righthand style and in male and female sizes.

STUDIO EQUIPMENT

1 SPRAY ADHESIVE
2 RUBBER CEMENT GLUE
3 INVISIBLE MENDING TAPE
4 CLEAR ADHESIVE TAPE
5 DOUBLE-SIDED TAPE
6 DRAFTING TAPE
7 GUMMED BROWN TAPE
8 STAPLERS
9 STAPLE REMOVER
10 BLADES
11 RETRACTABLE CRAFT KNIFE

12 CRAFT KNIFE
13 SCALPEL
14 STANLEY KNIFE
15 RETRACTABLE CRAFT KNIVE
16 FLEXICURVE
17 ADJUSTABLE TRIANGLE

18 METAL RULE
19 PLASTIC RULE
20 SCISSORS
21 TRANSLUCENT CUTTING MAT

22 CUTTING MAT
23 FRENCH CURVES
24 KNEADED ERASER
25 VINYL ERASER
26 GUM ERASER
27 INK ERASER
28 SANDPAPER BLOCKS

DRAWING & CALLIGRAPHY INSTRUMENTS

Charcoal · Pencils, graphite
sticks and leads · Fiber-tip and
felt-tip pens · Pens and nibs

Pencils, pens and other drawing instruments can be used either to create finished work or to make rough sketches. Traditional media, such as charcoal, are as popular as ever and the introduction of relatively new mediums, such as fiber-tip pens, provides the artist with an unprecedented choice of materials. Remember that pen and pencil marks vary enormously according to the surface they are made on, so always test them in conjunction with your support.

CHARCOAL

Charcoal is available in several different forms: natural sticks, compressed sticks, compressed pencils and powdered. It is usually made from willow and its production is limited to a few specialists. You may find that natural charcoal is messy and inconvenient to use, and prefer manufactured forms such as compressed charcoal or charcoal pencils. Both of these are made in a range of grades, usually from 2B to 2H in compressed charcoal, and soft, medium and hard in pencil charcoal. Berol's Blaisdell charcoal pencils are particularly useful because they are wrapped in a peel-off casing. Charcoal sticks can be bought in varying widths — thick, medium and thin.

List on p35
Photograph on p35

PENCILS, GRAPHITE STICKS AND LEADS

Pencil leads are made of mixed graphite and clay. The different grades are produced by varying the ratio of clay to graphite — the more graphite, the blacker and softer the pencil. 6B is extremely soft, HB is of medium strength and 6H is hard. A good pencil has the lead bonded to the cedar wood casing.

The top two grades of graphite pencils may be described as artists' and students' quality. The artists' quality usually runs from about 6H strength through F and HB to 6B. The students' quality generally runs from 4H to 4B.

Apart from standard drawing pencils there are some excellent specialist pencils available which are well worth trying out to see if they suit you. One popular type is the black-lead pencil sometimes called Black Prince or Black Beauty, usually of 3B thickness, which produces a soft black line.

Other types of black pencil are made by mixing black pigment with a chalky medium (pastel texture) or with wax (crayon texture). Examples can be found in the ranges offered by Faber-Castell, Conté and Koh-I-Noor Hardtmuth.

Carbon pencils, such as those made by Conté, are usually offered in 6 degrees of strength from 2H to 3B. Pure graphite sticks are offered by Faber-Castell in pencil thickness and polished like a pencil to keep the fingers clean. Like Conté, they also offer a $\frac{1}{2}$in hexagonal stick.

Thick refill leads, particularly in $\frac{1}{4}$in size, can sometimes be used instead of graphite sticks for sketching. Of the appropriate lead-holders, the best models are manufactured by Faber-Castell, Koh-I-Noor Hardtmuth and Conté. They can be fitted with soft wax-type crayon leads, chalk- or crayon-type leads, graphite leads (HB, 2B, 4B, 6B) and soft or medium charcoal leads.

List on pp36-37
Photograph on p37

FIBER-TIP AND FELT-TIP PENS

Fiber- and felt-tip pens are now increasingly used in design work. Fine fiber-tip pens are particularly conducive to rapid sketching. This type of pen usually has its tip supported by a metal sleeve, which gives added strength to the fiber. Until recently most of these pens were unsuitable for line and wash either because they used water-soluble ink or because the line faded after a few weeks exposure to light.

Today's pens, such as Sakura Pigma, are a better product. The ink is permanent and waterproof and gives a dense black line. They are offered in a choice of three line widths and a range of 4 colors. Similar types of pen are offered by Edding (the 1800 Profipen), Staedtler (Pancolor) and Rotring (Finograph).

Another recent development has been the advent of chisel-edged fiber-tip and felt-tip pens suitable for calligraphy. The Sanford range was the first to appear and is now available in many line widths and colors. They are also offered in a choice of permanent or water-soluble inks. Edding, Berol, Rexel and Hunt-Speedball also offer extensive ranges of these pens.

PENS AND NIBS

Dip, reservoir and fountain pens have been used by artists for many centuries. The basic technique with pen and ink is the use of line and dot which can create any number of different textures and effects on paper or board.

Reeds and quills

Reeds and quills are among the oldest implements used for writing and are still in use today. Should you decide to try cutting and using a reed, you will be continuing a tradition started 5000 years ago in Sumeria.

When you find swan quills in art materials shops they are usually from the US. The cheapest and commonest quills are turkey, whereas goose quills are more expensive, but well worth the extra money. Quills from the left wing suit a right-handed person and vice versa. This is because of the natural curvature of the quill, which, if incorrectly chosen, will tickle your nose.

Dip and reservoir pens

Today, a considerable variety of cheap and versatile dip pens are available. These are particularly good for the beginner. They include italic, round hand, script, poster, decro, scroll, copper plate, 5 line, drawing and mapping (crow quill) pens. Rexel manufacture a large range and Hunt-Speedball offer about 8 styles of nib in 42 variations. Both manufacturers offer loose nibs and holders, as well as sets.

Most dip pens will take any ink, and will rarely clog. Reservoirs may be fitted to some dip pens, or you can buy pens which are specifically designed with reservoirs attached. The Graphos range of reservoir pens is particularly good, offering a selection of 13 nibs and a reservoir that can be adjusted to regulate the ink feed.

A different style of dip pen is the brush pen. It has a metal nib consisting of two metal plates meeting together at the marking edge and should be used in the way you might use a rigid one-stroke brush. Brush pens are made in single line, double line and five line forms in widths varying from $\frac{1}{16}$in to 1in, offered by the Automatic Lettering Pen Co. Coit pens have toothed nibs that produce parallel strokes.

Fountain pens

Fountain pens should usually be filled with non-waterproof or drawing ink. Platignum offer a range of about a dozen nibs and three or four calligraphic sets, along with a black calligraphic fountain pen ink. Sheaffer offers three nib widths which fit into its No Nonsense pen.

The Pelikan Graphos is a fountain pen which accepts drawing ink and is offered with a range of 60 interchangeable nibs in 7 styles. It is suitable for technical drawings, sketching, lettering and calligraphy and comes in a range of line widths.

 Photographs on pp38-42

CHARCOAL

CHARCOAL STICKS

BURTON HOLT
Thin 4in, 5in
Medium 4in, 5in
Thick 5in
Scene Painters' Round and Wedge

PH COATE AND SON
Thin
Medium
Thick
Scene Painters'
Extra Thick

DALER-ROWNEY
Thin
Medium
Thick

FABER-CASTELL
Thin
Medium
Thick
Extra Thick

GRUMBACHER
Thin (extra soft)
Medium (square, round, jumbo)
Soft
Medium
Extra Hard

HOLBEIN
Semi-soft (Unryu-willow)
Soft (Willow)
Semi-hard (Mulberry)
Hard (Vine)
Semi-hard (Crapemyrtle)
Medium (Platanus)

KOH-I-NOOR HARDTMUTH
Thin
Medium
Thick
Extra Thick

KOH-I-NOOR PELIKAN
Thin
Medium
Thick
Extra Thick

WINSOR AND NEWTON
Thin
Medium
Thick

POWDERED CHARCOAL

GRUMBACHER

COMPRESSED CHARCOAL STICKS

BURTON HOLT
Thin 4in, 5in
Medium 4in, 5in
Thick 4in, 5in

CONTE
Extra Soft
Soft
Medium
Hard
Extra Hard

FABER-CASTELL
Extra Soft
Soft
Medium
Hard
Extra Hard

GRUMBACHER
Extra Soft
Soft
Medium
Medium Hard
Hard

KOH-I-NOOR HARDTMUTH
Thin
Medium
Thick
Extra Thick

KOH-I-NOOR PELIKAN
Extra Soft
Soft
Medium
Hard
Extra Hard

CHARCOAL PENCILS

listed overleaf

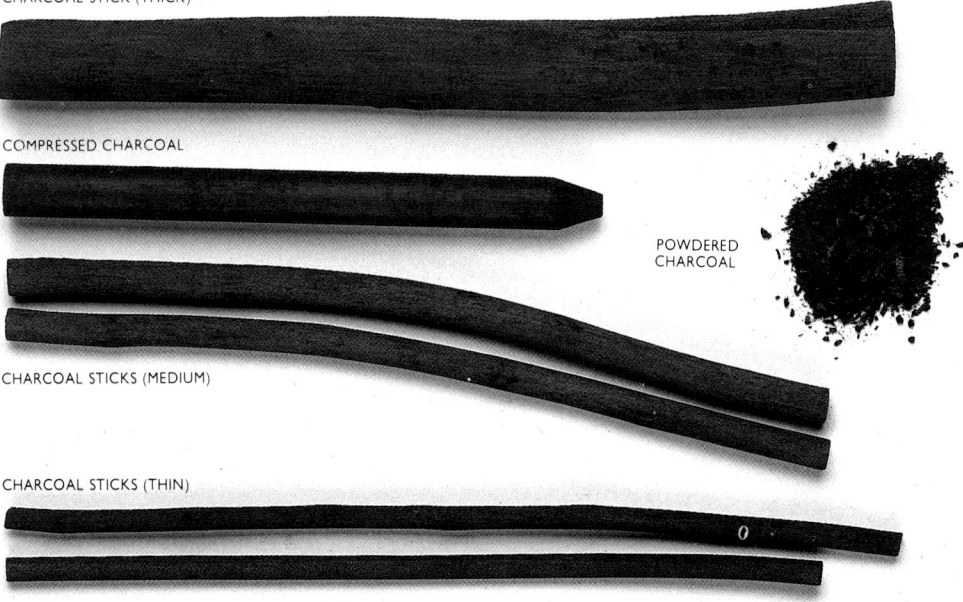

CHARCOAL STICK (THICK)

COMPRESSED CHARCOAL

POWDERED CHARCOAL

CHARCOAL STICKS (MEDIUM)

CHARCOAL STICKS (THIN)

CHARCOAL PENCILS

BEROL
Grades S/M/H

CONTE
Grades 2B/B/HB/H

DALER-ROWNEY
Grade 2B

EBERHARD-FABER
Grades 6B/4B/2B/HB

GENERAL
Grades 6B/4B/2B/HB
(also offer white charcoal)

GRUMBACHER
Grades S/M/H

KOH-I-NOOR HARDTMUTH
Size 4.5 mm

KOH-I-NOOR RAPIDOGRAPH
Grades 6B/4B/2B

ROYAL SOVEREIGN
Grades S/M/H

WINSOR AND NEWTON
Grades S/M

GRADE KEY
XS extra soft
S soft
M medium
H hard

OTHER PENCILS

SOFT SKETCHING PENCILS

BEROL
• Sketching Artists' Pencil Grade S

CARAN D'ACHE
• Black Beauty

CONTE
• Pierre Noire Grades 3B/2B/B/HB/H

DALER-ROWNEY
• Round Black Beauty Grade 4B
• Hexagonal Black Beauty Grade 4B
• Black Beauty Grade 4B

EBERHARD-FABER
• Ebony Graphite Pencil

FABER-CASTELL
• Pitt Artists' Sketching Pencil Grade 6B

GENERAL
• Layout Pencil Grade 6B

GRUMBACHER
• Midnight Sketching Pencil Grade S

KOH-I-NOOR HARDTMUTH
• Black Chalk Pencil
• Negro Drawing Pencil Grades 1/2/3/4/5

KOH-I-NOOR RAPIDOGRAPH
• Negro Pencil Grades 1/2/3
• Sketching Pencil
• Blackie Pencil

REXEL
• Sketching Pencil Grades S/M/H

SCHWAN-STABILO
• Stabilotone Graphite Pencil Grade S

THICK SKETCHING PENCILS

CARAN D'ACHE

FABER-CASTELL

GRUMBACHER
Grades 6B/4B/2B

KOH-I-NOOR HARDTMUTH
Grades 6B/4B/2B
(also offer Oval Sketching Pencil)

REXEL
Grades S/M/H

STAEDTLER

GRAPHITE PENCILS

MANUFACTURER	PENCIL	9B	EE 8B	EB 7B	6B	5B	4B	3B	2B	B	HB	F	H	2H	3H	4H	5H	6H	7H	8H	9H
BEROL	Venus Drawing Pencil				•	•	•	•	•	•	•		•	•	•	•	•	•	•		
	Turquoise Graphite Pencil				•	•	•	•	•	•	•	•	•	•	•	•	•	•	•	•	•
CARAN D'ACHE	Technograph Graphite Pencil				•	•	•	•	•	•	•	•	•	•	•	•	•	•	•	•	•
	Pro Juventute						•	•	•	•	•	•	•	•	•	•	•	•			
CONTE	Indiana							•	•	•	•		•	•	•	•					
	Criterium Sketching Pencil				•	•	•	•	•	•											
EBERHARD-FABER	Mongol Drawing Pencil								•	•	•	•	•	•	•	•	•				
	Microtomic Drawing Pencil					•	•	•	•	•	•	•	•	•	•	•	•	•	•		
FABER-CASTELL	Castell Drawing Pencil 9000		•	•	•	•	•	•	•	•	•	•	•	•	•	•	•	•	•	•	
	Goldfaber Drawing Pencil					•	•	•	•	•	•	•	•	•	•	•	•	•	•		
GENERAL	Kimberly Drawing Pencil			•	•	•	•	•	•	•	•	•	•	•	•	•	•	•			
KOH-I-NOOR HARDTMUTH	Graphite Drawing Pencil				•	•	•	•	•	•	•	•	•	•	•	•	•	•	•	•	•
REXEL	Derwent Graphite Pencil	•	•	•	•	•	•	•	•	•	•	•	•	•	•	•	•	•	•	•	•
	Five Star Graphite Pencil				•	•	•	•	•	•	•	•	•	•	•	•	•	•	•	•	•
ROYAL SOVEREIGN	RS 800 Graphite Pencil					•	•	•	•	•	•	•	•	•	•	•	•	•	•	•	•
ROWNEY	Victoria Drawing Pencil					•	•	•	•	•	•	•	•	•	•	•	•	•	•	•	•
SCHWANN-STABILO	Stabilo-micro 8000		•	•	•	•	•	•	•	•	•	•	•	•	•	•	•	•	•	•	•
STAEDTLER	Mars Lumograph Pencil 100		•	•	•	•	•	•	•	•	•	•	•	•	•	•	•	•	•	•	•
	Tradition 110 Pencil							•	•	•	•	•	•	•	•	•	•	•			

GRAPHITE STICKS AND CRAYONS

CONTE
- Graphite Stick
  Grades S/M

FABER-CASTELL
- Graphite Stick
  Grades 6B/3B/HB
- Pitt Graphite Crayon
  Grades 6B/4B/2B

KOH-I-NOOR HARDTMUTH
- Cyclop Graphite Stick
  Grades 6B/4B/2B/HB

KOH-I-NOOR RAPIDOGRAPH
- Graphite Stick
  Grades 6B/4B/2B
- Giant Graphite Stick
  Grades 6B/4B/2B

CARBON PENCILS AND STICKS

CONTE
- Carbon Pencil
  Grades
  3B/2B/B/HB/H/2H

KOH-I-NOOR RAPIDOGRAPH
- Carbon Pencil
  Grades S/M/H
- Carbon Stick
  Grades S/M/H

ROYAL SOVEREIGN
- Carbon Pencil
  Grades
  3B/2B/B/HB/H/2H

GRADE KEY
XS	extra soft
S	soft
M	medium
H	hard

LEADS

CARAN D'ACHE
- Graphite Leads
  Grades 6B/3B/HB
  Size 3mm

FABER-CASTELL
- Pitt Artists' Leads
  4 colours
  Size 5.6mm
- Pitt Charcoal Leads
  Grades S/M
- Pitt Leads
  Grades S/XS
- Castell Graphite Leads
  Grades 6B/4B/2B/HB
- Drawing Leads
  Grades 3B-5H
  Size 3.15mm

KOH-I-NOOR HARDTMUTH
- Graphite Leads
  Grades 6B/4B/2B
  Size 5.6mm

SCHWAN-STABILO
- Stabilo-micro Leads
  Grades 7B/6B/5B/4B
  Size 3.15mm

- Negro Drawing Leads
  Grades 1/2
  Size 5.6mm
- White Chalk Leads
  Size 3mm
- Charcoal Leads
  Grades 1/2
  Size 5.6mm
- Black Chalk Leads
  Grades 1/2
  Size 3mm
- Drawing Leads
  Grades 6B/4B
  Size 2.5mm

KOH-I-NOOR RAPIDOGRAPH
- Graphite Leads
  Grades 6B/4B/2B
  Size 0.22in
- Charcoal Leads
  Grades S/M/H
  Size 0.22in

SCHWAN-STABILO
- Stabilo-micro Leads
  Grades 7B/6B/5B/4B
  Size 3.15mm

LEADHOLDERS

CARAN D'ACHE
- Fixpencil 3
  Size 3mm

FABER-CASTELL
- Universal Leadholder
  Sizes 2–3.15mm

KOH-I-NOOR HARDTMUTH
- Plastic Leadholder
  Sizes 5.6mm
- Metal Leadholder
  Size 5.6mm
- Metal Leadholder
  Sizes 1.7–3.2mm
- Totiens Leadholder
  Sizes 1.7–3.2mm

KOH-I-NOOR RAPIDOGRAPH
- Universal Leadholder
  Size 0.22in
- Deluxe Leadholder
  Size 0.22in

SCHWAN-STABILO
- Stabilo 8900
  Leadholder
  Sizes 2–3.15mm

STAEDTLER
- Mars Pan Technico 787
  Leadholder
  Sizes 1.9–3.15mm

1 SOFT SKETCHING PENCIL
2 CHARCOAL PENCIL
3 THICK SKETCHING PENCIL
4 CARBON PENCIL
5 CARBON STICK
6 GRAPHITE PENCIL
7 GRAPHITE STICK
8 LEADS
9 LEADHOLDER
10 LEADHOLDER
11 LEAD
12 GRAPHITE PENCILS

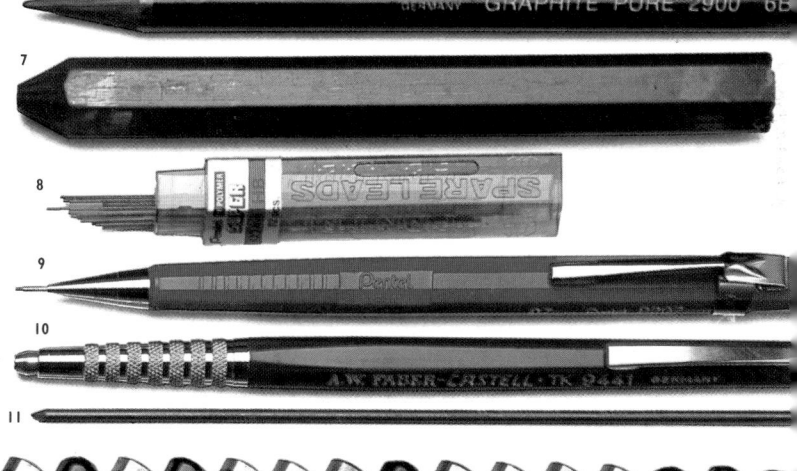

PENS AND NIBS

QUILL PENS

Quills are simple tools but are extremely adaptable because they can be cut to any angle to produce an infinite number of different effects. However, their soft tips require constant re-cutting. Traditional quill-cutting knives are available but craft knives will serve the purpose just as well.

QUILL

REED PEN WITH CAP

BAMBOO PEN

REED PENS

Reed pens can be brought from specialist art shops and, like quills, can be cut to any number of different angles. They produce a characteristic truncated line which can be very effective when used in conjunction with delicate ink drawing. However, the insensitivity of the material dictates that their use is limited.

DIP & RESERVOIR PENS

Dip pens are the most basic of manufactured pens and are very easy to use. They are extremely versatile because they can be used with any type of ink, and they rarely clog. The finer quality nibs should be replaced fairly regularly. Some dip pens can be bought with detachable reservoirs but more expensive are pens that have reservoirs attached, and these should be cleaned regularly and left covered to avoid blockage. The advantage of reservoir pens is that they can be used with waterproof inks which are available in a wide range of colors.

RESERVOIR

ITALIC NIBS/REXEL

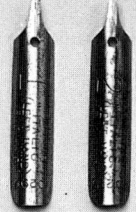   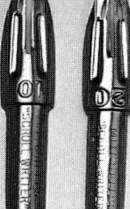

SCROLL NIBS/REXEL

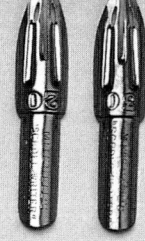

PENHOLDER/REXEL

ROUND-HAND NIBS/REXEL

 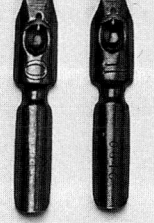  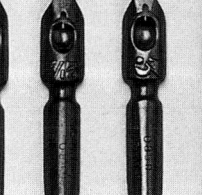

SCRIPT NIBS/REXEL

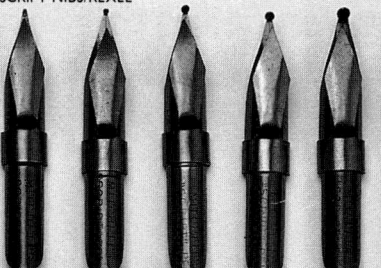

POSTER NIBS/REXEL

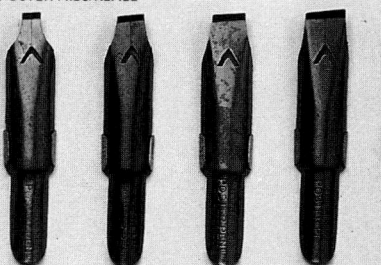 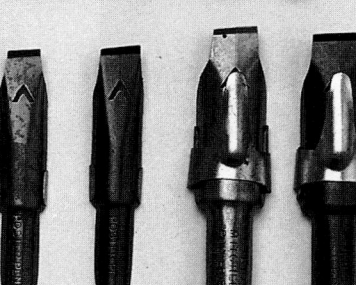

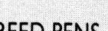

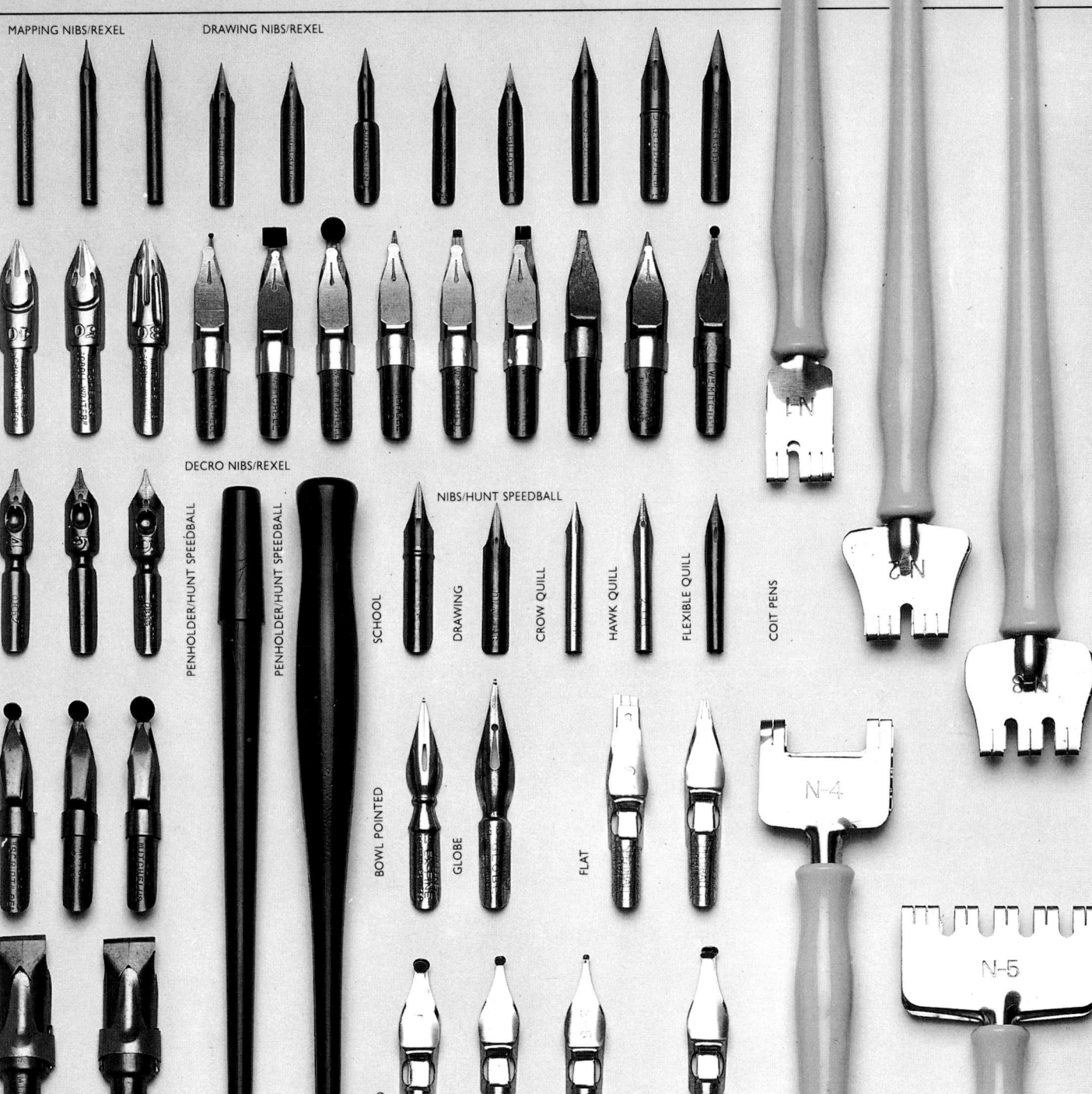

MAPPING NIBS/REXEL

DRAWING NIBS/REXEL

DECRO NIBS/REXEL

PENHOLDER/HUNT SPEEDBALL

PENHOLDER/HUNT SPEEDBALL

NIBS/HUNT SPEEDBALL

SCHOOL

DRAWING

CROW QUILL

HAWK QUILL

FLEXIBLE QUILL

COIT PENS

BOWL POINTED

GLOBE

FLAT

ROUND

OVAL

N-1

N-2

N-8

N-4

N-5

AUTOMATIC PENS

1

3

AUTOMATIC PEN

4 AUTOMATIC PEN

5 AUTOMATIC PEN MADE IN ENGLAND

6A AUTOMATIC PEN MADE IN ENGLAND

7 AUTOMATIC PEN MADE IN ENGLAND

8 AUTOMATIC PEN MADE IN ENGLAND

9 AUTOMATIC PEN MADE IN ENGLAND

10 AUTOMATIC PEN MADE IN ENGLAND

AUTOMATIC PEN

CALLIGRAPHY PEN/OSMIROID

OSMIROID

COPPERPLATE

ITALIC FINE

ITALIC MEDIUM

ITALIC BROAD

B2

B4

LEFTHAND NIBS

COPPERPLATE

ITALIC FINE

ITALIC MEDIUM

ITALIC BROAD

B2

B4

FOUNTAIN PENS

A fountain pen is a handy tool for outdoor sketching because it contains a built-in ink holder that can usually hold a good quantity of ink. This factor does have its disadvantages, however, because it can be a messy business changing nibs while the ink holder is still full. Ink is drawn up into the holder by suction through the nib. The choice of inks for these pens is limited and most types will take only non-waterproof or writing ink. Varieties of nib are also restricted, although the Rotring Artpen and the Isograph are both available with a choice of 9 different nibs.

SKETCHING E/F

SKETCHING F

LETTERING M

LETTERING B

LETTERING BB

VARIANT PEN/ROTRING

VARIANT AND CARTRIDGE

VARIANT NIB

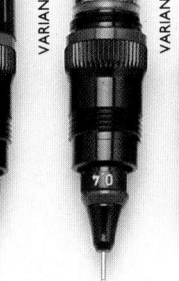

GRAPHOS PEN/ROTRING

RULING NIB/FINE

RULING AND POSTER NIB/BROAD

TUBULAR LETTERING AND STENCILING NIB

ARTPEN/ROTRING

CALLIGRAPHY 1.1

CALLIGRAPHY 1.5

CALLIGRAPHY 1.9

CALLIGRAPHY 2.3

ISOGRAPH PEN/ROTRING

rOtring *Art Pen*

rOtring *isograph*

CARTRIDGE

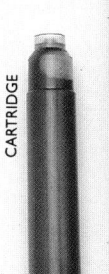

0.13

0.25

0.35

0.50

0.70

1.0

CALLIGRAPHY NIBS

LETTERING PEN/PLATIGNUM

1.0 1.5 2.0

LETTERING NIBS

ML BL BBL

SKETCHING NIBS

EF F

MC 120/PELIKAN

INK HOLDER

NIB REMOVER

Pelikan AG

FINE BROAD B2

B3 B4

INDIA INK PENS

Fountain pens that accept India ink are relative newcomers but have become very popular. India ink is the type most commonly used for drawing and, when diluted, can create interesting 'watercolor' effects. Depending on how much water is added to the ink, a considerable range of shades can be achieved.

ROLA MEDIUM ROLA BROAD

SKETCH SKETCH BOLD

INK HOLDER

OSMIROID

INDIA INK PEN/OSMIROID

INK HOLDER

CALLIGRAPHY PEN/PLATIGNUM

MEDIUM

FINE BROAD B3

NIB REMOVER

BRUSHES & PAINTING EQUIPMENT

Brushes · Palette and painting knives · Palettes · Miscellaneous equipment

There are four elements in the creation of a good painting: the painter's skill and imagination, the support, the quality of the color and the quality of the tools. Those tools are often the brushes, and they deserve close attention in their selection, use and maintenance. There is a wide selection of brushes and painting equipment on the market today and recent technological advances, particularly in the field of synthetics, means that the choice available is expanding all the time.

BRUSHES

Artists' brushes are made with natural hair, natural bristle, synthetic fiber or a mixture of natural hair and synthetic fiber. Generally, different materials are recommended for use with different media. Sable is best suited to watercolor, hog bristle is used for oil painting, and synthetic fibers complement acrylic paint. However, these categories are not finite, and, for example, a synthetic brush may work well with oil paint and watercolor. It is always advisable to experiment in order to find the brushes that best suit your technique.

Brush shapes and sizes vary according to their function. Round brushes are particularly suitable for watercolor and detailed work. Filberts, flats and brights are commonly used for oil and acrylic paints, and for applying areas of wash. The handle and the ferrule of a brush are also indicators of function and quality. Generally, oil and acrylic painting brushes have long handles and watercolor brushes have shorter handles. The metal surrounding the base of the brush, the ferrule, should be seamless, because otherwise it may split if the handle absorbs too much water and swells. Ferrules are usually made from either nickel-plated brass, brass tubes plated with gold, or solid cupro-nickel. Many lettering and lining brushes are made with quill ferrules because the long hair in these brushes is less likely to be damaged by a quill than by a metal ferrule.

List on pp47-61
Illustrations on pp 47-61

Brush maintenance

The following rules will extend the life and performance of your brushes:
1 Never leave your brushes standing on their hairs or bristles.
2 Clean brushes immediately after use in the appropriate solvent.
3 Make sure that every trace of pigment has been removed, right down to the ferrule, because particles of pigment are abrasive and will wear down the hair or bristle, causing breakage.
4 Wash the brush in warm water with soap.
5 Wipe the brush carefully with a soft cloth and shape it to its original position — this is called dressing the brush.
6 Let the brush dry naturally in room temperature, standing on its handle.

Hog bristle

Chinese hog is the most frequently used bristle in the better brushes, Chunking, Jynkeis and Hankow being most favored. The most suitable bristle comes from a narrow strip on each side of the hog's spine. Hog bristle differs from hair in two important respects. Instead of tapering to a point like natural hair it splits into a forked end with, perhaps, several tips — these are called flags. Bristle has exceptional spring — it is said that the world's first pocket watch employed a coiled hog bristle as a balance spring. The natural curve of the bristle is used to advantage in the construction of brushes, so that the bristles curve in toward the center of the working end, thereby keeping the working shape of the brush reasonably coherent and controlled. Quality hog bristle brushes are available in four basic shapes; round, filbert, long flat and bright (said by some to be named after a Mr Bright, and by others to come from the German breit, meaning broad or wide). They are particularly suitable for oil and acrylic painting because they demand a stiffer, more hardwearing brush.

Sable

The most suitable of natural hairs for watercolor is sable hair, although its sterling qualities are also appreciated by oil painters. This hair is derived from the Asiatic mink or weasel, genus Mustela. The very finest quality is known as Kolinsky or Tobolsky sable and comes from the tail of the mink Mustela sibirica. Weight for weight, Kolinsky sable hair is more valuable than gold.

Sable is admired for its ability to point, its ability to return to its original shape, its spring and its water-holding properties. When purchasing a sable brush, look for the whitish tips at the point of the brush, the characteristic mark of a true sable. Wash the brush well in clean water (most art shops will have water available), hold it by the end of the handle and tap the ferrule sharply against your index finger. It should come to a fine point.

Other natural hairs

Squirrel hair is another very soft natural hair. It points reasonably and retains water well. However, it lacks spring and is consequently less expensive than sable. It is excellent for broad washes and mops. French quill mops and china painting brushes are usually made from Kazan squirrel — named after the Russian town in the Volga basin. At the international fur auctions in autumn 1984 almost no Russian squirrel was on offer, and since then the price of squirrel has risen sharply.

Ox hair, or ox-ear hair, is sometimes called sabeline and is usually the dyed, white, ox-ear hair of Alpine cattle. It is much cheaper than sable, is noticeably stiffer to use and will not point to the degree that sable does. However, its greater rigidity is sometimes desirable. Ox hair is also used mixed with sable, particularly for brushes like the one-stroke.

Camel hair is one of the world's greatest misnomers; it is almost any hair except camel's. It is often pony hair taken from the pastern of Asian ponies, but alternatively can be inferior squirrel hair or even unstated mixtures of mysterious origin.

Mixtures of natural hair are usually to be found in the cheapest watercolor brushes. When purchasing a new watercolor brush, it is advisable to test it: wet it thoroughly, remove the excess water, point the brush and make some exploratory brushings on a surface, lifting the brush occasionally to observe its resilience. A good brush will recover its original shape immediately.

Synthetic fibers

Synthetic filaments have recently taken a strong hold on the brush market due to their cheapness, compared to sable, and their durability. In the early days of synthetics brushes were made from smooth nylon filaments. Both natural bristle and hair consist of a central medulla on which are many tiny scales; they also have small hollows which absorb liquid by capillary action. The natural products, therefore, have considerable liquid-holding capacity, whereas the early nylon filaments had none. Consequently, they were originally recommended only for acrylic paints, which were sticky enough to hold to the filaments.

In recent years a thin-tapered white filament which has good water-holding properties has been developed by a Japanese chemical company in combination with Robert Simmons of the US. Other brush manufacturers have dyed it a golden-red color to resemble sable or ox hair. A further improvement over the old nylon is that it tapers like a natural hair and, therefore, will point in a satisfactory way. It also has a structured hair-like surface which increases its water-retention capacity.

Blends of synthetic and sable are less satisfactory because the sable wears out before the synthetic content. Another problem is that the percentage ratio of sable to synthetic is rarely stated by the manufacturers offering such products, but it is widely believed that the usual mixture is, in fact, 90 percent synthetic to 10 percent sable.

Specialist brushes

There are many different types of specialist brushes on the market today that can be used to create interesting effects in your painting. Varnish brushes and a variety of decorating brushes make excellent mural or scenic brushes. They are usually made of bristle and are hardwearing, as are stencil brushes. Lettering and signwriting brushes can be used for fine art; the one-stroke is particularly useful for laying down broad flat washes and the long-haired pointed writer is good for detailed work. The fan blender — so called because of its shape — is available in natural and synthetic fibers and is effective at blending colors on your support.

Oriental brushes can be bought from art materials shops and from shops that specialize in Oriental goods. They frequently lack ferrules and the hair is set directly into the handle, which is normally made of either reed or bamboo. The better grades of brushes are made of mountain-goat hair as well as wolf, pony, badger, weasel, pine marten and bear. They are usually pencil-shaped or broad flat (hake) brushes.

PALETTE AND PAINTING KNIVES

The blades of palette and painting knives are usually made from flexible tempered steel but, more recently, have become available in a stainless steel range from Holbein.

Palette knives, as their name implies, are used for mixing colors on the palette. They are usually 4-6in long and available either straight or cranked. The cranked variety is particularly good at keeping your fingers out of the paint. Extensive ranges are offered by Maimeri and Holbein.

Painting knives vary in sizes of blade from $\frac{7}{8}$in-4in and are available in a considerable variety of shapes. The elongated diamond and the narrow leaf shapes are the most popular. Also known as painting trowels, they provide a useful alternative to brushes for the application of paint to the support, particularly for impasto effects. Talens offers 22 different shapes and Holbein offers an impressive 38 shapes.

 Photograph on p62

TYPES OF FILAMENTS

1 GOAT	5 SQUIRREL
2 HOG	6 SABLE
3 OX	7 MIXED HAIR
4 PONY/CAMEL	8 SYNTHETIC

PALETTES, TRAYS AND DISHES

Palettes are available in three basic shapes, about four different materials and an abundance of sizes. The best known is the traditional kidney-shaped palette, as used by the artist popularly depicted in cartoons with a Van Dyck beard, beret and large cravat. Usually smaller are the oval and rectangular palettes. All these shapes are available in wood, and usually in mahogany. A white background for color-mixing oils and acrylics is increasingly popular. Rectangular and oval shapes are available in white-enameled metal, and the rectangular shape is also manufactured with white melamine facing. The oval shape can be purchased in white plastic and is flexible enough to allow dried acrylic paint to be peeled off. Finally, the tear-off palette pads are easy to use, relatively cheap and save a lot of cleaning up. Most of the larger manufacturers offer a selection of palettes; particularly extensive ranges are offered by Talens and Holbein; Rowney market their unique Staywet palette for acrylic paints.

Paint-mixing trays and dishes are to the watercolorist what the palette is to the oil-painter. They are normally available in trays with five or six slanting divisions and are sometimes paired with circular wells. Cabinet saucers are available in a range of nesting sizes, sometimes with three or four divisions, and are available in white china and plastic. Although more expensive, the china dishes are preferable because their weight makes them more stable; also, the plastic trays tend to stain. However, there is a larger selection of plastic trays from suppliers such as Berol and Scholaquip Industries. Where there is no shortage of surface space, white saucers or dinner plates make good mixing dishes and spare added expense.

 *Photograph* on p63

OTHER EQUIPMENT

Although many painting accessories can be improvised, manufacturers produce a wealth of specialist equipment.

Sponges

Sponges are available in small sizes from art shops and in larger sizes from pharmacists. It is advisable to buy several natural sponges (synthetics are useless), since they have different shapes and textures. They are extremely useful for removing unwanted washes and for applying paint either in washes or in dabs.

Dippers and water bottles

Dippers are for holding mediums and solvents and have a spring clip which can be slipped onto the edge of the palette. The commonly available varieties are made of metal or plastic in single or double form. Holbein offers a range (called palette cups) with knurled screw-on lids in beautifully engineered nickel-plated brass.

Empty jars will serve well enough for water; or you can buy a collapsible plastic bottle or the nickeled brass bottle with knurled screw cap available from Holbein. The latter has a separate slide-on cover which can be clipped to the side of the watercolor box and filled from the bottle.

Brush holders

Brush holders come in several forms: some for keeping brushes in while you work and some for storage. A common variety is a large tin surmounted by an inverted metal "U" fitted with a spiral spring. This enables you to push the handle of the brush into the interstices of the spring, thereby suspending it in the solvent without resting the bristles or hair on the bottom of the tin while you work. Another variety, for the transport and storage of brushes, is an oblong box with spiral springs across the width of the box which hold the brushes in position and prevent damage. Plastic tubes can also be used to store brushes and may be further protected by inserting stiff cardboard. Rowney, Pébéo and ArtBin all offer a selection of containers.

The mahl stick

This instrument provides a stable support for the brush hand when painting detail. It is held in the hand not using the paint brush, and the padded end is rested against the canvas. Traditionally it is made from bamboo with a round cork end sometimes covered with chamois leather. It is also obtainable in aluminum with a rubber tip, made in three 12in sections which can be screwed together if desired, to make a 24in or 36in stick. Daler and Maimeri offer mahl sticks.

Glass mullers and mixing slabs

Glass mullers are used to grind colors and are not always easy to find. It may be worthwhile contacting general chemical or laboratory supplies companies. Glass mixing slabs should be thick — approx $\frac{1}{2}$-$\frac{3}{4}$in — and heavy enough to make them stable. It is a good idea to put the glass on a white surface or to paint the back of it white. Alternatively, a slab of white marble or lithographic stone may be used. It is desirable for these surfaces to have a certain amount of tooth, which can be created by grinding carborundum powder, mixed with water or turpentine, on them. Lukas offers a mixing slab 10 × 12$\frac{1}{2}$in and $\frac{5}{8}$in thick and two mullers of 2$\frac{1}{2}$in and 4in in diameter.

Empty boxes

Watercolor boxes can be acquired empty and fitted to your own specifications. Empty wooden boxes suitable for oils or acrylics are usually fitted with metal linings. Check that the tubes you wish to put into it will fit the space provided. Cornelissen offers a particularly well-made range. The modern alternative to the traditional sketching box is the large type of box containing trays which, in the larger sizes, open out on the cantilever principle. Flambeau Products' ArtBin range is extensive, well made and includes a box designed for pastels.

 Photograph on p64

BRUSHES FOR OIL AND ACRYLIC

HOG BRISTLE

BEROL

A SERIES 7
◆ Sizes 4, 6, 8, 10, 12, 14
A SERIES 8
◆ Sizes 4, 6, 8, 10, 12
C SERIES 9
◆ Sizes 4, 6, 8, 10, 12, 14
B SERIES Academy 12
Sizes S, M, L

BINNEY AND SMITH

C SERIES Liquitex 265
Sizes 1, 2, 4, 6, 8, 10
D SERIES Liquitex 270
★ Sizes 2, 4, 6, 8, 10
C SERIES Liquitex 868
★ Sizes 1, 4, 8

L CORNELISSEN

D SERIES S203
★ Sizes 000-8
A SERIES S222
★ Sizes 1-8
D SERIES S306
★ Sizes 1-8, 10, 12-18
C SERIES S307
★ Sizes 1-8, 10, 12-18
A SERIES S308
★ Sizes 1-8, 10, 12-18
B SERIES S309
★ Sizes 1-8, 10, 12-18

DALER-ROWNEY

C SERIES Bristlewhite 12
★ Sizes 1-6, 8-12
A SERIES Bristlewhite 24
★ Sizes 1-6, 8-12
C SERIES Bristlewhite 36
★ Sizes 1-6, 8-12
C SERIES Bristlewhite 48
★ Sizes 1-6, 8-12
A SERIES 56
Sizes 4, 6, 8-12
C SERIES 58
Sizes 4, 6, 8-12
C SERIES 110
Sizes 1-12

F SERIES 7460
Sizes 1-24
F SERIES 7467
Sizes 1-24
A SERIES 7720
Sizes 1-24
A SERIES 7767
Sizes 1-24
A SERIES 7768
Sizes 1-24
A SERIES 7779
◆ Sizes 1-24
A SERIES 7919
Sizes 1-24
A SERIES 7979
Sizes 1-24

DA VINCI

C SERIES Maestro 7000
★ Sizes 1-30
D SERIES Maestro 7100
★ Sizes 1-30
D SERIES Maestro 7200
★ Sizes 1-30
D SERIES Maestro 7300
★ Sizes 1-30
A SERIES Maestro 7600
★ Sizes 1-24
A SERIES Maestro 7700
★ Sizes 1-24
C SERIES Maestro 7900
★ Sizes 1-24
D SERIES 123
Sizes 1-24
D SERIES 7007
Sizes 0-16, 20, 24
C SERIES 7022
Sizes 1-24
C SERIES 7047
Sizes 1-20
D SERIES 7122
Sizes 1-24
C SERIES 7147
Sizes 1-20
D SERIES 7167
Sizes 1-26
C SERIES 7168
Sizes 1-24
D SERIES 7179
◆ Sizes 1-30
B SERIES 7425
Sizes 1-24

A SERIES 111
Sizes 1-12
B SERIES 115
Sizes 1-12
C SERIES 118
Sizes 1-12
C SERIES 577
Sizes 2, 4, 6, 8, 10, 12, 16
C SERIES 579
Sizes 1-12
F SERIES 851
Sizes 1/4, 1/2, 3/4, 1 in

C SERIES 2788 Speedart
Sizes 1/4-2 in
C SERIES 2789 Harmony
Sizes 1/4-2 in
D SERIES 4093B
Sizes 2, 4, 6, 8-24
C SERIES 4093F
Sizes 2, 4, 6, 8-24
A SERIES 4093R
Sizes 2, 4, 6, 8-24
D SERIES 4222B
Michelangelo
Sizes 1-8, 10, 12
C SERIES 4222F
Michelangelo
Sizes 1-8, 10, 12
D SERIES 4227B Mussini
★ Sizes 1-8, 10, 12
C SERIES 4227F Mussini
★ Sizes 1-8, 10, 12
A SERIES 4227R Mussini
★ Sizes 1-8, 10, 12
D SERIES 4228B
★ Pre-tested
Sizes 1-8, 10, 12
C SERIES 4228F
★ Pre-tested
Sizes 1-8, 10, 12
A SERIES 4228R
★ Pre-tested
Sizes 1-8, 10, 12
B SERIES 4229 Degas
Sizes 1-8, 10, 12
F SERIES 4231
★ Sizes 1-8
F SERIES 4230 Degas
★ Sizes 1-12
D SERIES 4670B Lyons
Sizes 0, 2, 4, 6, 8, 10,
12-20
C SERIES 4670F Lyons
Sizes 0, 2, 4, 6, 8, 10,
12-20
A SERIES 4670R
Sizes 0, 2, 4, 6, 8, 10,
12-20
F SERIES 6361
Sizes 1/4-2 in
C SERIES 6750
Esperanto
Sizes 1/4-1 in

DURO

F SERIES 1080
Sizes 1/4-1 in
F SERIES 1085
Sizes 1/4-1 in
C SERIES 5000
★ Sizes 1-12
C SERIES 5020
Sizes 1-12
D SERIES 5100
★ Sizes 1-12
D SERIES 5120
Sizes 1-12
A SERIES 5700
★ Sizes 1-12
A SERIES 5720
Sizes 1, 2, 4, 6, 8, 10, 12

GRUMBACHER

C SERIES 577F Eterna
◆ Sizes 0, 2, 4, 6, 8, 10,
12-20
C SERIES 579 Eterna
◆ Sizes 1-8, 10, 12
A SERIES 582 Eterna
◆ Sizes 1-8, 10, 12
D SERIES 1271B
★ Gainsborough
Sizes 1-8, 10, 12-20
C SERIES 1271F
★ Gainsborough
Sizes 1-8, 10, 12-20
A SERIES 1271R
Gainsborough
Sizes 1-8, 10, 12

HABICO

C SERIES 233
★ Sizes 1, 2, 4, 6, 8, 10,
12-24
D SERIES 235
★ Sizes 1, 2, 4, 6, 8, 10,
12-24
D SERIES 238
★ Sizes 1, 2, 4, 6, 8, 10,
12-24
A SERIES 240
★ Sizes 1, 2, 4, 6, 8, 10,
12-24
D SERIES 245
Sizes 1, 2, 4, 6, 8, 10,
12-24
D SERIES 250
Sizes 1, 2, 4, 6, 8, 10,
12-24
D SERIES 255
◆ Sizes 1, 2, 4, 6, 8, 10,
12-30
D SERIES 258
◆ Sizes 1, 2, 4, 6, 8, 10,
12-24
D SERIES 258K
◆ Sizes 1, 2, 4, 6, 8, 10,
12-24
B SERIES 260
Sizes 1, 2, 4, 6, 8, 10,
12-24
A SERIES 262
Sizes 1, 2, 4, 6, 8, 10,
12-24
A SERIES 263
Sizes 1, 2, 4, 6, 8, 10,
12-24

HAMILTON

A SERIES 311
Sizes 2, 4, 6, 8, 10, 12
C SERIES 313
Sizes 2, 4, 6, 8, 10, 12
F SERIES 328
Sizes 1/4-1 in
F SERIES 1313
Sizes 8, 10, 12

HANDOVER

B SERIES 314
Sizes 2-14
C SERIES 315
Sizes 2-14
A SERIES 316
Sizes 2-14

HOLBEIN

D SERIES K
★ Sizes 00-12
C SERIES K
★ Sizes 00-12
B SERIES K
★ Sizes 00-12
A SERIES K
★ Sizes 00-12
D SERIES EK
Sizes 0-24

A SERIES 265
◆ Sizes 1, 2, 4, 6, 8, 10,
12-24
A SERIES 270
◆ Sizes 1, 2, 4, 6, 8, 10,
12-24

KEY

Brush sizes
00000000, 0000000,
000000, 00000, 0000, 000,
00, 0, 1, 2, 3, 4, 5, 6, 7, 8,
9, 10, 11, 12, 14, 16, 18,
20, 22, 24, 26, 28, 30
(unless otherwise stated)

1/8, 1/4, 1/3, 3/8, 1/2, 3/4, 1, 1 1/4, 1 1/2,
2, 2 1/2, 3, 3 1/2, 4 in

10, 20, 30, 40, 50, 60, 70,
80, 90, 100 mm (unless
otherwise stated)

XS extra small   S   small
M   medium   L   large
XL extra large

Quill sizes
Lark (small), Crow, Duck,
Goose, Condor (large)

Quality
★ best quality
◆ school quality
(where indicated by
the manufacturer)

OIL AND
ACRYLIC

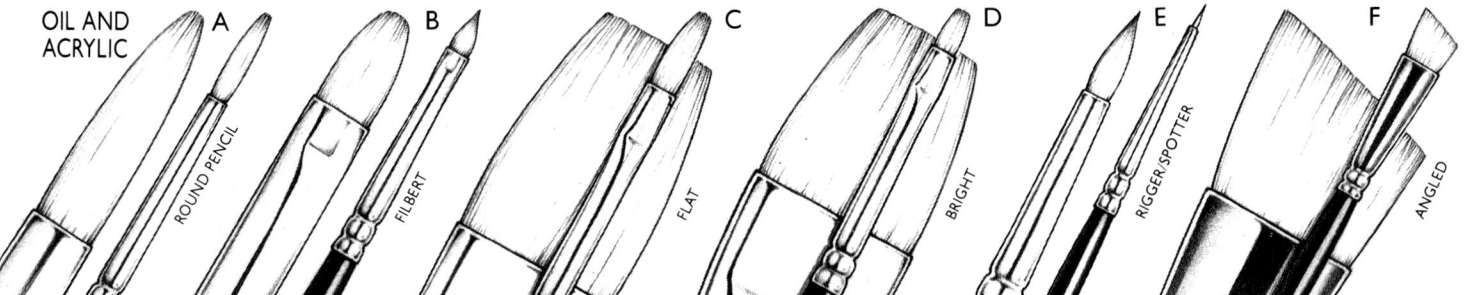

A ROUND PENCIL   B FILBERT   C FLAT   D BRIGHT   E RIGGER/SPOTTER   F ANGLED

C SERIES EK
Sizes 0-24
A SERIES EK
Sizes 0-24
F SERIES Z
Sizes 2, 4, 6, 8, 10, 12
C SERIES W
Sizes 1-12
D SERIES W
Sizes 1-12
A SERIES W
Sizes 1-12

ISABEY
A SERIES 6013
◆ Sizes 00-6, 8, 10, 12
A SERIES 6031
Sizes 1-6, 8, 10, 12
A SERIES 6036
Sizes 00-6, 8, 10, 12
A SERIES 6046
★ Sizes 1-8, 10, 12
C SERIES 6063
◆ Sizes 1-6, 8, 10, 12
C SERIES 6064
◆ Sizes 1-6, 8, 10, 12
C SERIES 6081
Sizes 1-6, 8, 10, 12
D SERIES 6082
Sizes 1-6, 8, 10, 12
B SERIES 6083
Sizes 1-6, 8, 10, 12
C SERIES 6086
Sizes 1-6, 8, 10, 12
D SERIES 6087
Sizes 1-6, 8, 10, 12
B SERIES 6088
Sizes 1-6, 8, 10, 12
C SERIES 6096
★ Sizes 1-8, 10, 12
D SERIES 6097
★ Sizes 1-8, 10, 12
B SERIES 6098
★ Sizes 1-8, 10, 12

JAKAR
C SERIES 632
Sizes 4, 6, 8, 10, 12

KIU FONG
C SERIES Hog Bristle
Sizes 1-12

LANGNICKEL
D SERIES Supreme 1AB
Sizes 1-6, 8, 10, 12-20
C SERIES Supreme 1AF
Sizes 1-6, 8, 10, 12-20
A SERIES Supreme 1AR
Sizes 1-6, 8, 10, 12-20
B SERIES Supreme 1AT
Sizes 1-6, 8, 10, 12-20
D SERIES Regis 400B
★ Sizes 0-8, 10, 12-20
C SERIES Regis 400F
★ Sizes 0-8, 10, 12-20
A SERIES Regis 400R
★ Sizes 0-8, 10, 12-20
B SERIES Regis 404T
★ Sizes 0-8, 10, 12
C SERIES Regis 406LF
★ Sizes 2, 4, 6, 8, 10, 12
B SERIES Regis 408LT
★ Sizes 2, 4, 6, 8, 10, 12
D SERIES King 410B
Sizes 0-8, 10, 12
C SERIES King 410F
Sizes 0-8, 10, 12
A SERIES King 410R
Sizes 0-8, 10, 12
B SERIES King 410T
Sizes 0-8, 10, 12

LEFRANC AND BOURGEOIS
A SERIES 87
Sizes 18, 21, 24
B SERIES J F Millet 109
★ Sizes 1-6, 8, 10, 12
C SERIES 731
Sizes 2, 4, 6, 8, 10, 12-16
C SERIES 741
Sizes 2, 4, 6, 8, 10, 12-16
C SERIES 742
Sizes 2, 4, 6, 8, 10, 12-16
C SERIES 751
Sizes 2, 4, 6, 8, 10, 12-16
C SERIES 752
Sizes 2, 4, 6, 8, 10, 12-16

A SERIES 753
Sizes 2, 4, 6, 8, 10, 12-16

LION BRUSH WORKS
B SERIES Trident 803
Sizes 1-12
A SERIES Trident 810
Sizes 1-12
D SERIES Trident 824
★ Sizes 1-12
C SERIES Trident 825
★ Sizes 1-12
B SERIES Trident 826
★ Sizes 1-12
A SERIES Trident 827
★ Sizes 1-12
C SERIES Trident 0808
Sizes 1-12

LUKAS
B SERIES 5481
★ Sizes 2, 4, 6, 8, 10, 12-20
D SERIES 5483
Sizes 2, 4, 6, 8, 10, 12-24
C SERIES 5485
Sizes 2, 4, 6, 8, 10, 12-24
C SERIES 5486
Sizes 2, 4, 6, 8, 10, 12-16

MAIMERI
C SERIES 976
Sizes $\frac{1}{2}$, $\frac{3}{4}$, 1, 1$\frac{1}{2}$, 2, 3 in
C SERIES 978
Sizes 2, 4, 6, 8, 10, 12
C SERIES 980
Sizes 2, 4, 6, 8, 10, 12
A SERIES 981
Sizes 2, 4, 6, 8, 10, 12
B SERIES 982
Sizes 2, 4, 6, 8, 10, 12

MARABU
C SERIES 2008
Sizes 2, 4, 6, 8, 10, 12-20

MARCUS ART
C SERIES Eterna 579
Sizes 2, 4, 6, 8, 10, 12
A SERIES Eterna 582
Sizes 2, 4, 6, 8, 10, 12

OCALDO
A SERIES D
Sizes 4, 6, 8, 10, 12, 14
C SERIES E
Sizes 4, 6, 8, 10, 12
A SERIES J
★ Sizes 4, 6, 8, 10, 12
C SERIES K
★ Sizes 4, 6, 8, 10, 12
B SERIES L
★ Sizes 4, 6, 8, 10, 12

PEBEO
A SERIES A8
Sizes 1, 2, 4, 6, 8, 10, 12-20
C SERIES A9
Sizes 1, 2, 4, 6, 8, 10, 12-20
A SERIES A10
★ Sizes 2, 4, 6, 8, 10, 12-20
D SERIES A11
★ Sizes 2, 4, 6, 8, 10, 12-20
B SERIES A12
★ Sizes 2, 4, 6, 8, 10, 12-20

PENNELLI CINGHIALE
E SERIES 124
★ Sizes 1-10
C SERIES 129
Sizes 2, 4, 6, 8, 10, 12-30
A SERIES 130
Sizes 2, 4, 6, 8, 10, 12-30
A SERIES 131
Sizes 12-30
C SERIES 132
Sizes 12-30
C SERIES 579
Sizes 1-12

A SERIES 582
Sizes 1-12
C SERIES 693
◆ Sizes 1-12

E PLOTON
B SERIES Lechertier 1
Sizes 0-12, 14-18
A SERIES Lechertier 2
Sizes 0-12, 14-18
C SERIES Lechertier 3
Sizes 0-12, 14-18
C SERIES Lechertier 4
Sizes 0-12, 14-18
F SERIES Hamilton 311
Sizes 2, 4, 6, 8, 10, 12
F SERIES Hamilton 313
Sizes 2, 4, 6, 8, 10, 12
F SERIES Hamilton 328
Sizes $\frac{1}{4}$, $\frac{1}{2}$, $\frac{3}{4}$, 1 in
F SERIES Hamilton 1900
Sizes $\frac{1}{2}$-4 in

PREMIER BRUSH CO
C SERIES P50
★ Sizes 1-6, 8, 10
A SERIES P53
Sizes 1-6, 8, 10
C SERIES P54
Sizes 1-6, 8, 10
F SERIES P55
Sizes $\frac{1}{4}$, $\frac{1}{2}$, $\frac{3}{4}$, 1 in
A SERIES P58
Sizes 1-6, 8, 10

PRO ARTE
A/C SERIES A (Jyukeis)
★ Sizes 1-8, 10, 12
A/C SERIES B (Chinese)
Sizes 1-8, 10, 12
C SERIES C
◆ Sizes 1-8, 10, 12

RAPHAEL
A SERIES 356
Sizes 1-12
C SERIES 357
Sizes 1-12
B SERIES 3577
Sizes 1-12

REEVES
A SERIES R11
Sizes 2, 4, 6, 8, 10
C SERIES R11
Sizes 2, 4, 6, 8, 10, 12
B SERIES R11
Sizes 2, 4, 6, 8, 10

ROBERT SIMMONS
D SERIES Signet 40B
★ Sizes 00-12
C SERIES Signet 40F
★ Sizes 00-12
A SERIES Signet 40R
★ Sizes 00-12
B SERIES Signet 42
★ Sizes 1-12
B SERIES Signet 43
★ Sizes 2, 4, 6, 8
D SERIES 41B
Interlocking
Sizes 00-12
C SERIES 41F
Interlocking
Sizes 00-12
A SERIES 41R
Interlocking
Sizes 00-12
D SERIES 45B Parisian
Sizes 1-8, 10, 12
C SERIES 45F Parisian
Sizes 1-8, 10, 12
A SERIES 45R Parisian
Sizes 1-8, 10, 12
D SERIES 44B
Sizes 2, 4, 6, 8-24
C SERIES 44F Majestic
Sizes 2, 4, 6, 8-24
A SERIES 44F
Sizes 2, 4, 6, 8-24
A SERIES 464 Soho
◆ Sizes 1-8, 10, 12
C SERIES 465 Soho
◆ Sizes 1-8, 10, 12
C SERIES 467 Soho
◆ Sizes 0, 2, 4, 6, 8-20
C SERIES 90 Fitch
Sizes $\frac{1}{4}$-1$\frac{1}{2}$ in
F SERIES 95 Angular Liner
Sizes $\frac{1}{4}$-1 in

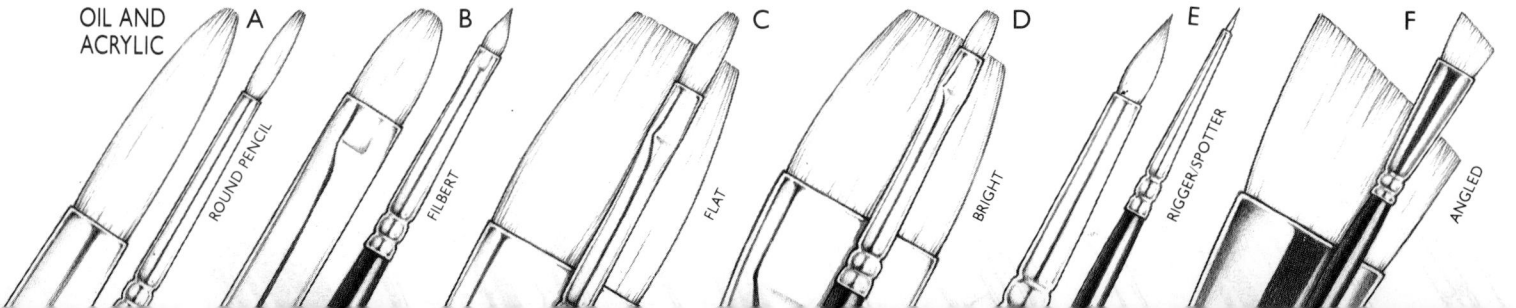

OIL AND ACRYLIC
A ROUND PENCIL
B FILBERT
C FLAT
D BRIGHT
E RIGGER/SPOTTER
F ANGLED

SIMONART

C SERIES 34
★ Sizes 1-6, 8, 10, 12
B SERIES 35
★ Sizes 1-6, 8, 10, 12
A SERIES 38
★ Sizes 1-6, 8, 10, 12
C SERIES 39
★ Sizes 1-6, 8, 10, 12
C SERIES 44
Sizes 1-8, 10, 12
A SERIES 48
Sizes 1-8, 10, 12

J P STEPHENSON

A SERIES Bristle
Sizes 2, 4, 6, 8, 10, 12

STRATHMORE ARTIST PRODUCTS

C SERIES Superior
★ Sizes 2, 4, 6, 8, 10, 12
D SERIES Superior
★ Sizes 2, 4, 6, 8, 10, 12
A SERIES Superior
★ Sizes 2, 4, 6, 8, 10, 12
B SERIES Superior
★ Sizes 2, 4, 6, 8, 10, 12
C SERIES Fine
Sizes 2-12
D SERIES Fine
Sizes 2-12
A SERIES Fine
Sizes 2-12

TALENS

D SERIES Rembrandt 200
★ Sizes 2, 4, 6, 8-24
A SERIES Rembrandt 201
★ Sizes 2, 4, 6, 8-24
B SERIES Rembrandt 208
★ Sizes 2, 4, 6, 8-24
C SERIES Rembrandt 220
◆ Sizes 2, 4, 6, 8-24
A SERIES Rembrandt 221
Sizes 2, 4, 6, 8-24
C SERIES Rembrandt 222
Sizes 2, 4, 6, 8-24

UTRECHT

C SERIES Rhenish 201
★ Sizes 1-6, 8, 10, 12
D SERIES Rhenish 202
★ Sizes 1-6, 8, 10, 12
C SERIES 203
★ Sizes 3, 6, 8, 10
B SERIES Rhenish 204
★ Sizes 1, 2, 4, 6, 8, 10, 12
A SERIES Rhenish 205
★ Sizes 0-2, 4, 6, 8, 10, 12
C SERIES 209
Sizes 1, 2, 4, 6, 8, 10, 12
D SERIES 210B
Sizes 14-24
D SERIES 209B
Sizes 1, 2, 4, 6, 8, 10, 12
B SERIES 209F
Sizes 1, 2, 4, 6, 8, 10, 12
A SERIES 209R
Sizes 1, 2, 4, 6, 8, 10, 12

L WARD AND CO

A SERIES Whistler S12
Sizes 16-30
D SERIES Whistler 302XL
Sizes 1-8, 10, 12, 14, 16, 18
C SERIES Whistler 303XL
Sizes 1-8, 10, 12, 14, 16, 18
A SERIES Whistler 304XL
Sizes 1-8, 10, 12, 14, 16, 18
B SERIES Whistler 305XL
Sizes 1-8, 10, 12, 14, 16, 18
D SERIES Whistler 306
★ Sizes 1-8, 10, 12
C SERIES Whistler 307
★ Sizes 1-8, 10, 12
A SERIES Whistler 308
★ Sizes 1-8, 10, 12
B SERIES Whistler 309
★ Sizes 1-8, 10, 12

WINSOR AND NEWTON

A SERIES A
Sizes 1-12
C SERIES A
Sizes 1-12
C SERIES AA
Sizes 1-12
B SERIES AO
★ Sizes 1-12
C SERIES B Flat
◆ Sizes 2, 4, 6, 8, 10, 12
A SERIES B Round
◆ Sizes 1-8
B SERIES CL
Sizes 1-12
D SERIES F
◆ Sizes 1-14
C SERIES O
Sizes 2, 4, 6, 8, 10, 12
C SERIES R
Sizes 2, 4, 6, 8, 10, 12

C SERIES Winsor Gold
★ BR
Sizes 2, 3 in
B SERIES Winsor Gold F
★ Sizes 2, 4, 6, 8, 10, 12
C SERIES Winsor Gold
★ LFL
Sizes 2, 4, 6, 8, 10, 12
A SERIES Winsor Gold R
★ Sizes 2, 4, 6, 8, 10, 12
C SERIES Winsor Gold
★ SFL
Sizes 2, 4, 6, 8, 10, 12-16

SABLE

BINNEY AND SMITH

A SERIES Liquitex 505
Sizes 0, 2, 4, 6, 10
A SERIES Liquitex 506
★ Sizes 0-2, 4, 6, 8, 10
D SERIES Liquitex 515
Sizes 1, 2, 4, 6, 10
D SERIES Liquitex 516
★ Sizes 2, 4, 6, 8, 10

L CORNELISSEN

A SERIES S17
★ Sizes 0-10
D SERIES S37
★ Sizes 2-12

DALER-ROWNEY

A SERIES 101 (Kolinsky)
★ Sizes 00-8, 10, 12
C SERIES 102 (Kolinsky)
★ Sizes 00-8, 10, 12
E SERIES 103 (Kolinsky)
★ Sizes 1-6
B SERIES 132
Sizes 2, 4, 6, 8, 10, 12
C SERIES 133
Sizes 1-6, 8, 10, 12
A SERIES 134
Sizes 1-6, 8, 10, 12

DA VINCI

A SERIES 1600 (Kolinsky)
★ Sizes 0-24

A SERIES 1604 (Kolinsky)
★ Sizes 0-24
A SERIES 1610 (Kolinsky)
Sizes 0-24
A SERIES 1640
Sizes 0-30
D SERIES 1800 (Kolinsky)
★ Sizes 0-24
B SERIES 1805 (Kolinsky)
★ Sizes 0-24
D SERIES 1810 (Kolinsky)
★ Sizes 0-30
B SERIES 1815 (Kolinsky)
★ Sizes 0-24
D SERIES 1840
Sizes 0-30
B SERIES 1842
Sizes 0-24
B SERIES 1843
Sizes 0-24
B SERIES 1845
Sizes 0-30

DURO

C SERIES 2110
★ Sizes 1-8, 10, 12
A SERIES 6600
★ Sizes 0-20
A SERIES 6610
Sizes 0-20
D SERIES 6800
★ Sizes 0-20
D SERIES 6810
Sizes 0-20

GRUMBACHER

D SERIES Renoir 626B
★ Sizes 00-8, 10, 12-20
D SERIES Renoir 626L
★ Sizes 1-8, 10, 12-20
A SERIES Renoir 626R
★ Sizes 00-8, 10, 12-20
B SERIES 1859
Sizes 3-8, 10, 12
D SERIES Corot 3611B
★ Sizes 00-8, 10, 12-20
A SERIES Corot 3611R
★ Sizes 00-8, 10, 12-20
D SERIES 3612B
★ Sizes 1-8, 10, 12

A SERIES 3612R
★ Sizes 1-8, 10, 12
D SERIES Franz Hals
★ 3617B
Sizes 1-8, 10, 12-20
A SERIES Franz Hals
★ 3617R
Sizes 1-8, 10, 12-20

HABICO

D SERIES 200 (Kolinsky)
★ Sizes 1, 2, 4, 6, 8, 10, 12-24
D SERIES 203
Sizes 1, 2, 4, 6, 8, 10, 12-24
D SERIES 208
Sizes 1, 2, 4, 6, 8, 10, 12-24
A SERIES 218 (Kolinsky)
★ Sizes 1, 2, 4, 6, 8, 10, 12-24
A SERIES 220
Sizes 1, 2, 4, 6, 8, 10, 12-24
A SERIES 225
Sizes 1, 2, 4, 6, 8, 10, 12-24
B SERIES 280 (Kolinsky)
★ Sizes 1, 2, 4, 6, 8, 10, 12-16
B SERIES 283
Sizes 1, 2, 4, 6, 8, 10, 12-20
B SERIES 285
Sizes 1, 2, 4, 6, 8, 10, 12-20

HANDOVER

A SERIES 300 (Kolinsky)
★ Sizes 00-8
D SERIES 305 (Kolinsky)
★ Sizes 2, 4, 6, 8, 10, 12

HOLBEIN

C SERIES N
Sizes 00-12
B SERIES N
Sizes 00-12
A SERIES N
Sizes 00-12

OIL AND ACRYLIC A ROUND PENCIL B FILBERT C FLAT D BRIGHT E RIGGER/SPOTTER F ANGLED

ISABEY

A SERIES 6116 (Kolinsky)
★ Sizes 2, 4, 6, 8, 10, 12-20
A SERIES 6118
Sizes 00-8, 10, 12-20
D SERIES 6164
Sizes 1-8, 10, 12-20
B SERIES 6165
Sizes 1-8, 10, 12-20
C SERIES 6166 (Kolinsky)
★ Sizes 2, 4, 6, 8, 10, 12-20
D SERIES 6167 (Kolinsky)
★ Sizes 2, 4, 6, 8, 10, 12-20
B SERIES 6168 (Kolinsky)
★ Sizes 2, 4, 6, 8, 10, 12

LANGNICKEL

C SERIES 511PB
Sizes 0-2, 4, 6, 8, 10, 12
A SERIES 512R
Sizes 0-16
A SERIES 514R
Sizes 0-10, 12-20
D SERIES 518B
★ Sizes 0-8, 10, 12-20
C SERIES 520F
Sizes 1-8, 10, 12
B SERIES 533T
★ Sizes 1-8, 10, 12, 18
F SERIES 937X
Sizes ¼-1¼ in

LEFRANC AND BOURGEOIS

A SERIES 79
Sizes 2, 4, 6, 8, 10, 12
C SERIES Constable 926
Sizes 4, 6, 8, 10, 12

LION BRUSH WORKS

A SERIES 625
Sizes 1-12
B SERIES 631
Sizes 1-16
D SERIES 632
Sizes 1-10, 12-16

L P BRUSH CO

A SERIES 3B
Sizes 8, 10, 12-20
A SERIES 4B
Sizes 8, 10, 12-20
B SERIES 35B
Sizes 8, 10, 12-20
C SERIES 36B
★ Sizes 8, 10, 12-20
A SERIES 41B
Sizes 8-14
A SERIES 45B
Sizes 8, 10, 12-20
A SERIES 46B
Sizes 8, 10, 12-20

E PLOTON

E SERIES Lechertier
Sizes 000-8
A SERIES Lechertier 1
Sizes 000-18
C SERIES Lechertier 2F
Sizes 10, 11
C SERIES Lechertier 2R
Sizes 000-8
B SERIES Lechertier 2ST
Sizes 000-18

PREMIER BRUSH CO

B SERIES P34
Sizes 1-6
C SERIES P34A
Sizes 1-6

PRO ARTE

A SERIES 3
Sizes 00-6
B SERIES 24
Sizes 2, 4, 6, 8, 10, 12
B SERIES 25 (Kolinsky)
★ Sizes 00-6
C SERIES 222
Sizes 0, 2, 4, 6, 8, 10, 12

ROBERSON AND CO

A SERIES BRU/70
Sizes 0-6
B SERIES BRU/72
Sizes 1-6
C SERIES BRU/74
Sizes 1-6

ROBERT SIMMONS

A SERIES Taubes
★ FT1/2/3
Sizes S, M, L
D SERIES 60B
Sizes 00-20
A SERIES 61R
Sizes 00-20
D SERIES Signet 65B
★ Sizes 1-12
A SERIES Signet 65R
★ Sizes 00-12
B SERIES Signet 66
★ Sizes 2, 4, 6, 8, 10, 12
B SERIES 67
Sizes 1-8, 10, 12
C SERIES 68L
Sizes 1-8, 10, 12-20
D SERIES 860BL
Empress
Sizes 2, 4, 6, 8, 10, 12-20

SIMONART

A SERIES 22 (Kolinsky)
Sizes 000-8, 10, 12
C SERIES 24 (Kolinsky)
Sizes 0-8, 10, 12
B SERIES 25 (Kolinsky)
Sizes 000-8, 10, 12

STRATHMORE ARTIST PRODUCTS

D SERIES Red Sable
Sizes 2, 4, 6, 8, 10, 12
A SERIES Red Sable
Sizes 2, 4, 6, 8, 10, 12

TALENS

C SERIES Rembrandt 240
Sizes 0, 2, 4, 6, 8, 10, 12-24
A SERIES Rembrandt 241
Sizes 0, 2, 4, 6, 8, 10, 12-24
B SERIES Rembrandt 245
Sizes 2, 4, 6, 8, 10, 12

UTRECHT

D SERIES Rhenish 211
Sizes 2, 4, 6, 8, 10, 12, 14, 16, 20
A SERIES 212
Sizes 2, 4, 6, 8, 10, 12, 14, 16, 20

WINSOR AND NEWTON

A/C SERIES 51
★ Sizes 00-12
D SERIES Newlyn 52
Sizes 1-12
B SERIES 53
Sizes 1-12
E SERIES 54
Sizes 00-6
A SERIES 66
Sizes 00-6

OX HAIR

DALER-ROWNEY

A SERIES 163
Sizes 4, 6, 8, 10, 12
B SERIES 166
Sizes 4, 6, 8, 10, 12

DA VINCI

A SERIES 1630
Sizes 0-24
A SERIES 1650 (Sabeline)
Sizes 0-24
A SERIES 1666
Sizes 0-24
A SERIES 1668
Sizes 0-24
A SERIES 1687
Sizes 0-24
D SERIES 1768
Sizes 1-30
D SERIES 1769
Sizes 1-24
D SERIES 1830
Sizes 0-20

D SERIES 1850 (Sabeline)
Sizes 0-24
B SERIES 1862
Sizes 0-28
B SERIES 1865
Sizes 0-30
D SERIES 1866
Sizes 0-24
B SERIES 1885
Sizes 0-24
D SERIES 1887
Sizes 0-24

DURO

E SERIES 2150 (Sabeline)
Sizes 1, 2, 4, 6, 8, 10, 12-20

GRUMBACHER

D SERIES 3608B (Sabeline)
Sizes 1-8, 10, 12-20
A SERIES 3608R (Sabeline)
Sizes 1-8, 10, 12-20

HABICO

D SERIES 210
Sizes 1, 2, 4, 6, 8, 10, 12-30
D SERIES 210A
Sizes 1, 2, 4, 6, 8, 10, 12-24
D SERIES 210B
Sizes 1, 2, 4, 6, 8, 10, 12-24
D SERIES 213
Sizes 1, 2, 4, 6, 8, 10, 12-30
D SERIES 213A
Sizes 1, 2, 4, 6, 8, 10, 12-24
D SERIES 213B
Sizes 1, 2, 4, 6, 8, 10, 12-24
D SERIES 214
Sizes 1, 2, 4, 6, 8, 10, 12-24
A SERIES 223
Sizes 1, 2, 4, 6, 8, 10, 12-24

A SERIES 228
Sizes 1, 2, 4, 6, 8, 10, 12-24
A SERIES 230
Sizes 1, 2, 4, 6, 8, 10, 12-24
B SERIES 287
Sizes 1, 2, 4, 6, 8, 10, 12-24

ISABEY

A SERIES 6117
Sizes 1-8, 10, 12-20
D SERIES 6160
Sizes 1-8, 10, 12-20
B SERIES 6161
Sizes 1-8, 10, 12-20

LANGNICKEL

D SERIES 525B (Sabeline)
Sizes 1-10, 12-24
A SERIES 526R
Sizes 2, 4, 6, 8, 10, 12-20, 24

LEFRANC AND BOURGEOIS

A SERIES 83
Sizes 2, 4, 6, 8, 10, 12

LION BRUSH WORKS

D SERIES Trident 732
Sizes 1-16

PREMIER BRUSH CO

C SERIES P17
Sizes 1-6, 8, 10
B SERIES P51
Sizes 1-6, 8, 10

ROBERT SIMMONS

D SERIES 63B (Sabeline)
Sizes 1-8, 10, 12-20
A SERIES 63R (Sabeline)
Sizes 1-8, 10, 12-20

STRATHMORE ARTIST PRODUCTS

D SERIES Sabeline
Sizes 2, 4, 6, 8, 10, 12

OIL AND ACRYLIC

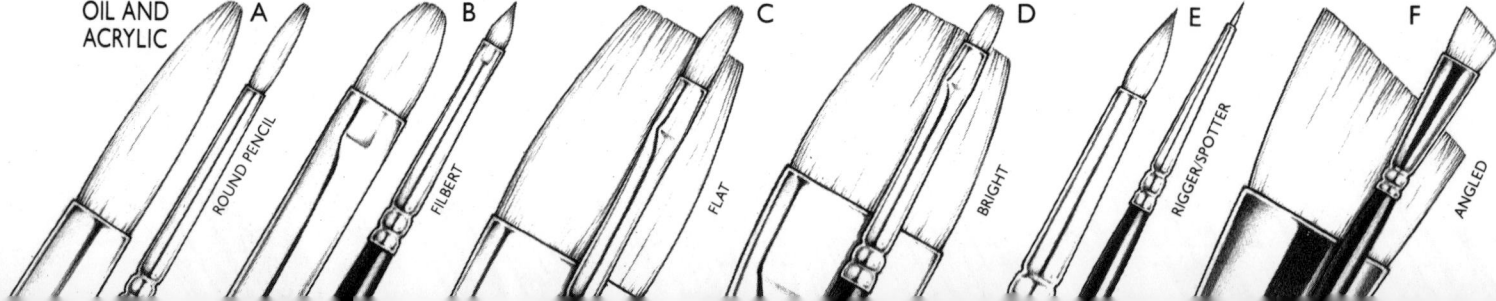

A ROUND PENCIL B FILBERT C FLAT D BRIGHT E RIGGER/SPOTTER F ANGLED

TALENS

C SERIES 230
Sizes 2, 4, 6, 8, 10, 12-24

A SERIES 231
Sizes 2, 4, 6, 8, 10, 12-24

B SERIES 232
Sizes 2, 4, 6, 8, 10, 12-24

UTRECHT

D SERIES 214 (Sabeline)
Sizes 1, 2, 4, 6, 8, 10, 12

A SERIES 215 (Sabeline)
Sizes 1, 2, 4, 6, 8, 10, 12

KEY

Brush sizes
00000000, 0000000, 000000, 00000, 0000, 000, 00, 0, 1, 2, 3, 4, 5, 6, 7, 8, 9, 10, 11, 12, 14, 16, 18, 20, 22, 24, 26, 28, 30 (unless otherwise stated)

$\frac{1}{16}$, $\frac{1}{8}$, $\frac{1}{4}$, $\frac{3}{8}$, $\frac{1}{2}$, $\frac{5}{8}$, $\frac{3}{4}$, $\frac{7}{8}$, 1, 1$\frac{1}{4}$, 1$\frac{1}{2}$, 2, 2$\frac{1}{2}$, 3, 3$\frac{1}{2}$, 4 in

10, 20, 30, 40, 50, 60, 70, 80, 90, 100 mm (unless otherwise stated)

XS extra small   S small
M medium   L large
XL extra large

Quill sizes
Lark (small), Crow, Duck, Goose, Condor (large)

Quality
★ best quality
◆ school quality
(where indicated by the manufacturer)

SYNTHETIC

BINNEY AND SMITH

D SERIES Liquitex 551
Sizes 1, 2, 4, 6, 8, 10

A SERIES Liquitex 552
Sizes 1, 2, 4, 6, 8, 10

D SERIES Liquitex 565
Sizes 1, 2, 4, 6, 8, 10

C SERIES Liquitex 570
Sizes 1, 2, 4, 6, 8, 10

DALER-ROWNEY

D SERIES Dalon D44
★ Sizes 1-6, 8, 10, 12, 14

A SERIES Dalon D66
★ Sizes 0-12

A SERIES 260
Sizes 0-12

C SERIES 280
Sizes 1-9

DA VINCI

A SERIES 1670 Nova
Sizes 0-12, 16, 20, 24

D SERIES 1870 Nova
Sizes 0-16, 20, 24

D SERIES 1872 Nova
Sizes 0-16, 20, 24

B SERIES 1875 Nova
Sizes 1-16, 20

B SERIES Maestro 7005
★ Sizes 1-24

D SERIES Maestro 7105
★ Sizes 1-24

D SERIES Maestro 7180
★ Sizes 1-24

A SERIES Maestro 7705
★ Sizes 1-20

A SERIES Maestro 7780
★ Sizes 1-20

DURO

C SERIES 9500
Sizes 2, 4, 6, 8, 10, 12

D SERIES 9000B
Sizes 2-8, 10, 12

C SERIES 9000F
Sizes 2-6, 8

GRUMBACHER

D SERIES 4567 Supreme
★ Sizes 14-20, 24, 28

B SERIES 4567B Hyplar
★ Sizes 1-8, 10, 12

C SERIES 4567F Hyplar
★ Sizes 1-8, 10, 12

A SERIES 4567R Hyplar
★ Sizes 00-8, 10, 12

C SERIES 4675F Hyplar
Sizes 2, 4, 6, 8, 10, 12-16

A SERIES 4675R Hyplar
Sizes 00-6, 8, 10, 12

D SERIES 4700B
Erminette
Sizes 1-8, 10, 12-16, 20

A SERIES 4700R
Erminette
Sizes 1-8, 10, 12

HABICO

D SERIES 204
Sizes 1, 2, 4, 6, 8, 10, 12-24

A SERIES 221
Sizes 1, 2, 4, 6, 8, 10, 12-24

D SERIES 241
★ Sizes 1, 2, 4, 6, 8, 10, 12-24

A SERIES 242
Sizes 1, 2, 4, 6, 8, 10, 12-24

D SERIES 254
Sizes 1, 2, 4, 6, 8, 10, 12-24

B SERIES 261
Sizes 1, 2, 4, 6, 8, 10, 12-24

HOLBEIN

C SERIES NY
Sizes 1-12

A SERIES NY
Sizes 1-12

C SERIES 151
★ Sizes 0-12

C SERIES 151-GF
Sizes 0-12

D SERIES 152
★ Sizes 0-12

D SERIES 152-GB
Sizes 0-12

A SERIES 155
★ Sizes 0-12

A SERIES 155-GR
Sizes 0-12

B SERIES 200F
Sizes 0-12

D SERIES 252-GB
Sizes 0-12

ISABEY

A SERIES 6511
Sizes 00-8, 10, 12-20

C SERIES 6561
Sizes 1-8, 10, 12-20

B SERIES 6571
Sizes 1-8, 10, 12-20

LANGNICKEL

B SERIES Snowhite 810
Sizes $\frac{3}{8}$-2 in

B SERIES Snowhite 811
Sizes $\frac{3}{8}$-2 in

C SERIES 820F
Sizes $\frac{1}{8}$-1 in

A SERIES 842R
Sizes 1, 2, 4, 6, 8, 10, 12, 14

C SERIES 876
Sizes 1-3 in

A SERIES Snowhite 4500
Sizes 1, 2, 4, 6, 8, 10, 12, 16, 20-24

D SERIES Snowhite 4510
Sizes 1, 2, 4, 6, 8, 10, 12, 16, 20-24

B SERIES Snowhite 4520
Sizes 1, 2, 4, 6, 8, 10, 12, 22, 24

C SERIES Snowhite 4590
Sizes 1, 2, 4, 6, 8, 10, 12, 16, 20

A SERIES Sunburst 2000
Sizes 000-6, 8, 10, 12, 16, 26, 30

D SERIES Sunburst 2010
Sizes 0, 1, 2, 4, 6, 8, 10, 12-20

D SERIES Sunburst 2015
Sizes 2, 4, 6, 8, 10, 12

B SERIES Sunburst 2020
Sizes 1, 2, 4, 6, 8, 10, 12

A SERIES Sunburst 2045
Sizes 0, 1, 2

F SERIES Sunburst 2060
Sizes $\frac{1}{8}$-1 in

LEFRANC AND BOURGEOIS

B SERIES 1981
Sizes 8, 10, 12-16

LION BRUSH WORKS

A SERIES Trident 828
Sizes 1-12

C SERIES Trident 829
Sizes 1-12

LUKAS

D SERIES 5441
Sizes 2, 4, 6, 8, 10, 12-16

A SERIES 5455
Sizes 00-6, 8, 10, 12, 14

OCALDO

A SERIES B
◆ Sizes 4, 6, 8, 10, 12, 14

C SERIES C
◆ Sizes 4, 6, 8, 10, 12

C SERIES N
Sizes 4, 6, 8, 10, 12

PEBEO

A SERIES A19 Polyamid
Sizes 2, 4, 6, 8, 10, 12-20

C SERIES A20 Polyamid
Sizes 2, 4, 6, 8, 10, 12-20

B SERIES A21 Polyamid
Sizes 2, 4, 6, 8, 10, 12-20

PREMIER BRUSH CO

C SERIES P42
Sizes 1-6, 8, 10

B SERIES P42A
Sizes 1-6, 8, 10

PRO ARTE

A SERIES 102
Sizes 0-8, 10, 12

E SERIES 104
Sizes 0-6

C SERIES 105
Sizes 0, 2, 4, 6, 8, 10, 12, 14

B SERIES 108
Sizes 2, 4, 6, 8, 10, 12, 14

A SERIES D
Sizes 1-8, 10, 12

ROBERT SIMMONS

D SERIES 47B Acrylette
Sizes $\frac{1}{8}$-1$\frac{1}{2}$ in

C SERIES 47F Acrylette
Sizes $\frac{1}{8}$-1$\frac{1}{2}$ in

D SERIES 760B White Sable
Sizes 1-4, 6, 8, 10, 12-16, 20

A SERIES 761R White Sable
Sizes 1-4, 6, 8, 10, 12

B SERIES 767 White Sable
Sizes 1, 2, 4, 6, 8, 10, 12, 14

C SERIES 1411
Sizes 1-6, 8, 10, 12, 14

A SERIES 1411R
Sizes 0-6, 8, 10, 12, 14

D SERIES 1425B
★ Sizes 1-12

C SERIES 1425F
★ Sizes 1-12

A SERIES 1425R
★ Sizes 1-12

D SERIES 1430B Tynaloc
★ Sizes 0-4, 6, 8, 10, 12

C SERIES 1430F Tynaloc
★ Sizes 0-4, 6, 8, 10, 12

A SERIES 1430R Tynaloc
★ Sizes 0-4, 6, 8, 10, 12

OIL AND ACRYLIC

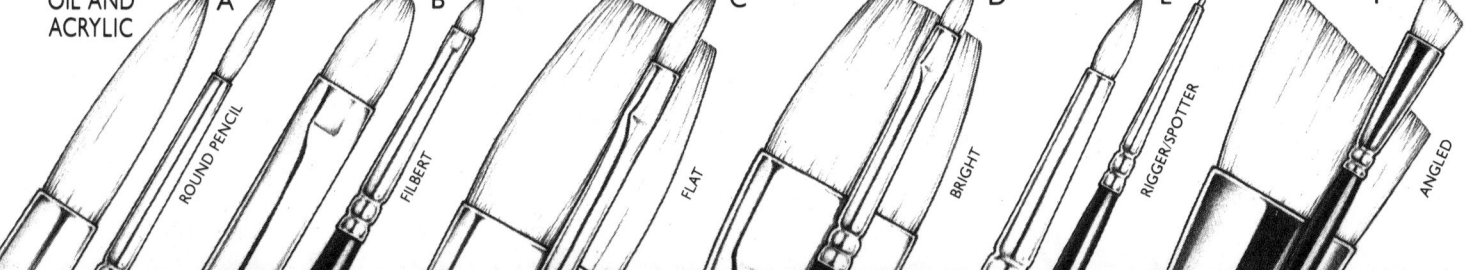

A ROUND PENCIL B FILBERT C FLAT D BRIGHT E RIGGER/SPOTTER F ANGLED

STRATHMORE ARTIST PRODUCTS

D SERIES White
Sizes 0-8, 10, 12

A SERIES White
Sizes 0-8, 10, 12

TALENS

C SERIES 294
Sizes 0, 2, 4, 6, 8, 10, 12-24

A SERIES 295
Sizes 0, 2, 4, 6, 8, 10, 12-24

UTRECHT

I SERIES 231
Sizes 2, 4, 6, 8, 10, 12, 14, 16, 20

D SERIES 232
Sizes 2, 4, 6, 8, 10, 12, 14, 16, 20

A SERIES 233
Sizes 2, 4, 6, 8, 10, 12

B SERIES 235 Sablette
Sizes 1, 2, 4, 6, 8, 10

L WARD AND CO

D SERIES Whistler 310
Sizes 0, 2, 4, 6, 8, 10, 12

MARTIN/F WEBER

A SERIES Jenkins E

WINSOR AND NEWTON

A SERIES 20
Sizes 1-8

SYNTHETIC AND SABLE MIX

PRO ARTE

C SERIES 97
Sizes 2, 4, 6, 8, 10, 12-16

A SERIES 98
Sizes 000-6, 8

L WARD AND CO

R SERIES Regency Plus 45
Sizes 0, 2, 4, 6, 8, 10, 12-20

WINSOR AND NEWTON

R SERIES Sceptre 404
Sizes 0-6, 8

C SERIES Sceptre 505
Sizes 0-6, 8

KEY

Brush sizes
00000000, 0000000, 000000, 00000, 0000, 000, 00, 0, 1, 2, 3, 4, 5, 6, 7, 8, 9, 10, 11, 12, 14, 16, 18, 20, 22, 24, 26, 28, 30 (unless otherwise stated)

$\frac{1}{8}$, $\frac{1}{4}$, $\frac{1}{2}$, $\frac{3}{8}$, $\frac{5}{8}$, $\frac{3}{4}$, $\frac{7}{8}$, 1, $1\frac{1}{4}$, $1\frac{1}{2}$, 2, $2\frac{1}{2}$, 3, $3\frac{1}{2}$, 4 in

10, 20, 30, 40, 50, 60, 70, 80, 90, 100 mm (unless otherwise stated)

XS extra small   S small
M medium   L large
XL extra large

Quill sizes
Lark (small), Crow, Duck, Goose, Condor (large)

Quality
★ best quality
♦ school quality
(where indicated by the manufacturer)

BRUSHES FOR WATERCOLOR AND WATER-BASED PAINTS

SABLE

BEROL

A SERIES 1
Sizes 2, 4, 6, 8

BINNEY AND SMITH

A SERIES Liquitex 9
★ Sizes 00-2, 4, 6

D SERIES Liquitex 160
★ Sizes $\frac{1}{8}$, $\frac{1}{4}$, $\frac{1}{2}$, $\frac{3}{4}$, 1 in

A SERIES Liquitex 511
★ Sizes 00-2, 4, 6

B SERIES Liquitex 520
★ Sizes 00000, 000

A SERIES Liquitex 527
Sizes 0, 1, 2, 4, 6

H SERIES Liquitex 547
★ Sizes $\frac{1}{2}$, $\frac{3}{4}$ in

H SERIES Liquitex 548
★ Sizes $\frac{1}{2}$, 1 in

A SERIES Liquitex 592
Sizes 2, 4, 6, 8, 10, 12

J SERIES Liquitex 597
Sizes 1, 3, 5

L CORNELISSEN

B SERIES S22 (Kolinsky)
★ Sizes 00-4

A SERIES S80 (Kolinsky)
★ Sizes 000-14

A SERIES S80A
★ (Kolinsky)
Sizes 000-8, 10, 12

D SERIES One-stroke
★ (Kolinsky)
Sizes $\frac{1}{8}$-1 in (also $\frac{3}{16}$ in)

R SERIES Pocket Sable
★ (Kolinsky)
Sizes 0-12

DALER-ROWNEY

A SERIES Diana
★ (Kolinsky)
Sizes 00-14

A SERIES 34
Sizes 00-8, 10, 12

A SERIES 40 (Kolinsky)
★ Sizes 00-14

C SERIES 43 (Kolinsky)
★ Sizes 0-6

B SERIES 46 (Kolinsky)
★ Sizes 00-6

DA VINCI

A SERIES Maestro 10
★ (Kolinsky)
Sizes 00000-24

A SERIES Maestro 11
★ (Kolinsky)
Sizes 000-24

A SERIES Maestro 12
★ (Kolinsky)
Sizes 00000-24

A SERIES Maestro 14
★ (Kolinsky)
Sizes 10, 12-16

A SERIES Maestro 15
★ (Kolinsky)
Sizes 1-6

A SERIES Maestro 17
★ (Kolinsky)
Size 9

B SERIES Maestro 1505
★ (Kolinsky)
Sizes 00000-12

B SERIES Maestro 1506
★ (Kolinsky)
Sizes 00000-12

B SERIES Maestro 1515
★ (Kolinsky)
Sizes 000-12

A SERIES 13
Sizes 10-24

A SERIES 15 (Kolinsky)
Sizes 1-16

A SERIES Compact 901
(Kolinsky)
Size 4

A SERIES Compact 902
(Kolinsky)
Size 4

D SERIES 1300 (Kolinsky)
Sizes 2-20

D SERIES 1310 (Kolinsky)
Sizes 2-20

D SERIES 1311 (Kolinsky)
Sizes 2-20

A SERIES Pocket 1503
(Kolinsky)
Sizes 1-6, 8, 10, 12

A SERIES 1504 (Kolinsky)
Sizes 000-12

A SERIES 1510 (Kolinsky)
Sizes 00000-12

A SERIES 1520
Sizes 000-16

A SERIES 1526
Sizes 000-6, 8

A SERIES 1546
Sizes 000-16

DURO

A SERIES 6500
★ Sizes 000-12

A SERIES 6510
Sizes 000-12

A SERIES 6520
Sizes 000-12

B SERIES 6750
★ Sizes 00000-5

GRUMBACHER

A SERIES 177
Sizes 000-8

B SERIES Spot-rite 178
Sizes 10/0, 00000–5

A SERIES Rubens 187
★ (Kolinsky)
Sizes 000-8, 10, 12

A SERIES Beaux Arts 190
Sizes 000-8, 10, 12

A SERIES 197
Sizes 000-8, 10, 12

A SERIES 615
Sizes 000-8, 10, 12

A SERIES 815
Sizes 000-8, 10, 12

A SERIES Sir Raeburn 3545
Sizes 00-8, 10, 12

D SERIES 4117
Sizes $\frac{1}{8}$-$1\frac{1}{2}$ in

D SERIES 4119
Sizes $\frac{1}{8}$-$1\frac{1}{2}$ in

E SERIES Aquarelle 6143
Sizes $\frac{1}{2}$, $\frac{3}{4}$, 1 in

HABICO

A SERIES 100 (Kolinsky)
★ Sizes 000-12

A SERIES 105 (Kolinsky)
★ Sizes 000-12

A SERIES 110 (Kolinsky)
★ Sizes 000-12

B SERIES 115 (Kolinsky)
★ Sizes 000-6

A SERIES 120
Sizes 000-12

A SERIES 122
Sizes 000-12

A SERIES 125
Sizes 000-12

D SERIES 300
Sizes $\frac{1}{16}$-1 in (also $\frac{3}{16}$, $\frac{5}{16}$, $\frac{7}{16}$, $\frac{9}{16}$ in)

D SERIES 305
Sizes $\frac{1}{8}$-$1\frac{1}{2}$ (also $\frac{1}{16}$, $\frac{3}{16}$, $\frac{5}{16}$, $\frac{7}{16}$, $\frac{9}{16}$ in)

HAMILTON

A SERIES 450
Sizes S1-10

D SERIES 453
Sizes $\frac{1}{8}$-$\frac{3}{4}$ in

C SERIES 459
Sizes 1-10

HANDOVER

A SERIES 33 (Kolinsky)
★ Sizes 00-8

A SERIES 66 (Kolinsky)
★ Sizes 00-12

B SERIES 99 (Kolinsky)
★ Sizes 00-8

D SERIES 2104
Sizes $\frac{1}{16}$-1 in

D SERIES 2115 (Kolinsky)
★ Sizes $\frac{1}{16}$-1 in

HOLBEIN

A SERIES N
Sizes 00-12

WATERCOLOR AND WATER-BASED

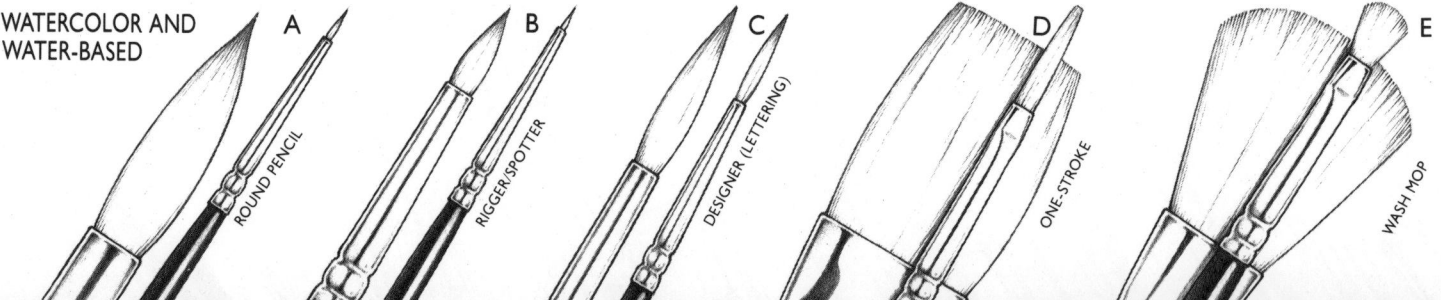

A ROUND PENCIL
B RIGGER/SPOTTER
C DESIGNER (LETTERING)
D ONE-STROKE
E WASH MOP

ISABEY
A SERIES 6222
Sizes 1-6
A SERIES 6223
Sizes 00-10, 12, 14
A SERIES 6225
Sizes 2, 4, 6, 8, 10, 12-20
A SERIES 6226 (Kolinsky)
★ Sizes 00-14
A SERIES 6227 (Kolinsky)
★ Sizes 00-14
A SERIES 6229 (Kolinsky)
★ Sizes 00-8
J SERIES 6238
Sizes 2, 4, 6, 8
A SERIES 6707 (Kolinsky)
★ Sizes 7, 9
A SERIES 6725
Sizes 1-12
A SERIES 6727 (Kolinsky)
★ Sizes 1-12

JAKAR
A SERIES 650
Sizes 000-6

LANGNICKEL
A SERIES 99 (Kolinsky)
★ Sizes 000-8
A SERIES 133
Sizes 1-6, 8
A SERIES 134
Sizes 1-6, 8
A SERIES 135
Sizes 1-6
D SERIES 206
Sizes $\frac{1}{8}$-1 in
D SERIES 209
Sizes $\frac{1}{8}$-1$\frac{1}{2}$ in (also $\frac{3}{16}$, $\frac{5}{16}$ in)
B SERIES 621
Sizes 0000000-8
B SERIES 622
Sizes 0-6
A SERIES 623N
Sizes 00000-8, 10, 12
A SERIES 625
Sizes 0000-8, 10, 12
B SERIES 640
Sizes 000-6, 8
A SERIES 700 (Kolinsky)
★ Sizes 000-8, 10, 12

T N LAWRENCE
A SERIES 112
Sizes 00-2, 4, 5, 7, 8, 10-12

LEFRANC AND BOURGEOIS
A SERIES 669
Sizes 2, 4, 6, 8, 10, 12, 14
A SERIES 1109
★ Sizes 1-6, 8

LION BRUSH WORKS
A SERIES Trident 616
Sizes 00-12
A SERIES Trident 617
★ Sizes 00-12
A SERIES Trident 618
★ (Kolinsky)
Sizes 000-12
D SERIES Trident 640
Sizes $\frac{1}{8}$-1 in (also $\frac{3}{16}$ in)
A SERIES Trident 694
Sizes 0-10
D SERIES Trident 0640
Sizes $\frac{1}{8}$-1 in (also $\frac{3}{16}$ in)

L P BRUSH CO
A SERIES 1A
★ Sizes 000-12
A SERIES 30
Sizes 00-12
B SERIES 36
Sizes 00-4
A SERIES 37/64
Sizes 000-8
A SERIES 38/39
Sizes 000-12
A SERIES 41
Sizes 1-12
A SERIES 45/46
Sizes 1-12
A SERIES 65
★ Sizes 000-12
A SERIES 21
◆ Sizes 1-12
D SERIES 42
Sizes $\frac{1}{8}$-$\frac{1}{2}$ in (also $\frac{3}{16}$ in)
D SERIES 42B
Sizes $\frac{1}{4}$-1$\frac{1}{4}$ in

D SERIES 47
Sizes $\frac{1}{8}$-1 in (also $\frac{3}{16}$ in)
D SERIES 62
Sizes $\frac{1}{8}$-1 in
(also $\frac{1}{16}$, $\frac{3}{16}$ in)

LUKAS
A SERIES 5451 (Kolinsky)
★ Sizes 0000-8, 10, 12
J SERIES 5494
Size S

MAIMERI
A SERIES 970
Sizes 0-8
A SERIES 989 (Kolinsky)
★ Sizes 000-10, 12
A SERIES 990
Sizes 000-12

MARABU
A SERIES 2006
Sizes 0000-8, 10, 12

OCALDO
A SERIES Q
Sizes 00-8

PEBEO
A SERIES A16
Sizes 2, 4, 6, 8, 10, 12-20
H SERIES A17
Sizes 2, 4, 6, 8, 10, 12-20
G SERIES A18
Sizes 2, 4, 6, 8, 10, 12-20
B SERIES 409 (Kolinsky)
★ Sizes 0-2, 4
A SERIES 424 (Kolinsky)
★ Sizes 00-10

PELIKAN
A SERIES Master-class 55
Sizes 0-6, 8

PENNELLI CINGHIALE
A SERIES 370
Sizes 00-10, 12-20

H SERIES 371
★ Sizes 1-10, 12-16
J SERIES 372
★ Sizes 4, 6, 8, 10, 12, 14
A SERIES S303
Sizes 1-10, 12

E PLOTON
A SERIES Lechertier
Red Sable
Sizes 000-18
D SERIES Lechertier
Sable
Sizes $\frac{1}{8}$-$\frac{1}{2}$ in
(also $\frac{3}{16}$, $\frac{5}{16}$, $\frac{7}{16}$ in)
E SERIES Lechertier
Ox hair
Sizes $\frac{5}{8}$, $\frac{3}{4}$, $\frac{7}{8}$, 1, 2, 3 in
E SERIES Lechertier
Sable
Sizes $\frac{1}{2}$, $\frac{3}{4}$, 1, 1$\frac{1}{4}$, 1$\frac{1}{2}$, 2 in
C SERIES Sable Designer
Sizes 00-8
B SERIES Sable Spotter
Sizes 00-8
B SERIES Sable Rigger
Sizes 000-8

PREMIER BRUSH CO
A SERIES 22S
Sizes 000-6
A SERIES P23
Sizes 000-10, 12
C SERIES P.DES 23
Sizes 00-6
B SERIES P27
Sizes 00-6
A SERIES 33A
⚓ Sizes 1-6
A SERIES P33
Sizes 00000-14

PRO ARTE
A SERIES 1 (Kolinsky)
★ Sizes 000-12
A SERIES 1A (Kolinsky)
★ Sizes 000-12
A SERIES 2A (Kolinsky)
★ Sizes 000-12
A SERIES 3
Sizes 0000-8, 10, 12

D SERIES 11
Sizes $\frac{1}{8}$-$\frac{5}{8}$ in (also $\frac{3}{16}$ in)

REEVES
A SERIES R2
Sizes 00-2, 4, 6, 8, 10, 12

ROBERSON AND CO
A SERIES BRU/1
Sizes 00-8, 10, 12
H SERIES Cotman BR/7
Sizes 3, 7, 9-12
B SERIES Cosway BR/13
Sizes 00-4

ROBERT SIMMONS
B SERIES BH Lancer
Sizes 000-4
D SERIES 21
Sizes $\frac{1}{8}$-1$\frac{1}{2}$ in
A SERIES 55 Skyscraper
Sizes $\frac{1}{2}$, $\frac{3}{4}$, 1 in
A SERIES 70
★ Sizes 000-8, 10, 12
J SERIES 80
Sizes 000-8
A SERIES 81
Sizes 0000000-5
A SERIES 82
◆ Sizes 000-8, 10, 12
A SERIES 84
Sizes 000-8, 10, 12
A SERIES 1610
◆ Sizes 000-12

SIMONART
A SERIES 21 (Kolinsky)
★ Sizes 000-8, 10, 12
A SERIES 26 (Kolinsky)
★ Sizes 000-6
B SERIES 27 (Kolinsky)
★ Sizes 000-6

J P STEPHENSON
A SERIES Sable
Sizes 00, 1, 3, 5, 7

STRATHMORE ARTIST PRODUCTS
A SERIES Kolinsky
★ Sizes 000-12

A SERIES Red Sable
Sizes 000-12
J SERIES Wash
Sizes $\frac{3}{4}$, 1, 1$\frac{1}{2}$ in

TALENS
A SERIES Rembrandt 100
★ (Kolinsky)
Sizes 000-12
A SERIES 110
Sizes 000-12
B SERIES 111R
Sizes 0-6
A SERIES 310
Sizes 2, 4, 6, 8, 10, 12

UTRECHT
A SERIES Vermeer 221
★ Sizes 0000-4, 6, 8, 10, 12

L WARD AND CO
B SERIES Whistler 53 City
Sizes 000-6
A SERIES Whistler 55 City
Sizes 000-6
A SERIES Whistler 100
Sizes 000-8, 10, 12
J SERIES Whistler 101
Sizes 000-6
A SERIES Whistler 777
★ (Kolinsky)
Sizes 000-6

WINSOR AND NEWTON
A SERIES Pocket Sable
C SERIES 3A
Sizes 0-8
A SERIES 7 (Kolinsky)
★ Sizes 000-14
B SERIES 12
★ Sizes 000-6
A SERIES 16
Sizes 00-12
B SERIES 29
Sizes 00-6
A SERIES 33
Sizes 00-12
D SERIES 608
Sizes $\frac{1}{8}$-$\frac{5}{8}$ in
(also $\frac{3}{16}$, $\frac{5}{16}$ in)

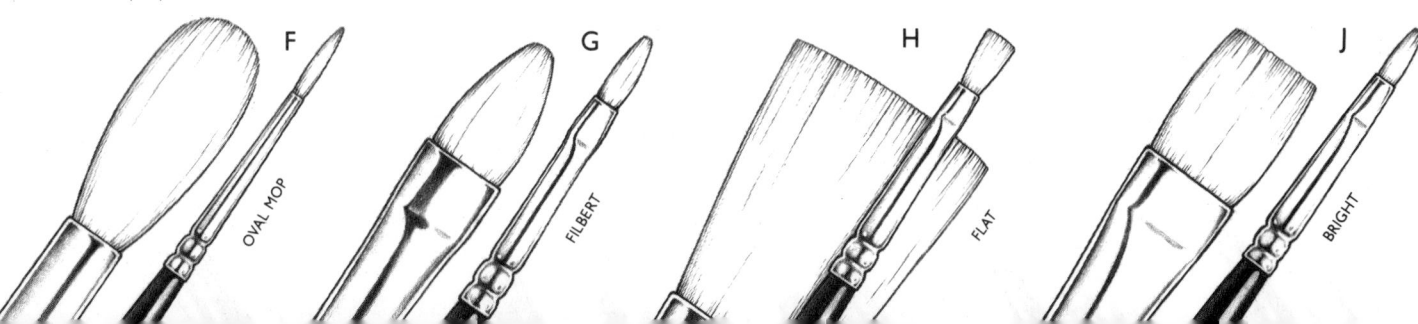

F OVAL MOP   G FILBERT   H FLAT   J BRIGHT

OX HAIR

BEROL
A SERIES 2 (Sablette)
Sizes 2, 4, 6, 8

BINNEY AND SMITH
D SERIES Liquitex 170
Sizes $\frac{1}{4}$, $\frac{1}{2}$, $\frac{3}{4}$, 1 in

DALER-ROWNEY
A SERIES 162
Sizes 4, 6, 8, 10, 12
H SERIES 164
Sizes $\frac{3}{16}$, $\frac{3}{8}$-1 in
G SERIES 165
Sizes 4, 6, 8, 10, 12

DA VINCI
E SERIES 416
Sizes 0-6, 8, 10, 12
F SERIES 806
Sizes 10/14
D SERIES 1350 (Sabeline)
Sizes 2-24
D SERIES 1351 (Sabeline)
Sizes 2-24
D SERIES 1352 (Sabeline)
Sizes 2-24
D SERIES 1366
Sizes 2-20
D SERIES 1367
Sizes 2-20
A SERIES 1530
Sizes 000-20
A SERIES 1550 (Sabeline)
Sizes 000-24
A SERIES 1566
Sizes 00-24
A SERIES 1587
Sizes 00-30

DURO
D SERIES 3360
Sizes $\frac{1}{8}$-1 in
D SERIES 3370
Sizes $\frac{1}{8}$-1 in
H SERIES 1437
Sizes $\frac{1}{8}$-1 in

GRUMBACHER
A SERIES 874 (Sabeline)
Sizes 1-8, 10, 12-20, 24-28
D SERIES 4116 (Sabeline)
Sizes $\frac{1}{8}$-1$\frac{1}{2}$ in
E SERIES 6142 (Sabeline)
Sizes $\frac{1}{2}$, $\frac{3}{4}$, 1 in
D SERIES 6654
Sizes $\frac{1}{8}$-1 in
D SERIES 6658
Sizes $\frac{1}{8}$-1$\frac{1}{2}$ in
D SERIES 6661
Sizes $\frac{1}{8}$-1$\frac{1}{2}$ in
D SERIES 6844
Sizes $\frac{1}{8}$-1 in

HABICO
A SERIES 130
Sizes 000-20
A SERIES 135
Sizes 000-20
J SERIES 205
Sizes 1, 2, 4, 6, 8, 10, 12-24
D SERIES 305
Sizes $\frac{1}{8}$-1$\frac{1}{2}$ in
(also $\frac{1}{16}$, $\frac{3}{16}$, $\frac{5}{16}$, $\frac{7}{16}$, $\frac{9}{16}$ in)
D SERIES 310
Sizes $\frac{1}{16}$-1 in
(also $\frac{1}{16}$, $\frac{3}{16}$, $\frac{5}{16}$, $\frac{7}{16}$, $\frac{9}{16}$ in)
D SERIES 315
Sizes $\frac{1}{16}$ in
(also $\frac{1}{16}$, $\frac{3}{16}$, $\frac{5}{16}$, $\frac{7}{16}$, $\frac{9}{16}$ in)
D SERIES 320
Sizes $\frac{1}{16}$-1$\frac{1}{2}$ in
(also $\frac{1}{16}$, $\frac{3}{16}$, $\frac{5}{16}$, $\frac{7}{16}$, $\frac{9}{16}$ in)
D SERIES 325
Sizes $\frac{1}{16}$-1 in
(also $\frac{1}{16}$, $\frac{3}{16}$, $\frac{5}{16}$, $\frac{7}{16}$, $\frac{9}{16}$ in)
J SERIES 585
Sizes 0-4
E SERIES 630
Sizes 2, 4, 6, 8, 10, 12
E SERIES 665
Sizes 2, 4, 6, 8, 10, 12-18

HAMILTON
D SERIES 454
Sizes $\frac{1}{8}$-$\frac{3}{4}$ in

HANDOVER
A SERIES 102
Sizes 10, 12-16
D SERIES 2105
Sizes $\frac{1}{8}$-1 in
D SERIES 2106
Sizes $\frac{1}{8}$-1 in

ISABEY
A SERIES 6218
Sizes 1-6, 8, 10, 12
J SERIES 6233
Sizes 2, 4, 6, 8

LANGNICKEL
D SERIES 200
Sizes $\frac{1}{8}$-2 in (also $\frac{5}{16}$ in)
D SERIES 203
Sizes $\frac{1}{8}$-2 in
(also $\frac{3}{16}$, $\frac{5}{16}$ in)
D SERIES 204
Sizes $\frac{1}{8}$-1 in
D SERIES 219 (Sabeline)
Sizes $\frac{1}{8}$-1 in
(also $\frac{3}{16}$, $\frac{5}{16}$ in)
D SERIES 228 (Sabeline)
Sizes $\frac{1}{8}$-2 in
A SERIES 666 (Sabeline)
Sizes 1-8, 10, 12-24
E SERIES Porpoise 722
Size 1 in
E SERIES Dolphin 724
Size 1 in
E SERIES 727 (Sabeline)
Size 1 in
E SERIES 759 (Sabeline)
Sizes 0-6
E SERIES 777 (Sabeline)
Sizes $\frac{1}{4}$, $\frac{1}{2}$, $\frac{3}{4}$, 1 in

LION BRUSH WORKS
A SERIES Trident 716
Sizes 1-12
D SERIES Trident 740
Sizes $\frac{1}{8}$-1 in (also $\frac{3}{16}$ in)
D SERIES Trident 743
Sizes $\frac{1}{8}$-1 in (also $\frac{3}{16}$ in)

LUKAS
A SERIES 5452
Sizes 1-6, 8, 10

D SERIES 5462
Sizes 1-6, 8, 10
G SERIES 5473
Sizes 2, 4, 6, 8, 10, 12-18
J SERIES 5475
Sizes 2, 4, 6, 8, 10, 12-18

OCALDO
A SERIES 1
Sizes 2, 4, 6, 8, 10

PEBEO
A SERIES A13
Sizes 2, 4, 6, 8, 10, 12-20
J SERIES A14
Sizes 2, 4, 6, 8, 10, 12-20
G SERIES A15
Sizes 2, 4, 6, 8, 10, 12-20
H SERIES 223
Sizes $\frac{1}{4}$, $\frac{1}{2}$, $\frac{3}{4}$, 1 in
A SERIES 224
Sizes 2, 4, 7, 9, 11, 16

PELIKAN
A SERIES Studio 50
Sizes 1-6, 8, 10, 12

PENNELLI CINGHIALE
A SERIES 170
Sizes 00-24
H SERIES 171
Sizes 1-24
J SERIES 172
Sizes 2, 4, 6, 8, 10, 12-24
E SERIES 176
Sizes 8, 10, 12-20
E SERIES 276
Sizes 2, 4, 6, 8, 10, 12, 14
A SERIES S301
Sizes 000-12
H SERIES S302
Sizes 1, 2, 4, 6, 8, 10, 12

D SERIES S304
Sizes 00-6, 8, 10, 12

PREMIER BRUSH CO
A SERIES P14
Sizes 1-6
A SERIES P15
Sizes 00-6
D SERIES P19
Sizes $\frac{1}{8}$-1 in
(also $\frac{3}{16}$, $\frac{5}{16}$ in)

PRO ARTE
A SERIES 5
Sizes 10, 12-16
D SERIES 13
Sizes $\frac{1}{8}$-1 in (also $\frac{3}{16}$ in)

ROBERT SIMMONS
D SERIES 22 (Sabeline)
Sizes $\frac{1}{8}$-1$\frac{1}{2}$ in
D SERIES 23
Sizes $\frac{1}{8}$-1$\frac{1}{2}$ in
D SERIES 25
Sizes $\frac{1}{8}$-1$\frac{1}{2}$ in
D SERIES 26
Sizes $\frac{1}{8}$-1 in
F SERIES 53 (Sabeline)
Sizes 0, 1, 2, 4, 6, 8, 10
E SERIES 56 Skyscraper
Sizes $\frac{1}{2}$, $\frac{3}{4}$, 1 in
A SERIES 86 (Sabeline)
Sizes 00-16, 26, 30
A SERIES 869 Goliath
Sizes 36, 40

STRATHMORE ARTIST PRODUCTS
A SERIES Sabeline
Sizes 1-12
J SERIES Sabeline
Sizes $\frac{1}{2}$, $\frac{3}{4}$, 1 in
H SERIES Ox Hair
Sizes 1$\frac{1}{2}$, 2 in

TALENS
A SERIES 120
Sizes 1-12
A SERIES 301
Sizes 2, 4, 6, 8, 10, 12-16

A SERIES 304
Sizes 2, 4, 6, 8, 10, 12-16

L WARD & CO
E SERIES Whistler 190
Sizes 2, 4, 6, 8

WINSOR AND NEWTON
G SERIES 40
Sizes 4, 6, 8, 10, 12
D SERIES 628
Sizes $\frac{1}{8}$-1 in (also $\frac{3}{16}$ in)

SQUIRREL

L CORNELISSEN
E SERIES S51
Sizes L, XL
E SERIES S72
Sizes 2, 4, 6, 8, 10, 12

DALER-ROWNEY
A SERIES 25
Sizes 1-12
E SERIES 28
Sizes $\frac{1}{4}$-$\frac{3}{4}$ in

DA VINCI
E SERIES 411
Sizes 0-6, 8, 10, 12
E SERIES 710
Sizes 0-20, 25
E SERIES 713
Sizes 0-20, 25
E SERIES 803
Sizes 0-8, 10, 12
A SERIES 1596
Sizes 0-16
A SERIES 1597
Sizes 0-24

GRUMBACHER
A SERIES Le Mer 6017
Sizes 4, 6, 8, 12, 16, 20, 24

WATERCOLOR AND WATER-BASED

A ROUND PENCIL

B RIGGER/SPOTTER

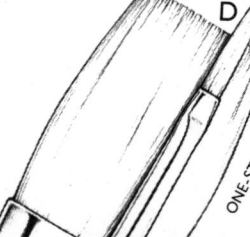
C DESIGNER (LETTERING)

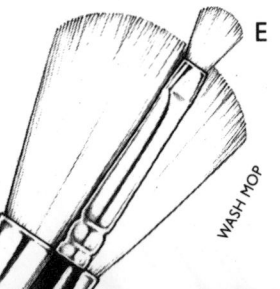
D ONE-STROKE

E WASH MOP

HABICO
A SERIES 140
Sizes 1-20
F SERIES 141
Sizes 1-8, 10, 12
E SERIES 600
Sizes 2, 4, 6, 8, 10, 12
E SERIES 610
Sizes 2, 4, 6, 8, 10, 12-24

HAMILTON
A SERIES 483
Sizes 1-10, 12
E SERIES 513
Sizes 2, 4, 6, 8, 10, 12
E SERIES 522
Sizes 2, 4, 6, 8, 10, 12
J SERIES 493

ISABEY
A SERIES 6215
Sizes 2, 4, 6, 8, 10, 12-20
A SERIES 6219
Sizes 1-6, 8, 10, 12
B SERIES 6220
Sizes 1-6
A SERIES 6221
Sizes 1-14
A SERIES 6234
Sizes 000-8
E SERIES 6235
Sizes 2, 4, 6, 8
J SERIES 6236
Sizes 2, 4, 6, 8
A SERIES 6715
Sizes 2, 4, 6, 8, 10, 12
H SERIES 6721
Sizes 1-12
H SERIES 6722
Sizes 1-12
H SERIES 6723
Sizes 1-12
B SERIES 6731
Sizes 1-12
A SERIES 6732
Sizes 1-12
A SERIES 6733
Sizes 1-12
A SERIES 6735
Sizes 1-12

JAKAR
A SERIES 6201
Sizes 2-8

LEFRANC AND BOURGEOIS
A SERIES 666
Sizes 2, 4, 6, 8, 10, 12-20

LION BRUSH WORKS
E SERIES Trident 238
A SERIES Trident 362
Sizes 0-12
A SERIES Trident 368
Sizes 1-12
G SERIES Trident 375
Sizes $\frac{3}{8}, \frac{1}{2}, \frac{3}{4}$ in
E SERIES Trident 376
Sizes 14-18
E SERIES Trident 377
Sizes 14-18
E SERIES Trident 1264
Sizes 2, 4, 6, 8, 10, 12

MAIMERI
E SERIES 967
Size 4
A SERIES 998
Sizes 1-10, 12

MARABU
A SERIES 2005
Sizes 1, 2, 4, 6, 8, 10, 12

PEBEO
A SERIES 401
Sizes 2, 4, 6, 8, 10, 12-20

E PLOTON
E SERIES 44A Edma
$\frac{1}{2}, \frac{3}{4}$, 1, $1\frac{1}{2}$, 2, 3, 4
E SERIES Edma 72
Sizes 2, 4, 6, 8, 10, 12-14
E SERIES 82 Edma
$\frac{1}{2}, \frac{3}{4}$, 1, $1\frac{1}{2}$, 2, 3, 4

PREMIER BRUSH CO
A SERIES P11
Sizes 00-10
A SERIES P16
Sizes 1-12
D SERIES P21
Sizes $\frac{1}{4}$-1 in
A SERIES P25
Sizes 1-12
E SERIES P68
Sizes 2, 4, 6, 8, 10
E SERIES P69

PRO ARTE
A SERIES 6
Sizes 00-8
A SERIES 7
Sizes 2, 4, 6, 8, 10, 12-16
E SERIES 50
Sizes L, XL
E SERIES 333

ROBERT SIMMONS
F SERIES 52
Sizes 0-4, 6
A SERIES 88
Sizes 1-12
A SERIES 89 Mountain
Sizes 3, 6

SIMONART
A SERIES 352
Sizes 1-8

STRATHMORE ARTIST PRODUCTS
A SERIES Squirrel
Sizes 1-12

L WARD AND CO
E SERIES Whistler 64
Sizes 2, 4, 6, 8, 10, 12

WINSOR AND NEWTON
A SERIES 36 Poster
Sizes 1-6

CAMEL/PONY

BINNEY AND SMITH
A SERIES Liquitex 1107
Sizes 1, 2, 4, 6, 8, 10
A SERIES Liquitex 1120
Sizes 1, 2, 4, 6, 8, 10, 12

DURO
A SERIES 1010
Sizes 0-12
A SERIES 1020
Sizes 0-12

GRUMBACHER
E SERIES Meissoner 55
Sizes $\frac{1}{4}$-1 in
E SERIES Artcraft 172
Sizes 20, 24, 30, 36
E SERIES 319 Finest
Sizes 1-6
A SERIES 1091 Quality
Sizes 1-8, 10, 12
A SERIES 1095 Quality
Sizes 1-8, 10, 12
A SERIES 1096 Quality
Sizes 1-8, 10, 12
E SERIES 1920 Quality
Sizes 1-6
A SERIES 3017 Finest
Sizes 0-8, 10, 12
E SERIES 3422 Finest
Sizes 0-8, 10, 12
A SERIES 4017 Finest
Sizes 0-8, 10, 12
A SERIES 4020 Select
Sizes 1-8, 10, 12
A SERIES 5017 Select
Sizes 1-8, 10, 12
E SERIES 6201 Finest
Sizes 1-6
E SERIES 6205 Select
Sizes 1-6
A SERIES 9620 Finest
Sizes 1-8, 10, 12

ISABEY
A SERIES 6211
Sizes 2, 4, 6, 10, 12-20
A SERIES 6217
Sizes 1-6, 8, 10, 12

A SERIES 6232
Sizes 0-8
J SERIES 6417
Sizes 2, 4, 6, 8

JAKAR
A SERIES 610
Sizes 1-7

LANGNICKEL
A SERIES M-1
Sizes 1-12
H SERIES M8
Sizes $\frac{1}{4}$-1 in
A SERIES 14B
Sizes 1-8, 10, 12
F SERIES 758
Sizes 1-6, 8, 10
F SERIES 1357
Sizes $\frac{1}{4}, \frac{1}{2}, \frac{3}{4}$, 1 in

LION BRUSH WORKS
E SERIES Trident 237
G SERIES Trident 374
Sizes $\frac{3}{8}, \frac{1}{2}, \frac{3}{4}$ in

MARABU
A SERIES 2003
Sizes 1, 2, 4, 6, 8, 10, 12

PREMIER BRUSH CO
A SERIES P10
Sizes 1-6
A SERIES P12
Sizes 1-6, 8, 10

A SERIES P13 (Double-Ended)
Sizes 3/4, 4/5, 5/6, 6/7, 7/8

PRO ARTE
A SERIES 26
Sizes 1-8, 10, 12

TALENS
SERIES 150
Sizes 1-14

UTRECHT
A SERIES 226
Sizes 1-12

SYNTHETIC

BEROL
A SERIES Sprite 4
Sizes 0, 2, 4, 6, 8, 10, 12
E SERIES Sprite 5
Sizes S, M, L
D SERIES Sprite 6
Sizes S, M, L
H SERIES Gold Tip 15
Sizes S, M, L

BINNEY AND SMITH
A SERIES Liquitex 550
Sizes 1, 2, 4, 6, 8
D SERIES Liquitex 554
Sizes $\frac{1}{4}, \frac{1}{2}, \frac{3}{4}$, 1 in

KEY

Brush sizes
00000000, 0000000, 000000, 00000, 0000, 000, 00, 0, 1, 2, 3, 4, 5, 6, 7, 8, 9, 10, 11, 12, 14, 16, 18, 20, 22, 24, 26, 28, 30 (unless otherwise stated)

$\frac{1}{8}, \frac{1}{4}, \frac{1}{3}, \frac{3}{8}, \frac{5}{8}, \frac{3}{4}, \frac{7}{8}$, 1, $1\frac{1}{4}, 1\frac{1}{2}$, 2, $2\frac{1}{2}$, 3, $3\frac{1}{2}$, 4 in

10, 20, 30, 40, 50, 60, 70, 80, 90, 100 mm (unless otherwise stated)

XS extra small   S   small
M   medium   L   large
XL extra large

Quill sizes
Lark (small), Crow, Duck, Goose, Condor (large)

Quality
★ best quality
♦ school quality
(where indicated by the manufacturer)

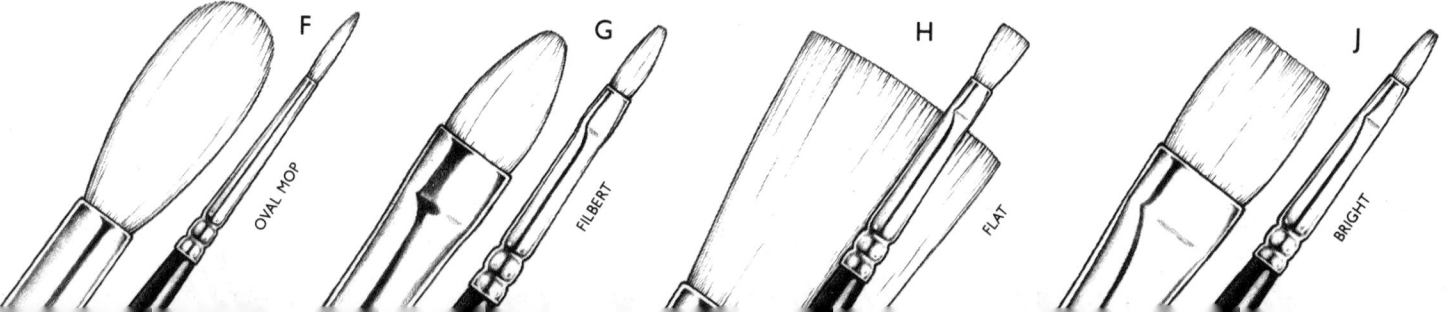

F OVAL MOP
G FILBERT
H FLAT
J BRIGHT

E SERIES Liquitex 555
Sizes 2, 4, 6, 8, 10
H SERIES Liquitex 558
Sizes $\frac{1}{2}$, $\frac{3}{4}$, 1 in

L CORNELISSEN
A SERIES S101
Sizes 0000-8, 10, 12-16
D SERIES S106
Sizes $\frac{1}{8}$-2 in (also $\frac{3}{16}$ in)

DALER-ROWNEY
J SERIES Dalon D22
Sizes $\frac{1}{2}$, $\frac{3}{4}$, 1 in
A SERIES Dalon D77
Sizes 00000-20
H SERIES Dalon D88
Sizes $\frac{1}{8}$-1$\frac{1}{2}$ in
A SERIES 270
Sizes 0-12

DA VINCI
E SERIES Maestro 16
Sizes 4, 8, 12, 16, 20
E SERIES Nova 18
Sizes 8, 16, 18, 20
D SERIES Nova 1370
Sizes 2-16, 20
A SERIES Nova 1570
Sizes 000-6, 8, 10, 12-20
A SERIES Nova 1572
Sizes 000-6, 8, 10, 12-20

GRUMBACHER
A SERIES 4701 Erminette
Sizes 000-8, 10, 12, 14
D SERIES Aquarelle 4703
Sizes $\frac{1}{8}$, $\frac{1}{4}$, $\frac{1}{2}$, $\frac{3}{4}$, 1, 1$\frac{1}{2}$ in
E SERIES Aquarelle 4704
Sizes $\frac{1}{2}$, $\frac{3}{4}$, 1 in
E SERIES Aquarelle 4755
Sizes $\frac{1}{2}$, $\frac{3}{4}$, 1 in

HABICO
A SERIES 123
Sizes 000-12

HOLBEIN
H SERIES 151S
Sizes 0-12
H SERIES 151S-GF
Sizes 0-12
J SERIES 152S
Sizes 0-12
J SERIES 152S-GB
Sizes 0-12
A SERIES 155S
Sizes 0-12
A SERIES 155S-GR
Sizes 0-12
D SERIES 500
Sizes $\frac{1}{8}$, $\frac{1}{4}$, $\frac{1}{2}$, $\frac{3}{4}$, 1 in
A SERIES 655
Sizes 000-12
A SERIES 655-GR
Sizes 000-12
D SERIES 1151-GS
Sizes $\frac{1}{8}$-1 in

ISABEY
A SERIES 6521
Sizes 00-6, 8, 10, 12, 14
H SERIES 6541
Sizes 2, 4, 6, 8

JAKAR
SERIES 640
Sizes 000-6

LANGNICKEL
D SERIES Sunburst 2070
Sizes 0, 1, 2
E SERIES Sunburst 2075
Sizes $\frac{1}{4}$, $\frac{1}{2}$, $\frac{3}{4}$, 1 in
F SERIES Sunburst 2080
Sizes $\frac{1}{2}$, $\frac{3}{4}$, 1 in
A SERIES Snowhite 4000
Sizes 1, 2, 4, 6, 8, 10, 12, 16, 20-24
J SERIES Snowhite 4010
Sizes 1, 2, 4, 6, 8, 10, 12, 16, 20-24
G SERIES Snowhite 4020
Sizes 1, 2, 4, 6, 8, 10, 12, 22, 24
D SERIES Snowhite 4070

H SERIES Snowhite 4090
Sizes 1, 2, 4, 6, 8, 10, 12, 16, 20

LUKAS
E SERIES 5492
Size 1

MAIMERI
A SERIES 996
Sizes 00000-12
H SERIES 996
Sizes $\frac{1}{4}$, $\frac{1}{2}$, $\frac{3}{4}$, 1 in

MARCUS ART
A SERIES Roymac 3550
Sizes 000-4, 6, 8, 10, 12

OCALDO
A SERIES M
Sizes 0-2, 4, 6, 8

PENNELLI CINGHIALE
A SERIES 570
Sizes 0-2, 4, 6, 8, 10, 12-20
H SERIES 571
Sizes 1, 2, 4, 6, 8, 10, 12-20

PREMIER BRUSH CO
A SERIES P41
Sizes 00000-12
A SERIES P42
Sizes 000-6
D SERIES P43
Sizes $\frac{1}{8}$-1 in

PRO ARTE
A SERIES 31
Sizes 1-8, 10, 12
A SERIES 101 Prolene
Sizes 0000-8, 10, 12-16
D SERIES 106 Prolene
Sizes $\frac{1}{8}$-1 in

REEVES
A SERIES R16
Sizes 00-2, 4, 6, 8, 10

ROBERT SIMMONS
A SERIES BHW White Sable
Sizes 000-4
E SERIES 278W White Sable
Sizes 1, 1$\frac{1}{2}$, 2 in
D SERIES 721 White Sable
Sizes $\frac{1}{8}$, $\frac{1}{4}$, $\frac{1}{2}$, $\frac{3}{4}$, 1, 1$\frac{1}{2}$ in
B SERIES 731 White Sable
Sizes 1, 2, 4, 6, 8, 10-16
F SERIES 752 White Sable
Sizes $\frac{1}{4}$, $\frac{1}{2}$, $\frac{3}{4}$, 1 in
E SERIES 755 White Sable
Sizes $\frac{1}{2}$, $\frac{3}{4}$, 1 in
H SERIES 762B White Sable
Sizes 1, 2, 4, 6, 8, 10, 12
A SERIES 785 White Sable
Sizes 00000000-6, 8, 10, 12, 14
E SERIES 789 White Sable
Sizes 26, 30, 36

STRATHMORE ARTIST PRODUCTS
A SERIES White
Sizes 1-12
J SERIES Wash
Sizes $\frac{1}{2}$, $\frac{3}{4}$, 1 in

TALENS
A SERIES 191
Sizes 0-12

UTRECHT
E SERIES 40 Sablette
Size 40
D SERIES 223
Sizes $\frac{1}{4}$, $\frac{1}{2}$, $\frac{3}{4}$, 1 in
A SERIES 224
Sizes 2, 4, 7, 9, 11, 16
D SERIES 230 Sablette
Sizes $\frac{1}{8}$, $\frac{1}{4}$, $\frac{1}{2}$, $\frac{3}{4}$, 1 in

A SERIES 228 Sablette
Sizes 0-2, 4, 6, 7, 8, 10, 12
A SERIES 234
Sizes 0-2, 4, 6, 8, 10, 12

L WARD AND CO
A SERIES Whistler 44
Sizes 0, 2, 4, 6, 8, 10, 12
A SERIES Whistler 54
Sizes 000-8, 10, 12

WINSOR AND NEWTON
D SERIES 638
Sizes $\frac{1}{8}$-1 in

SYNTHETIC AND SABLE MIX

BINNEY & SMITH
F SERIES Liquitex 589
Sizes $\frac{1}{2}$, $\frac{3}{4}$, 1 in
A SERIES Liquitex 590
Sizes 00-2, 4, 6, 8, 10, 12
D SERIES Liquitex 594
Sizes $\frac{1}{4}$, $\frac{1}{2}$, $\frac{3}{4}$, 1 in
H SERIES Liquitex 598
Sizes $\frac{1}{2}$, $\frac{3}{4}$, 1 in
B SERIES Liquitex 599
Sizes 00000, 000, 0

L CORNELISSEN
H SERIES S97
Sizes 0, 2, 4, 6, 8, 10, 12, 14, 16
A SERIES S98
Sizes 000-6/8
D SERIES S99
Sizes $\frac{1}{8}$-$\frac{5}{8}$ in (also $\frac{3}{16}$ in)
A SERIES S100
Sizes 000-8, 10, 12-16

PRO ARTE
D SERIES 99
Sizes $\frac{1}{8}$-$\frac{5}{8}$ in (also $\frac{3}{16}$ in)

SIMONART
A SERIES 11
Sizes 000-8, 10, 12-16
A SERIES 12
Sizes 000-8, 10, 12-16
D SERIES 13
Sizes $\frac{1}{8}$-$\frac{5}{8}$ in (also $\frac{3}{16}$, $\frac{5}{16}$, $\frac{7}{16}$, $\frac{9}{16}$ in)
H SERIES 14
Sizes 0, 2, 4, 6, 8, 10, 12-16
D SERIES 323
Sizes $\frac{1}{8}$-$\frac{5}{8}$ in (also $\frac{3}{16}$, $\frac{5}{16}$, $\frac{7}{16}$, $\frac{9}{16}$ in)

L WARD AND CO
A SERIES Regency Plus 45
Sizes 0, 2, 4, 6, 8, 10, 12-20

KEY

Brush sizes
00000000, 0000000, 000000, 00000, 0000, 000, 00, 0, 1, 2, 3, 4, 5, 6, 7, 8, 9, 10, 11, 12, 14, 16, 18, 20, 22, 24, 26, 28, 30 (unless otherwise stated)

$\frac{1}{8}$, $\frac{1}{4}$, $\frac{1}{2}$, $\frac{3}{8}$, $\frac{3}{4}$, $\frac{7}{8}$, 1, 1$\frac{1}{4}$, 1$\frac{1}{2}$, 2, 2$\frac{1}{2}$, 3, 3$\frac{1}{2}$, 4 in

10, 20, 30, 40, 50, 60, 70, 80, 90, 100 mm (unless otherwise stated)

XS extra small   S small
M medium   L large
XL extra large

Quill sizes
Lark (small), Crow, Duck, Goose, Condor (large)

Quality
★ best quality
♦ school quality
(where indicated by the manufacturer)

WATERCOLOR AND WATER-BASED

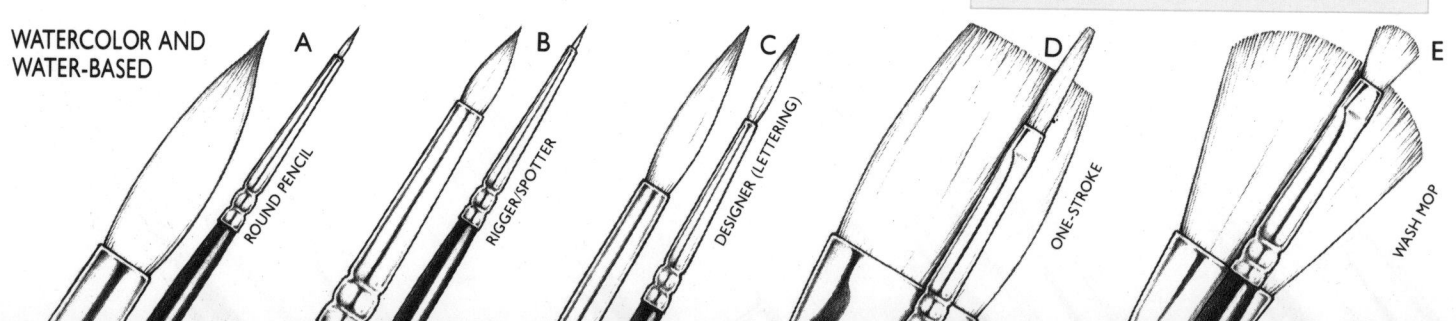

A ROUND PENCIL   B RIGGER/SPOTTER   C DESIGNER (LETTERING)   D ONE-STROKE   E WASH MOP

WINSOR AND NEWTON

A SERIES Sceptre 101
Sizes 00-10, 12, 14

A SERIES Sceptre 202
Sizes 0-6

D SERIES Sceptre 606
Sizes $\frac{1}{8}$-$\frac{3}{4}$ in

SABLE AND OX HAIR

DALER-ROWNEY

D SERIES 55
Sizes 2, 4, 6, 8, 10, 12

A SERIES 56
Sizes 2, 4, 6, 8

DA VINCI

A SERIES Maestro 20
Size 8

LION BRUSH WORKS

D SERIES Trident 642
Sizes $\frac{1}{8}$-1 in (also $\frac{3}{16}$ in)

D SERIES Trident 0642
Sizes $\frac{1}{8}$-1 in (also $\frac{3}{16}$ in)

OCALDO

A SERIES 0
Sizes 0-2, 4, 6, 8

PRO ARTE

D SERIES 12
Sizes $\frac{1}{8}$-1 in (also $\frac{3}{16}$ in)

SIMONART

D SERIES 321
Sizes $\frac{1}{8}$-1 in

WINSOR AND NEWTON

A SERIES 35
Sizes 1-12

NATURAL HAIR BLENDS

BEROL

A SERIES 3
Sizes 2, 4, 6, 8, 10

A SERIES Academy 10
Sizes 2, 4, 6, 8, 10, 12

BINNEY AND SMITH

F SERIES 120 Liquitex
Size 1 in

DALER-ROWNEY

A SERIES 60
Sizes 1-10, 12

HOLBEIN

H SERIES 300-H
(Ox/nylon)
Sizes 0-10

A SERIES 300-R
(Ox/nylon)
Sizes 0-10

H SERIES 1221
Sizes 0-12

ISABEY

A SERIES 6111
Sizes 2, 4, 6, 8, 10, 12-20

J SERIES 6162
Sizes 2, 4, 6, 8, 10, 12-20

G SERIES 6163
Sizes 2, 4, 6, 8, 10, 12-20

A SERIES 6213
(Squirrel/pony)
Sizes 2, 4, 6, 8, 10, 12-20

LANGNICKEL

A SERIES Royal Sable 5500
Sizes 0-6, 8, 10, 12-30

A SERIES Royal Sable 5505
Sizes 0-6, 8, 10, 12-30

J SERIES Royal Sable 5510
Sizes 0-8, 10, 12-32, 44

J SERIES Royal Sable 5515
Sizes 0-8, 10, 12-32, 44

G SERIES Royal Sable 5520
Sizes 0-8, 10, 12-24

G SERIES Royal Sable 5525
Sizes 1-8, 10, 12-22

H SERIES Royal Sable 5590
Sizes 2, 4, 8, 10, 12, 16, 20, 30, 44

D SERIES 250 (Camel/ox)
Sizes $\frac{1}{8}$-$1\frac{1}{2}$ in

A SERIES 260
Sizes $\frac{1}{4}$, $\frac{1}{2}$, $\frac{3}{4}$, 1 in

A SERIES 266
Sizes $\frac{1}{4}$, $\frac{1}{2}$, $\frac{3}{4}$, 1 in

A SERIES Sunburst 3000
Sizes 0000000, 00000, 0000, 000-6, 8, 10, 12, 16, 20, 26, 30

A SERIES Sunburst 3005
Sizes 2, 4, 6, 8, 10, 12, 20

J SERIES Sunburst 3015
Sizes 2, 4, 6, 8, 10, 12

J SERIES Sunburst 3010
Sizes 0-2, 4, 6, 8, 10, 12-20

G SERIES Sunburst 3020
Sizes 1, 2, 4, 6, 8, 10, 12

A SERIES Sunburst 3045
Sizes 0-2

A SERIES Sunburst 3500
Sizes 0, 2, 4, 6, 8, 10, 12, 20

J SERIES Sunburst 3510
Sizes 0, 2, 4, 6, 8, 10, 12, 20

G SERIES Sunburst 3520
Sizes 1-4, 6, 8, 10, 12

D SERIES Sunburst 3070
Sizes $\frac{1}{4}$, $\frac{1}{2}$, $\frac{3}{4}$, 1 in

E SERIES Sunburst 3075
Sizes $\frac{1}{4}$, $\frac{1}{2}$, $\frac{3}{4}$, 1 in

F SERIES Sunburst 3080
Sizes $\frac{1}{2}$, $\frac{3}{4}$, 1 in

LEFRANC AND BOURGEOIS

H SERIES 928
Sizes 4, 6, 8, 10, 12

LION BRUSH WORKS

A SERIES Trident 525
Sizes 1-12

G SERIES Trident 531
Sizes 1-16

J SERIES Trident 532
Sizes 1-16

A SERIES Trident 619
Sizes 1-12

MAIMERI

H SERIES 977
Sizes $\frac{1}{2}$-3 in

A SERIES 999
Sizes $\frac{1}{4}$-$\frac{3}{4}$ in

MARCUS ART

H SERIES Roymac 3500B
Sizes 1, 2, 4, 6, 8, 10, 12

OCALDO

A SERIES A
Sizes 2, 4, 6, 8, 10, 12

PEBEO

A SERIES A22
Sizes 000-5

PELIKAN

A SERIES 23
Sizes 1-6, 8, 10, 12

A SERIES 25
Sizes 2, 4, 6, 8, 10, 12

A SERIES 42
Sizes 2, 4, 6, 8, 10, 12

E PLOTON

E SERIES 9 Edma Mop
Sizes 1-6, 8, 10, 12-16

E SERIES 34 Edma Mops
Sizes 1-6, 8, 10

PRO ARTE

E SERIES 320
Sizes M. L

ROBERSON & CO

A SERIES BRU/25
Sizes 1-10, 12

E SERIES BRU/26
Sizes $\frac{1}{2}$, 1, $1\frac{1}{2}$, 2 in

E SERIES BRU/27
Sizes $\frac{1}{4}$-$\frac{5}{8}$ in

E SERIES BRU/30
Sizes $\frac{1}{4}$-$\frac{5}{8}$ in

TALENS

A SERIES 115
Sizes 1-12

E SERIES 130
Sizes 0-6

L WARD & CO

A SERIES Whistler 51
Sizes 2, 4, 6, 8, 10, 12

MARTIN/F WEBER

E SERIES Jenkins A
Size $2\frac{1}{2}$ in

WINSOR AND NEWTON

H SERIES 14A
Sizes S, L, XL

H SERIES 14B
Sizes S, L

A SERIES 32
Sizes 1-12

OTHER HAIRS

L CORNELISSEN

E SERIES S975 (Goat)
Sizes 6, 12

DALER-ROWNEY

E SERIES 34G (Goat)
Sizes 4, 6, 8, 10, 12

A SERIES 38 (Goat)
Sizes 2, 4, 6

A SERIES 57 (Ringcat)
Sizes 1-10, 12

E SERIES 63
(Squirrel/goat)
Size L

E SERIES 66
(Squirrel/goat)
Size XL

DA VINCI

E SERIES 92 (Badger)
Size 5

E SERIES 750 (Goat)
Sizes 1-20, 25

GRUMBACHER

E SERIES 910 (Badger)
Sizes 2, 4, 6

HABICO

E SERIES 675 (Goat)
Sizes 2, 4, 6, 8, 10, 12

E SERIES 683 (Goat)
Sizes 2, 4, 6, 8, 10, 12-24

E SERIES 690 (Badger)
Sizes 3, 4 in

E SERIES 693 (Badger)
Sizes 3, 4 in

HOLBEIN

H SERIES H (Badger)
Sizes 1-12

G SERIES H (Badger)
Sizes 1-12

A SERIES H (Badger)
Sizes 1-12

KIU FONG

A SERIES Horse hair
Sizes 1-11

H SERIES Horse hair
Sizes 1-11

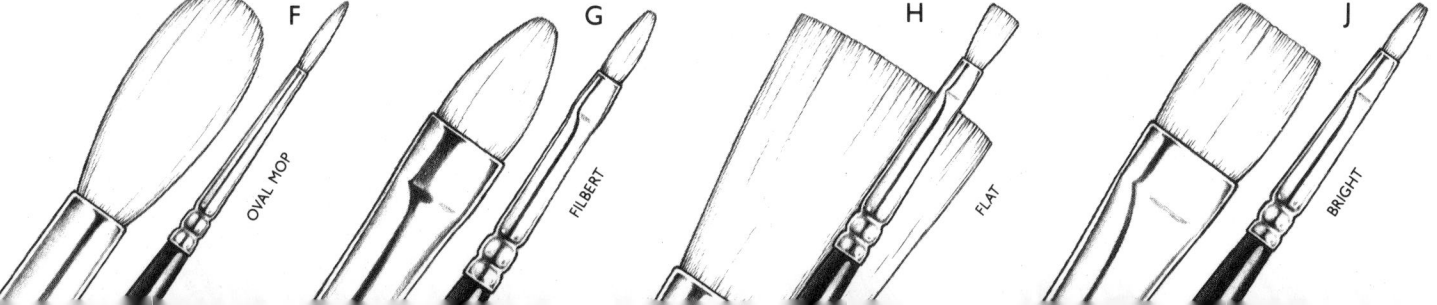

F OVAL MOP G FILBERT H FLAT J BRIGHT

LANGNICKEL
B SERIES 344 (Fitch)
Sizes 10, 12, 16
B SERIES 346 (Fitch)
H SERIES 982
Sizes $\frac{1}{4}$-1 in
E SERIES 1501
Sizes S, M, L
E SERIES 1554
Sizes S, M, L

LEFRANC AND BOURGEOIS
H SERIES 927 (Polecat)
Sizes 4, 6, 8, 10, 12

LION BRUSH WORKS
E SERIES Trident 239 (Goat)
Sizes 0, 2, 4, 6, 8, 10, 12-16
E SERIES Trident 474 (Bear)
E SERIES Trident 1267 (Goat)
Sizes 2, 4, 6, 8, 10, 12

PENNELLI CINGHIALE
A SERIES 270 (Fitch)
Sizes 1, 2, 4, 6, 8, 10, 12-20
H SERIES 271 (Fitch)
Sizes 1, 2, 4, 6, 8, 10, 12-18
J SERIES 272 (Fitch)
Sizes 2, 4, 6, 8, 10, 12-18

E PLOTON
I SERIES Lechertier Badger
Sizes 2$\frac{1}{2}$, 3, 4 in
I SERIES Lechertier Badger
Sizes 1, 1$\frac{1}{2}$-3 in
A SERIES Lechertier Badger
Sizes 2, 4, 6, 8, 10, 12

SIMONART
E SERIES Goat
Sizes 0, 2, 4, 6, 8, 10, 12-24

MARTIN/F WEBER
J SERIES Jenkins B
G SERIES Jenkins C
H SERIES Jenkins D

TALENS
D SERIES 250 (Iltis)
Sizes 2, 4, 6, 8, 10, 12-24

HOG BRISTLE

BEROL
H SERIES Artists' 11
Sizes 4, 6, 8, 10, 12

PELIKAN
H SERIES 613F
Sizes 2, 4, 6, 8, 10, 12-16

PENNELLI CINGHIALE
H SERIES S77
Sizes 0, 2, 4, 6, 8, 10, 12-16
A SERIES 766
Sizes 2, 4, 6, 8, 10, 12-16

E PLOTON
A SERIES Lechertier 4
Sizes 1, 2, 4, 6, 8, 10, 12

WINSOR AND NEWTON
G SERIES 27
Sizes 2, 4, 6, 8

VARNISH BRUSHES

BEROL
SERIES 18 (Bristle)
Sizes S, M, L

DALER-ROWNEY
SERIES 151 (Hog)
Sizes 1, 1$\frac{1}{2}$, 2in

DA VINCI
SERIES 513 (Squirrel)
Sizes $\frac{1}{2}$-4 in
SERIES 520 (Fitch)
Sizes $\frac{1}{2}$-4 in
SERIES 530 (Ox)
Sizes $\frac{1}{2}$-4 in
SERIES 560 (Ox)
Sizes $\frac{1}{2}$-4 in
SERIES 570 (Ox)
Sizes $\frac{1}{2}$-4 in
SERIES 2470 (Hog)
Sizes $\frac{1}{2}$-5 in
SERIES 2471 (Hog)
Sizes $\frac{1}{2}$-5 in

GRUMBACHER
SERIES 3634 (Badger)
Sizes 1, 2, 3
SERIES 3640 (Hog/ox)
Sizes 1-3 in
SERIES 3647 (Hog/ox)
Sizes 1-2$\frac{1}{2}$ in
SERIES 3661 (Camel)
Sizes $\frac{1}{2}$-3 in
SERIES 3669 (Fitch)
Sizes 1, 2, 3
SERIES 4846 (Hog)
Sizes $\frac{1}{2}$-2 in

HABICO
SERIES 865 (Bristle)
Sizes $\frac{1}{2}$, $\frac{3}{4}$, 1-3 in

LANGNICKEL
SERIES 878 (Bristle/ox)
Sizes 1, 2, 2$\frac{1}{2}$ in

LUKAS
SERIES 5491 (Bristle)
Size 3

PEBEO
SERIES A25 (Bristle/synthetic)
Sizes 30, 40, 50 mm

PENNELLI CINGHIALE
SERIES 405 (Ox)
Sizes 20-100 mm
SERIES 406 (Ox)
Sizes 20-100 mm

E PLOTON
SERIES Whistler (Bristle) Spalter
Sizes 120, 150, 180 mm

PRO ARTE
SERIES 21 (Ox)
Sizes 1, 1$\frac{1}{2}$, 2 in

ROBERSON AND CO
SERIES BRU/55
Sizes 1, 1$\frac{1}{2}$, 2, 3 in

TALENS
SERIES 303 (Ox)
Sizes $\frac{1}{8}$-1$\frac{1}{2}$ in
SERIES 360 (Bristle)
Sizes $\frac{1}{2}$, 1, 2, 3 in
SERIES 365 (Goat)
Sizes $\frac{1}{2}$, 1, 2, 3 in

L WARD & CO
SERIES S40 Lily (Hog)
Sizes 20–50, 70, 100 mm
SERIES S41 Lily (Hog)
Sizes 30, 50, 80 mm
SERIES S57 Lily (Hog)
Sizes 1$\frac{1}{2}$-3 in

WINSOR AND NEWTON
SERIES K (Hog)
Sizes 1, 2, 3 in

STENCIL BRUSHES

BEROL
SERIES 16
Sizes M, L

DALER-ROWNEY
SERIES 393
Sizes 2, 4, 6

DA VINCI
SERIES 111
Sizes 6, 10, 14
SERIES 112
Sizes 2, 5, 8
SERIES 113
Sizes 2-24

DURO
SERIES 1075
Sizes 4, 6, 10, 12

GRUMBACHER
SERIES 1131
Sizes 00-8, 10, 12

HABICO
SERIES 800
Sizes 1-6, 8, 10, 12-20
SERIES 805
Sizes 5, 6, 7, 8, 10

HAMILTON
SERIES 349
Sizes 4, 6, 8, 10

ISABEY
SERIES 6418
Sizes 2-10

LANGNICKEL
SERIES 674
Sizes 0, 2, 4, 6, 8, 10, 12-20
SERIES 676
Sizes 0, 2, 4, 6, 8, 10, 12-20
SERIES 678
Sizes 1$\frac{1}{8}$ in
SERIES 679
Sizes 1, 1$\frac{1}{2}$, 2 in

LUKAS
SERIES 5493
Size 8

MAIMERI
SERIES 971
Sizes $\frac{1}{4}$, $\frac{1}{2}$, $\frac{3}{4}$, 1 in

OCALDO
SERIES Q
Sizes 1, 2, 3

PEBEO
SERIES A24
Sizes 2, 4, 6

ROBERT SIMMONS
SERIES 96 (Hog)
Sizes 1-6, 8
SERIES 960 Decorator
Sizes $\frac{3}{8}$-1$\frac{1}{4}$ in

TALENS
SERIES 350
Sizes 2, 4, 6, 8, 10, 12, 14

L WARD & CO
SERIES Whistler 65
Sizes 2, 6, 8, 10, 12-24

WINSOR AND NEWTON
SERIES S4
Sizes 2, 4, 6

VARNISH

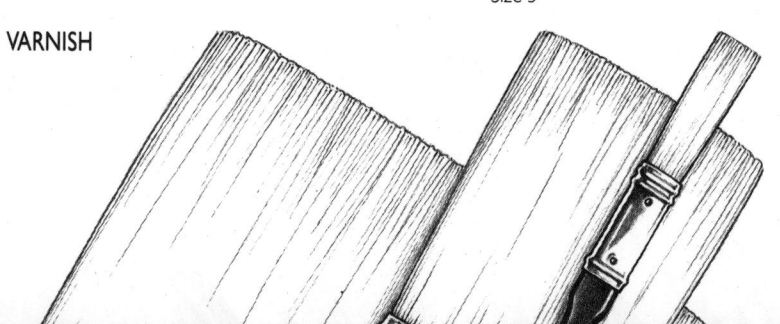

STENCIL

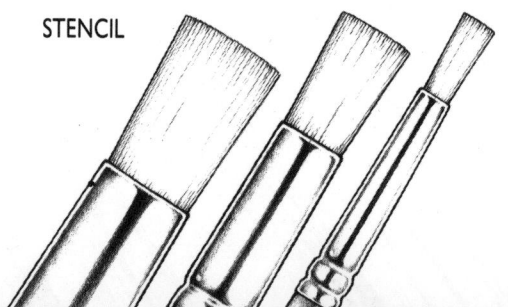

BRUSHES FOR LETTERING

BINNEY AND SMITH

A SERIES Liquitex 553
(Sablon)
Sizes 1, 2, 4, 6

A SERIES Liquitex 591
Sizes 2, 4, 6

A SERIES Liquitex 593
Sizes 2, 4, 6

DALER-ROWNEY

A SERIES Dalon D99
Sizes 1-6

DA VINCI

D SERIES 700 (Squirrel)
Sizes 0-4

B SERIES 1100 (Kolinsky)
Sizes 1-24

A SERIES 1105 (Kolinsky)
Sizes 1-14

B SERIES 1110 (Kolinsky)
Sizes 1-24

B SERIES 1111 (Kolinsky)
Sizes 1-24

A SERIES 1115 (Kolinsky)
Sizes 00-24

B SERIES 1150 (Sabeline)
Sizes 1-30

B SERIES 1151 (Sabeline)
Sizes 1-30

A SERIES 1152 (Sabeline)
Sizes 1-30

A SERIES 1200 (Kolinsky)
Sizes 1-24

C SERIES 1203 (Kolinsky)
Sizes 1-20

B SERIES 1206 (Kolinsky)
Sizes 1-24

B SERIES 1209 (Kolinsky)
Sizes 1-24

A SERIES 1210 (Kolinsky)
Sizes 1-24

A SERIES 1250 (Sabeline)
Sizes 1-24

A SERIES 1267 (Ox)
Sizes 1-24

B SERIES 1285 (Ox)
Sizes 1-24

A SERIES 1287 (Ox)
Sizes 1-24

A SERIES 1289 (Ox)
Sizes 1-24

A SERIES 1400 (Kolinsky)
Sizes 1-9

B SERIES 1406 (Kolinsky)
Sizes 1-9

A SERIES 1410 (Kolinsky)
Sizes 1-9

B SERIES 1416 (Kolinsky)
Sizes 1-9

A SERIES 1450 (Sabeline)
Sizes 0000-9

B SERIES 1469 (Ox)
Sizes 0-9

B SERIES 1499 (Squirrel)
Sizes 0-9

DURO

A SERIES 2270 (Sable)
Sizes 1-6

GRUMBACHER

B SERIES 40 (Sable)
Sizes 2, 4, 6, 8, 10, 12,
14

B SERIES 303G (Camel)
Sizes 0-8, 10, 12-20

A SERIES 297G (Camel)
Sizes 0-8, 10, 12

D SERIES 1010 (Squirrel)
Sizes 00-4

B SERIES 2356 (Sable)
Sizes 1-8

B SERIES 2357 (Sable)
Sizes 1-8, 10, 12

A SERIES 4702
(Erminette)
Sizes 1-6

B SERIES 52555G
(Camel)
Sizes 1-8, 10, 12

A SERIES 7357 (Sable)
Sizes 1-6

A SERIES 7356 (Sable)
Sizes 1-6

B SERIES 9355 (Sable)
Sizes 1-8, 10, 12-20

B SERIES 9358 (Sable)
Sizes 1-8, 10, 12

B SERIES 9452 (Sabeline)
Sizes 1, 2, 4, 6, 8, 10,
12-20

B SERIES 9454 (Ox)
Sizes 1, 2, 4, 6, 8, 10, 12

B SERIES 9455 (Sable)
Sizes 1-8, 10, 12-20

HABICO

A SERIES 330 (Sable)
Sizes 1, 2, 4, 6, 8, 10,
12-20

A SERIES 335 (Sable)
Sizes 1, 2, 4, 6, 8, 10,
12-20

A SERIES 340
(Sable imitation)
Sizes 1, 2, 4, 6, 8, 10,
12-20

A SERIES 350
(Sable imitation)
Sizes 1, 2, 4, 6, 8, 10,
12-24

A SERIES 355 (Ox)
Sizes 1, 2, 4, 6, 8, 10,
12-20

A SERIES 356 (Ox)
Sizes 1, 2, 4, 6, 8, 10,
12-24

A SERIES 400 (Kolinsky)
Sizes 1, 2, 4, 6, 8, 10,
12-24

B SERIES 400A
(Kolinsky)
Sizes 1, 2, 4, 6, 8, 10,
12-24

A SERIES 405
(Sable imitation)
Sizes 1, 2, 4, 6, 8, 10,
12-24

B SERIES 405A
(Sable imitation)
Sizes 1, 2, 4, 6, 8, 10,
12-24

A SERIES 410 (Ox)
Sizes 1, 2, 4, 6, 8, 10,
12-24

A SERIES 415 (Ox)
Sizes 1, 2, 4, 6, 8, 10,
12-24

A SERIES 420
(Sable imitation)
Sizes 1, 2, 4, 6, 8, 10,
12-24

A SERIES 430 (Kolinsky)
Sizes 1-9

A SERIES 432 (Sable)
Sizes 1-9

A SERIES 435
(Sable imitation)
Sizes 1-9

A SERIES 440 (Ox)
Sizes 1-9

A SERIES 445 (Kolinsky)
Sizes 1-9

A SERIES 450
(Sable imitation)
Sizes 1-9

A SERIES 455 (Ox)
Sizes 1-9

B SERIES 460 (Kolinsky)
Sizes 1-9

B SERIES 465
(Sable imitation)
Sizes 1-9

B SERIES 470 (Ox)
Sizes 1-9

B SERIES 475 (Ox)
Sizes 1-9

B SERIES 480 (Squirrel)
Sizes 1-9

HAMILTON

A SERIES 460 (Sable)
Sizes Lark, Swan

A SERIES 461 (Sable)
Sizes Lark, Swan

A SERIES 463 (Ox)
Sizes Lark, Swan

A SERIES 465 (Sable)
Sizes Lark, Swan

HANDOVER

B SERIES 2100 (Kolinsky)
Sizes 00-8

B SERIES 2101
(Sable/ox)
Sizes 1-8

B SERIES 2102 (Kolinsky)
Sizes 00-8

B SERIES 2111 (Ox)
Sizes 8-16

B SERIES 2112 (Kolinsky)
Sizes 00-8

B SERIES 2114
(Sable/ox)
Sizes Lark–Condor

HOLBEIN

A SERIES 1355
(Nylon)
Sizes 0-6

A SERIES 1355-GL
(Nylon)
Sizes 1, 3, 5

ISABEY

B SERIES 6311 (Sabeline)
Sizes 2, 4, 6, 8, 10,
12-20

B SERIES 6316 (Kolinsky)
Sizes 2, 4, 6, 8, 10,
12-20

A SERIES 6317 (Kolinsky)
Sizes 2, 4, 6, 8, 10,
12-20

B SERIES 6318 (Kolinsky)
Sizes 2, 4, 6, 8, 10,
12-20

B SERIES 6411 (Sabeline)
Sizes 2, 4, 6, 8, 10, 12,
14

B SERIES 6531 (Synthetic)
Sizes 2, 4, 6, 8, 10,
12-16

LANGNICKEL

B SERIES 60 (Sable)
Sizes 1-8, 10, 12-20

B SERIES 65S (Sable)
Sizes 1-8, 10, 12-20

B SERIES 150 (Sable)
Sizes 1-8, 10, 12-20

B SERIES 163 (Sable)
Sizes 1-8, 10, 12-20

B SERIES Shorty 164
Sizes 1-8, 10, 12-20

B SERIES 167 (Sable)
Sizes 1-8, 10, 12-20

B SERIES 306 (Camel)
Sizes 0-4, 6, 8, 10

B SERIES 350 (Camel)
Sizes 1-16

B SERIES 370 (Camel)
Sizes 1-6

B SERIES 381 (Camel)
Sizes 2, 4, 6, 8, 10,
12-24

A SERIES 387 (Camel)
Sizes 1, 2, 4, 6

A SERIES 388 (Camel)
Sizes 1, 2, 4, 6

A SERIES 660 (Sable)
Sizes 0-4

A SERIES 661 (Sable)
Sizes 0-4

KEY

Brush sizes

00000000, 0000000,
000000, 00000, 0000, 000,
00, 0, 1, 2, 3, 4, 5, 6, 7, 8,
9, 10, 11, 12, 14, 16, 18,
20, 22, 24, 26, 28, 30
(unless otherwise stated)

$\frac{1}{8}, \frac{1}{4}, \frac{1}{2}, \frac{3}{8}, \frac{5}{8}, \frac{3}{4}, \frac{7}{8}, 1, 1\frac{1}{4}, 1\frac{1}{2},$
$2, 2\frac{1}{2}, 3, 3\frac{1}{2}, 4$ in

10, 20, 30, 40, 50, 60, 70,
80, 90, 100 mm (unless
otherwise stated)

XS extra small   S small
M medium   L large
XL extra large

Quill sizes

Lark (small), Crow, Duck,
Goose, Condor (large)

Quality

★ best quality
♦ school quality
(where indicated by
the manufacturer)

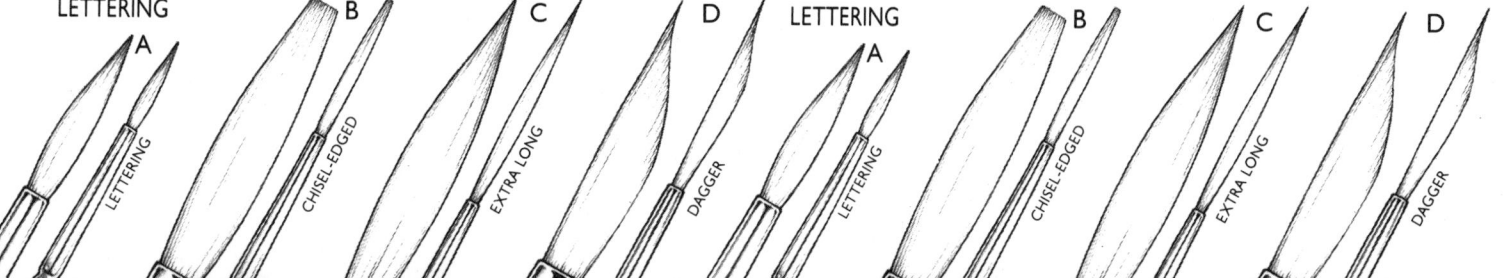

LETTERING   A   B   C   D   LETTERING   A   B   C   D

LETTERING   CHISEL-EDGED   EXTRA LONG   DAGGER   LETTERING   CHISEL-EDGED   EXTRA LONG   DAGGER

A SERIES 670 (Sable)
Sizes 1-6, 8
A SERIES 671 (Sable)
Sizes 1-6, 8
D SERIES 748 (Ox)
Sizes 00-4
D SERIES 749 (Camel)
Sizes 00-4
B SERIES 1300 (Camel)
Sizes 0-8, 10, 12-20
A SERIES 1390 (Camel)
Sizes 1-16
A SERIES 1391 (Camel)
Sizes 1-6
A SERIES Sunburst 2040
(Taklon)
Sizes 0000000000,
00-2, 4, 6
A SERIES Sunburst 2050
(Taklon)
Sizes 0000000000,
00-2, 4, 6
A SERIES Sunburst 3040
(Hair/Taklon)
Sizes 0000000000,
00-2, 4, 6
A SERIES Sunburst 3050
(Hair/Taklon)
Sizes 0000000000,
00-2, 4, 6
B SERIES 15300 (Camel)
Sizes 0-8, 10, 12-24

LION BRUSH WORKS

A SERIES Trident 610
(Sable)
Sizes 0-7
A SERIES Trident 610M
(Sable/ox)
Sizes 0-7
B SERIES Trident 612
(Sable)
B SERIES Trident 612M
(Sable/ox)
A SERIES Trident 635
(Sable)
Sizes 0-10, 12
A SERIES Trident 635M
(Sable/ox)
Sizes 0-10, 12

B SERIES Trident 637
(Sable)
Sizes 0-8, 10
B SERIES Trident 637A
(Sable)
Sizes 0-8, 10
B SERIES Trident 637P
(Sable)
Sizes 0-6, 8
B SERIES Trident 639
(Sable/ox)
Sizes 0-8, 10
B SERIES Trident 714
(Ox)
Sizes 6, 8, 10, 12-16
B SERIES Trident 737
(Ox)
Sizes 0-8, 10
B SERIES Trident 0637
(Sable)
Sizes 0-8, 10
B SERIES Trident 0639
(Sable/ox)
Sizes 0-8, 10

MAIMERI

A SERIES 966 (Squirrel)
A SERIES 968 (Sable)
Size 2
A SERIES 969 (Sable)
Size 2
B SERIES 974 (Sable)
Sizes 0-10, 12

PENNELLI CINGHIALE

A SERIES 265 (Ox)
Sizes 2, 4, 6, 8, 10,
12-24

E PLOTON

A SERIES Lechertier
(Sable)
Sizes 00-8
B SERIES Lechertier
(Sable/ox)
Sizes 000-8

PREMIER BRUSH CO

A SERIES P24 (Sable)
Sizes 0-9

B SERIES P35 (Sable)
Sizes 1-16
B SERIES P35m
(Sable/ox)
Sizes 1-16
A SERIES P37 (Sable)
Sizes 1-8
A SERIES P37A
Sizes 1-8
B SERIES P38 (Sable)
Sizes 1-11

PRO ARTE

A SERIES 9 (Ox)
Sizes XS, S, M, L
B SERIES 10 (Ox)
Sizes 0-10, 12-16
B SERIES 10A (Sable/ox)
Sizes 1-12

ROBERSON AND CO

A SERIES BRU/3/CROW
(Sable)
Sizes Crow, Duck,
Goose
B SERIES BRU/5/LARK
(Sable)
Sizes Lark, Crow,
S Duck, L Duck,
S Goose, Goose,
L Goose
A SERIES BRU/6/CROW
(Ox)
Sizes Crow, Duck,
Goose

ROBERT SIMMONS

A SERIES Taubes FT4
B SERIES 30 (Sable)
Sizes 1-8, 10, 12-20
B SERIES 31 (Sable)
Sizes 1-8, 10, 12-20
B SERIES 32 (Sable)
Sizes 1-8, 10, 12
B SERIES 33 (Sable)
Sizes 1-8
B SERIES 35 (Sable)
Sizes 1-8, 10, 12

B SERIES 37 (Sabeline)
Sizes 1-10, 12
B SERIES 38 (Sabeline)
Sizes 1, 2, 4, 6, 8, 10,
12-20
A SERIES 50 (Sable)
Sizes 0-6
A SERIES 51 (Sable)
Sizes 00-4
B SERIES 98G (Squirrel)
Sizes 0-8, 10, 12
D SERIES 101 (Squirrel)
Sizes 00-4
B SERIES 304 (Sable)
Sizes 1, 2, 4, 6, 8, 10,
12, 14
B SERIES 730 White
Sable (Synthetic)
Sizes 1, 2, 4, 6, 8, 10,
12
A SERIES 750 White
Sable (Synthetic)
Sizes 1-4, 6

SIMONART

C SERIES 313 (Sable/ox)
Sizes 1-8, 10, 12
C SERIES 337
(Sable/ester)
Sizes 1-8, 10, 12

STRATHMORE ARTIST PRODUCTS

B SERIES Red Sable
Sizes 1-12

UTRECHT

A SERIES 229 (Sablette)
Sizes 1, 2, 4, 6, 8

L WARD & CO

A SERIES Whistler 200
Sizes 1-6, 8, 10, 12
B SERIES Whistler 201
Sizes ⅛-1 in
A SERIES Whistler 202
(Sable)
Sizes Lark, L Swan
A SERIES Whistler 203
(Ox)
Sizes 1-6

B SERIES Whistler 204
Sizes ⅛-1 in
B SERIES Whistler 206
Sizes ⅛-1 in
A SERIES Whistler 222
Sizes 1-6, 8, 10, 12

WINSOR AND NEWTON

A SERIES 2 (Sable)
Sizes Lark, Goose
A SERIES 19 (Sable)
Sizes 1-6
B SERIES 19L (Ox/sable)
Sizes 1-6
A SERIES Sceptre 303
(Synthetic/sable)
Sizes 0-3

SCENIC AND MURAL BRUSHES

HANDOVER
SERIES H313
(Hog hair)
Sizes 2-12

LANGNICKEL
SERIES 830 (Bristle)
Sizes ¼, ½, ¾, 1, 1½, 2, 3 in

OCALDO
SERIES H
Sizes 1, 2 in

ROBERT SIMMONS
SERIES Signet 40
Sizes 14-24
SERIES 41 Interlocked
Sizes 14-24

L WARD AND CO
SERIES S57 Sax (Bristle)
Sizes 1½, 2, 3 in

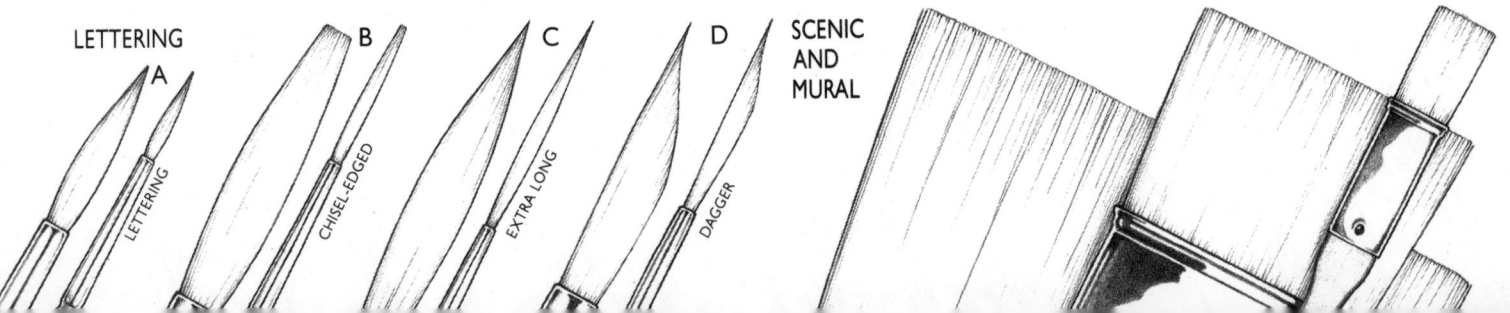

LETTERING   A   B   C   D   SCENIC AND MURAL

LETTERING   CHISEL-EDGED   EXTRA LONG   DAGGER

FAN BRUSHES

BINNEY AND SMITH
SERIES Liquitex 556
(Sablon)
Sizes 1, 3
SERIES Liquitex 596
Sizes 1, 3, 5
SERIES Liquitex 665
(Hog)
Sizes 2, 6
SERIES Liquitex 742
(Badger)
Sizes 2, 4, 6

L CORNELISSEN
SERIES SE (Hog)
Sizes S, M, L
SERIES S55 (Sable)
Sizes 1-6

DALER-ROWNEY
SERIES Dalon D55
Sizes 1-6
SERIES Bristlewhite
B84
Sizes 2, 4, 6
SERIES 114 (Hog)
Sizes 2, 4, 6
SERIES 131 (Sable)
Sizes 2, 4, 6

DA VINCI
SERIES 402 (Synthetic)
Sizes 1-5
SERIES 404 (Hog)
Sizes 1-5
SERIES 405 (Kolinsky)
Sizes 1-5
SERIES 406 (Ox)
Sizes 1-5
SERIES 407 (Squirrel)
Sizes 1-5

GRUMBACHER
SERIES 1060 (Hog)
Sizes 3-6
SERIES 1061 (Sable)
Sizes 1-6
SERIES 1062 (Fitch)
Sizes 3, 6

HOLBEIN
SERIES T (Badger)
Sizes 2, 4, 6, 8, 10, 12
SERIES U (Hog)
Sizes 2, 4, 6, 8, 10, 12
SERIES 777GR (Nylon)
Sizes 0, 2, 4, 6, 8, 10, 12
SERIES 4710 (Hog)
Sizes 3, 6

ISABEY
SERIES 6089 (Hog)
Sizes 3-6
SERIES 6581 (Synthetic)
Sizes 3, 6

LANGNICKEL
SERIES 505FB (Sable)
SERIES Sunburst 2020
(Taklon)
Sizes 1, 3, 6
SERIES Snowhite 4030
(Taklon)
Sizes 2, 4, 6
SERIES Snowhite 4530
(Taklon)
Sizes 2, 4, 6
SERIES Royal Sable
5530 (Mixed hair)
Sizes 2, 4, 6, 8, 10, 12,
20, 30

LUKAS
SERIES 5495 (Synthetic)
Size 4

PEBEO
SERIES A23 (Synthetic)
Sizes 10, 12, 12/12

PREMIER BRUSH CO
SERIES P44 (Nylon)
Sizes 2, 4, 6
SERIES P52 (Hog)
Sizes 2, 4, 6

PRO ARTE
SERIES Series E (Hog)
Sizes S, M, L

ROBERT SIMMONS
SERIES 48 (Hog)
Sizes 2, 4, 6
SERIES 49 (Fitch)
Sizes 2, 4, 6
SERIES 748 (Synthetic)
Sizes 2, 4, 6
SERIES 748L
Sizes 2, 4, 6

TALENS
SERIES 280 (Hog)
Sizes 2, 4
SERIES 281 (Synthetic)
Sizes 2, 4

UTRECHT
SERIES 208 (Hog)
Sizes 2, 4, 6
SERIES 227 (Sablette)
Sizes 2, 4, 6

WINSOR AND NEWTON
SERIES J (Hog)
Sizes 1-6
SERIES 55 (Sable)
Sizes 1-6

ORIENTAL BRUSHES

L CORNELISSEN
A SERIES Japanese
Sizes Selection
B SERIES Japanese Hake
Size 2 in

FABER-CASTELL
B SERIES 6652
Size 2 in

GRUMBACHER
A SERIES 287 (Camel)
Sizes 000-8, 10, 12
A SERIES 289 (Camel)
Sizes 00-6
A SERIES 628 (Sable)
Sizes 1-6

HOLBEIN
A SERIES BB
(Brown hair)
Sizes 000-6, 8, 10, 12-16
A SERIES BDB Double-ended
A SERIES 1110-L Duplex
A SERIES 1110-S Duplex
A SERIES BW
(White hair)
Sizes 000-6, 8, 10, 12-16
A SERIES 1210
(White hair)
Sizes A, B, C, D, E
A SERIES 1211
(White hair)
Sizes A, B, C, D
A SERIES 1212
(White hair)
Sizes A, B, C, D, E
A SERIES 1213
(White hair or badger)
Size 1
A SERIES 1214
(Brown hair)
Sizes B, C, D
A SERIES 1215
(White hair)
Sizes A, B, C

A SERIES 1216
(White hair)
Size C
A SERIES 1217
(Brown hair)
Sizes B, C, D
B SERIES 1220
Sizes $\frac{5}{8}$, 1-3$\frac{1}{2}$, 4$\frac{1}{4}$, 4$\frac{3}{4}$, 6 in
B SERIES 1265-L (Horse)
B SERIES 1265-S (Horse)
A SERIES 1267L
(Horse/wool)
A SERIES 1267M
(Horse/wool)
A SERIES 1267S
(Horse/wool)
A SERIES 1268
(Horse/badger)
A SERIES 1280
(Brown hair)
Sizes B, C, D
A SERIES 1281
(Brown hair)
Sizes A, B, C, D
A SERIES 1282
(White hair)
Sizes B, C, D

KIU FONG
B SERIES 302
Sizes 1-4$\frac{1}{2}$ in

LANGNICKEL
A SERIES JB
Sizes S, M, L
A SERIES JW (Goat)
Sizes S, M, L
A SERIES TJ-6 Double-ended (Brown hair)
A SERIES TJ-12 Double-ended (White hair)
A SERIES 634 Double-ended
A SERIES 635 Brush and Pen
A SERIES 636

B SERIES 787
Sizes 1, 1$\frac{3}{8}$, 1$\frac{3}{4}$, 2$\frac{1}{2}$, 3$\frac{3}{8}$,
4$\frac{1}{2}$ in
B SERIES 788
Sizes 1-3$\frac{1}{2}$ in
B SERIES 797
Sizes 44, 55, 77
A SERIES 798
(Brown hair)
B SERIES 799
Sizes 33, 66

LASCAUX
A SERIES Japanese
(Goat hair)
Sizes 1, 2, 3 in

T N LAWRENCE
A SERIES A (Mixed hair)
A SERIES B (Goat)
A SERIES C (Mixed hair)

ROBERT SIMMONS
A SERIES 75 Double-ended
A SERIES 76 Brush and Pen
A SERIES 78
(Brown hair)
Sizes 1-6
A SERIES 79 (White hair)
Sizes SM, S, M, L

TALENS
A SERIES 321
(Mixed hair)
A SERIES 322 Double-ended (Mixed hair)

L WARD & CO
A SERIES Whistler Ishima
Sizes 12 approx
A SERIES Whistler
Shikish
Sizes 6 approx
A SERIES Whistler Reed
SERIES Whistler
Bamboo
Sizes 0-6, 8

FAN

ORIENTAL

A

ROUND PENCIL

B

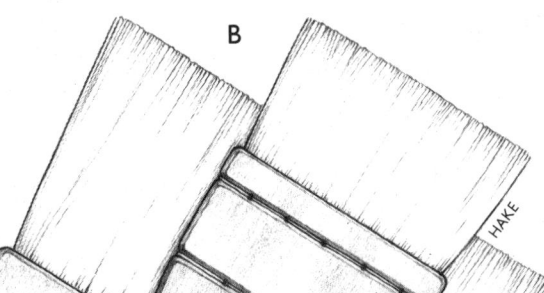

HAKE

PALETTE AND PAINTING KNIVES

Tempered and stainless steel are commonly used for the blades of palette and painting knives. Palette knives are used for mixing paint directly on the palette and generally have broad rounded blades. Painting knives, however, have cranked handles and are much more varied in shape. They are used for the application and removal of paint from the support. The diamond-shaped knives are effective for creating rich impastos; the toothed knives can be used to create interesting parallel-line effects. Extensive ranges of painting and palette knives are offered by Talens and Maimeri, both with solid wooden handles.

PALETTE KNIVES

PAINTING KNIVES

PAINTING KNIVES

PALETTES

1 WHITE PLASTIC PALETTE
2 SMALL OVAL PALETTE
3 OLD MASTER'S PALETTE
4 CERAMIC MIXING TRAY
5 CIRCULAR MIXING TRAY
6 CERAMIC MIXING TRAY
7 MAHOGANY PALETTE

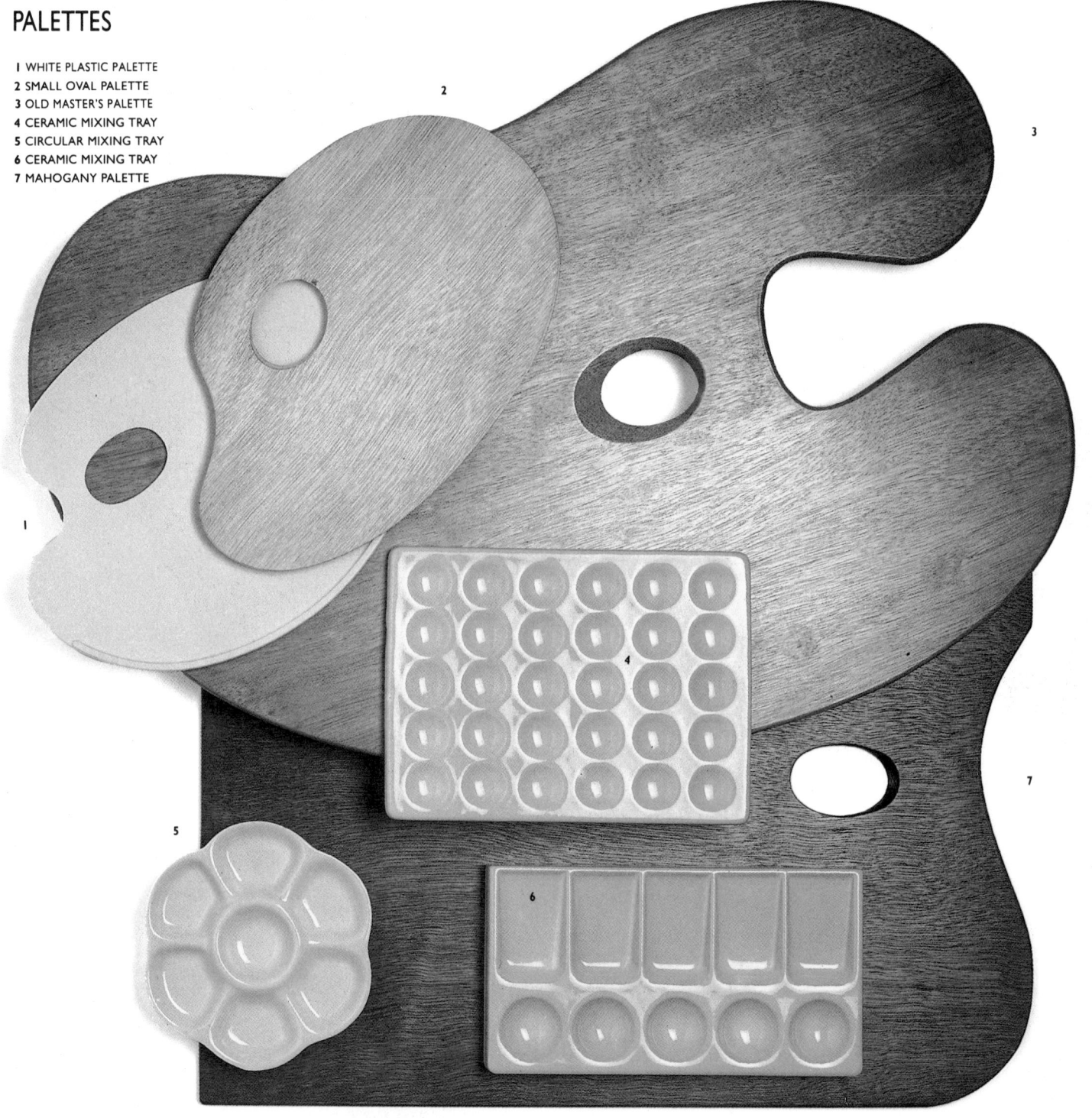

PAINTING EQUIPMENT

1 DOUBLE-SIDED PAINT BOX
2 CANTILEVERED PAINT BOX
3 WATERCOLOR SKETCHING BOX
4 OIL-PAINT BOX
5 WATERCOLOR BOX
6 BRUSH HOLDER
7 PALETTE CUPS
8 COLLAPSIBLE WATER BOTTLE
9 GLASS MIXING SLAB
10 GLASS MULLER
11 MAHL STICK
12 NATURAL SPONGES

COLOR
& MEDIA

Paints and pigments • Painting
sets • Inks • Soft pastels, oil
pastels and oil painting sticks •
Colored pencils • Crayons •
Mediums, additives and
fixatives

You, the artist, have at your disposal an enormous range of paints and other media to choose from. This part of the book contains charts illustrating the available ranges of paints and pigments, inks, pastels and colored pencils, and is designed to help you in your selection. An additional section outlines the various mediums, additives and grounds — a knowledge of which is essential for the good quality of your painting.

PAINTS AND PIGMENTS

A paint is made by mixing dry powder pigment in a liquid in order to make the color easy to manipulate and control, and to cause it to stick to the surface of the support. The liquid medium binds the particles of pigment and may vary in nature from the dry solidity of a pastel to the wetness of ink. It should be able to adhere mechanically to the tooth of the support and, in some cases, chemically to the substance of the support. A dryish medium, such as soft pastel, will cling better to a paper surface of some roughness or tooth rather than a smooth texture, whereas watercolor will take well on smooth as well as rough paper.

Experienced artists may want to make their own paints; this is desirable because the exact constituents of the paint are then known, unlike some manufactured paints.

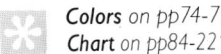

Colors on pp74-79
Chart on pp84-221

Testing Paints

Some manufacturers indicate the amount of pigment in their paints. However, simple tests that you can do to check the pigment content of any permanent artists' colors in tubes are as follows:

Mass tone

Taking a few brands of similar types of paint and with the same claimed pigment composition, squeeze the paints straight from the tube, and spread them out thickly with a palette knife. Compare them for intensity, brilliance and cleanness of color — the most brilliant will be the best quality paint.

Under tone

With a palette knife, scrape the paint very thinly on smooth white paper and look at it for the same qualities as mass tone. Again, the cleanest color will indicate the best paint.

Color strength

Take one level teaspoon of the first test color and three level teaspoons of white paint, being careful to smooth out any bubbles. Mix the paint with a palette knife until all the streaks have been blended in and spread it out smoothly on one half of a sheet of white paper. Take the second test color and repeat the procedure using the same amount of white. Spread it out smoothly on the other half of the same sheet of paper and then compare the two samples. The sample with a smaller percentage of color pigment will appear paler.

Dry ground pigments

Natural pigments are usually classified as inorganic and organic, depending on their origin. Inorganic (or mineral) pigments include native (or natural) earths, such as raw umber and ocher, and calcined native earths, such as burnt umber and burnt sienna. Synthetic iron oxides, such as Mars black, Mars brown, Mars red and Mars yellow sometimes replace some of the traditional native earth colors such as English red, Indian red and Venetian red. Mineral colors include cadmium yellow and red, cerulean blue, chrome yellow, cobalt blue, chromium oxide, titanium dioxide and lapis lazuli.

Organic pigments are of animal, vegetable or synthetic origin. Animal-derived pigments are made mainly from calcined bones and include ivory black, and caput mortuum (mummy brown) which was traditionally made from the ground bones of Egyptian mummies. Originally, Indian yellow (a lake of euxanthic acid) was derived from the urine of cows fed on mango leaves. Charcoal, gamboge (yellow gum resin) and madder root are all examples of vegetable-derived pigments.

Synthetic organic pigments today form a large part of the colorman's selection. They bring to the modern artist's palette a range of colors of great beauty, permanence and strength of color. They were first made in the 1950s and for a while received a slow reception. There were initial doubts as to their permanence, and some of their generic terms, such as aniline and coal-tar, had acquired a pejorative meaning. In recent years, however, modern chemistry has overcome problems of permanence in many instances, and these pigments have found increasing acceptance.

Synthetic organic pigments and dyes are made by distilling coal-tar, and from certain residues of petroleum. These raw materials are processed into intermediate compounds and dyes and pigments are made by various combinations of these compounds. The names of some of these pigments may be recognized as forming part of a longer chemical name, such as aniline, anthracene and beta (ß) naphthol. Azo, for example, refers to nitrogen and indicates chemical reactions such as nitration, and prefixes such as mono, di, tri, tetra and sesqui refer to variations in number of elements in a compound, such as mono-azo, di-azo and sesquioxide.

Alizarin crimson, also known as alizarin carmine, alizarin red, alizarin scarlet, alizarin lake, crimson lake and crimson alizarin, is a synthetic organic pigment made from anthracene, and is a lake color. A lake pigment is made by the precipitation of dye — transparent color — onto an inert pigment or base.

Common synthetic organic pigments include quinacridone red, alizarin crimson, arylamide red, arylamide yellow, azo red, azo yellow, carbazole dioxazine purple, flavanthrone yellow, Hansa yellow, indanthrone blue, iso violanthrone violet, lithol red, naphthol red, permanent magenta, permanent rose, perylene red, phthalocyanine blue, phthalocyanine green, quinacridone magenta, quinacridone red, quinacridone violet, thio indigo red-violet and toluidine red.

Various fugitive synthetic organic pigments are used in gouaches, where permanence is of secondary importance. Artists' quality pigments, such as the quinacridones and phthalocyanines, have greater permanence — the phthalocyanines, particularly, have enormous color strength in concentrated form.

Of the various forms of inert pigments, calcium carbonate (chalk), which occurs in many mineral bases, is used extensively in artists' materials. Chalk forms the basis of most pastels and crayons, and, when used in glue and other aqueous mediums, makes good grounds for tempera and oil painting. Whiting, which contains chalk, can be used for gesso grounds, and marble dust, used as part of the ground for mural or pastel painting, gives sparkle to colors. Gypsum is effective for very smooth grounds, and powdered pumice stone may be used to give tooth to the surface of supports for pastel, crayon or charcoal.

The most commonly found inert pigment is barytes, more often described in color composition lists by its chemical name of barium sulphate. Blanc fixe is another form of barium sulphate, but it is artificially prepared and is considerably finer and fluffier than barytes. Both are white powders with no coloring power. Barytes is almost always used as a filler or extender in the cheaper kinds of paint. It is almost transparent in oils, giving a slightly muddy tone to the color.

Aluminum hydroxide, usually known as alumina, alumina base or alumina hydrate, is also an artificially made white powder and light in weight. It has a tremendous capacity for absorbing oil and does not disguise the color so that a darkening of linseed oil in the paint, for example, is very apparent. It is most commonly found as a base for alizarin crimson.

Oil paints

Oil paints are pigments mixed usually with linseed oil, poppy oil or safflower oil. They are available in two grades, artists' and students' quality. Artists' quality paints are the more expensive because they contain the best pigments and the least amount of extender, and some colors are available in this quality only. They take longer to dry and are, therefore, most suited to studio work.

Students' colors generally contain the cheaper pigments and more extender. They are coarser in texture but are extremely useful for beginners.

The traditional drying oil medium in which pigments are ground is cold pressed linseed oil. Today, however, commercial considerations usually dictate that refined linseed oil be used. Cold pressed linseed oil is superior to refined linseed oil in its working qualities, resistance to embrittlement and retention of flexibility. It is recommended for home grinding; it is hard to locate a range of prepared artists' oil colors that use it.

Poppy oil is often used for whites and for some of the lighter, brighter colors because of its pale color and non-yellowing qualities. However, it is slower drying than linseed oil and, more seriously, is prone to embrittlement.

Safflower oil is used in the same way as poppy oil. Oil paints containing it have been available for only 30 years, and this is generally thought to be too short a period for them to be considered proven. This oil suffers from the same defects as poppy oil but to a slightly lesser extent.

Getting the correct balance of medium and pigment consistent with good handling and adhesion to the paint surface is of vital importance. Pigments absorb varying amounts of medium. Venetian red, for example, needs only a small amount of oil to become workable, whereas raw umber needs almost double the quantity. Viridian and cobalt blue need large quantities of oil to achieve a similar handling quality, consistency or feel. Too little medium will produce a paint film which becomes brittle and will crack and flake over the years; too much may enfeeble its color strength and lessen its permanence.

Colors have different degrees of permanence, and manufacturers should indicate whether their paint is permanent or non-permanent. Rowney use a star rating for their paints: four stars indicate that the paint is permanent, whereas one star indicates that the paint is relatively fugitive.

The well-known Belgian manufacturer, Blockx,

make good paints and claim that their oil colors are made with only the best oils and pigments. Pigment concentrations are invariably taken as far as possible, and fillers, extenders and dryers are apparently never used. Old-fashioned stone mills and slow grinding processes help to prevent the pigment from burning and to give the paint a soft, buttery quality. Their paints are certainly greatly admired and have been used by artists such as Paul Signac, René Magritte and Salvador Dali. Similarly, Utrecht, J P Stephenson and Michael Harding claim maximum content of top grade pigments and minimum amounts of extender in their paints.

Alkyd paints

The word "alkyd" is derived from "alcid", meaning a mixture of alcohol and acid — alkyds are produced from polyhydric alcohol and polybasic acid. The oil-modified alkyds are combined with a drying oil such as linseed oil to make the paint. Alkyd paints are not water-based but are soluble in turpentine and can be mixed with oils. You can use them on any primed support suitable for oils or acrylics. Like acrylics, however, they are not easy to manipulate, but are handy paints for artists who want a waterproof surface and a hard edge. The paint is usually expected to dry in about 18 hours and is a good compromise between relatively long-drying oil colors and fast-drying acrylic colors. Alkyd colors are offered by Winsor and Newton and by the PDQ Artists Oil Paints Co.

Watercolor

Watercolor is one of the oldest painting media — it was used by the paleolithic cave painters of Lascaux, who ground their natural pigments with water and used gum, starch or honey to bind them. In today's commercially produced watercolors the pigments are essentially the same as those in oil colors but lead-based pigments are normally eschewed. In addition, the constituents of watercolor paints include a binder such as gum arabic or gum Senegal and a moisturizer (usually glycerine). The wetting agent is traditionally ox-gall, which, in combination with the glycerine, helps the paint to overcome the water surface-tension, and makes rapid absorption of the paint into the water possible, improving the flow of the paint. Dextrin is used in some colors to enhance texture. Sodium orthophenylphenate is a preservative added to watercolors, but a few drops of oil of cloves will do the job just as well. The transparent watercolors can be made opaque by the addition of Chinese white.

You can buy pure watercolor paints in a number of forms, the most common being in tubes and semi-moist pans. Tubed watercolors are particularly useful in the studio, where larger quantities of paint may be required. When painting out-of-doors, pans of semi-moist paint are recommended because they are lighter to carry and can be stored in tins or boxes with lids that can be used as palettes.

Gouache

Gouache (also known as designers' color) is a water-based paint which generally contains the same ingredients as watercolor. The great difference is the opacity of gouache, effected by the addition of inert white pigments such as blanc fixe or precipitated chalk. The brilliance and opacity of the colors are due to the reflectivity of the white inert pigment. This pigment replaces the white of the paper that is used to such advantage in watercolor painting. The smooth uniformity of gouache and the fact that one opaque color can be laid on top of another are useful features of this paint. However, some of the particularly brilliant hues are fugitive and are useful only where the necessity for permanence is less important. Pigments in gouache are less finely ground than those in watercolor paints.

Egg-tempera

All the prepared egg-tempera paints readily available are based on an egg-oil emulsion. This prevents them from drying to a brittle film, as pure egg-tempera does. These paints will serve as an underpainting for oils or as a medium in their own right. Rowney and

Sennelier are well-known manufacturers of egg-tempera. J P Stephenson is less well known but is well respected as a manufacturer and offers a customer service to artists with special requirements.

Casein

Casein paint is based on the curds of milk, with glycerine added to improve handling. It is strongly adhesive and dries quickly. Casein colors are more brittle than pure egg-tempera but work quite well on rigid supports such as masonite, plywood or painting boards. The best-known manufacturers are Shiva, which offers a range of 34 colors in tubes, and Pelikan which offers a range of 38 colors available in jars, tins and aerosol sprays.

Silk colors

Silk colors are paints specially made for using on silk fabric. They have been treated as a serious medium for some time in parts of Europe and the trend is now picking up, as evidenced in the work of Jean Françoise-Paris, the well-known Swiss silk painter who today commands substantial prices for his work.

Silk colors tend to run or spread through the fibers of the silk, rather like a watercolor wet-in-wet technique. This tendency is controlled with a liquid outliner called gutta. Beautiful effects can be achieved with good silk colors such as Sennelier's Tinfix or the more concentrated Super Tinfix, but both of these need steam fixing. An excellent alternative is Deka Silk, which you can fix with an iron.

Acrylic paints

Acrylic paints are made of pigment dispersed or suspended in an acrylic resin made by polymerization of acrylic and methacrylic acid. While some traditionalist oil painters insist that acrylics lack the luminosity and warmth of oil colors, there is little doubt that they have a great future. The strength and flexibility of the paint film, its resistance to pollutants, its speed of drying, and, therefore, its suitability for building up layers of glazes, make it very attractive for both original and restoration

work. Today, very little serious oil or fresco restoration is undertaken in anything other than acrylics. Most importantly, the milky, whitish medium dries into a clear film which permits light to penetrate to and reflect from the pigment particles deep in the paint film, conferring great brilliance on the colors.

Golden Artist Colors are acrylics of a particularly high standard. Their pigments are rated as excellent and their cadmiums are all chemically pure, whereas most major brands contain large quantities of barium sulphate. Lascaux acrylic colors have a high concentration of pure pigment and use top quality binding mediums. They retain their colorfastness when diluted and are also economical to use. Lascaux's Artists' Acrylic Color range is lime-resistant, weatherproof and lightfast, and thus suitable for use on outside murals.

Scholastic paints

There is a considerable number of what might be called scholastic paints, some of which are useful for sketching and for color notes. These paints are relatively inexpensive and can be bought in all art material stores.

PVA (polyvinyl acetate) and vinyl paints are made with cheaper pigments than those used in acrylics and are consequently less permanent. They are quick-drying and hardwearing and can be used on any support suitable for acrylics. Vinyl paints are water-soluble and are good for covering large areas. Poster paints are a cheaper form of gouache and should essentially be used for preliminary work.

Substantial ranges of these paints are offered by Berol, Scholaquip, Calder, Marabu, Marcus Art, Rich-Art, Pentel and Teranishi Chemicals, all of which specialize in this sector of the market. Good ranges are also available from the more general manufacturers — for example, Winsor and Newton's poster and vinyl colors, Rowney's ranges of powder poster paints, PVA and Redicolor, Lascaux's Decora and gouache tempera, Lefranc and Bourgeois' Flash vinyl and Poly-flashe,

Schminke's Kuppers' Akademie gouache, Feine Studien's Aquarelle colors and Lukas' Plakat tempera.

PAINTING SETS

The rule to remember when choosing a painting set is to buy the best quality you can afford. If you are working out-of-doors, choose one that contains everything you are likely to need without being so big that it is unwieldy or too heavy to carry. Most manufacturers offer an excellent range of sets:

MANUFACTURER	OIL	ACRYLIC	WATERCOLOR	GOUACHE	PASTEL
WINSOR & NEWTON	15	1	25	3	
ROWNEY	20	3	23	1	6
SCHMINCKE	26	3	21	5	8
LUKAS	19	8	13	3	
SENNELIER	6		6		14
LEFRANC & BOURGEOIS	13		1		9
GRUMBACHER	30	14	11	6	20

INKS

Ink, by definition, is usually considered to be a transparent color. However, some brands now available use opaque pigments, these include Higgins Pigment Ink, Magic Color Ink and Pêbêo Colorex Technic Ink. This pigment renders them considerably more lightfast — pigments are normally more permanent than dyes. The pigmented inks, therefore, might be better described as "liquid water colors." Despite this classification, some inks, such as the non-waterproof India ink used for calligraphy, are lightfast, whereas some so-called permanent colors are fugitive. In inks, the word "permanent," in fact, means water-resistant or waterproof, and the ink is usually spirit- or shellac-based.

Many inks are suitable only for use with particular pens. For example, most of the artists' inks on the market cannot be used in fountain pens; only fountain pen ink can.

However, Osmiroid has recently brought out a calligraphic ink for fountain pens in a range of five colors. It is advisable when buying ink to look for the exact specifications for what you want it to do.

Chinese sticks are available pre-ground, or you can buy the grinding stone and the sticks and grind your own in water.

 **Colors** on pp80-81
Chart on pp222-243

SOFT PASTELS, OIL PASTELS AND OIL PAINTING STICKS

Soft pastels are usually made of pigment mixed with a medium and binder of precipitated chalk, gum tragacanth and a preservative such as beta naphthol or sodium orthophenyl-phenate. Water is added during their production, but most of it evaporates when the extruded pastel is drying out, prior to packing. They are probably the closest to pure unadulterated pigment, with the minimum of medium — hence their purity of color.

The basic range of any manufacturer's pastels consists of a relatively small number of colors, each one available in several shades (apart from black and white). The largest range commonly available is Sennelier's A L'Ecu, consisting of 83 basic colors extending to 522 shades. Another French company with an equally well-known pastel is Lefranc & Bourgeois, with their Girault range of 300 shades.

Oil pastels are made in a similar way to soft pastels, but oil is used when mixing them instead of water. They are available in sets such as those offered by Sakura, Pentel, the Teranishi Chemical Co and Filia. In addition to their oil pastel range of 48 standard colors, Sennelier manufactures 5 metallic colors and 16 iridescent colors.

A comparative rarity are oil painting sticks, which are essentially oil paint in solid form. No fixative is necessary after using them because the colors dry overnight to a permanent flexible film. While still moist the colors can be blended with your finger or a paintbrush.

Thinned with turpentine, they can be used in conjunction with regular oil paints. Generally, artists' and students' colors are lightfast but the fluorescent sticks are fugitive. Shiva makes a range of 31 artists' quality colors, a colorless blender and a set of fluorescent colors.

Handy tools used in conjunction with pastels are stumps and tortillons. Stumps are shaped like pencils and are made of pulped gray paper sharpened at both ends, and they come in a range of sizes. Tortillons are made of the same material rolled to form an extended cone rather like a short pencil with an elongated point. You can use these tools to spread and blend pastel colors; they also help you to keep your fingers clean, although you may prefer to use your fingers.

 Colors on p82
Chart on pp244-267

COLORED PENCILS

Colored pencils are rarely considered as a serious medium and have in the past more generally been used for color notes and sketches. However, they are gaining popularity among illustrators and graphic artists as a medium in their own right. When buying them, remember that the more expensive pencils are, the more permanent they are likely to be.

Colored pencils are available in three main varieties; the crayon, pastel and aquarelle types. The crayon type is made by mixing pigment with a medium of non-greasy waxes and clay. Examples of crayon pencils are best exemplified by the 72 colors of the Derwent Series 19 Artists' Pencil, the Derwent Series 18 Studio Pencil, the Rowney Victoria Color Pencil and the Staedtler Mars Lumochrom.

A softer pencil is the pastel type, in which the pigment is mixed with a dense, chalky medium. They are manufactured in a range of up to 60 colors. The pencil version of the Conté carré crayon is available in restricted colors of very dense black (such as Conté's "Pierre Noir"), white, sanguine, sepia and bistre. The black crayon is obtainable in grades of softness, and the sanguine comes in several shades.

The pigment in aquarelle pencils is mixed with a medium of handling qualities similar to those of crayon pencils but is water-soluble. The quality of a good aquarelle pencil is simple to test — scribble with it and run a wet brush over the mark. If traces of the original scribble are visible then the pencil is of poor quality. If, however, the scribble disappears and you are left with a color wash, then the pencil is of good quality.

The most famous of the aquarelle pencils are the Caran d'Ache Prismalo I and II. The Faber-Castell Albrecht Dürer, the Derwent Watercolor, the Staedtler Karat and the Koh-I-Noor Hardtmuth Mona Lisa Watercolor are all examples of good quality aquarelle pencils. The largest range is the Schwan-Stabilo Stabilotone, offered in 55 colors.

Colors on p83
Chart on pp268-283

CRAYONS

The most common artists' crayons are those of pigment mixed with a dense, chalky medium similar to pastel pencils, such as the Faber-Castell Polychromos pastel or the Carb-Othello by Schwan-Stabilo. The Conté type of crayon has long been a popular medium — Toulouse-Lautrec used them to great effect, as have many other artists.

These crayons come in black (several grades), white (several grades), sanguine, bistre, gray and sepia, and are made by Conté, Faber-Castell and Koh-I-Noor Hardtmuth. A less common type of crayon is the aquarelle variety (included in the Colored pencils, leads and water-soluble crayons chart).

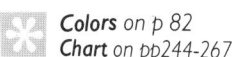
Colors on p 82
Chart on pp244-267

PAINT MEDIUMS, ADDITIVES AND FIXATIVES

Anyone who has ever been inside an art materials shop will no doubt have been amazed at the quantity of little bottles on offer and, perhaps, will have wondered what they

are all for. The purpose of this section is to tell you what all those little bottles contain and how you can use them. Drying oils, for example, can be used for grinding your own colors or may be added to manufactured paints. Siccatives can be mixed with paint to affect the drying time, whereas solvents are used to thin paint or to clean brushes. Varnishes and fixatives can provide a finishing touch to your painting that may ensure protection and greater permanence.

Natural drying oils

All drying oils are basically intended for the grinding of oil colors and should be added sparingly and with discretion to prepared oil (and alkyd) colors.

Cold pressed linseed oil

An oil that reduces the consistency of the paint and brushmarks but increases transparency and gloss. It is generally considered the best for pigment grinding.

Poppy seed oil

This oil is less siccative than linseed oil and is less likely to yellow. It is good for grinding whites and pale colors but not for grounds.

Safflower oil

Less siccative than linseed oil, safflower oil is less inclined to yellow. It is best for grinding light colors, especially blues and whites. However, it cracks more easily than linseed oil, so avoid using it for grounds.

Sun bleached linseed oil

Prolonged bleaching action of the sun's rays produces this paler oil, which has a faster drying rate than refined linseed oil. It improves flow.

Sun bleached poppy oil

This has qualities similar to those of regular poppy seed oil but is even paler.

Sun thickened linseed oil

Faster drying than unprocessed oils, this oil is excellent for preparing oil mediums. It improves paint flow.

Walnut oil

Together with poppy and safflower oil, this oil is best for light colors and whites. It yellows less than linseed oil but more than safflower oil and dries relatively fast.

Chemically processed drying oils

Drying linseed oil

This oil is darker in color than refined linseed oil but contains manganese driers and is faster drying.

Drying poppy oil

A pale oil which resists yellowing, drying poppy oil increases the drying rate of oil and alkyd colors but reduces consistency.

Refined linseed oil

This is considered inferior to cold pressed linseed oil, but has a similar action. It tends to slow the drying rate of oil colors.

Stand (or polymerized) linseed oil

This oil retards the drying of oils and alkyds, improves flow, and imparts a durable, flexible finish to the paint. It does not yellow and is suitable for ground preparations and in tempera egg-oil emulsions.

Balsams

Balsams or oleoresins are the viscous liquids usually secreted by coniferous trees. They mix well with oils, solvents and varnishes but not with water.

Canada balsam

A viscous liquid extracted from the balsam fir (*Abies balsamea*) native to Canada and eastern United States. It can be used as an adhesive or may be substituted for Strasbourg turpentine.

Copaiba (or Copaiva) balsam

A balsam from the South American genus *Copaifera*. It is often used in the restoration of pictures. When diluted with turpentine, it can be applied very thinly to dried out parts of the paint film and allows varnishing and overpainting quite happily.

Strasbourg turpentine

A resin derived from the silver fir (*Abies pectinata*) found in the Austrian Tyrol and Italy. It is basically similar to Venice turpentine but has a different odor and color. It is a less popular turpentine now, and is quite hard to find.

Venice (or Venetian) turpentine

The natural resin extracted from the Austrian larch (*Larix decidua*). Sold in its pure, undiluted state (eg by Sennelier) it has the consistency of honey, a pleasant pine aroma and a light color. It is used as a plasticizing agent in varnishes. When used with stand oil, polymerized linseed oil or sun-thickened oil, it imparts good brushing qualities and an acceptably tough, non-yellowing finish with, if so desired, an enamel surface.

Siccatives

Siccatives, or dryers, are metallic salts that are mixed with paint or varnish to assist drying but may affect permanence adversely.

Brown Courtrai siccative

The dark brown color of this siccative, which contains lead oxide and manganese oxide, renders it useless for light colors. It has strong siccative properties but induces brittleness.

Cobalt dryer (cobalt linoleate)

This dryer is less harmful than brown Courtrai siccative or Haarlem siccative because it is less brittle (eg Winsor and Newton's Strong drying oil No 2).

Dutch siccative

This is actually a misnomer; it is an extremely oily copal-based varnish and amber in color. It can be mixed with colors or used as a finishing varnish and may be thinned with petrol or turpentine.

Haarlem siccative

Very similar in action to brown Courtrai siccative.

Japan dryer

An alkyd resin-based liquid dryer for artists' oils.

Strong drying oil No 1

Winsor and Newton's lead-oxide linseed dryer. It hardens the paint film to a more brittle finish and tends to darken.

White Courtrai siccative

This siccative's main action is to improve hardening. It contains no lead oxide and does not affect light colors.

Solvents and Diluents

Acrylic varnish remover

A solvent specifically designed to remove acrylic varnish.

Artgel

An artists' hand cleaner made by Winsor and Newton, similar to industrial hand cleaners such as Swarfega. Grumbacher offers a similar product.

Artists' picture cleaner/Oil painting restorer

A Copaiba balsam of pine oil with ammonia, typically dipentine.

Artists' mineral spirit

This solvent has qualities similar to those of turpentine but is less "wet" and has a less pronounced smell.

Artwipes

Tissues impregnated with solvent for cleaning oil and alkyd colors from your hands, manufactured by Winsor and Newton.

Brush cleaner and preserver

A cleaner that is effective at its job and is thoroughly recommended, available from B & J Industries.

Essence of petroleum

This substance keeps paint workable for longer than petroleum but does not alter the final appearance of the paint.

Hand soap

A specially developed and very effective artists' hand cleaner, available from B & J Industries.

Oil of spike lavender

A less volatile diluent than turpentine and nicer smelling.

Paint remover

A liquid paint cleaner made from trichloro-ethylene, useful for removing oil, alkyd and acrylic colors from brushes, etc.

Petroleum

A mineral solvent that is more oily than turpentine. It keeps paint workable longer and makes color more mat.

Turpentine

A volatile distillate of pine resin, also known as spirits of turpentine, English distilled turpentine and rectified spirits of turpentine. It has better wetting properties than other alternatives and can be used to dilute oil colors and to clean brushes.

Turpentine substitute

Synonymous with spirit mineral, but less expensive to buy and more readily available.

Mediums

Acrylic flow release

Eases color flow without diluting color strength. Good for washes.

Acrylic gel medium

A paste-like medium that imparts transparency and gloss to acrylic and watercolor paints.

Acrylic medium (gloss and mat)

Thin milky liquids which dry to a strong transparent film. They may be used with any water-based paints.

Acrylic retarder

This medium slows the drying time of acrylic colors.

Acrylic water tension breaker

Assists the absorption of water into the paint.

Acrylizing medium

This is a resin medium designed to change gouache into a water-resistant medium for use on foil, acetate etc. It permits overpainting and is available from Rowney.

Amber liquids

Fossil resins derived from conifers. If cooked at high temperatures, they can be coaxed into hot fatty oils or a heated oil varnish such as copal. The result is usually very dark and when used over layers of soft paint forms a very hard, splintery skin.

Aquapasto

Gum arabic and silica combined to make a translucent jelly for giving an impasto effect to water-based colors.

Artists' mat medium

A medium used to make oils as well as alkyds mat.

Artists' painting medium

A general-purpose painting medium for oils and alkyds made from stand oil and petroleum distillate. It thins well, is resistant to cracking and does not yellow.

Casein tempera binder

A casein solution in water with special oil-emulsifying additives available from Talens. A thickener and matting agent, it is used to make casein tempera colors by mixing with artists' oil color.

Colorless paint medium/ketone resin
An excellent vehicle for oils that is strongly siccative, gives depth and sheen and is virtually colorless.

Copal oil mediums Nos 1 and 2
These consist of linseed oil, gum copal and turpentine or petroleum distillate. Both mediums increase gloss and transparency but No 1 will dry more quickly.

Crystal medium for transparent oil paints
A thixotropic gel medium based on poppy oil and colloidal silica used only for artists' quality transparent oil colors.

Dutch brilliant
A moisture-resistant medium useful for glazes. It intensifies colors, leaves a gloss finish, enhances color transparency and imparts luminosity.

Flemish medium/Megilp
Linseed oil and mastic resin combined with zinc oxide and turpentine to form a jelly like base that imparts a buttery texture to the paint. Similar to Sennelier's Thickening medium.

Flemish siccative/Copal oil medium No 1
Based on copal gum, this medium increases gloss and transparency but has a tendency to darken and embrittle. Shortens drying time.

Glycerine
A moisturizer that along with pigment and binder is used to make watercolors.

Gum arabic
A pale gum solution that increases the gloss and transparency of watercolors and improves wetting.

Gum water
A diluted version of gum arabic.

Haarlem Duroziez siccative/Copal oil medium No 2
A medium based on copal gum with characteristics similar to those of Flemish siccative but less concentrated and slower drying.

Impasto medium
A thicker version of Flemish medium, similar to Rembrandt painting paste.

Lake medium for transparent oil paints
A medium designed to improve the flow of transparent color from the brush.

Lascaux acrylic emulsion
A translucent medium for mixing with powder colors and extenders to make acrylic colors, primers, etc.

Lascaux Plastik A
Acrylic modeling paste, ground finely with calcite extenders. It can be used to make bas relief and heavy textures and may be mixed directly with colors or used by itself and painted over afterward.

Lascaux Plastik B
Similar to the above but with the addition of 30 percent silica sand.

Liquin
An alkyd medium that is quick-drying and imparts better flow properties to oils and alkyds. It enhances transparency and resists yellowing.

Modeling paste
A paste for making acrylic relief surfaces.

Nacryl acrylic medium
Similar to a- gloss medium, this additive enhances water resistance.

Oil of cloves
A painting medium available from art material shops and pharmacists. The best variety comes from clove tree blossoms and is light in hue; the darker variety comes from the branches. It has an incisive odor and evaporates slowly although, mixed with zinc oxide white, it can stay wet for up to six weeks. It is best used very sparingly in "alla prima" techniques on layered paint surfaces because it tends to coalesce the top and lower layers. Like other semi-volatile oils, such as lavender oil and spike oil, it is useful in restoration.

Oil vehicles Nos 1A and 2A
Sun-thickened oils mixed with turpentine. They thin pale oil colors and can be used for oiling out. No 1A, with linseed oil, dries more quickly than No 2I, with poppy oil.

Oleopasto
An alkyd-based impasto medium. It resists yellowing and is quick-drying.

Ox-gall liquid
A medium that increases wetness.

Siccative medium for oil paints
A stand oil and synthetic resin-based medium.

Turner transparent medium
Used with glazes, this medium is transparent and luminous. It preserves the texture of the paint and imparts a silky finish.

Venetian medium/Opal medium
A combination of beeswax, stand oil and turpentine which dries evenly into a satiny, opalescent mat film and is capable of impasto treatment. Sennelier's Satin varnish is similar.

J G Vibert painting varnish
Combined with a ketone acrylic and poppy oil base, this medium makes paint smoother to handle. It remains workable for longer than straight ketone resin.

Watercolor medium No 1
A binder for watercolors. Talens manufacture a designers' color medium for use with gouache.

Watercolor medium No 2
Similar to Watercolor medium No 1 but imparts greater brilliance to colors.

Win-gel
This universally useful medium is quick drying and smooths brushwork. It is good for glazing and fine detail, and increases transparency and gloss.

Xavier de Langlais egg medium
An egg-, linseed oil- and wax-based emulsion. It increases smoothness of paint paste and speeds up setting. Thin with water before mixing with the paint. A small quantity added to paint (4 or 5 drops per dab) gives a gloss, whereas double that amount gives a mat finish.

Varnishes and Fixatives

Acrylic satin varnish
Similar to acrylic varnish but leaves a satin finish.

Acrylic varnish (gloss or mat)
Protects dry acrylic paints and dries quickly to a gloss or mat finish.

Art masking fluid
A usually latex-based fluid used to mark off areas needing protection when applying water-based paints.

Artists' gloss varnish
A high-gloss ketone resin and mineral spirit varnish which dries quickly to a non-yellowing glossy film that does not embrittle.

Artists' mat varnish
Ketone resin and wax blended in mineral spirit. It is quick drying and more durable than wax-based varnishes.

Artists' picture varnish
An aerosol ketone resin and mineral spirit blend, similar to Artists' gloss and mat varnish.

Artists' retouching varnish/J G Vibert retouching varnish
This resin-based varnish provides temporary protection for recently finished work. It is quick drying.

Barbola varnish
Designed to varnish barbola paste as well as wood, metal, paper, china and glass.

Beeswax
Can be made into varnish with the addition of mineral spirit.

Dammar crystal varnish
A traditional varnish based on dammar resin. Dammar is derived from certain firs; Batavia (or Sumatra) and Singapore are considered the best varieties. Turpentine is the traditional solvent used with it. It makes a pale yellow varnish which dries quickly to a high gloss finish. It is used traditionally with oils and alkyds but is also used for prints, maps and drawings on paper.

Fixative
Vinyl resin and methylated spirits. Fixes pastel, charcoal, pencil, crayon and chalk drawings. It can be applied from the bottle with a spray diffuser or by aerosol.

Glossy acrylic varnish
A finishing varnish for oil and alkyd colors which dries quickly to a tough, resistant film. It is available from Sennelier and Grumbacher. Thin with turpentine.

Griffin picture varnish
A ketone resin in mineral spirit solution with stand oil. It is a permanent, non-yellowing, non-blooming varnish. Dries moderately quickly to a high-gloss flexible film.

Heat-resisting varnish
A tung oil/phenolic varnish that dries to a heat- and water-resistant glossy finish, for decorative work. Good for outdoor work.

Isolating Varnish
A vinyl resin that prevents penetration of other varnishes into the paint film. Prevents white spots from forming when a mat varnish is used on a mat paint. Thin with methylated spirits.

Japan (Writer's) gold size
An oil-modified copal resin in mineral spirit with the addition of driers. It is designed for oil gilding.

Lascaux acrylic glaze (gloss and mat)
An acrylic resin based on solvents. Used for sealing murals, sculptures, acrylics, tempera, frescos, well-dried oil paintings and as a fixative for charcoal, pastel and pencil drawings.

Lascaux acrylic resin
A pure butyl-methacrylate thermoplastic acrylic resin. It resists aging and color change and is effective for conserving and consolidating paint layers and as a final varnish.

Lascaux acrylic transparent varnish (gloss and mat)
A varnish thinned in water which dries to a hard flexible film. Excellent for transparent colors and general use.

Lascaux acrylic varnish mat
Of similar composition to the above. Soluble in mineral spirit, this varnish is age- and light-resistant. It can be used to varnish oils, acrylics, tempera and gouache.

Lascaux retouching varnish
Based on PVA butyrate synthetic resin. It is age- and light-resistant as well as flexible and adhesive. Good as a binder with powder pigments for retouching and painting, and as an intermediate varnish.

Lascaux-Fix
A crystal clear solvent-based acrylic resin. Fixes all common drawing media, watercolor, ink, tempera and well-dried oil colors.

Mastic varnish (double or picture)
Mastic resin dissolved in turpentine. A traditional varnish for thick films on oils and alkyds painted on inflexible grounds. It is dark yellow and dries quickly to a high gloss but embrittles and darkens with age, and is prone to blooming. Pure mastic can be bought from Grumbacher and Cornelissens.

Mat acrylic varnish
As above, but mat. Available from Sennelier and Lefranc & Bourgeois.

Modeling varnish
Vinyl resin with alcohol and glycol solvents. A clear liquid which forms a protective varnish for models etc painted with water-based paints.

Oil copal varnish
A traditional medium with constituents similar to those of gold size but darker. It tends to darken and embrittles with time.

Picture copal varnish
A slightly lighter varnish with constituents similar to oil copal varnish. It is prone to cracking.

Rembrandt picture varnish/J G Vibert picture varnish
A synthetic resin base that dries quickly to a gloss finish and is non-yellowing.

Satin acrylic varnish
Similar to glossy acrylic varnish but gives a satin finish. Available from Sennelier.

Superfine retouching varnish
Dammar resin with mineral spirit. A traditional dammar varnish for reviving dull spots in oil paintings and for temporary protection. Dries fast.

Wax varnish (Matwax varnish)
Beeswax dissolved in mineral spirit. A white paste — gently rubbed onto a paint film, it dries to a mat finish. Can be polished to a soft sheen with a soft cloth or brush. Lefranc & Bourgeois' Ceronis varnish is similar.

Weather-resisting varnish
Oil-modified alkyd resin in mineral spirit with driers. Useful for decorative work in exposed conditions. It is pale yellow and dries to a clear, tough film.

White mat picture varnish
A variation of wax varnish with beeswax and dammar resin. Not susceptible to polishing.

PAINT AND PIGMENT COLORS

These color samples relate to the Paints and Pigments Chart (see pp84-221). The number beside a paint or pigment in the chart corresponds to a numbered color sample below. Obviously, the colors have been reproduced within the limitations of four-color printing and can serve only as an approximation. Black, white, metallic, fluorescent and iridescent colors have been omitted.

54 55 56 57 58 59 60

68 69 70 71 72 73 74

82 83 84 85 86 87 88

96 97 98 99 100 101 102

61 62 63 64 65 66 67

75 76 77 78 79 80 81

89 90 91 92 93 94 95

103 104 105 106 107 108 109

INK COLORS

These color samples relate to the Inks Chart (see pp222-243). The number beside a paint or pigment in the chart corresponds to a numbered color sample below. Colors have been reproduced within the limitations of 4-color printing and are approximate. Black, white and metallic colors have been omitted.

| 1 | 2 | 3 | 4 | 5 | 6 |

| 17 | 18 | 19 | 20 | 21 | 22 | 23 | 24 | 25 | 26 |

| 37 | 38 | 39 | 40 | 41 | 42 | 43 | 44 | 45 | 46 |

| 57 | 58 | 59 | 60 | 61 | 62 | 63 | 64 | 65 | 66 |

| 77 | 78 | 79 | 80 | 81 | 82 | 83 | 84 | 85 | 86 |

| 97 | 98 | 99 | 100 | 101 | 102 | 103 | 104 | 105 | 106 |

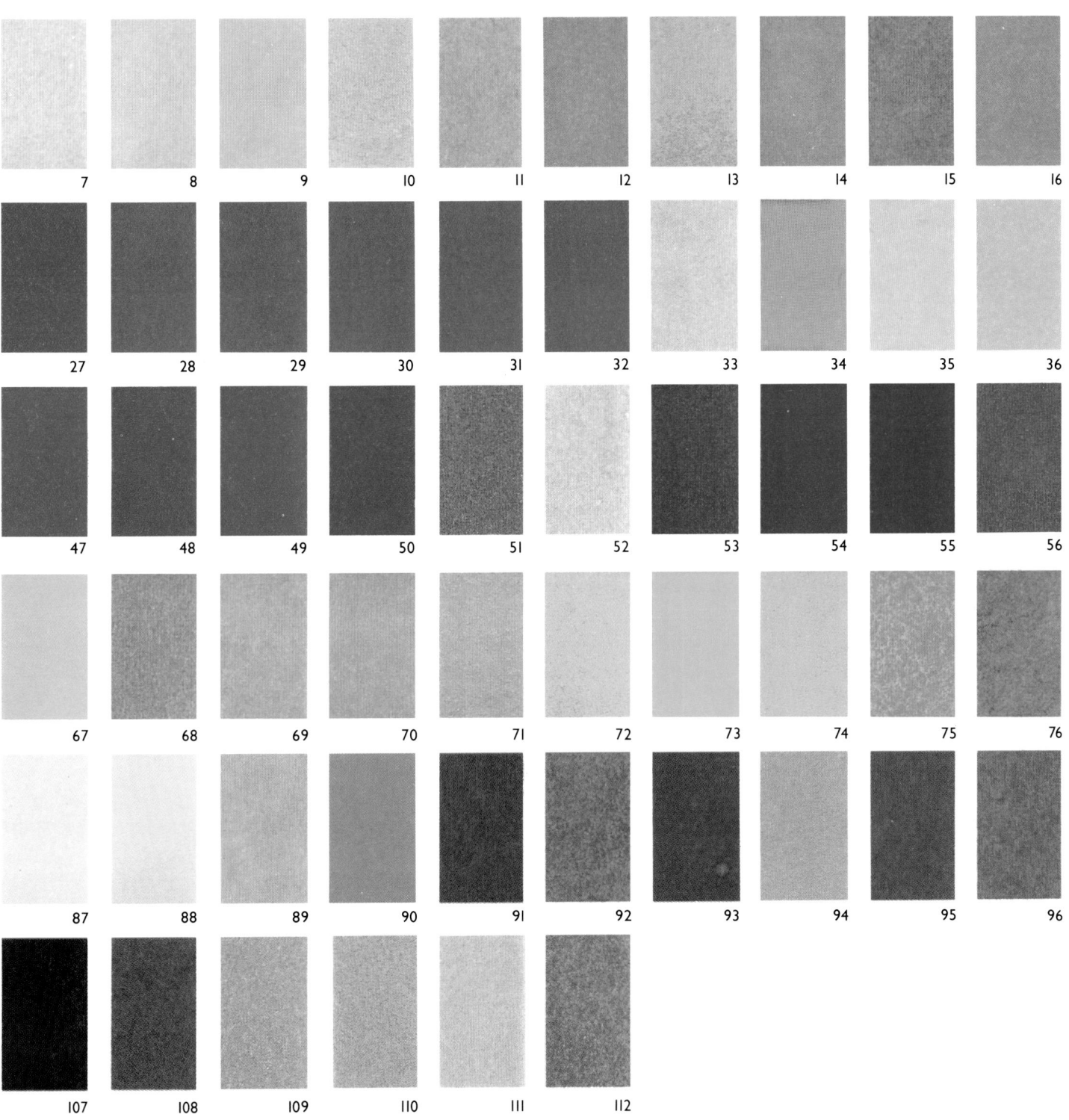

PASTEL AND CRAYON COLORS

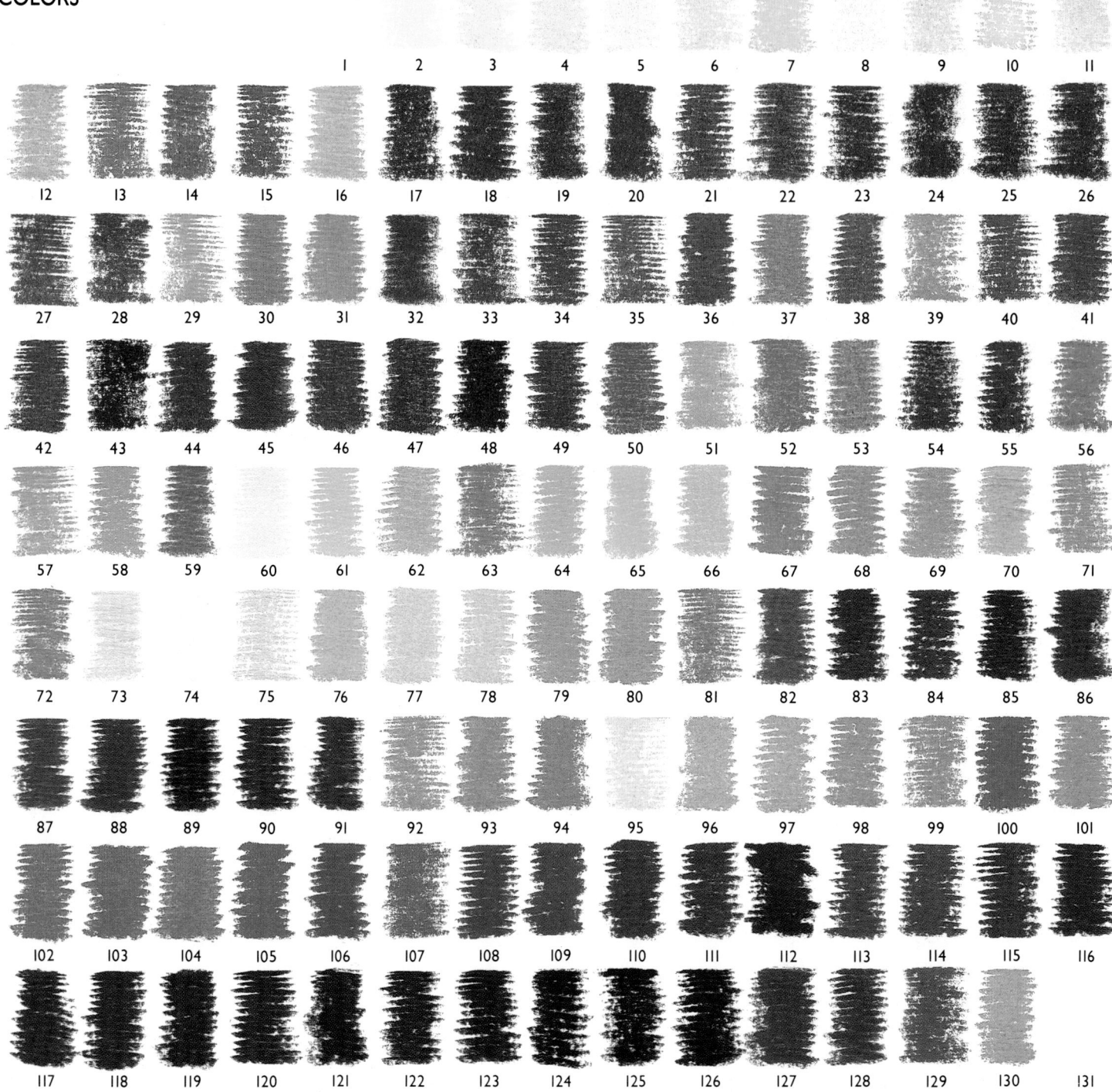

PENCIL, LEAD AND WATER-SOLUBLE CRAYON COLORS

1	2	3	4	5	6	7	8	9	10
11	12	13	14	15	16	17	18	19	20	21	22	23	24
25	26	27	28	29	30	31	32	33	34	35	36	37	38
39	40	41	42	43	44	45	46	47	48	49	50	51	52
53	54	55	56	57	58	59	60	61	62	63	64	65	66
67	68	69	70	71	72	73	74	75	76	77	78	79	80
81	82	83	84	85	86	87	88	89	90	91	92	93	94
95	96	97	98	99	100	101	102	103	104	105	106	107	108
109	110	111	112	113	114	115	116	117	118	119	120	121	122
123	124	125	126	127	128	129	130	131	132	133	134	135	136
137	138	139	140	141	142	143	144	145	146	147	148	149	150
151	152	153	154	155	156	157	158	159	160	161	162	163	164
165	166	167	168	169	170	171	172	173	174	175	176	177	178
179	180	181	182	183	184	185	186	187	188	189	190	191	192

HOW TO USE THE PAINTS & PIGMENTS CHART

1 2 3 4 5

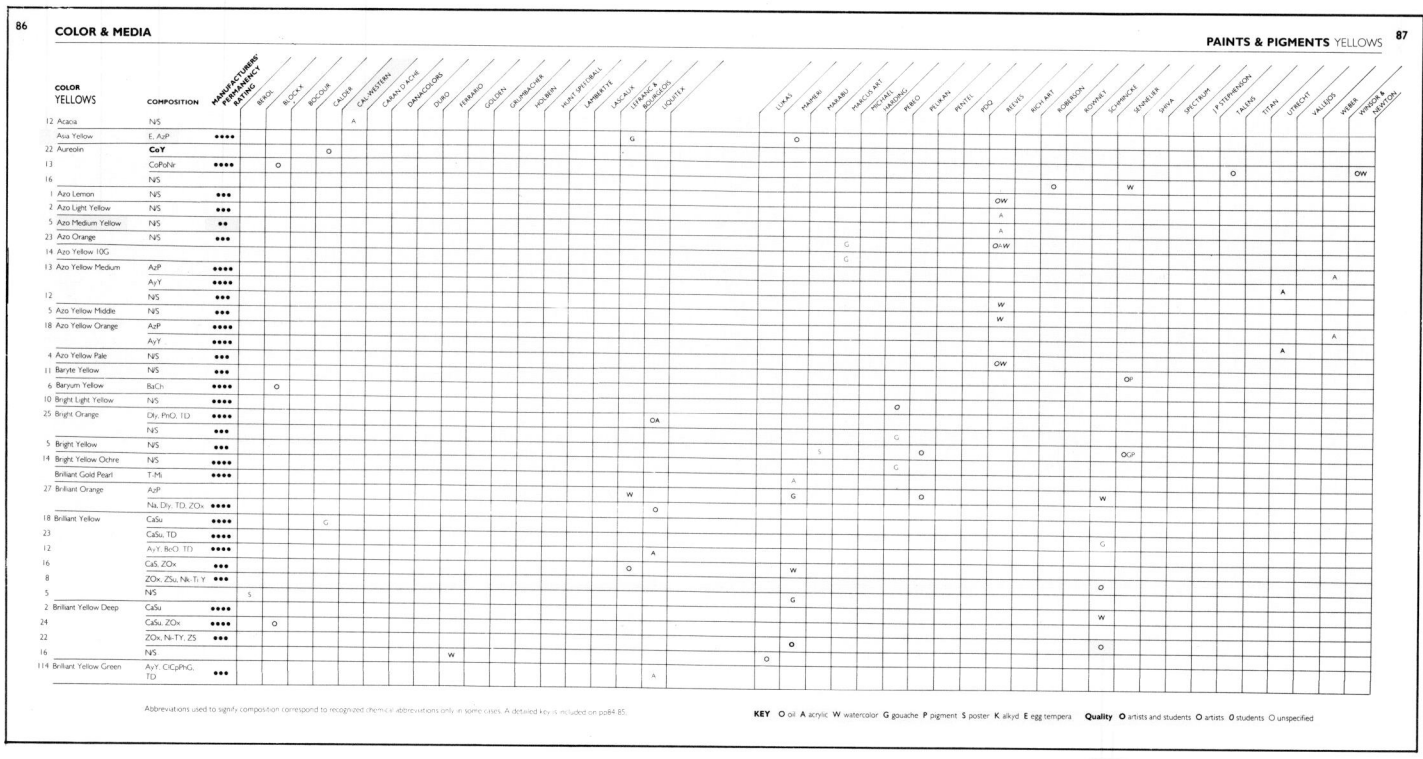

6

COMPOSITION KEY

A Acid	**B** Brown	**Cc** Calcined	**Db** Dibromoanthanthrone	**Fe** Ferric	**L** Lake		
Aa Alizarin	**Ba** Barium	**Cd** Compound	**Dg** Dry binding	**Fl** Flake	**La** Lamp		
Ac Actimate	**Bc** Basic	**Ce** Carbonate	**Dh** Dinydroxide		**Lb** Lignite-based		
Ae Aniline	**Be** Benzimidazolone	**Ch** Chromate	**Di** DIN	**G** Green	**Le** Lead		
Ah Anhydrous	**Bg** Bronze powder with	**Ci** Carminic	**Dk** Dark	**Gn** Genuine	**Lh** Lithopone		
Ai Aluminate	dry binding	**Cl** Chlorinated	**Dl** Diarylide	**Gr** Ground	**Li** Lithol		
Ak Alkali	**Bi** Bluish	**Cm** Carbamide	**Dn** Dinitraline	**Gu** Gum	**Ll** Lapis Lazuli		
Al Aluminum	**Bk** Black	**Cn** Carbon	**Dx** Dioxazine		**Lm** Lemon		
Am Antiomonal	**Bl** Blue	**Co** Cobalt	**Dy** Dyestuff	**H** Hue	**Ln** Linear		
An Antimony	**Bn** Bronze	**Cp** Copper	**Dz** Dibenzoate	**Hc** Hydrocarbon	**Lq** Laquered		
Ans Anilines	**Bo** Bones	**Cq** Charcoal		**Hn** Hansa	**Lt** Light		
Ao Ammonium	**Br** Bright	**Cr** Chrome	**E** Earth	**Hs** Hydrous	**Lu** Luminous		
Ap Amorphous	**Bs** Burnt Sienna	**Cs** Crimson	**E-D** EURO-DIN	**Hx** Hydroxide			
Ar Arylamide	**Bt** Beta	**Ct** Crystallized	**En** English	**Hy** Hydrated	**M** Madder		
Ars Arylamides	**Bu** Burnt	**Cu** Chromium	**Ex** Extender		**Mc** Metallic		
As Asphalt	**Bz** Benzoate	**Cy** Cyan		**In** Indanthrene	**Me** Methane		
At Anthraquinone		**Cz** Carbazole	**F** Flavanthrone	**Ir** Iron	**Mg** Manganate		
Au Alumina	**C** Complex		**Fa** Fanal	**Is** Isoviolanthrene	**Mga** Magenta		
Ay Arylide	**Ca** Cadmium	**D** Dioxide	**Fc** Ferrocyanide	**Iv** Ivory	**Mh** Methyl		
Az Azo	**Cb** Carboxylic	**Da** Davy's Grey			**Mi** Mica		

1 The number beside each paint or pigment relates to a numbered color sample (see pp 74-79).

2 Paints and pigments are listed alphabetically down the page. They are divided up into nine groups consisting of yellows, reds, violets, blues, greens, browns, blacks, whites and miscellaneous colors. The name of each paint corresponds to the name used by the manufacturer. To establish which manufacturer produces a particular color, follow the relevant column horizontally across the chart.

3 The composition of each type of paint or pigment is shown in abbreviated form. The full name for each constituent can be found in the Composition Key (see below). **Bold** type indicates the recognized standard composition, and N/S appears in the chart where the composition is unknown. The abbreviations used in the Paints and Pigments chart are related where possible to the accepted symbol system for chemical compositions. However, in some places other symbols have been used because of limited space.

4 Paints and pigments have different degrees of permanence and many manufacturers indicate this information on their packaging. In this chart the classification is as follows:
●●●● Permanent
●●● Permanent in full strength
●● Moderately permanent
● Fugitive
Where no indication of degree of permanence is shown, the information is unknown. If a color with the same pigmentation is available in watercolor and oil (or acrylic), the latter will be more lightfast due to the protection the appropriate binder renders to the pigment.

5 Manufacturers are listed alphabetically along the top of the chart. To establish which colors are produced by a manufacturer, follow the relevant column vertically down the chart.

6 An entry in the chart indicates that the manufacturer at the top of the vertical column produces the color at the far left of the horizontal column. **Bold** type indicates artists' and students' quality, **medium** type indicates artists' quality only, *italic* type indicates students' quality only, and light type indicates unspecified quality.
O oil
W watercolor
K alkyd
A acrylic
P pigment
S poster
E egg tempera
G gouache

Ml Molybdo	Or Organic	Ps Phosphate	Ru Rutile	Sx Sesquioxide	V Viridian
Mn Manganese	Ox Oxide	Pt Permanent	Rw Raw	Sy Synthetic	Vg Vegetable
Mo Molybdate		Pu Phosphorus		Sz Slate	Vi Violet
Mr Mercury	P Pigment	Pv PTMA Violet	S Salt		Vr Vermilion
Ms Mars	Pa Para	Pw Powder	Sa Saturn	T Titanium	Vt Vitrified
Mt Metallized	Pc PTMA Complex	Py Poly	S-A-S-S Sodium-Aluminium-Silica-Sulphur Complex	Ta Tartrazine	
	Pd Product	Pyt Pyrophosphate		Td Traditional	W White
Na Naphthol	Pe Perylene	Pz Pyrazdone		Th Thioindigoid	We Wet Bronze Powder for oil painting
Ni Nitroso	Ph Phthalocyanine		Sc Silicate	Ti Titanate	
Nk Nickel	Pk Pink	Q Quinacridone	Sd Sodium	Tl Translucent	Wi Winsor
Nl Natural	Pm Phosphomolybdo-tungstic acid	Qt Quinophtalone	Se Selenide	Tm Trimethylmethane	Wo Wood
NN Nitroso-Naphthol			Sh Shade	Tn Tin	
Np Naples	P-M Phospho-Molybdo	R Red	Si Sienna	To Toluidine	X Xanthene
Nr Nitrate	P-M-T Phosopho-Molybdo-Tungsten	Rb Red B	Sl Sulphate	Tp Triphenylmethane	
Nt Nitraline		Rd Reddish	Sn Stannate	Tr Transparent	Y Yellow
	Pn Perinone	Re Resin	Sp Sepia	Tt Tartrazine	Yw Yellowish
O Orange	Po Potassium	Rh Rhodamine	S-S Sulpho-Selenide		
Oc Ochre	Pp Purple	Ro Rose	St Strontium	U Ultramarine	Z Zinc
Op Opaque	Pr Prussian	Rt Root	Su Sulphide	Um Umber	

COLOR
YELLOWS

#	Color	Composition	Manufacturers' Permanency Rating	BEROL	BLOCKX	BOCOUR	CALDER	CAL-WESTERN	CARAN D'ACHE	DANACOLORS	DURO	FERRARIO	GOLDEN	GRUMBACHER	HOLBEIN	HUNT SPEEDBALL	LAMBERTYE	LASCAUX	LEFRANC & BOURGEOIS	LIQUITEX
12	Acacia	N/S					A													
	Asia Yellow	E, AzP	••••															G		
22	Aureolin	**CoY**					O													
13		CoPoNr	••••		O															
16		N/S																		
1	Azo Lemon	N/S	•••																	
2	Azo Light Yellow	N/S	•••																	
5	Azo Medium Yellow	N/S	••																	
23	Azo Orange	N/S	•••																	
14	Azo Yellow 10G	N/S																		
13	Azo Yellow Medium	AzP	••••																	
		AyY	••••																	
12		N/S	•••																	
5	Azo Yellow Middle	N/S	•••																	
18	Azo Yellow Orange	AzP	••••																	
		AyY	••••																	
4	Azo Yellow Pale	N/S	•••																	
11	Baryte Yellow	N/S	•••																	
6	Baryum Yellow	BaCh	••••		O															
10	Bright Light Yellow	N/S	••••																	
25	Bright Orange	Dly, PnO, TD	••••																OA	
		N/S	•••																	
5	Bright Yellow	N/S	•••																	
14	Bright Yellow Ochre	N/S	••••																	
	Brilliant Gold Pearl	T-Mi.	••••																	
27	Brilliant Orange	AzP																W		
		Na, Dly, TD, ZOx	••••																O	
18	Brilliant Yellow	CaSu	••••				G													
23		CaSu, TD	••••																	
12		AyY, BeO, TD	••••																A	
16		CaS, ZOx	•••															O		
8		ZOx, ZSu, Nk-Ti Y	•••																	
5		N/S		S																
2	Brilliant Yellow Deep	CaSu	••••																	
24		CaSu, ZOx	••••		O															
22		ZOx, Ni-TY, ZS	•••																	
16		N/S									W									
114	Brilliant Yellow Green	AyY, ClCpPhG, TD	•••																A	

Abbreviations used to signify composition correspond to recognized chemical abbreviations only in some cases. A detailed key is included on pp84-85.

LUKAS	MAIMERI	MARABU	MARCUS ART	MICHAEL HARDING	PEBEO	PELIKAN	PENTEL	PDQ	REEVES	RICH ART	ROBERSON	ROWNEY	SCHMINCKE	SENNELIER	SHIVA	SPECTRUM	J P STEPHENSON	TALENS	TITAN	UTRECHT	VALLEJO	WEBER	WINSOR & NEWTON
	O																						
																		O					OW
											O			W									
									OW														
									A														
									A														
			G						OAW														
			G																				
																						A	
																				A			
									W														
									W														
																						A	
																				A			
									OW														
														OP									
					O																		
					G																		
		S				O								OGP									
					G																		
	A																						
	G					O							W										
													G										
	W												O										
	G												W										
	O												O										
O																							

KEY O oil A acrylic W watercolor G gouache P pigment S poster K alkyd E egg tempera   **Quality** O artists and students O artists O students O unspecified

#	COLOR	COMPOSITION	MANUFACTURERS' PERMANENCY RATING	BEROL	BLOCKX	BOCOUR	CALDER	CAL-WESTERN	CARAN D'ACHE	DANACOLORS	DURO	FERRARIO	GOLDEN	GRUMBACHER	HOLBEIN	HUNT SPEEDBALL	LAMBERTYE	LASCAUX	LEFRANC & BOURGEOIS	LIQUITEX
114	Brilliant Yellow Green (Contd)	AyY, CICP PhG, TD, ZOx																	O	
8	Brilliant Yellow Light	ZOx, CaSu	●●●	O																
5		CaSuBa, TD	●●●●																	
2		TD, CaSu	●●●																	
2		ZOx, Ni-TY	●●●																	
8		AyY10G, TDZOx	●●●																O	
3		N/S		O								W								
132	Bronze Yellow	SyHyIrOx, NIIrOxMn	●●●●																A	
140	Burnt Yellow Ochre	IrOx	●●●●																	
13	Buttercup	N/S																		
25	C.P. Cadmium Orange	CaS-S	●									A								
16	C.P. Cadmium Yellow Dark	CaSu	●									A								
4	C.P. Cadmium Yellow Light	CaZSu	●									A								
12	C.P. Cadmium Yellow Medium	CaSu	●									A								
	Cadmium Deep	N/S									O									
6	Cadmium Lemon	**CaSu**	●●●●			OAW														
3		CaS, AzY	●●●															G		
3		AzY.				WS														
2	Cadmium Lemon (Azo)	AzP	●●●																	
12	Cadmium Lemon Yellow	N/S																		
	Cadmium Light	N/S									O									
	Cadmium Middle	N/S									O									
27	Cadmium Orange	**CaS**	●●●●			OAWG														
31		CaS-S	●●●●										O				O	A	OAW	
23		CaS-S, Ex	●●●●																	
		CaS-S Ba	●●●●																	
25		CaS, CaSe	●●●																	
19		OrP, CaSu, CaSe	●●●																	
20		CaS-S, BaSl	●●●							OA			OA							
20		CaSe or CaS-S	●●●																	
19		CaS-S, CaS, BaSu	●●●										W							
19		Ans, Ars	●●										W							
19		AzR				WS														
26		N/S			OAW			O			O				OAW		W			
19	Cadmium Orange (Azo)	AzP	●●●																	

Abbreviations used to signify composition correspond to recognized chemical abbreviations only in some cases. A detailed key is included on pp84-85.

LUKAS	MAIMERI	MARABU	MARCUS ART	MICHAEL HARDING	PEBEO	PELIKAN	PENTEL	PDQ	REEVES	RICH ART	ROBERSON	ROWNEY	SCHMINCKE	SENNELIER	SHIVA	SPECTRUM	JP STEPHENSON	TALENS	TITAN	UTRECHT	VALLEJO	WEBER	WINSOR & NEWTON
	O																	O					
																					O		
												W											
												O											
OG						O									O								
												W											
																							S
																		OAW	O				OW
																		O					
G																							
																					A		
	OAW																						
												OGP						A					
												A											
																					OA		
																		OW					OW
												O											
																				OA			
																			O				
O			O					K	A		O		S		O	O					A		
																		O					

KEY O oil A acrylic W watercolor G gouache P pigment S poster K alkyd E egg tempera **Quality** **O** artists and students **O** artists *O* students O unspecified

COLOR	COMPOSITION	MANUFACTURERS' PERMANENCY RATING	BEROL	BLOCKX	BOCOUR	CALDER	CAL-WESTERN	CARAN D'ACHE	DANACOLORS	DURO	FERRARIO	GOLDEN	GRUMBACHER	HOLBEIN	HUNT SPEEDBALL	LAMBERTYE	LASCAUX	LEFRANC & BOURGEOIS	LIQUITEX
20 Cadmium Orange (Imit.)	AzP	•••																	
30 Cadmium Orange Deep	CaS-S	••••															A		
28 Cadmium Orange Light	CaS-S	••••														O	A		
19 Cadmium Orange Medium	CaS-S	••••															A		
18 Cadmium Yellow	CaSu	••••			OAW														
18	AzY				WS														
18	CaSu, BaSl																		
13	N/S															O			
12 Cadmium Yellow (Azo)	AzP	•••																	
18 Cadmium Yellow Dark	CaSu	••••																	
17 Cadmium Yellow Dark (Imit.)	AzP	•••																	
19 Cadmium Yellow Deep	CaSu	••••		O	OAW													OW	OW
21	CaSuBa, CaS-S Ba	••••																	
14	CaSu, AzY	••••																G	
17	CaS-S	••••										O				O			
11	CaSu, CaS-S	•••										W							
10	CaSu, BaSl	•••										A							
10	CaS-S, BaSu, BaSl	•••										O							
10	Ans, Ars	••										W							
10	AzY						S												
26	N/S				OAW						W					OAW			
19 Cadmium Yellow Deep (Azo)	AzP	•••																	
18 Cadmium Yellow Deep (Subst.)	N/S																		
17 Cadmium Yellow Gold	CaSu	•••														O			
18	N/S	••••														W			
10 Cadmium Yellow Lemon	CaSu	••••										O						OW	
3	CaSu, ZSu	••••														O			
5	OrP, CaSu	•••																	
5	CaSu, CaS-S, BaSl	•••										W							
13	N/S										OAW					OAW			
13 Cadmium Yellow Lemon (Subst.)	N/S																		
5 Cadmium Yellow Light	CaSu	••••		O												O	A	OAW	
3	CaSuBa	••••																	

Abbreviations used to signify composition correspond to recognized chemical abbreviations only in some cases. A detailed key is included on pp84-85.

LUKAS	MAIMERI	MARABU	MARCUS ART	MICHAEL HARDING	PEBEO	PELIKAN	PENTEL	PDQ	REEVES	RICH ART	ROBERSON	ROWNEY	SCHMINCKE	SENNELIER	SHIVA	SPECTRUM	J P STEPHENSON	TALENS	TITAN	UTRECHT	VALLEJO	WEBER	WINSOR & NEWTON
G	O																						
												OW											
												OW											
																	O	OW					
																				OA			
			O							O					O								
																		O					
	AW																						
	O																						
	O		O									OWGP						OAW					OW
																					O		
OW											O	S	OWPE		O						A		
																		O					
													OGP										
	OAW																						
													OWP										
													O										
O												S	OWP										
													OP										
	OAW											OWGP						OAW	O				
																					OA		

KEY O oil A acrylic W watercolor G gouache P pigment S poster K alkyd E egg tempera   **Quality** O artists and students O artists *O* students ○ unspecified

No.	COLOR	COMPOSITION	MANUFACTURERS' PERMANENCY RATING	BEROL	BLOCKX	BOCOUR	CALDER	CAL-WESTERN	CARAN D'ACHE	DANACOLORS	DURO	FERRARIO	GOLDEN	GRUMBACHER	HOLBEIN	HUNT SPEEDBALL	LAMBERTYE	LASCAUX	LEFRANC & BOURGEOIS	LIQUITEX
2	Cadmium Yellow Light (contd)	CaSu, BaSl	••••							OA			A							
7		CaS-S, BaSl	••••										O							
13		CaZSu	••••																WA	
2		CaSu, CaS-S	•••										OW							
5		CaSu, AzY	•••															G		
16		OrP, CaSu	•••																	
6		N/S	•••		OWA				O						OA	OAW				
5	Cadmium Yellow Light (Azo)	AzP	•••																	
13	Cadmium Yellow Light (Subst.)	N/S																		
12	Cadmium Yellow Light Imit.	AzP	•••																	
12	Cadmium Yellow Medium	CaSu	••••	O												O	A		OW	W
3		CaSu, BaSl	••••							OA			A							
		CaSuBa	••••																	
17		CaSu, CaS-S	•••										OW							
12		CaSu, AzY																G		
17		CaSu, CaS-S, BaSu	•••										O							
15		CaZSu	••••																	AO
10		Ans, Ars	••										W							
15		N/S			OWA				O						OAW	W				
14	Cadmium Yellow Medium (Subst.)	N/S																		
17	Cadmium Yellow Middle	CaSu	••••																	
10		N/S									A									
19	Cadmium Yellow Orange	CaSu	••••																OW	
19		CaSu, AzY	••••															G		
25		CaS-S, CaSu, BaSu											O							
		CaS-S	••••	O																
23		N/S									WA						OA			
23	Cadmium Yellow Orange (Subst.)	N/S	•••																	
5	Cadmium Yellow Pale	CaSu	•••	O		OWG										O		O		
6		CaS-S, BaS	•••										O							
5		Ans, Ars	••										W							
5		N/S			OA											W				
	Cadmium Yellow-Orange	N/S					O													
138	Capucine Yellow Deep	RoM, IrOx	••••				O													
137	Capucine Yellow Light	RoM, IrOx	••••				O													
4	Carthusian Yellow	AzY, Ph																G		
7	Chartreuse Yellow	N/S	••••																	

Abbreviations used to signify composition correspond to recognized chemical abbreviations only in some cases. A detailed key is included on pp84-85.

	LUKAS	MAIMERI	MARABU	MARCUS ART	MICHAEL HARDING	PEBEO	PELIKAN	PENTEL	PDQ	REEVES	RICH ART	ROBERSON	ROWNEY	SCHMINCKE	SENNELIER	SHIVA	SPECTRUM	J P STEPHENSON	TALENS	TITAN	UTRECHT	VALLEJO	WEBER	WINSOR & NEWTON
																					AG			
													O											
	OA								K				S	WPE	O									
																				O				
														OGP										
		O																						
		O																		O				
																					OA			
																						OA		
									K					OP	O									
														OP										
													OWG											
	O								A															
														OWPE										
														OP										
			O																					OW
									A		O			O										
				O																				

KEY O oil A acrylic W watercolor G gouache P pigment S poster K alkyd E egg tempera   **Quality** **O** artists and students O artists *O* students ○ unspecified

No.	COLOR	COMPOSITION	MANUFACTURERS' PERMANENCY RATING	Berol	Blockx	Bocour	Calder	Cal-Western	Caran d'Ache	Danacolors	Duro	Ferrario	Golden	Grumbacher	Holbein	Hunt Speedball	Lambertye	Lascaux	Lefranc & Bourgeois	Liquitex
32	Chinese Orange	N/S	●●●																	
16	Chrome Deep	**LeCh**	●●																	
5	Chrome Lemon	**LeCh**	●●●																	
5		LeCh, LeSu	●●																	
5		LeCh, Le	●																	
14	Chrome Lemon Deep	N/S																		
28	Chrome Orange	LeCh	●●●																	
25		OrP	●●●																	
26		LeCh, LeMo	●●																	
26		N/S																		
27	Chrome Orange Deep	N/S																		
11	Chrome Yellow	LeCh	●●																	
14		N/S																		
14	Chrome Yellow Dark	**LeCh**	●●●																	
25	Chrome Yellow Deep	**LeCh**	●●●															OG		
19		OrP	●●●																	
23		N/S										O				O				
2	Chrome Yellow Lemon	LeCh	●●●																	
9		OrP	●●●																	
7		AzP	●●															W		
11		N/S										W								
15	Chrome Yellow Light	**LeCh**	●●●															OWG		
21		N/S										O				O				
18	Chrome Yellow Medium	**LeCh**	●●															OG		
19	Chrome Yellow Middle	N/S										O								
18-20	Chrome Yellow Nos 1—3	F	●●●●													O				
25	Chrome Yellow Orange	**LeCh**	●●															OG		
23	Dark Cadmium Yellow	N/S	●●●●																	
	Dark Yellow	N/S																		
22	Deep Cadmium Yellow	N/S	●●●●																	
18	Deep Yellow	N/S	●●																	
17	Delta Yellow	AzP	●●●●															O		
	Diarylide Yellow	N/S	●										A							
12	Diazo Yellow Red	AzP																		
135	Ferrite Yellow	IrOx	●●●●																	
37	Fire Orange	LuSh	●●●●																	

Abbreviations used to signify composition correspond to recognized chemical abbreviations only in some cases. A detailed key is included on pp84-85.

LUKAS	MAIMERI	MARABU	MARCUS ART	MICHAEL HARDING	PEBEO	PELIKAN	PENTEL	PDQ	REEVES	RICH ART	ROBERSON	ROWNEY	SCHMINCKE	SENNELIER	SHIVA	SPECTRUM	J P STEPHENSON	TALENS	TITAN	UTRECHT	VALLEJO	WEBER	WINSOR & NEWTON
														OW									
																							O
																		O					
																							O
																							W
																O							
	OW												OP					O					
													WS										
																							OW
											O					O							
																O							
																							OW
											O		S										
OW																							
	O												OP					O					W
													W										
O														OWGP		O							
	O												O										
													W										
														P									
	OW												OP					O					
O														OP									
	O												O										
													W										
O																							
A																							
			W							S													
			OA																				
AWG																							
		G																					
													P										

KEY O oil A acrylic W watercolor G gouache P pigment S poster K alkyd E egg tempera **Quality** O artists and students O artists O students O unspecified

COLOR	COMPOSITION	MANUFACTURERS' PERMANENCY RATING	BEROL	BLOCKX	BOCOUR	CALDER	CAL-WESTERN	CARAN D'ACHE	DANACOLORS	DURO	FERRARIO	GOLDEN	GRUMBACHER	HOLBEIN	HUNT SPEEDBALL	LAMBERTYE	LASCAUX	LEFRANC & BOURGEOIS	LIQUITEX
5 Flanders Yellow	AzP	●●●●																OW	
39 Flesh Colour	NpRdY																		
39	TD, CaSu, CaSe	●●																	
41 Flesh Colour 1 (Light)	CaS-S, TD	●●																	
40 Flesh Colour 4 (Deep)	CaS-S, TD	●●																	
21 Flesh Yellow	ZOx, CaS-S, TD	●●●●							O										
16 Gallstone	AtP	●●●●															W		
14 Gamboge	GuRe	●●																	
17	Ans, Ars, IrOx	●●●●										W							
16	OrP	●●●																	
16	Ans, Ars	●●										W							
16	AzY					W													
21	N/S									OW									
15 Gamboge (Subst.)	AzY, Ph	●●●●															W		
14 Gamboge (Hue)	N/S	●●																	
14 Gamboge (Imit.)	AzP	●●●																	
10 Gold	IrOx, TD, Mi	●●●●									O								
132 Gold Ochre	E	●●●●	O																
137	IrOx	●●●●																	
135	IrOx, E	●●●●																	
135	E, IrOx, Fl	●●●●														O			
135	N/S									O									
132 Gold Ochre Transparent	IrOx	●●●●									O								
16 Gold Yellow	LeCh	●●															OW		
19	N/S	●●●●														W			
19 Golden Cadmium Yellow	N/S	●●●●																	
18 Golden Chrome Yellow	N/S	●●●●																	
135 Golden Ochre	E	●●●●																	
17 Golden Yellow	LeCh	●●															G		
13	Ans, Ars	●●										W							
18	N/S																AG		
6 Grumbacher Transparent Yellow	CaSu, CaS-S	●●●										O							
31 Hansa Orange	Ans, Ars	●●●										A							
19	Hn, Y3R	●●●●																	
9 Hansa Yellow	AyYG	●●●																W	
5	N/S			W				O											
5 Hansa Yellow Deep	N/S			A															
9 Hansa Yellow Light	AyY, 10G	●●●						A											O

Abbreviations used to signify composition correspond to recognized chemical abbreviations only in some cases. A detailed key is included on pp84-85.

LUKAS	MAIMERI	MARABU	MARCUS ART	MICHAEL HARDING	PEBEO	PELIKAN	PENTEL	PDQ	REEVES	RICH ART	ROBERSON	ROWNEY	SCHMINCKE	SENNELIER	SHIVA	SPECTRUM	J P STEPHENSON	TALENS	TITAN	UTRECHT	VALLEJO	WEBER	WINSOR & NEWTON
		G																					
												O											
												O											
												O											
																							W
																		W					
					W																		
									W														
	OW																						
	W																						O
																		O					
																		W					
OWG														W									
																			O				
					G																		
					G																		
	OW												OWP		O								
																					A		S
																				A			
				O																			
																			O				
																						A	

KEY O oil A acrylic W watercolor G gouache P pigment S poster K alkyd E egg tempera   **Quality** O artists and students O artists O students O unspecified

No.	COLOR	COMPOSITION	MANUFACTURERS' PERMANENCY RATING	BEROL	BLOCKX	BOCOUR	CALDER	CAL-WESTERN	CARAN D'ACHE	DANACOLORS	DURO	FERRARIO	GOLDEN	GRUMBACHER	HOLBEIN	HUNT SPEEDBALL	LAMBERTYE	LASCAUX	LEFRANC & BOURGEOIS	LIQUITEX
11	Hansa Yellow Light (contd)	Ans, Ars	●●●										A							
5		AyY	●●●●																	
5		HnYR, ZW	●●																	
1		N/S			A							A								
6	Hansa Yellow Medium	AyYGX	●●●●							A			A							O
5		N/S									A									
19	Hansa Yellow Orange	N/S							O											
2	Hansa Yellow Pale	AyY	●●●●																	
12	Helios Yellow	AzP	●●●●															OW		
	Imdazole Vat Orange	N/S																		
6	Imitation Naples Yellow	N/S	●●●																	
29	Indanthrene Orange	InP	●●●●																	
26	Indian Yellow	OrP	●●●●																	
19		TtY	●●●																	
21		AzP	●●●															OW		
26		AzP, Ex	●●●																	
16		CaSu, OrP	●●●																	
14		Ans, Ars	●●										W							
23		N/S									OW					O				
16	Indian Yellow (Imit.)	AzYP	●●●															OG		
132	Indian Yellow (Subst.)	N/S																		
136	Indian Yellow Stable	E, F	●●●●													O				
8	Ivory	BrNpY																		
14	Japanese Yellow Deep	AzYp	●●●															OG		
15	Japanese Yellow Lemon	AzP	●●●●															G		
9	Japanese Yellow Light	AzP	●●●															OG		
27	Japanese Yellow Orange	AzYP	●●															O		
22	Jaune Brillant	CaY, FLW, Vr	●●●																	
10	King's Yellow	AyYGX, TD, ZOx	●●●●							O										
32	Lambertye Orange	N/S	●●●●														OW			
3	Lemon	AzP				OAG														
13		CaYLe																		
4		N/S						AG						A						
1	Lemon Cadmium Yellow	N/S	●●●●																	
	Lemon Chrome Yellow	N/S	●●●●																	
139	Lemon Ochre	IrOx	●●●●															G		
1	Lemon Yellow	**BaCh**	●●●																	
		AzP	●●●●																	

Abbreviations used to signify composition correspond to recognized chemical abbreviations only in some cases. A detailed key is included on pp84-85.

Lukas	Maimeri	Marabu	Marcus Art	Michael Harding	Pebeo	Pelikan	Pentel	PDQ	Reeves	Rich Art	Roberson	Rowney	Schmincke	Sennelier	Shiva	Spectrum	J P Stephenson	Talens	Titan	Utrecht	Vallejo	Weber	Winsor & Newton
																				A			
																				O			
								K													A		
								K															
																				A			
OAW																							
								K															
					G																		
	O		G																				
													OWG					OW				O	OW
													OA										
													P					O					
					O						O			G	O								
OAW	OW																						
														OWPE									
		G																					
																							O
		G																					
		S																					
			AWG		O																		
		O																					
																							OWK
																		A					

KEY O oil A acrylic W watercolor G gouache P pigment S poster K alkyd E egg tempera   **Quality** O artists and students O artists O students O unspecified

#	COLOR	COMPOSITION	MANUFACTURERS' PERMANENCY RATING	BEROL	BLOCKX	BOCOUR	CALDER	CAL-WESTERN	CARAN D'ACHE	DANACOLORS	DURO	FERRARIO	GOLDEN	GRUMBACHER	HOLBEIN	HUNT SPEEDBALL	LAMBERTYE	LASCAUX	LEFRANC & BOURGEOIS	LIQUITEX
6	Lemon Yellow (contd)	HnY 10G, ZOx	●●●																	
7		AoAc	●●●													O				
4		Ans, Ars	●●●										OW							
7		Ans, Ars TD, LeCh	●●●										G							
6		AyY	●●●●																A	
6		LeCh, AzP	●●																G	
2		N/S	●●●	S		OW										W	W	AG		
4	Lemon Yellow Hansa	AyY 10G, TD, ZOx	●●●																	O
13		AyY 10G	●●●																	W
3	Lemon Yellow Japanese	AzP	●●●●															O		
10	Light Cadmium Yellow	N/S	●●●●																	
3	Light Chrome Yellow	N/S	●●●●																	
132	Light Orange	F, AzP	●●●●													O				
23		N/S																		
12	Light Yellow	AzP	●●●●																	
3		BrCaY																		
5		N/S														W		S		
140	Mars Orange	**IrOx**	●●●●		O													OW		
142		N/S																		
131	Mars Yellow	**IrOx**	●●●●		O									O		O		O		
		SyHyIrOx, NlHyIrOx	●●●●																O	
147		N/S				OA														
136	Mars Yellow (Subst.)	N/S	●●●●																	
138	Mars Yellow Deep	N/S																		
138	Mars Yellow-Orange	IrOx	●●●●		O															
10	Medium Yellow	DKCaY																		
5		N/S																		
10	Middle Cadmium Yellow	N/S	●●●●																	
12	Middle Chrome Yellow	N/S	●●●●																	
139	Monaco Yellow	E, AzP	●●●●															G		
12	Naples Yellow	Nk, TY	●●●●																	
8		TD, CaSu	●●●●																	
11		NK, TY, OrP	●●●																	
22		Ans, Ars, TD	●●●										G							
7		Ans, Ars, IrOx	●●●										w							
1		CaSu, BaSl, ZOx	●●●										O							
21		CaSu, IrOx, ZOX	●●●		O															
15		LeAmY	●●●●																O	

Abbreviations used to signify composition correspond to recognized chemical abbreviations only in some cases. A detailed key is included on pp84-85.

LUKAS	MAIMERI	MARABU	MARCUS ART	MICHAEL HARDING	PEBEO	PELIKAN	PENTEL	PDQ	REEVES	RICH ART	ROBERSON	ROWNEY	SCHMINCKE	SENNELIER	SHIVA	SPECTRUM	J P STEPHENSON	TALENS	TITAN	UTRECHT	VALLEJO	WEBER	WINSOR & NEWTON
																						O	
P	OWG			O			S				O		OWGPE								A		
				OAW																			
				G																			
				G																	A		
A																							
	G																						
OAWG									S														
	O																						
OA		G	O																O				O
											O			O									
											O		WP								A		
													O										
																					A		
	G																						
	S																						
				G																			
				O																			
													AWG										
																				O			
													O										
																							W

KEY O oil A acrylic W watercolor G gouache P pigment S poster K alkyd E egg tempera **Quality** O artists and students O artists O students O unspecified

COLOR		COMPOSITION	MANUFACTURERS' PERMANENCY RATING	BEROL	BLOCKX	BOCOUR	CALDER	CAL-WESTERN	CARAN D'ACHE	DANACOLORS	DURO	FERRARIO	GOLDEN	GRUMBACHER	HOLBEIN	HUNT SPEEDBALL	LAMBERTYE	LASCAUX	LEFRANC & BOURGEOIS	LIQUITEX
24	Naples Yellow (contd)	CaY, LtR, FIW, YOc	•••																	
7		IrOx, CaS-S, CaSu, BaSl	•••										W							
24		IrOx				G														
7		IrOx, AzY					OAW													
18		N/S			OA															
11	Naples Yellow Bright	N/S										O				OW			O	
21	Naples Yellow Dark	CaSu, ZOx	••••																	
12	Naples Yellow Deep	CaS-S, ZOx	••••																	
24		CaSe, TD	••••																	
22		Nk, TY	••••																	
17		ZOx, AzP	••••																	
24		N/S									O									
21	Naples Yellow Genuine	**AmLe**	•••																	
21	Naples Yellow Hue	TD, CaSuBa, IrOx	••••																	
15		HnYR, YOx, ZW	•••																	
21		AyY, NlHylrOx, ZOx	•••																O	
12	Naples Yellow Imitation	CaSu, ZSu	••••															W		
41		AzP	••															G		
11	Naples Yellow Light	CaSu, ZOx	••••																	
10		TLNk, I	••••																	
24		ZOx, AzP	•••																	
24		N/S									OA									
8	Naples Yellow Light Ex.	CaSu, ZOx	••••																	
21	Naples Yellow Middle	N/S																		
12	Naples Yellow Pale	ZOx, OrP	••••																	
41		N/S																		
24	Naples Yellow Red Ex.	CaSu, ZOx	••••																	
23	Naples Yellow Reddish	CaS-S, TD	••••																	
39		CaS-S, ZOx	••••																	
24		CaSu, ZOx	••••																	
24		TD, IrOx, CaSu	••••																	
24		TD, CaSu	••••																	
18		ZOx, CaSu	••••																	
40		ZOx, OrP	••••																	
		N/S									OAW									
15	Naples Yellow Shade	Z, IrOx	••••															O		

Abbreviations used to signify composition correspond to recognized chemical abbreviations only in some cases. A detailed key is included on pp84-85.

LUKAS	MAIMERI	MARABU	MARCUS ART	MICHAEL HARDING	PEBEO	PELIKAN	PENTEL	PDQ	REEVES	RICH ART	ROBERSON	ROWNEY	SCHMINCKE	SENNELIER	SHIVA	SPECTRUM	J P STEPHENSON	TALENS	TITAN	UTRECHT	VALLEJO	WEBER	WINSOR & NEWTON
																							O
	G			O				K					OWGPE	O		O			O				K
	O																						
																		O					
																		A					
													O										
	O												O										
O											O												
	W																						
																						O	
																				O			
																		OW					
													O										
	O																						
O																							
																		O					
											O												
	O																						
											O												
																		O					
																		A					
	O																	O					
																		W					
													W										
																			O				
													O										
O	O																						

KEY O oil A acrylic W watercolor G gouache P pigment S poster K alkyd E egg tempera   **Quality** O artists and students O artists O students O unspecified

No.	COLOR	COMPOSITION	MANUFACTURERS' PERMANENCY RATING	BEROL	BLOCKX	BOCOUR	CALDER	CAL-WESTERN	CARAN D'ACHE	DANACOLORS	DURO	FERRARIO	GOLDEN	GRUMBACHER	HOLBEIN	HUNT SPEEDBALL	LAMBERTYE	LASCAUX	LEFRANC & BOURGEOIS	LIQUITEX
2	Naples Yellow Shade (contd)	IrOx, QtY	••••																A	
21	Naples Yellow Stable	E/F	••••												O					
17	New Gamboge	ArY, ToR	••••																	
21		N/S														W				
7	Nickel Yellow	NkTi	••••																OA	
5		Nk, An, Tc	••••																	
	Norma Yellow	AzP, TD	••••																	
133	Opaque Deep Chrome Yellow	CrLeSu	••••																	
139	Opaque Mars Yellow	IrOx	••••																	
26	Orange	AzR				OAG														
27		PzO	•••																A	
17		N/S					A	AG										AG		S
25	Orange (Spectrum)	N/S																		
25	Orange Cadmium Yellow	N/S	••••																	
31	Orange Deep	AzP	••••												O					
26	Orange GG (Light)	CaS-S																		
17	Orange Lead (Imit.)	AzP, TD	•••															G		
	Orange Madder	N/S																		
	Orange Ochre	N/S																A		
132	Orange Oxide	SylrOx	•									A								
25	Orange R (Light)	CaSu																		
26	Oriental Yellow	N/S	•••																	
133	Oxide Yellow	IrOx																A		
22	Permanent Dark Yellow	N/S	••••																	
132	Permanent Indian Yellow	FY	••••																O	
2	Permanent Lemon	N/S																		
1	Permanent Lemon Yellow	N/S	••••																	
13	Permanent Light Lemon Yellow	N/S	••••																	
13	Permanent Light Yellow	N/S	••••																	
26	Permanent Orange	OrP	••••																	
25		AzY, Ex	••••																	
28		N/S	••••																	
7	Permanent Yellow	AzY				OWA														
15		N/S																		
11	Permanent Yellow Deep	AzP	••••																	
19		OrP	••••																	
15		AzY	•••																	

Abbreviations used to signify composition correspond to recognized chemical abbreviations only in some cases. A detailed key is included on pp84-85.

	LUKAS	MAIMERI	MARABU	MARCUS ART	MICHAEL HARDING	PEBEO	PELIKAN	PENTEL	PDQ	REEVES	RICH ART	ROBERSON	ROWNEY	SCHMINCKE	SENNELIER	SHIVA	SPECTRUM	J P STEPHENSON	TALENS	TITAN	UTRECHT	VALLEJO	WEBER	WINSOR & NEWTON
																							W	
													O											
													P											
													O											
			O																					
			O																					
	AWG	S		O				S							S							A		
											S													
				OAW																				
			G																					
												O												
			G																					
				OA																				
				W																				
																								S
				W																				
				W																				
				W																				
													OWG							A				
													P											
				W																				
								S				O												
													O											
													WG											
													P											

KEY O oil A acrylic W watercolor G gouache P pigment S poster K alkyd E egg tempera   **Quality** O artists and students O artists O students O unspecified

No.	COLOR	COMPOSITION	MANUFACTURERS' PERMANENCY RATING	BEROL	BLOCKX	BOCOUR	CALDER	CAL-WESTERN	CARAN D'ACHE	DANACOLORS	DURO	FERRARIO	GOLDEN	GRUMBACHER	HOLBEIN	HUNT SPEEDBALL	LAMBERTYE	LASCAUX	LEFRANC & BOURGEOIS	LIQUITEX
17	Perm Yellow Deep (contd)	N/S																		
1	Permanent Yellow Lemon	AzP	●●●																	
	Permanent Yellow Light	OrP	●●●●																	
3		CaSu, Ex	●●●●																	
2		AzP	●●●●																	
3		AzY, Ex	●●●																	
5	Permanent Yellow Middle	AzP	●●●●																	
11		N/S																		
5	Permanent Yellow Pale	N/S																		
23	Permasol Yellow Deep	N/S																		
1	Permasol Yellow Light	N/S																		
12	Permasol Yellow Medium	N/S																		
132	Permasol Gold Ochre	N/S																		
27	Permasol Orange	N/S																		
26	Permasol Red Orange	N/S																		
20	Persian Orange Deep	AzP	●●●															G		
23	Persian Orange Light	AzP	●●●●															G		
20	Persian Yellow Deep	AzP	●●●															G		
1	Persian Yellow Lemon	AzP	●●●●															G		
6	Persian Yellow Light	AzP	●●●●															G		
15	Persian Yellow Medium	AzP	●●●															G		
2	Primary Yellow	AzYP	●●●●															G		
25	Pure Cadmium Orange	CaS-S	●●●●																	
12	Pure Cadmium Yellow	CaSu	●●●●																	
22	Pure Dark Cadmium Yellow	AzY	●●●●																	
3	Pure Lemon Cadmium Yellow	AzY	●●●●																	
7	Pure Middle Cadmium Yellow	AzY	●●●●																	
145	Quinacridone Burnt Orange	Q	●										A							
140	Quinacridone Gold	Q	●										A							
138	Raw Bergamo	E	●●●●																	
133	Raw Sienna	E	●●●●																	
153		IrOx	●●●●			OAWG				OA			A	OAWG						OAW
144		E, IrOx	●●●●														O			
146		N/S			OAW		A		O		OAW					OAW	OAW			
135	Raw Sienna Deep	E	●●●●																	
133	Raw Sienna Light	E	●●●●																	
25	Red Orange	N/S																		S

Abbreviations used to signify composition correspond to recognized chemical abbreviations only in some cases. A detailed key is included on pp84-85.

LUKAS	MAIMERI	MARABU	MARCUS ART	MICHAEL HARDING	PEBEO	PELIKAN	PENTEL	PDQ	REEVES	RICH ART	ROBERSON	ROWNEY	SCHMINCKE	SENNELIER	SHIVA	SPECTRUM	J P STEPHENSON	TALENS	TITAN	UTRECHT	VALLEJO	WEBER	WINSOR & NEWTON
							S																S
												A											
												G											
												A											
												OW											
												P											
												W											
																							S
																							S
															O								
															O								
															O								
															O								
															O								
															O								
				OAG																OA			
																				OA			
				O																			
				O																			
				O																			
	O																						
	OAW		O										OWGP					OW	O				OWK
																			A			OA	
OG				OAWG					OAW	S	O			OWPE		O					A		
	O																						
	O																						
		S																					

KEY O oil A acrylic W watercolor G gouache P pigment S poster K alkyd E egg tempera   **Quality** O artists and students O artists O students O unspecified

COLOR	COMPOSITION	MANUFACTURERS' PERMANENCY RATING	BEROL	BLOCKX	BOCOUR	CALDER	CAL-WESTERN	CARAN D'ACHE	DANACOLORS	DURO	FERRARIO	GOLDEN	GRUMBACHER	HOLBEIN	HUNT SPEEDBALL	LAMBERTYE	LASCAUX	LEFRANC & BOURGEOIS	LIQUITEX
26 Red Orange (Spectrum)	N/S																		
8 Rembrandt Yellow	CaSu, ZOx, CrOx	●●●●																	
15 Roberson's Yellow	N/S																		
19 Saffron	N/S	●●●●																	
18 Sahara Yellow	AzP	●●●															OW		
17	AyY	●●●															A		
12 Senegal Yellow	AzP	●●●															O		
27 Shiva Orange	N/S																		
4 Shiva Yellow Citron	N/S																		
1 Shiva Yellow Light	N/S																		
2 Shiva Yellow Medium	N/S																		
Shiva Yellow Pale	N/S																		
1 Spectrum Lemon Yellow	N/S																		
Spectrum Orange	N/S																		
11 Spectrum Yellow	N/S																		
23 Spectrum Yellow Deep	N/S																		
15 Stil de Grain Jaune	OrP	●●																	
140 Stil de Grain Yellow	E, F	●●●●												O					
7	AzP, InP	●●●																	
7	Nk, AoP	●●●																	
7	P-ML	●●●																	
10 Strontia Yellow	N/S	●●●																	
2 Strontian Yellow	StCh	●●															O		
1 Strontium Yellow	ZOx, AyY FGL	●●●●							O										
114 Sulphur Yellow	AzNkP	●●●●															O		
20 Talens Orange	AzP	●●●																	
19	AzP, OrP	●●●																	
11 Talens Yellow	AzP	●●●																	
23 Talens Yellow Deep	AzP	●●●																	
3 Talens Yellow Lemon	AzP	●●●																	
5 Talens Yellow Light	AzP	●●●																	
5 Titan Yellow Lemon	OrP	●●●																	
15 Titan Yellow Medium	OrP	●●●																	
31 Titan Yellow Orange	OrP	●●●																	
6 Titanium Nickel Yellow	Nk, An, TOx																		
135 Translucent Orange Oxide	IrOx	●●●●																	
21 Translucent Yellow Oxide	IrOx	●●●●																	
10 Transparent Azo Lemon Yellow	AzP	●●●																	

Abbreviations used to signify composition correspond to recognized chemical abbreviations only in some cases. A detailed key is included on pp84-85.

	LUKAS	MAIMERI	MARABU	MARCUS ART	MICHAEL HARDING	PEBEO	PELIKAN	PENTEL	PDQ	REEVES	RICH ART	ROBERSON	ROWNEY	SCHMINCKE	SENNELIER	SHIVA	SPECTRUM	J P STEPHENSON	TALENS	TITAN	UTRECHT	VALLEJO	WEBER	WINSOR & NEWTON
											S								O					
												O												
					G																			
																O								
																O								
																O								
																O								
																O								
																	O							
																	O							
																	O							
																	O							
																		O						
	O																							
	W																							
	O																							
														OP										
																			W					
																			O					
																			OW					
																			OAW					
																			OW					
																			OAW					
																				O				
																				O				
																				O				
	O																							
												O												
												O												
			O																					

KEY O oil A acrylic W watercolor G gouache P pigment S poster K alkyd E egg tempera **Quality** O artists and students O artists O students O unspecified

No.	COLOR	COMPOSITION	MANUFACTURERS' PERMANENCY RATING	BEROL	BLOCKX	BOCOUR	CALDER	CAL-WESTERN	CARAN D'ACHE	DANACOLORS	DURO	FERRARIO	GOLDEN	GRUMBACHER	HOLBEIN	HUNT SPEEDBALL	LAMBERTYE	LASCAUX	LEFRANC & BOURGEOIS	LIQUITEX
139	Transparent Gold Ochre	E	●●●●																	
		N/S																		
6	Transparent Gold Yellow	FY	●●●															O		
21	Transparent Indian Yellow	AzP	●●●																	
138	Transparent Oxide Yellow	IrOx	●●●●																	
19	Transparent Yellow	AzP	●●●															O		
		NrCoPo	●●●●		O															
	Transparent Yellow Iron Oxide	IrOx																		
21	Turner's Yellow	AyY, SyHyIrOx	●●●																A	
7	Ultramarine Yellow	N/S									O									
3	Utrecht Orange	HnY3R, HnYR																		
15	Utrecht Yellow	HnYR, TW																		
3	Vat Orange	At										A								
26	Vivid Red Orange	N/S																	OA	
17	Winsor Fast Orange	NaCbAP	●●●																	
2	Winsor Fast Yellow	AzMeP	●●●																	
4	Winsor Lemon	ArY	●●●																	
27	Winsor Orange	BoN ArR, ArY	●●●																	
2	Winsor Yellow	ArY	●●●																	
3	Yellow	E-D																		
		QtY	●●●●															A		
16		N/S						AG											S	
12	Yellow (Spectrum)	N/S																		
10	Yellow 10G (Lemon Yellow)	CaSu																		
14	Yellow Brown	N/S																	S	
138	Yellow Burnt Ochre	E	●●●●																	
7	Yellow Citron	HnY10G, TD	●●●																	
		HnYG, NKAzY																		
17	Yellow Deep	Ans, Ars	●●●										G							
		N/S	●●●●													W				
13	Yellow G (Mid Yellow)	CaSu																		
12	Yellow Lake	N/S									O									
9	Yellow Lemon	N/S														W				
13	Yellow Light	AoA	●●●													O				
21		Ans, Ars	●●●										G							
12		N/S	●●●●													W				
5	Yellow Light Hansa	AyY	●●●												A				A	
21	Yellow Medium	Ans, Ars	●●●										G							

Abbreviations used to signify composition correspond to recognized chemical abbreviations only in some cases. A detailed key is included on pp84-85.

	LUKAS	MAIMERI	MARABU	MARCUS ART	MICHAEL HARDING	PEBEO	PELIKAN	PENTEL	PDQ	REEVES	RICH ART	ROBERSON	ROWNEY	SCHMINCKE	SENNELIER	SHIVA	SPECTRUM	J P STEPHENSON	TALENS	TITAN	UTRECHT	VALLEJO	WEBER	WINSOR & NEWTON
		O																						
												O												
			O																					
																		OAW						
	O																							
			G																					
																					A			
																					A			
																								K
																								K
																								O
																								O
																								OW
		G														S								
											S													
			G																					
													OG											
																							O	
																							O	
			G																					
														W										

KEY O oil A acrylic W watercolor G gouache P pigment S poster K alkyd E egg tempera   **Quality** O artists and students O artists O students O unspecified

	COLOR	COMPOSITION	MANUFACTURERS' PERMANENCY RATING	BEROL	BLOCKX	BOCOUR	CALDER	CAL-WESTERN	CARAN D'ACHE	DANACOLORS	DURO	FERRARIO	GOLDEN	GRUMBACHER	HOLBEIN	HUNT SPEEDBALL	LAMBERTYE	LASCAUX	LEFRANC & BOURGEOIS	LIQUITEX
14	Yellow Medium (contd)	AoAt	•••													O				
10	Yellow Medium Azo	AyY	••••																A	
5	Yellow Medium Hansa	N/S													A					
134	Yellow Ochre	**E**	••••															OG		
135		IrOx	••••	O		OAWG				OA		A						AW		
133		E, IrOx	••••												O					
139		NlHylrOx	••••																	OW
132		N/S			OAW				O		OAW			O	OAW	OAW		AG		W
131	Yellow Ochre 1	E, IrOx	••••																	
133	Yellow Ochre 2	E	••••																	
138	Yellow Ochre Deep	IrOx	••••											O						
133	Yellow Ochre Light	**E**	••••															O		
135		IrOx	••••								OA									
21	Yellow Ochre Pale	**E**	••••																	
133		IrOx	••••																	
		N/S									O									
136	Yellow Ochre Reddish	IrOx	••••																	
23	Yellow Orange (Spectrum)	N/S																		
19	Yellow Orange Azo	Ay	••••																A	
17	Yellow Orange Hansa	N/S													A					
134	Yellow Oxide	SyHylrOx	•••									A							A	
19	Yellow R (Yellow-Orange)	CaS																		
133	Yellow Raw Ochre	**E**	••••																	
13	Zinc Yellow	ZCh	•••																	
2		Ans, Ars	••••											O						
13		AzP	••••																	
12		N/S				OA					O									
5	Zinc Yellow Hue	AyY10G + 5GX, TD, ZOx	•••																O	
11		HnY, ZW																		

REDS

	COLOR	COMPOSITION	RATING	BEROL	BLOCKX	BOCOUR	CALDER	CAL-WESTERN	CARAN D'ACHE	DANACOLORS	DURO	FERRARIO	GOLDEN	GRUMBACHER	HOLBEIN	HUNT SPEEDBALL	LAMBERTYE	LASCAUX	LEFRANC & BOURGEOIS	LIQUITEX
53	Acra Crimson	QV	••••																	OW
46	Acra Red	QR	••••																	AW
47		QV	••••																	O
54	Acridone Red	LnQ	••••																	
48	Alizarin Carmine	At	•••																	
53		AaL	•••															O		
50	Alizarin Crimson	**Aa**	•••			OAWG														

Abbreviations used to signify composition correspond to recognized chemical abbreviations only in some cases. A detailed key is included on pp84-85.

Lukas	Maimeri	Marabu	Marcus Art	Michael Harding	Pebeo	Pelikan	Pentel	PDQ	Reeves	Rich Art	Roberson	Rowney	Schmincke	Sennelier	Shiva	Spectrum	J P Stephenson	Talens	Titan	Utrecht	Vallejo	Weber	Winsor & Newton
WOG			O										GP										OWK
																		OAW	O	A		OA	
																			O				
	A	S		OAW			S	K	OAW	S	O		OWGPE		O	O	O						S
													W										
													W										
O	O																						
																		O	O				
	O																						
																							O
																			O				
										S													
			G																				
													O										O
	O																						
													O										
																				O			

Bottom section:

Lukas	Maimeri	Marabu	Marcus Art	Michael Harding	Pebeo	Pelikan	Pentel	PDQ	Reeves	Rich Art	Roberson	Rowney	Schmincke	Sennelier	Shiva	Spectrum	J P Stephenson	Talens	Titan	Utrecht	Vallejo	Weber	Winsor & Newton
																						A	
																							W
	OW																						
			O																				

KEY O oil A acrylic W watercolor G gouache P pigment S poster K alkyd E egg tempera   **Quality** O artists and students O artists O students O unspecified

	COLOR	COMPOSITION	MANUFACTURERS' PERMANENCY RATING	BEROL	BLOCKX	BOCOUR	CALDER	CAL-WESTERN	CARAN D'ACHE	DANACOLORS	DURO	FERRARIO	GOLDEN	GRUMBACHER	HOLBEIN	HUNT SPEEDBALL	LAMBERTYE	LASCAUX	LEFRANC & BOURGEOIS	LIQUITEX
	Alizarin Crimson (contd)	AaL																	O	
53		Aa, ToR	•••																	
53		At	•••																	
50		SyM	•••																	
53		AaLqAu	••														O			
149		At, Au	••							O			OA W						OW	
139		At, Au, PaNt	••										G							
50		N/S			AW				O					G	OW					
50	Alizarin Crimson Golden	At, Au	••										OW							
47	Alizarin Madder	AaM	•••																	
53		N/S									O									
53	Alizarin Madder Lake Deep	AaL	•••																	
47		AaL	••																	
44	Alizarin Madder Lake Light	AaL, OrP	•••																	
46	Alizarin Madder Lake Middle	AaL	••																	
48	Alizarin Red	N/S																		
50	Alizarin Red Lake	N/S																		
38	Alizarin Rose	N/S																		
48	Alizarin Scarlet Lake	N/S																		
38	Alps Red	N/S	•••											OA						
35	Angelico Red	AzP	••••															OW		
47	Antique Rose Madder	AaL	•••																	
38	Azo Carmine BB	AzP																		
33	Azo Crimson	N/S	•••																	
35	Azo Red	N/S	••																	
44	Azo Red Deep	N/S	•••																	
43	Azo Red Middle	N/S	•••																	
141	Barn Red	CaZSu, NllrOx Mn, Na	••••																	O
52	Bellini Red	Q				W														
48	Bellini Rose Red	Q				W														
38	Bengal Pink	AeL	•															G		
38	Bengal Pink Lake	N/S	•																	
54	Bengal Red II	N/S																		
60	Bengal Rose	RhP, ChPaNt	••										G							
55		TpDy	•																	
28	Blazing (Light) Red	N/S																		
52	Bocour Red	N/S				A														
48	Bocour Rose Red	N/S				A														

Abbreviations used to signify composition correspond to recognized chemical abbreviations only in some cases. A detailed key is included on pp84-85.

LUKAS	MAIMERI	MARABU	MARCUS ART	MICHAEL HARDING	PEBEO	PELIKAN	PENTEL	PDQ	REEVES	RICH ART	ROBERSON	ROWNEY	SCHMINCKE	SENNELIER	SHIVA	SPECTRUM	J P STEPHENSON	TALENS	TITAN	UTRECHT	VALLEJO	WEBER	WINSOR & NEWTON
																							G
																							OAWK
																		O					
																				OA	OA		
									OW						O						A		
																	O						
W													P										
													O										
W													O										
													O										
								K						O									
														P									
									O														
														P									
						G																	
	O																						
			G																				
									A														
									W														
									O														
									O														
			G																				
					G																		
													S										
																							G
										S													

KEY O oil A acrylic W watercolor G gouache P pigment S poster K alkyd E egg tempera **Quality** O artists and students O artists O students O unspecified

No.	COLOR	COMPOSITION	MANUFACTURERS' PERMANENCY RATING	BEROL	BLOCKX	BOCOUR	CALDER	CAL-WESTERN	CARAN D'ACHE	DANACOLORS	DURO	FERRARIO	GOLDEN	GRUMBACHER	HOLBEIN	HUNT SPEEDBALL	LAMBERTYE	LASCAUX	LEFRANC & BOURGEOIS	LIQUITEX
59	Bordeaux Red	FaR	••																G	
52		N/S													A		O			
32	Breughel Red	AzP	••••																OAW	
50	Bright Red	PeR	••••																OAW	
35		ToAz	•••														O			
31		ToR	•••																	
37		To, Na	••			A				O							W			
135	Bright Red Ochre	N/S	••••																	
26	Bright Vermilion	CaVr																		
23		N/S																		
146	Brilliant Carmine (Red)	BaLiR, Rh, ChPaNtR	•											G						
46	Brilliant Pink	N/S	•												O					
6	Brilliant Red	AzP	•••				OP												G	
35		N/S		S																
153	Brownish Madder	N/S																		O
143	Brownish Madder (Aliz.)	SyM, IrOx	•••																	
26	Cadmium Light Red	**CaS-S**	•••																	
	Cadmium Medium Red	N/S																		
35	Cadmium Red	**CaS-S**	•••		O															
		CaS-S, BaSl	••••																	
38		CaSe					OW													
38		CaSu					A													
38		AzR					W													
28		N/S				O									G					
32	Cadmium Red (Azo)	AzP, OrP	•••																	
28	Cadmium Red (Hue)	BtNaR	••																	
60	Cadmium Red Bordeaux	**CaS-S**																A		
48	Cadmium Red Burgundy	N/S																		
48	Cadmium Red Carmine	CaS-S	••••														O		W	
52	Cadmium Red Dark	CaS-S	•							O			G							
52	Cadmium Red Deep	**CaS-S**	••••											W			O		O	OW
38		CaS-S, Ex	••••																	
31		CaS-S, AzP																	G	
142		CaS-S Ba	••••																A	
59		CaS-S, BaSl	•••									O								
35		AzR	•••									W								
37		OrP, CaSe	•••				OWG													
37		CaSu					A													

Abbreviations used to signify composition correspond to recognized chemical abbreviations only in some cases. A detailed key is included on pp84-85.

Lukas	Maimeri	Marabu	Marcus Art	Michael Harding	Pebeo	Pelikan	Pentel	PDQ	Reeves	Rich Art	Roberson	Rowney	Schmincke	Sennelier	Shiva	Spectrum	J P Stephenson	Talens	Titan	Utrecht	Vallejo	Weber	Winsor & Newton
G					G								S										
																							OW
																						OA	
				G																			
	G																						
	S																						
A													W										
										S													
																		W					
			O														O						
							K																
W			O								O	OAW				O		W					OWK
																			OA				
W								A															
												O											
																		O					
																					A		
OA			O								O	OA	OWGP			O		OAW	O				OWG
													A										
																						O	

KEY O oil A acrylic W watercolor G gouache P pigment S poster K alkyd E egg tempera   **Quality** O artists and students O artists O students O unspecified

COLOR	COMPOSITION	MANUFACTURERS' PERMANENCY RATING	BEROL	BLOCKX	BOCOUR	CALDER	CAL-WESTERN	CARAN D'ACHE	DANACOLORS	DURO	FERRARIO	GOLDEN	GRUMBACHER	HOLBEIN	HUNT SPEEDBALL	LAMBERTYE	LASCAUX	LEFRANC & BOURGEOIS	LIQUITEX
37 Cadmium Red Deep (contd)	N/S				AW						OA		OWG	W	OAW	A			
36 Cadmium Red Deep (Azo)	AzP, OrP	•••																	
32 Cadmium Red Light	**CaS-S**	••••									A	W			O		O	OAW	
29	CaS-S, Ex	••••																	
38	CaS-S Ba	••••															A		
26	OrP, CaSe	•••																	
20	CaS-S, AzP	••••															G		
32	CaS-S, BaSl	•••							OA				OA						
26	Ans, Ars, NaR	••										W							
31	N/S				AW			O		OA			OAW	OA	OAW	A			
27 Cadmium Red Light (Azo)	AzP	•••																	
35 Cadmium Red Light (Subst.)	N/S																		
48 Cadmium Red Medium	**CaS-S**	••••									A	W			O		O	AW	
44	CaS-S Ba	••••																	
52	CaS-S, BaSl	••••							OA				OA						
52	N/S				AW			O						OA	W	A			
38 Cadmium Red Medium Deep	CaS-S	••••																	O
35 Cadmium Red Medium Light	CaS-S	••••																	O
29 Cadmium Red Middle	N/S												A						
29 Cadmium Red Orange	**CaS-S**	••••		O											O			OW	
30	N/S											OW	O						
34 Cadmium Red Orange (Subst.)	N/S																		
27 Cadmium Red Pale	CaS-S	••••																	
26	Ans, Ars, NaR	••										W							
	N/S																		
38 Cadmium Red Permanent	CaS-S	••••													O				
48 Cadmium Red Purple	CaS-S	••••															O		
47	N/S	••••											OAWG						
Cadmium Red Purple (Subst.)	N/S																		
31 Cadmium Red Scarlet	CaS-S	••••																	
35	CaS-S, AzP	••••															G		
26 Cadmium Scarlet	**CaS-S**	•••	·																
29	N/S														W				
33 Cadmium Vermilion	CaS-S Ba, CaSuB	••••																	
37	CaS-S, BaSl	•••										O							
32	N/S																		
35 Cadmium Vermilion Red	CaS-S	••••															W		

Abbreviations used to signify composition correspond to recognized chemical abbreviations only in some cases. A detailed key is included on pp84-85.

LUKAS	MAIMERI	MARABU	MARCUS ART	MICHAEL HARDING	PEBEO	PELIKAN	PENTEL	PDQ	REEVES	RICH ART	ROBERSON	ROWNEY	SCHMINCKE	SENNELIER	SHIVA	SPECTRUM	J P STEPHENSON	TALENS	TITAN	UTRECHT	VALLEJO	WEBER	WINSOR & NEWTON
OAW															O						A		
																	O						
	OA											OWGP						OAW	O				
												A											
																						OA	
												O											
OAW														P									
																	O						
														P									
	O																		O				
																						OA	
																					A		
	O																						
														P									
												OWGP	OAWP										
															O								
																			O				
	OA													P									
														P									
															O				O				
											OA												
																						O	
	O																				A		

KEY O oil A acrylic W watercolor G gouache P pigment S poster K alkyd E egg tempera **Quality** O artists and students O artists 0 students O unspecified

No.	COLOR	COMPOSITION	MANUFACTURERS' PERMANENCY RATING	BEROL	BLOCKX	BOCOUR	CALDER	CAL-WESTERN	CARAN D'ACHE	DANACOLORS	DURO	FERRARIO	GOLDEN	GRUMBACHER	HOLBEIN	HUNT SPEEDBALL	LAMBERTYE	LASCAUX	LEFRANC & BOURGEOIS	LIQUITEX
31	Cadmium Vermilion Red Light	CcCaMrSu	••••																O	
29	Cadmium Yellow Red	CaSu	••••															W		
153	Caput Mortuum	IrOx	••••													O				
145		N/S									OW									
139	Caput Mortuum Deep	IrOx	••••																	
144		N/S																		
148	Caput Mortuum Light	IrOx	••••																	
		N/S																		
150	Caput Mortuum Violet	IrOx	••••																	
142	Carmine	PrNaAz	••••													O				
35		OrP	••••																	
36		SyM	•••																	
33		OrP	•••																	
52		OrP, Q	•••																	
50		AaL, Ar	•••																	
37		MtAzP	•										W							
31		DkCaR																		
52		N/S						AG			OAW			OWG		OAW				
52	Carmine (Alizarin)	ArR	•••																	
48	Carmine (Hue)	AaL, Pc	•••																	
52	Carmine (Imit.)	ToP	•••															G		
50	Carmine (Red Medium)	N/S																		
53	Carmine Alizarin	SyM	•••																	
31	Carmine Extra Fine	GnCiA	••															G		
48	Carmine Lake	N/S																		
48	Carmine Lake (Alizarin)	AaL	••															O		
57	Carmine Madder	DhAt	••••		O															
35	Carmine Red	OrP	•••																	
52		N/S															AG			
31	Cartham Pink Lake	N/S	•																	
33	Carthamine Pink Lake	N/S																		
	Cerise	LP				S														
59	Chapel Rose	N/S	•••											A						
31	China Red	ToP									W							G		
34	Chinese Red	Na, ZOx	••••											O					O	
48		ToP	•••															G		
38	Chinese Red Vermilion	AzP	••															O		
31	Chinese Vermilion	N/S	•••											O						
34	Chinese Vermilion Ex.	OrP	•••																	

Abbreviations used to signify composition correspond to recognized chemical abbreviations only in some cases. A detailed key is included on pp84.

LUKAS	MAIMERI	MARABU	MARCUS ART	MICHAEL HARDING	PEBEO	PELIKAN	PENTEL	PDQ	REEVES	RICH ART	ROBERSON	ROWNEY	SCHMINCKE	SENNELIER	SHIVA	SPECTRUM	J P STEPHENSON	TALENS	TITAN	UTRECHT	VALLEJO	WEBER	WINSOR & NEWTON
												AG										S	
												O											
O																							
												OS											
O																							
												OS											
												OW											
																	O						
																	W						
																	A						
											O												
	G																						
O	OAWG	S			O	OG	S																
											W												
											O												
			G																				
																	O						
					OG	G																	
												OAWS											
WG																							
					G																		
						G																	
																	O						

KEY O oil A acrylic W watercolor G gouache P pigment S poster K alkyd E egg tempera   **Quality** O artists and students O artists O students O unspecified

	COLOR	COMPOSITION	MANUFACTURERS' PERMANENCY RATING	BEROL	BLOCKX	BOCOUR	CALDER	CAL-WESTERN	CARAN D'ACHE	DANACOLORS	DURO	FERRARIO	GOLDEN	GRUMBACHER	HOLBEIN	HUNT SPEEDBALL	LAMBERTYE	LASCAUX	LEFRANC & BOURGEOIS	LIQUITEX
32	Chinese Vermilion (Subst.)	N/S																		
54	Compose Rose	N/S	●●●											A						
32	Coral Red	In	●●●●															OW		
28		N/S	●●●											O						
50	Crimson	ArR	●●●																	
		LP				S														
35		N/S		S																
53	Crimson Alizarin	AaL	●●●																	
48	Crimson Lake	AaL, Q	●●●																	
48		AaL, Pc	●●●																	
60		AaL, ThR	●●																	
52		AaL	●●															OWG		
50		OrP																		
59		N/S												OW						
52	Crimson Lake Permanent	AaL	●●															O		
61	Crimson Red	N/S																		
34	Dark Cadmium Red	N/S	●●●●																	
140	Dark Madder	N/S																		
38	Dark Madder Lake	N/S	●●●																	
37	Dark Oriental Red	N/S	●●●●																	
38	Dark Red	N/S																		S
26	Dark Vermilion	DkCaVr																		
52	Deep Brilliant Red	NaCmCs, ThV	●●●																OA	
48		NaCm, ThV, ZOx, TD																	O	
49	Deep Cadmium Red	N/S	●●●																	
38	Deep Madder	N/S																		
57		AaL	●●															OW		
52	Deep Madder Lake	QMga, ThV, TD	●●●●																	
38	Deep Magenta	Q, Td, ZOx	●●●●																	O
31	Deep Oriental Red	N/S	●●●																	
60	Deep Rose	OrP	●●●																	
43	Dutch Vermilion Ex.	OrP	●●●																	
147	English Red	**IrOx**	●●●●															O		
141		N/S															AG			
147	English Red Deep	**IrOx**	●●●●																	
140	English Red Light	**IrOx**	●●●●										W							
44	English Rose	N/S										W								
33	Extra Fine Carmine	N/S	●●●																	
54	Fast Light Carmine	N/S	●●●●																	

Abbreviations used to signify composition correspond to recognized chemical abbreviations only in some cases. A detailed key is included on pp84-85.

LUKAS	MAIMERI	MARABU	MARCUS ART	MICHAEL HARDING	PEBEO	PELIKAN	PENTEL	PDQ	REEVES	RICH ART	ROBERSON	ROWNEY	SCHMINCKE	SENNELIER	SHIVA	SPECTRUM	J P STEPHENSON	TALENS	TITAN	UTRECHT	VALLEJO	WEBER	WINSOR & NEWTON
													P										
											A												
																					A		
											OW												
											O												
											O												
											W												
																			O				
												OW											
									S														
			OG																				
	G																						
			G																				
			O																				
									S														
	G																						
			A																				
					G																		
			O																				
			O																				
																	O						
																	O						
	O											A							O				
					OG																		
OAW												OW											
OWG												OWP							O		A		
			G																				
			A																				

KEY O oil A acrylic W watercolor G gouache P pigment S poster K alkyd E egg tempera **Quality** O artists and students O artists O students O unspecified

COLOR	COMPOSITION	MANUFACTURERS' PERMANENCY RATING	BEROL	BLOCKX	BOCOUR	CALDER	CAL-WESTERN	CARAN D'ACHE	DANACOLORS	DURO	FERRARIO	GOLDEN	GRUMBACHER	HOLBEIN	HUNT SPEEDBALL	LAMBERTYE	LASCAUX	LEFRANC & BOURGEOIS	LIQUITEX
71 Fast Madder Lake	N/S	●●●●																	
39 Figurine Pink	N/S	●●●●																	
Fire (Permanent Light) Red	N/S																		
32 Fire Red	N/S					A		O											
34 Flame Red	PaNtR, Ans, Ars	●●										G							
37	N/S												AG						
32 Flame Red B (Red Light)	CaS-S																		
39 Flesh	TD, ZOx, CaS-S, CaSeBa	●●●●																	
39	IrOx, CaS-S, ZOx	●●●										O							
39	N/S																		
40 Flesh Colour	ZSu, CaSu, CaSe	●●																	
39	N/S																		
146 Flesh Ochre	E	●●●●															O		
133	TD, IrOx	●●●●										G							
40 Flesh Tint	IrOx, LeT, ZW	●●●																	
55 Floral Pink	Na, ZOx	●●●																	
33 French Red Vermilioned	AzP	●●											O				O		
33 French Vermilion (Subst.)	N/S																		
32 French Vermilion	N/S	●●●●											O						
61 Garnet	Q	●●●●															A		
60 Garnet Red	Q	●●●●															O		
50 Geranium	N/S	●●											G						
44 Geranium Lake	P-M-T	●●●●																	
32	OrP	●●●																	
37	AzP	●●●															G		
61	At, Au	●●							O										
53	ToR	●										W							
31	N/S									OW									
44 Geranium Lake (Anil.)	N/S	●																	
44 Geranium Pink	N/S	●																	
31 Geranium Lake Pale	Ls	●																	
46 Geranium Pink Lake	N/S	●																	
37 Geranium Red	AaL	●●●															O		
31	N/S												O						
50 Grumbacher Red	NaR	●●●										OAW							
49	BaLiR, To, Pa, NtR, Ans, Ars	●●										G							
36 Harrison Red	ToR	●●●							O										

Abbreviations used to signify composition correspond to recognized chemical abbreviations only in some cases. A detailed key is included on pp84-85.

LUKAS	MAIMERI	MARABU	MARCUS ART	MICHAEL HARDING	PEBEO	PELIKAN	PENTEL	PDQ	REEVES	RICH ART	ROBERSON	ROWNEY	SCHMINCKE	SENNELIER	SHIVA	SPECTRUM	J P STEPHENSON	TALENS	TITAN	UTRECHT	VALLEJO	WEBER	WINSOR & NEWTON
					O																		
					G																		
								K															
						G																	
			G																				
																						O	
										S					O						A		
													OA										
OG		S			OG	G																	
O																		O					
	AWG											O											
																						O	
														P									
					O																		
					OA																		
	OWG																						
																		O	O				
	O																						
OG					O									P									
														W									
														O									G
					G																		
											O		S										

KEY O oil A acrylic W watercolor G gouache P pigment S poster K alkyd E egg tempera   **Quality** O artists and students O artists O students O unspecified

No.	COLOR	COMPOSITION	MANUFACTURERS' PERMANENCY RATING	BEROL	BLOCKX	BOCOUR	CALDER	CAL-WESTERN	CARAN D'ACHE	DANACOLORS	DURO	FERRARIO	GOLDEN	GRUMBACHER	HOLBEIN	HUNT SPEEDBALL	LAMBERTYE	LASCAUX	LEFRANC & BOURGEOIS	LIQUITEX
37	Helios Red	N/S																		
146	Indian Red	**IrOx**	••••	O		O								OW						
141		S-A-S-S	••••																	
147		SyRIrOx	••••																	OW
143		N/S			AW						O			OW						
146	Indian Red Light	IrOx	••••																	
29	Indo Orange Red	PnO	••••																A	
36	Japanese Red Deep	AzR	••															O		
34	Japanese Red Light	AzR	••															O		
50	Lambertye Red	PtAz	••••														O			
50		N/S	••••														W			
	Lamp Red	IrOx	•••							O										
28	Lead Red	N/S																		
32	Light Cadmium Red	N/S	••••																	
39	Light Magenta	QMGa, Na, TD	••••																A	
39		Na, QV, TD, ZOx	••••																O	
31	Light Oriental Red	N/S	••••																	
148	Light Oxide Red	**IrOx**	••••																	
40	Light Portrait Pink	Na, QMga, TD	••••																A	
40		Na, PhO, TD, ZOx	••••																O	
141	Light Red	IrOx	••••	O		OAW							W							
140		E	••••																	
140		N/S												OW						
152	Light Red (English Red Light)	IrOx, YwH	••••										O							
52	Light Red Bright	N/S	••											O						
140	Light Red Oxide	SyRIrOx, SyHyIrOx	••••																W	
47	Lightproof Rose	OrP	•••																	
44	Madder Carmine	OrP	•••																	
52		AtL	•••																	
43		AaL	••															OW		
52	Madder Carmine Deep	OrP																		
57	Madder Deep	N/S	•••													W				
30	Madder Lake	AaL	•••																	
50		N/S														W				
	Madder Lake Carmine	OrP	••••																	
50	Madder Lake Deep	SyM	•••																	
52		AaL	••															G		
		N/S														O				

Abbreviations used to signify composition correspond to recognized chemical abbreviations only in some cases. A detailed key is included on pp84-85.

	LUKAS	MAIMERI	MARABU	MARCUS ART	MICHAEL HARDING	PEBEO	PELIKAN	PENTEL	PDQ	REEVES	RICH ART	ROBERSON	ROWNEY	SCHMINCKE	SENNELIER	SHIVA	SPECTRUM	J P STEPHENSON	TALENS	TITAN	UTRECHT	VALLEJO	WEBER	WINSOR & NEWTON
					O							OW	AGP			O			OW				O	OWK
		O																						
							G					O										A		
													O											
																					A	A		
														OP										
					OAG																			
						O																		
																			OAW					
												OW												
					O																			
										O		O				O	O							OWK
													G											
													AW											
																								G
																				O				
							O																	
													O											
													A											
																			OW					
													W	W										
	OG	W											OW											

#	COLOR	COMPOSITION	MANUFACTURERS' PERMANENCY RATING	BEROL	BLOCKX	BOCOUR	CALDER	CAL-WESTERN	CARAN D'ACHE	DANACOLORS	DURO	FERRARIO	GOLDEN	GRUMBACHER	HOLBEIN	HUNT SPEEDBALL	LAMBERTYE	LASCAUX	LEFRANC & BOURGEOIS	LIQUITEX
52	Madder Lake Garnet	AaL, FaVi	••																G	
	Madder Lake Golden	N/S	•••																	
44	Madder Lake Light	AaL, Q	•••																	
		Q	•••																	
49		SyM	•••																	
50		AaL, FaPk	••																G	
54	Madder Lake Pink	N/S	•••																	
	Madder Lake Red	AaL	•••																	
31	Madder Lake Rose	N/S															O			
52	Madder Red	AaL, AzP	•••																	
31	Madder Rose	AaLqAu	••														O			
66	Magenta	OrP	•••																	
58		Rh, DzL	•																	
64		Q					A				O							AG	A	S
58	Magenta Lake	P-M-T	•••																	
		N/S									W									
55	Magenta Red	RhL	•																G	
140	Mahogany Red	IrOx	••••																O	
48	Maroon	N/S																		
146	Mars Red	**IrOx**	••••	O						A				O			O		OG	
140		N/S																		
58	Medium Magenta	QMga, TD	••••																	OA
58		QMga, TD, ZOx	••••																	O
39	Medium Portrait Pink	SyRIrOx ZOx	••••																	O
30	Middle Oriental Red	N/S	••••																	
52	Monaco Madder	N/S									O									
36	Naphthol Crimson	NaCmCs	•••													A				A
35	Naphthol ltr Red Light	N/S							O											
	Naphthol Red	NaR																		
	Naphthaol Red Crimson	NaR	••••																	
	Naphthol Red Deep	NaR																		
35	Naphthol Red Light	NaR	••••							A										A
36		NaR, ZW	••									A				A				
37		N/S										A				A				
38	Naphthol Red Medium	N/S										A								
32	Opaque Cadmium Vermilion	CaS-S																		
139	Opaque Mars Red	**IrOx**																		
44	Opera	N/S	•								W									

Abbreviations used to signify composition correspond to recognized chemical abbreviations only in some cases. A detailed key is included on pp84-85.

LUKAS	MAIMERI	MARABU	MARCUS ART	MICHAEL HARDING	PEBEO	PELIKAN	PENTEL	PDQ	REEVES	RICH ART	ROBERSON	ROWNEY	SCHMINCKE	SENNELIER	SHIVA	SPECTRUM	J P STEPHENSON	TALENS	TITAN	UTRECHT	VALLEJO	WEBER	WINSOR & NEWTON
														W									
													G										
																			W				
																		O					
														OW									
													A										
O													OAS										
													WGS										
					G																		G
																					A		
	O																						
	G																						
										S													
	OA		G									O											O
					O						O					O							
					O																		
																							A
																				A			
																				A			
																				A			
																				A		A	
																				O			
			O																				
			O																				

KEY O oil A acrylic W watercolor G gouache P pigment S poster K alkyd E egg tempera **Quality** O artists and students O artists O students O unspecified

COLOR	COMPOSITION	MANUFACTURERS' PERMANENCY RATING	BEROL	BLOCKX	BOCOUR	CALDER	CAL-WESTERN	CARAN D'ACHE	DANACOLORS	DURO	FERRARIO	GOLDEN	GRUMBACHER	HOLBEIN	HUNT SPEEDBALL	LAMBERTYE	LASCAUX	LEFRANC & BOURGEOIS	LIQUITEX
35 Orange Red	N/S	●●●											A						
28 Orange Red Indo	N/S													A					
137 Orient Earth	N/S														O				
47 Oriental Red	AzP	●●●															A		
150 Oxide Red Deep	IrOx															A			
142 Oxide Red Light	IrOx															A			
40 Peach	AzR				OAS														
52 Peony Red	N/S	●●											O						
52 Permanent Carmine	N/S							O											
46	Q	●●●●															W		
44 Permanent Geranium	Q, Db	●●●																	
44 Permanent Madder Red 1	Q	●●●																	
52 Permanent Madder Red 2	OrP	●●●																	
46 Permanent Magenta	Q	●●●			OAWG														
57	Q, Di	●●●																	
58	Q, T															A			
48	N/S													W	W				
149 Permanent Maroon	AzC															A			
30 Permanent Red	OrP	●●●●																	
29	BtNaR	●●																	
52	AzR				OAW														
47	N/S														W				
26 Permanent Red 1	OrP	●●●																	
26	OrP, Ex	●●●																	
29 Permanent Red 2	OrP	●●●																	
29	OrP, Ex	●●●																	
34 Permanent Red 3	OrP, Ex	●●●																	
34	OrP	●●●●																	
53 Permanent Red Deep	AzP	●●●																	
49	OrP	●●																	
47 Permanent Red Light	AzP	●●●																	
44 Permanent Rose	Q	●●●●																	
46	OrP	●●●●																	
48	At	●●●●																	
50	N/S													W	W	W			
54 Permanent Rose Deep	Q	●●●●													O	A			
51 Permanent Rose Light	Q, T															A			
47 Permanent Scarlet	N/S	●●●●																	

Abbreviations used to signify composition correspond to recognized chemical abbreviations only in some cases. A detailed key is included on pp84-85.

	LUKAS	MAIMERI	MARABU	MARCUS ART	MICHAEL HARDING	PEBEO	PELIKAN	PENTEL	PDQ	REEVES	RICH ART	ROBERSON	ROWNEY	SCHMINCKE	SENNELIER	SHIVA	SPECTRUM	J P STEPHENSON	TALENS	TITAN	UTRECHT	VALLEJO	WEBER	WINSOR & NEWTON
					G																			
					W																			
												O												
													O											
													O											
												O												
												OW												
					AW																			
													A											
												W												
											O													
																						A		
		O																						
													OW											
													P											
													OW											
													P											
													P											
													OW											
																			A					
	OW												O											
	OW																			A				
												AW												OW
													W											
													O											
	O										O													
					W																			

KEY O oil A acrylic W watercolor G gouache P pigment S poster K alkyd E egg tempera **Quality** O artists and students O artists O students O unspecified

#	COLOR	COMPOSITION	MANUFACTURERS' PERMANENCY RATING	BEROL	BLOCKX	BOCOUR	CALDER	CAL-WESTERN	CARAN D'ACHE	DANACOLORS	DURO	FERRARIO	GOLDEN	GRUMBACHER	HOLBEIN	HUNT SPEEDBALL	LAMBERTYE	LASCAUX	LEFRANC & BOURGEOIS	LIQUITEX
	Permasol Magenta	N/S																		
	Permasol Pink	N/S																		
34	Permasol Red	N/S																		
37	Permasol Red Deep	N/S																		
31	Permasol Red Scarlet	N/S																		
36	Persian Red Deep	AzP	●●●																G	
33	Persian Red Light	AzP	●●●																G	
60	Perylene Red	N/S	●●●												O					
56	Phoenician Red	AeL																	G	
48	Phthalo Red	N/S						A												
50	Phthalo Red Rose	Q	●●●●																	
39	Pink	N/S							A											
56	Pink Brilliant	N/S																		
140	Pink Earth Transparent	IrOx																		
48	Pink Madder	At, Rb, Q	●●										O	O						
44		N/S	●●●																	
33	Pink Madder Lake	N/S	●●●●																	
51	Pink Tyrian	AeL, FaR																	G	
139	Portrait (Red Oxide)	IrOx	●●●●										A							
39	Portrait Pink	N/S	●●●●																A	
141	Pouzolles Red	N/S	●●●●																	
138	Pozzouli Earth	E	●●●●																	
139		IrOx	●●●●																	
138		N/S	●●																	
	Pure Cadmium Red	CaS-S	●●●●																	
35	Pure Dark Cadmium Red	N/S	●●●●																	
29	Pure Light Cadmium Red	N/S	●●●●																	
63	Purple Red	N/S																		
49	Quinacra Red	Q																AG		
50	Quinacridone Crimson	Q	●									A								
51	Quinacridone Magenta	N/S	●●●																	
49	Quinacridone Red	LnQ	●●●●							O		A								
44		N/S														A				
35	Quinacridone Red Light	Q	●									A								
46	Quinacridone Rose	Q	●●●●																	
38	Red	N/S	●	S																S
35	Red (Spectrum)	N/S																		S
60	Red Bordeaux	N/S																A		

Abbreviations used to signify composition correspond to recognized chemical abbreviations only in some cases. A detailed key is included on pp84-85.

LUKAS	MAIMERI	MARABU	MARCUS ART	MICHAEL HARDING	PEBEO	PELIKAN	PENTEL	PDQ	REEVES	RICH ART	ROBERSON	ROWNEY	SCHMINCKE	SENNELIER	SHIVA	SPECTRUM	J P STEPHENSON	TALENS	TITAN	UTRECHT	VALLEJO	WEBER	WINSOR & NEWTON
														O									
														O									
														O									
														O									
														O									
																						O	
G								O	S														
					G																		
																			O				
				W																			
				O																			
				A																			
	OW													O									
														O			O						
W	W													O									
																					OA		
				O																			
				O																			
																					A		
			G					A															A
	O																						
							K																
	OA													S							A		
									S														

KEY O oil A acrylic W watercolor G gouache P pigment S poster K alkyd E egg tempera   **Quality** O artists and students O artists O students O unspecified

#	COLOR	COMPOSITION	MANUFACTURERS' PERMANENCY RATING	BEROL	BLOCKX	BOCOUR	CALDER	CAL-WESTERN	CARAN D'ACHE	DANACOLORS	DURO	FERRARIO	GOLDEN	GRUMBACHER	HOLBEIN	HUNT SPEEDBALL	LAMBERTYE	LASCAUX	LEFRANC & BOURGEOIS	LIQUITEX
32	Red Cadmium	N/S	●●●●																	
38	Red Deep Permanent	N/S																		
26	Red Lead Imit.	AzP	●●●																	
53	Red Light	PaNtR, BaLiR, ToR, Ans, Ars	●										G							
139	Red Ochre	**E**	●●●●											OA		OW		OWG		
143		IrOx	●●●●															A		
25	Red Orange	SaR																		
143	Red Oxide	Sy, IrOx	●●●●									A								A
52		N/S										A			A					
47	Red Rose	RhP, PaNtR	●										G							
35	Red Vermilion	PeR	●●●																	
46	Red Vermilioned	AzP	●●●															O		
60	Rembrandt Rose	Q	●●●●															G		
46	Rose	N/S															G			
33	Rose Carthame	L	●																	
33		AeL	●●															G		
34	Rose Carthamus	AeL	●															W		
43	Rose Dore	RoM	●●●																	
43		N/S									O									
43	Rose Dore (Alizarin)	AaL, BtNaR	●●●																	
38	Rose Dore Madder	AaL	●●															O		
148	Rose Grey No 1	N/S	●●●●											O						
139	Rose Grey No 2	N/S	●●●●											O						
33	Rose Madder	Aa	●●●				O											W		
44		Q	●●●																	
44		SyM	●●●																	
59		At	●●	O						O	W			OW						
46		MRt	●●								W									
47		AaL	●●															O		
47		SyDhAtAu	●●																OW	
60		N/S			AW			O		O				OW						W
33	Rose Madder (Quinacridone)	Q	●●●																	
47	Rose Madder Alizarin	At	●●●																	
38	Rose Madder Antique	SyM	●●●																	
47	Rose Madder Carmine	N/S									O									
52	Rose Madder Deep	AaL	●●●																	
47		MRt	●●																	

Abbreviations used to signify composition correspond to recognized chemical abbreviations only in some cases. A detailed key is included on pp84-85.

LUKAS	MAIMERI	MARABU	MARCUS ART	MICHAEL HARDING	PEBEO	PELIKAN	PENTEL	PDQ	REEVES	RICH ART	ROBERSON	ROWNEY	SCHMINCKE	SENNELIER	SHIVA	SPECTRUM	J P STEPHENSON	TALENS	TITAN	UTRECHT	VALLEJO	WEBER	WINSOR & NEWTON
				W																			
														P									
	O																						
	G				O									WP									
		GS																					
																				A		A	
																	OAW						
																					A		
													S										W
																							OW
											O												
												OW											
OW													O					W					
																		O					
																					O		
																							OW
											O				O								
												O											
																							W
																		O					
OW																							
																							O

KEY O oil A acrylic W watercolor G gouache P pigment S poster K alkyd E egg tempera   **Quality** O artists and students O artists O students O unspecified

No	COLOR	COMPOSITION	MANUFACTURERS' PERMANENCY RATING	BEROL	BLOCKX	BOCOUR	CALDER	CAL-WESTERN	CARAN D'ACHE	DANACOLORS	DURO	FERRARIO	GOLDEN	GRUMBACHER	HOLBEIN	HUNT SPEEDBALL	LAMBERTYE	LASCAUX	LEFRANC & BOURGEOIS	LIQUITEX
52	Rose Madder Deep (contd)	DhAt	••••		O						OAW									
46	Rose Madder Genuine	**MRt**	••																	
53	Rose Madder Light	AaL	•••																	
34	Rose Madder Light (Alizarin)	SyM	•••																	
48	Rose Madder Pale	DhAt	••••		O															
54	Rose Malmaison	RhL	•																	
45		AeL	•																W	
44	Rose Red	N/S																		
56	Rose Tyrien	RhL	•																	
44		AeL	•																WG	
37	Rowney Red	Db	•••																	
54	Rowney Rose	Q	•••																	
45	Ruby Lake	Q	•••																	
56	Ruby Lake Deep	Q	••••																	
51	Ruby Lake Light	Q	•••																	
57	Ruby Madder	N/S	••••																	
36	Ruby Red	Q	••••																OW	
35	Ruby Red Deep	AzP, FaPk	•••																G	
30	Ruby Red Light	AzP	•••																G	
29		Na, DIY, ZOx, TD	•••																	O
	Salmon Pink	N/S																		
26	Saturn Red	OrP, TD	•••																	
25		N/S																		
44	Scarlet	AzP	•••														O			
36		BrCaR																		
34		N/S						G									W			
48	Scarlet Alizarin	AaL, BtNaR	•••																	
	Scarlet Earth	N/S															O			
30	Scarlet Lake	Ar	•••																	
30		ChPaNtR	•••																	
45		OrP	•••																	
48		AzR	•••			OWGS														
48		NaR, Q, Ans, Ars	•••										W							
37		Aa, BlNaR	••																	
32		N/S												OW						
144	Scarlet Red	ToR, BaLiR, Ans, Ars	•										G							
34		NkTiY, BeO, Na	••••																A	
28	Scarlet Vermilion	**MrSu**	•••																	

Abbreviations used to signify composition correspond to recognized chemical abbreviations only in some cases. A detailed key is included on pp84-85.

LUKAS	MAIMERI	MARABU	MARCUS ART	MICHAEL HARDING	PEBEO	PELIKAN	PENTEL	PDQ	REEVES	RICH ART	ROBERSON	ROWNEY	SCHMINCKE	SENNELIER	SHIVA	SPECTRUM	J P STEPHENSON	TALENS	TITAN	UTRECHT	VALLEJO	WEBER	WINSOR & NEWTON
																							OK
OWG																							
																	O						
																							G
															O								
																							G
											O												
											O												
												O											
												O											
												O											
				W																			
																					A		
												O											
					G																		
	G																						
	S							W															
										O	OW												
											O												**OW**
																							G
												W											
											W												
										O													
											OW												OW

KEY O oil A acrylic W watercolor G gouache P pigment S poster K alkyd E egg tempera **Quality** O artists and students O artists O students O unspecified

#	COLOR	COMPOSITION	MANUFACTURERS' PERMANENCY RATING	BEROL	BLOCKX	BOCOUR	CALDER	CAL-WESTERN	CARAN D'ACHE	DANACOLORS	DURO	FERRARIO	GOLDEN	GRUMBACHER	HOLBEIN	HUNT SPEEDBALL	LAMBERTYE	LASCAUX	LEFRANC & BOURGEOIS	LIQUITEX
31	Scarlet Vermilion (contd)	OrP	●●●●																	
		N/S									OW									
30	Shiva Astra Red Light	N/S																		
50	Shiva Red Crimson	N/S																		
34	Shiva Red Medium	N/S																		
	Sign Cerise	N/S																		
	Sign Magenta	N/S																		
	Sign Red	N/S																		
35	Signal Red	N/S															AG			
61	Solferino	N/S																		
61	Solferino Lake	P-M-T	●●●																	
56	Solferino Lake (Tyrian Pink)	N/S																		
53	Solid Carmine	OrP																		
50	Spectrum Red	AzP	●●●			G														
37		ToR, RL	●●●																	
		N/S																		
38	Spectrum Red Deep	N/S																		
35	Spectrum Red No 1	N/S																		
37	Spectrum Red No 2	N/S																		
34	Spectrum Scarlet	N/S																		
30	Speedball Red	N/S													OW					
52	Stephenson's Madder	Ar	●●●																	
28	Super Azo Vermilion	AzP																		
27	Talens Red Deep	AzP	●●●																	
21	Talens Red Light	AzP	●●●																	
37	Talens Red Purple	AzP	●●●																	
140	Terra Rosa	IrOx	●●●●										O							
141		N/S	●●●●											O						
141	Terra Rosa (Flesh Ochre)	IrOx	●●●●										O							
141	Terre Rosa	**E**	●●●●															O		
48	Thalo Crimson	Rb, Q	●●●										A**W**							
61	Thalo Red	Rb, Q	●●●										**W**							
52	Thalo Red Rose	Rb, Q	●●●										O							
53		Q	●●●										O							
52	Thio-Indigo Red	N/S																		
30	Titan Red Deep	OrP																		
43	Titan Red Scarlet	OrP																		
35	Titan Red Rose	OrP																		

Abbreviations used to signify composition correspond to recognized chemical abbreviations only in some cases. A detailed key is included on pp84-85.

	LUKAS	MAIMERI	MARABU	MARCUS ART	MICHAEL HARDING	PEBEO	PELIKAN	PENTEL	PDQ	REEVES	RICH ART	ROBERSON	ROWNEY	SCHMINCKE	SENNELIER	SHIVA	SPECTRUM	J P STEPHENSON	TALENS	TITAN	UTRECHT	VALLEJO	WEBER	WINSOR & NEWTON
																O								
																O								
																O								
											S													
											S													
											S													
							G																	
		O																						
														P										
																				O				
																								G
																	O							
																	O							
																	O							
																	O							
																	O							
																		O						
			G																					
																			OW					
																			OW					
																				O				
																								O
																						A		
																				O				
																				O				
																				O				

KEY O oil A acrylic W watercolor G gouache P pigment S poster K alkyd E egg tempera **Quality** O artists and students O artists O students O unspecified

No.	Color	Composition	Manufacturers' Permanency Rating	Berol	Blockx	Bocour	Calder	Cal-Western	Caran d'Ache	Danacolors	Duro	Ferrario	Golden	Grumbacher	Holbein	Hunt Speedball	Lambertye	Lascaux	Lefranc & Bourgeois	Liquitex
137	Translucent Red Oxide	**IrOx**	●●●●																	
48	Transparent Quina Magenta	Q																		
61	Transparent Garnet	AzR	●●●				O													
61		Th	●●											O				O		
140	Transparent Oxide Red	**IrOx**	●●●●																	
39	Transparent Red	AzR	●●●				O											O		
36		N/S	●●											O						
56	Transparent Rose	N/S	●●											O						
34	Transparent Vermilion	N/S	●●											O						
36	Turkish Red	AzP	●●●															G		
52	Uccello Red	AzR	●●●															W		
64	Ultramarine Red	Q	●●●●																	
65		SyU	●●●●																	
34	Utrecht Red	NaR, HnYR	●●●●																	
144	Venetian Red	**E**	●●●●		O															
141		IrOx	●●●●				O						O				O	OW	O	
140		E, IrOx	●●●●															G		
148		N/S				AW		A	O					O		OW				
141	Venice Red	N/S									O									
32	Vermilion	MrSu	●●		O															
33		OrP, MIR	●●●●																	
34		AzR	●●●				OAWS									O		G		
36		N/S		S	W			AG						OW	W	W	AG		S	
30	Vermilion (Deep)	N/S																		
28	Vermilion (Genuine)	**MrSa**	●●●																	
27	Vermilion (Hue)	PaNtR, Ans, Ars	●										w							
36		BaLiR, PaNtR, Ans, Ars	●										G							
26	Vermilion (Imit.)	IrOx	●●																	
38	Vermilion (Tint)	N/S												OW						
26	Vermilion Clear	N/S														O				
32	Vermilion Deep	**MrSu**	●●●																	
30		OrP	●●●																	
32		N/S									O									
21	Vermilion Deep (Hue)	Ans, Ars, NpR	●●●										w							
43	Vermilion Deep Imit.	AzP	●●●																	
30	Vermilion Hue	NpR	●●																	
38		N/S	●●●																	
28	Vermilion Light	**MrSu**	●●●																	

Abbreviations used to signify composition correspond to recognized chemical abbreviations only in some cases. A detailed key is included on pp84-85.

LUKAS	MAIMERI	MARABU	MARCUS ART	MICHAEL HARDING	PEBEO	PELIKAN	PENTEL	PDQ	REEVES	RICH ART	ROBERSON	ROWNEY	SCHMINCKE	SENNELIER	SHIVA	SPECTRUM	J P STEPHENSON	TALENS	TITAN	UTRECHT	VALLEJO	WEBER	WINSOR & NEWTON
												O											
		O																					
																		OW					
				G																			
O																							
												P											
																				A			
O			O								OAW							O			O		W
		G																					
				W						O			P	O		O							
																							OW
												W											
																		OW					
W				O	O				S	O													
		G																					
			O																				
OG											OA												
OW																							
												O											
					G																		
OG																							
																					O		
								OW															
OW																							

KEY O oil A acrylic W watercolor G gouache P pigment S poster K alkyd E egg tempera   **Quality** O artists and students O artists O students O unspecified

#	COLOR	COMPOSITION	MANUFACTURERS' PERMANENCY RATING	BEROL	BLOCKX	BOCOUR	CALDER	CAL-WESTERN	CARAN D'ACHE	DANACOLORS	DURO	FERRARIO	GOLDEN	GRUMBACHER	HOLBEIN	HUNT SPEEDBALL	LAMBERTYE	LASCAUX	LEFRANC & BOURGEOIS	LIQUITEX
29	Vermilion Light (contd)	OrP	●●●																	
26	Vermilion Light (Imit.)	AzP	●●●																	
28	Vermilion Pale	N/S																		
43	Vermilion Red	AzP	●●●															W		
29		N/S	●●●																	
30	Vermilion Red Tone	LeMo, OrP	●●●●																	
28		OrP	●●●●																	
20	Vivid Red Orange	Na, DiY	●●●●																A	
20		Na, DiY, TD, ZOx	●●●																	O
145	Wine Red	BaLiR, Pm	●										G							

VIOLETS

#	COLOR	COMPOSITION	MANUFACTURERS' PERMANENCY RATING	BEROL	BLOCKX	BOCOUR	CALDER	CAL-WESTERN	CARAN D'ACHE	DANACOLORS	DURO	FERRARIO	GOLDEN	GRUMBACHER	HOLBEIN	HUNT SPEEDBALL	LAMBERTYE	LASCAUX	LEFRANC & BOURGEOIS	LIQUITEX
59	Acra Violet	QMga	●●●●																	AW
58		QVi	●●●●																	O
60	Acridone Violet	Q	●●●●																	
59	Alizarin Violet	N/S	●●●																	
59	Alizarin Violet Lake	N/S	●●●																	
61	Bayeux Violet	InVi	●●●															OWG		
61	Bellini Violet	N/S			O															
66	Blue Violet	N/S																		
78		S-A-S-S																		S
66	Blue Violet (Anil.)	Ae	●																	
76	Blue Violet (Spectrum)	N/S																G		
61	Bocour Violet	N/S				AW														
59	Bordeaux	AzP	●●●													OW				
67	Bright Violet	N/S									w									
89	Brilliant Blue Purple	S-A-S-S, TD	●●●●																	
80		S-A-S-S, TD, ZOx	●●●●																	OA
60	Brilliant Purple	RhP, ClPa NtR, Pu	●																	
68		DxPp, TD	●●●										G							
64		DxPp, TD, ZOx	●●●●																A	O
58		N/S																		
73	Brilliant Violet	Dx	●●●●													O				
72		Pm	●										G							
38	Cadmium Purple	CaS-S	●●●●		O															
148	Cadmium Red Purple	N/S														O				
149	Caput Mortuum Violet	**IrOx**	●●●●																	
71	Carbazole Violet	CzOx	●●●						A											

Abbreviations used to signify composition correspond to recognized chemical abbreviations only in some cases. A detailed key is included on pp84-85.

	LUKAS	MAIMERI	MARABU	MARCUS ART	MICHAEL HARDING	PEBEO	PELIKAN	PENTEL	PDQ	REEVES	RICH ART	ROBERSON	ROWNEY	SCHMINCKE	SENNELIER	SHIVA	SPECTRUM	J P STEPHENSON	TALENS	TITAN	UTRECHT	VALLEJO	WEBER	WINSOR & NEWTON
														O										
		OG																						
							G																	
														GS										
					WG																			
														O										
														AW										

	LUKAS	MAIMERI	MARABU	MARCUS ART	MICHAEL HARDING	PEBEO	PELIKAN	PENTEL	PDQ	REEVES	RICH ART	ROBERSON	ROWNEY	SCHMINCKE	SENNELIER	SHIVA	SPECTRUM	J P STEPHENSON	TALENS	TITAN	UTRECHT	VALLEJO	WEBER	WINSOR & NEWTON
																						A		
														O										
														WP										
		G																						
														A										
														G										
											S													
														S										
		G																						
														W										
														W										
																			O					

KEY O oil A acrylic W watercolor G gouache P pigment S poster K alkyd E egg tempera   **Quality** O artists and students O artists O students O unspecified

COLOR	COMPOSITION	MANUFACTURERS' PERMANENCY RATING	BEROL	BLOCKX	BOCOUR	CALDER	CAL-WESTERN	CARAN D'ACHE	DANACOLORS	DURO	FERRARIO	GOLDEN	GRUMBACHER	HOLBEIN	HUNT SPEEDBALL	LAMBERTYE	LASCAUX	LEFRANC & BOURGEOIS	LIQUITEX
69 Carbazole Violet (contd)	N/S							O											
62 Cobalt Red Violet	**CoPs**	●●●●															O		
65 Cobalt Violet	**CoPs**	●●●●				O						W							
58	CoAoPs, MaAoPs	●●●●																	
62	CoPs, CoAoPs	●●●●																	W
66	OrP	●●●																	
57	N/S			OAW						W					O				
68 Cobalt Violet (Hue)	CoPs, MaAoPs	●●●●										O	G						
64	MaAoPs, ZOx	●●●																	
62	Pv	●																	
70 Cobalt Violet (Imit.)	DxP, AzP, ZOx	●●●●																	
58	MnPs	●●															G		
65 Cobalt Violet (Subst.)	N/S	●●●																	
64 Cobalt Violet (Tint)	N/S												O						
65 Cobalt Violet Dark	**CoPs**	●●●●																	
	N/S									W									
63 Cobalt Violet Deep	**CoPs**	●●●●		O								O			O		O		
64	N/S												O						
62 Cobalt Violet Deep (Imit.)	RhL, AzR	●●●															G		
	N/S	●●●																	
61 Cobalt Violet Deep (Subst.)	N/S	●●●																	
62 Cobalt Violet Hue	RhL, S-A-S-S, MhV, P	●●																	
57 Cobalt Violet Light	CoPs, CoAoPs	●●●●								W		O						O	
62	CoPsAi, CoAoPs	●●●●																	
62	CoPs, CtAo																		
61	N/S												OW						
62 Cobalt Violet Light (Subst.)	N/S	●●●																	
62 Cobalt Violet Light Opaque	**CoPs**	●●●●																	
64 Cobalt Violet Light Shade	CoPs, Q	●●●															O		
64 Cobalt Violet Light Tint	N/S	●											O						
Cobalt Violet Light Toxic	N/S	●●●●																	
61 Cobalt Violet Light Transparent	**CoPs**	●●●																	
61 Cobalt Violet Pale	**CoPs**	●●●●																	
58 Cobalt Violet Reddish	CoAoPs	●●●●																	
58 Compose Bordeaux	N/S	●●											A						

Abbreviations used to signify composition correspond to recognized chemical abbreviations only in some cases. A detailed key is included on pp84-85.

LUKAS	MAIMERI	MARABU	MARCUS ART	MICHAEL HARDING	PEBEO	PELIKAN	PENTEL	PDQ	REEVES	RICH ART	ROBERSON	ROWNEY	SCHMINCKE	SENNELIER	SHIVA	SPECTRUM	J P STEPHENSON	TALENS	TITAN	UTRECHT	VALLEJO	WEBER	WINSOR & NEWTON
	W		O								OW	G											OW
P																		W					
												O											
				W		S	K	O							O		P				A		
																		O					
											O	S											
	O																						
													O										
																							O
	O												OW					O	O				
OW														WP									
O													OG										
																						O	
																		O					
																			O				
															O								
													OG										
												O											
													W										
													O										
	O																						
																		O					

KEY O oil A acrylic W watercolor G gouache P pigment S poster K alkyd E egg tempera **Quality** O artists and students O artists O students O unspecified

COLOR	COMPOSITION	MANUFACTURERS' PERMANENCY RATING	BEROL	BLOCKX	BOCOUR	CALDER	CAL-WESTERN	CARAN D'ACHE	DANACOLORS	DURO	FERRARIO	GOLDEN	GRUMBACHER	HOLBEIN	HUNT SPEEDBALL	LAMBERTYE	LASCAUX	LEFRANC & BOURGEOIS	LIQUITEX
64 Compose Violet	N/S	•											A						
63 Dark Cobalt Violet	N/S	•••																	
68 Deep Violet	Dx	•••																	
69 Dioxazine Purple	DxPp	•••		A														OA	
69	CzDxVi	••••									A								
64	N/S																		W
64 Dioxazine Violet	N/S													A					
66 Egypt Violet	AzP, CzVi	••••															OAW		
144 English Red Violet	IrOx																		
61 Garnet Lake	N/S																		
58 Genuine Red Violet	QP	••••																	
68 Glowing Violet	U	••																	
60 Grey Violet	N/S	•••											W						
62 Grumbacher Purple	Dx	•••									A								
58 Helios Purple	N/S	••																	
63 Heliotrope	N/S																		
59 Indanthrene Violet	In	••••																	
64 Lambertye Violet	Dx	••••													OW				
64 Lavender	N/S																		
88 Light Blue Violet	S-A-S-S, TD, DxPp	•••																A	
80	S-A-S-S, TD	••••																O	
62 Light Cobalt Violet	N/S	•••																	
64 Light Purple	BzL	••																	
62	RhL, FaVi	•															G		
63 Lightproof Violet	OrP	••••																	
67 Light Violet	DxPp, Q	••••															A		
62 Lilac	N/S						A												
64 Manganese Violet	MaPs	••••													O				
66	MaAoPs	••••										O							
59	MnAoPyt	••••																O	
60	N/S			O															
148 Mars Violet	IrOx	••••	O												O		O		
61	SyM, IrOx	••••																	
144	RIrOx, BiH	••••									OA								
60	N/S												OAW		OW				
62 Mauve	Dx	•••										W							
69	Q, DxP, TpL, Ph	•																	
64	Q, DxP	•••																	
70	N/S			W															

Abbreviations used to signify composition correspond to recognized chemical abbreviations only in some cases. A detailed key is included on pp84-85.

LUKAS	MAIMERI	MARABU	MARCUS ART	MICHAEL HARDING	PEBEO	PELIKAN	PENTEL	PDQ	REEVES	RICH ART	ROBERSON	ROWNEY	SCHMINCKE	SENNELIER	SHIVA	SPECTRUM	J P STEPHENSON	TALENS	TITAN	UTRECHT	VALLEJO	WEBER	WINSOR & NEWTON
					OG																		
												A	S										
			G																			A	
																				A			
																							S
									A														
								K															
																			O				
O																							
													O										
													W										
														OW									
					G																		
O																							
										S													
					OAG																		
																							G
													G										
G	G				G	G															A		
	O																						
																				O			
															O		P						
	O	G	O									O											
																		O					
									O					A		O							
																					A		
																							W
																		W					
W	G					S																	

KEY O oil A acrylic W watercolor G gouache P pigment S poster K alkyd E egg tempera   **Quality** O artists and students O artists O students O unspecified

COLOR	COMPOSITION	MANUFACTURERS' PERMANENCY RATING	BEROL	BLOCKX	BOCOUR	CALDER	CAL-WESTERN	CARAN D'ACHE	DANACOLORS	DURO	FERRARIO	GOLDEN	GRUMBACHER	HOLBEIN	HUNT SPEEDBALL	LAMBERTYE	LASCAUX	LEFRANC & BOURGEOIS	LIQUITEX
61 Mauve (True Purple)	RhL, S-A-S-S	●●																	
69 Mauve Blue Shade	Dx, Ph, Q	●●●																	
63 Mauve Red Shade	Dx, Ph	●●●																	
68 Mineral Violet	MaPs	●●●●																	
66	N/S										w		OW	O					
Mineral Violet Deep	N/S										w								
70 Mineral Violet No 1	MnPs	●●●●															O		
64 Mineral Violet No 2	MnPs	●●●●															O		
80 Mountain Violet	S-A-S-S	●										G							
Opera	N/S																		
66 Parma Violet	XDyL	●																	
61	N/S	●●																	
66 Parma Violet (Anil.)	Ae	●																	
69 Permanent Blue Violet	DxP	●●●●																	
62 Permanent Light Violet	DxPp, ClCpPhB, TD	●●●																A	
62	DxPp, S-A-S-S, TD, ZOx	●●●●																	O
58 Permanent Lilac	Q, T															A			
64 Permanent Mauve	MnPs	●●●●																	
69	Dx	●●●																	
57 Permanent Purple	Q	●●●														A			
65 Permanent Red Violet	Q, DxP	●●●																	
54 Permanent Violet	QP	●●●●			G												OAW		
69	Q, DxP	●●●●																	
64	OrP	●●●●																	
69	Dx, Q	●●●																	
	CzDxVi, UVi																		
63	N/S	●●●											w						
66 Permanent Violet Deep	Is, T															A			
67 Permanent Violet Light	Is, T															A			
73	N/S													A					
58 Persian Violet	FaR	●●															G		
64 Persian Violet Deep	FaR	●●															G		
58 Persian Violet Light	FaR	●●															G		
66 Platinum Violet	N/S						O												

Abbreviations used to signify composition correspond to recognized chemical abbreviations only in some cases. A detailed key is included on pp84-85.

LUKAS	MAIMERI	MARABU	MARCUS ART	MICHAEL HARDING	PEBEO	PELIKAN	PENTEL	PDQ	REEVES	RICH ART	ROBERSON	ROWNEY	SCHMINCKE	SENNELIER	SHIVA	SPECTRUM	J P STEPHENSON	TALENS	TITAN	UTRECHT	VALLEJO	WEBER	WINSOR & NEWTON
																						O	
																							O
																							O
											O												
				O				O					OWP		O								
							S																
																							G
	G				G									G									
																		A					
					AW																		
																							OW
											O												
										O								OA					
										A													
											O							O					
	A																						
										OWG													
											A												
																				A			
A																					A		
										OG											A		

COLOR	COMPOSITION	MANUFACTURERS' PERMANENCY RATING	BEROL	BLOCKX	BOCOUR	CALDER	CAL-WESTERN	CARAN D'ACHE	DANACOLORS	DURO	FERRARIO	GOLDEN	GRUMBACHER	HOLBEIN	HUNT SPEEDBALL	LAMBERTYE	LASCAUX	LEFRANC & BOURGEOIS	LIQUITEX
62 Prism Violet	DxPp, QMga, TD	●●●																A	
62	DxPp, QMga, TD, ZOx	●●●●																	O
59 Phthalo Violet	Ph													O					
58 Purple	N/S			S			G												
39 Purple Lake	Aa, Q	●●●																	
61	AaL, OrL	●●●																	
61	BzL	●●																	
61	AaL, ThR, SyAaLs	●●																	
54 Purple Lake Madder	FaViR	●●															G		
129 Purple Madder (Alizarin)	CsL, VgBk	●●							O										
59 Purple Madder Alizarin	AaL, OrL	●●●																	
50	SyM, Q	●●●																	
66 Purple Violet	Dx	●●●●													O				
58	OrP	●●																	
62 Quinacra Violet	Q	●●●●																	
54 Quinacridone Red Violet	Q																		
57 Quinacridone Violet	Q	●●●●						O			A								
59	N/S																A		
59 Red Violet	Q	●●●																	
62	DxPpQ																A		
58	N/S														W	G		S	
Red Violet (Anil.)	Ae	●																	
58 Red Violet (Spectrum)	N/S																		
62 Reddish Violet	CoVi																		
64	N/S																		
57 Rose Violet	N/S	●●●											O						
71 Rowney Red Violet	Q	●●●																	
57 Rubine	N/S	●																	
64 Shiva Astra Violet	N/S																		
67 Shiva Violet Deep	N/S																		
66 Shiva Violet Light	N/S																		
Sign Violet	N/S																		
62 Spectrum Cobalt Violet (Syn)	N/S																		
67 Spectrum Violet	Tp, XL	●																	
	N/S																		

Abbreviations used to signify composition correspond to recognized chemical abbreviations only in some cases. A detailed key is included on pp84-85.

LUKAS	MAIMERI	MARABU	MARCUS ART	MICHAEL HARDING	PEBEO	PELIKAN	PENTEL	PDQ	REEVES	RICH ART	ROBERSON	ROWNEY	SCHMINCKE	SENNELIER	SHIVA	SPECTRUM	J P STEPHENSON	TALENS	TITAN	UTRECHT	VALLEJO	WEBER	WINSOR & NEWTON
	G				G	G			OW														S
												W											O
																						WG
												O											
												W											OW
																		W					
													W							A			
																					A		
	OA																						
																							S
												A											
														W									
														G									
										S													
		G																					
		GS																					
												O											
					G																		
															O								
															O								
															O								
										S						O							
																O							
																							G
																O							

KEY O oil A acrylic W watercolor G gouache P pigment S poster K alkyd E egg tempera **Quality** O artists and students O artists O students O unspecified

#	COLOR	COMPOSITION	MANUFACTURERS' PERMANENCY RATING	BEROL	BLOCKX	BOCOUR	CALDER	CAL-WESTERN	CARAN D'ACHE	DANACOLORS	DURO	FERRARIO	GOLDEN	GRUMBACHER	HOLBEIN	HUNT SPEEDBALL	LAMBERTYE	LASCAUX	LEFRANC & BOURGEOIS	LIQUITEX
71	Speedball Violet (Diox.)	Dx													W					
	Stable Violet	S-A-S-S, Az	••															O		
54		FaR																G		
62		N/S	•											O						
69	Thalo Purple	DxVi, S-A-S-S	•••										W							
	Thalo Violet	At, Ths	•••										O							
	Thio Indigo Violet	N/S																		
64	Thio Violet	Ths	•••										OW							
55		LiQ	•••										A							
66	Titan Violet	OrP																		
62	Transparent Violet	IsVi	•••			O												O		
65		N/S	••											O		O				
66	Transparent Vivid Violet	Cz-DxP	••••																	
62	Ultramarine Pink	DxVi, LnVl	••••															G		
63	Ultramarine Rose Light	PyPsAu	••••													O				
70	Ultramarine Violet	U	••••																	
76		SyU	••••																	
77		PsCuAlSi	••••													O				
66		S-A-S-S	•••										O							OW
64		N/S									W									
69	Violet	DxP	••••																	
69		OrP	•••																	
		Q				A														
		LP				WS														
69		N/S		S			A	G						A			A			S
63	Violet (Spectrum)	N/S																		
76	Violet (Thalo Purple)	DxVi, Ph	•••										W							
68	Violet Alizarin	Q, Dx, CnBk	•••																	
61	Violet Bluish	N/S																		
66	Violet Bright	N/S									A									
67	Violet Carmine	OrP	••																	
70	Violet Extra-Deep	FaVi	••															G		
65	Violet Extra-Light	AeL	•															W		
62	Violet Grey	N/S	••											O						
66	Violet Lake	P-M-T P	••••																	
69		DxP	••••																	
69		OrP	••																	

Abbreviations used to signify composition correspond to recognized chemical abbreviations only in some cases. A detailed key is included on pp84-85.

	LUKAS	MAIMERI	MARABU	MARCUS ART	MICHAEL HARDING	PEBEO	PELIKAN	PENTEL	PDQ	REEVES	RICH ART	ROBERSON	ROWNEY	SCHMINCKE	SENNELIER	SHIVA	SPECTRUM	J P STEPHENSON	TALENS	TITAN	UTRECHT	VALLEJO	WEBER	WINSOR & NEWTON
				G																				
																				O				
				O																				
													WG											
													P							O				
	P																							
		O																			O			
	O																					A		
																			W					
																			O					
		AWG	G				OG															A		S
								S																
										O			W											
	G																							
																				O				W
		OW																						
		O																						
								O																

KEY O oil A acrylic W watercolor G gouache P pigment S poster K alkyd E egg tempera   **Quality** **O** artists and students O artists *O* students ○ unspecified

No.	COLOR	COMPOSITION	MANUFACTURERS' PERMANENCY RATING	BEROL	BLOCKX	BOCOUR	CALDER	CAL-WESTERN	CARAN D'ACHE	DANACOLORS	DURO	FERRARIO	GOLDEN	GRUMBACHER	HOLBEIN	HUNT SPEEDBALL	LAMBERTYE	LASCAUX	LEFRANC & BOURGEOIS	LIQUITEX
63	Violet Lake (contd)	Rh L	•															G		
69		N/S														OA				
60	Violet Madder	N/S									W					O				
	Violet Oxide	SylrOx	•									A								
62	Violet Rose	N/S													A	OA				
57	Violet Rose Madder	N/S									O									
66	Winsor Fast Violet	DxVi	•••																	
66	Winsor Violet	Q, Ph	•••																	

BLUES

No.	COLOR	COMPOSITION	MANUFACTURERS' PERMANENCY RATING	BEROL	BLOCKX	BOCOUR	CALDER	CAL-WESTERN	CARAN D'ACHE	DANACOLORS	DURO	FERRARIO	GOLDEN	GRUMBACHER	HOLBEIN	HUNT SPEEDBALL	LAMBERTYE	LASCAUX	LEFRANC & BOURGEOIS	LIQUITEX
	Alizarin Blue Lake	N/S	•••																	
82	Anthraquinone Blue	InAtP										A								
85	Antwerp Blue	AklrFc, Al	••																	
78		Ph	••••															W		
	Aquamarine Blue	N/S																		
77	Ash Blue	S-A-S-S, TD	••••															G		
78	Astral Blue	N/S																		
86	Azure Blue	BaMg	••••															OG		
91		ZS, OrP	••••																	
74		S-A-S-S																G		
90		Ph, ZTW	••																	
84		TpL	•																	
87		N/S																A		
91	Azure Blue (Manganese)	N/S																		
78	Azure Cobalt	CoBl, V	••••																	
82	Bellini Blue	Ph				O														
80	Blockx Blue	CpPh	••••		O															
76	Blue	ATm, Ph	•••										G							
91		Dn																		
91		E																		
79		N/S		S															S	
75	Blue (Spectrum)	N/S																		
73	Blue B (Mid-Blue)	CoAlS																		
94	Blue G (Blue Green)	CoAlCrS																		
91	Blue Grey	N/S													OW					
81	Blue Lake	Ph					GS													
92		N/S																		

Abbreviations used to signify composition correspond to recognized chemical abbreviations only in some cases. A detailed key is included on pp84-85.

LUKAS	MAIMERI	MARABU	MARCUS ART	MICHAEL HARDING	PEBEO	PELIKAN	PENTEL	PDQ	REEVES	RICH ART	ROBERSON	ROWNEY	SCHMINCKE	SENNELIER	SHIVA	SPECTRUM	J P STEPHENSON	TALENS	TITAN	UTRECHT	VALLEJO	WEBER	WINSOR & NEWTON
OWG	O					G																	
																							K
																							O

LUKAS	MAIMERI	MARABU	MARCUS ART	MICHAEL HARDING	PEBEO	PELIKAN	PENTEL	PDQ	REEVES	RICH ART	ROBERSON	ROWNEY	SCHMINCKE	SENNELIER	SHIVA	SPECTRUM	J P STEPHENSON	TALENS	TITAN	UTRECHT	VALLEJO	WEBER	WINSOR & NEWTON
												O											
																							OW
																					AS		
						O																	
													GS										
													O										
																							G
G														O									
														P									
																							O
	G																						
	G																						
																S							
							S																
		O																					
		O																					
					O																		
	G																						S

KEY O oil A acrylic W watercolor G gouache P pigment S poster K alkyd E egg tempera **Quality** O artists and students O artists O students O unspecified

COLOR	COMPOSITION	MANUFACTURERS' PERMANENCY RATING	BEROL	BLOCKX	BOCOUR	CALDER	CAL-WESTERN	CARAN D'ACHE	DANACOLORS	DURO	FERRARIO	GOLDEN	GRUMBACHER	HOLBEIN	HUNT SPEEDBALL	LAMBERTYE	LASCAUX	LEFRANC & BOURGEOIS	LIQUITEX
87 Blue Verditer (Imit.)	CoPs	••••																W	
83 Bocour Blue	N/S			AW															
86 Bright Turquoise	N/S																		
91 Brilliant Blue	Dn																		
	PhTo																A		
89	ClCpPhBl+G,	••••																A	
90	ClCpPhBl, TD, ZOx	••••																	O
73	N/S		S																
91 Cerulean Blue	**CoSn**	••••															A	OW	
81	CoOx, TnOx	••••																	OW
91	CoOx, CrOx	••••				OWG													
91	CoCuOx	••••																A	
87	CoP	••••																	
78	ZOx, Ph	••••																	
86	CoSn, CoAl Ox	••••																	
	SnCo, ZOx	••••		O															
87	Ph	••••										O							
88	Co, Z, CrAi	••••										A							
92	U, Ph	••••												O					
92	Sd, Al, SuSc, Ph	••••																	
92	Ph, Td	•••										W							
87	Ph, ZOx, Cb	•••										G							
91	TD, CoAi	•••																	
79	CoAi	•									A								
85	N/S			OAW			O		OAW				OAWG	OW	OW				OAW
87 Cerulean Blue (Hue)	S-A-S-S	•••											G						
78	PhTD																		
78 Cerulean Blue (Imit.)	Ph, TD	••••															A		
91	Ph, ZOx	•••															G		
91 Cerulean Blue (Phthalo)	Ph, ZOx	••••															O		
89 Cerulean Blue (Tint)	N/S	•											O						
85 Cerulean Blue Hue	Ph	••••							O										
86	S-A-S-S, ClCpPhG, TD	••••																A	
91	ClCpPhBl, ZOx	••••																	O
	PhB, ZW	••••																	
86	N/S																A		
90 Cerulean Blue Phthalo	Ph, TD	••••																	

Abbreviations used to signify composition correspond to recognized chemical abbreviations only in some cases. A detailed key is included on pp84-85.

LUKAS	MAIMERI	MARABU	MARCUS ART	MICHAEL HARDING	PEBEO	PELIKAN	PENTEL	PDQ	REEVES	RICH ART	ROBERSON	ROWNEY	SCHMINCKE	SENNELIER	SHIVA	SPECTRUM	J P STEPHENSON	TALENS	TITAN	UTRECHT	VALLEJO	WEBER	WINSOR & NEWTON
		G																					
		G																					
													W										
	OAW		O										P				O	OAW					OWGK
													A										
													W										
													OG										
																						O	
													OS										
													G										
OAW				OWG	G	S	K								O								A
																		A					
																				O			
									W														
																		W					

KEY O oil A acrylic W watercolor G gouache P pigment S poster K alkyd E egg tempera   **Quality** **O** artists and students O artists *O* students ◦ unspecified

COLOR	COMPOSITION	MANUFACTURERS' PERMANENCY RATING	BEROL	BLOCKX	BOCOUR	CALDER	CAL-WESTERN	CARAN D'ACHE	DANACOLORS	DURO	FERRARIO	GOLDEN	GRUMBACHER	HOLBEIN	HUNT SPEEDBALL	LAMBERTYE	LASCAUX	LEFRANC & BOURGEOIS	LIQUITEX
Cerulean Blue Tint	Ph				O														
90 Cerulean Imit.	Ph, ZOx	●●●																	
75 Cinereous Blue	N/S	●●●●																	
75 Cinereous Blue (Perm.)	N/S	●●●●																	
79 Cobalt	N/S						AG												
78 Cobalt Blue	CoOx, AlOx	●●●●										A	OW						OAW
91	CoAi	●●●●		O												O		OW	
81	S-A-S-S, Ph	●●●●																	
87	CoAu, U	●●●																	
91	S-A-S-S	●●●											W						
75	Co ZAu																A		
79	U					W													
79	N/S		S		OAW				O	AW			OAWG	OAW	OAW		G		
73 Cobalt Blue (Hue)	S-A-S-S	●●●											G						
79	U, Ph	●●●																	
77 Cobalt Blue (Imit.)	U, ZOx	●●●●																	
75	S-A-S-S, Ph, ZOx	●●●●																O	
87	PhTD																G		
85 Cobalt Blue (Subst.)	N/S																		
76 Cobalt Blue (Tint)	N/S													OW					
73 Cobalt Blue (Ultra)	SyU	●●●●																	
77	SyU, ZOx	●●●●																	
77 Cobalt Blue Deep	CoOx, AlOx	●●●●											O						
77	CoAi	●●●●																	
74	N/S										O		O						
72 Cobalt Blue Hue	InBl, TD	●●●●							A										
72	Ph, Q, ZOx	●●●●							O										
77	S-A-S-S																		
78 Cobalt Blue Light	CoOx, AlOx	●●●●											O						
89	CoAi	●●●●																	
77	S-A-S-S	●●●●														O			
78	N/S									O									
86 Cobalt Blue Pale	N/S													O					
87 Cobalt Blue Tone	U, BaMg	●●●●																	
77 Cobalt Blue Verit.	CoAi	●●●●															G		
77 Cobalt Substitute	U, BaMg	●●●●																	
94 Cobalt Turquoise	N/S													O					
91 Coeruleum	CoSn	●●●●																	

Abbreviations used to signify composition correspond to recognized chemical abbreviations only in some cases. A detailed key is included on pp84-85.

LUKAS	MAIMERI	MARABU	MARCUS ART	MICHAEL HARDING	PEBEO	PELIKAN	PENTEL	PDQ	REEVES	RICH ART	ROBERSON	ROWNEY	SCHMINCKE	SENNELIER	SHIVA	SPECTRUM	J P STEPHENSON	TALENS	TITAN	UTRECHT	VALLEJO	WEBER	WINSOR & NEWTON
	OG																						
														G									
														W									
	A																					A	
				O								OAW	GP					AW					
																						O	
													OA										
		S			OW	OG	S	K															
												O											
													W										
	OG																						
G														O									
W																							
																		O					
																		W					
													OW					O	O				
OW	W												S								A		
																				OA			
	OW												OW					O	O				
O													S										
						G																	
													O										
													P										
																					A		
												OAW											

KEY O oil A acrylic W watercolor G gouache P pigment S poster K alkyd E egg tempera **Quality** O artists and students O artists O students O unspecified

COLOR	COMPOSITION	MANUFACTURERS' PERMANENCY RATING	BEROL	BLOCKX	BOCOUR	CALDER	CAL-WESTERN	CARAN D'ACHE	DANACOLORS	DURO	FERRARIO	GOLDEN	GRUMBACHER	HOLBEIN	HUNT SPEEDBALL	LAMBERTYE	LASCAUX	LEFRANC & BOURGEOIS	LIQUITEX
87 Coeruleum Blue	N/S	●●●●																	
87 Coeruleum (Hue)	Ph, CoBl	●●●																	
87	Ph, IrOx, ZOx, BoBk	●●●																	
94 Compose Blue	N/S	●											OW						
89, 91 Compose Blue Nos 1+2	N/S	●●											A						
84 Copper Phthalocyanine Blue	CpPh	●●																	
93 Cyan	Ph	●●●●																AG	
90	N/S	●●●																	
86 Cyan Blue	N/S																		
77 Cyanin Blue	N/S	●●●●																	
85 Dark Blue	N/S																		S
73 Dark Cobalt Blue	N/S	●●●●																	
93 Dark Turquoise	N/S																		
75 Dark Ultramarine	N/S																		
73 Dark Ultramarine Blue	N/S	●●●●																	
80 Dark Ultramarine Lake	N/S	●●●●																	
80 Deep Blue	N/S																A		
70 Deep Ultramarine	S-A-S-S	●●●●															G		
75 Delft Blue	S-A-S-S	●●●●															G		
92 France Blue	Ph	●●●●															G		
85 French Ultramarine	S-A-S-S											OW							
73 French Ultramarine Blue	N/S																		
74 French Ultramarine Deep	S-A-S-S	●●●●		O															
73 French Ultramarine Light	S-A-S-S	●●●●		O															
Helio Gen Blue	N/S									AW									
84 Hoggar Blue	Ph	●●●●															OAWG		
80 Hortensia Blue	Ph	●●●●															OW		
85 Hydranger Blue	N/S	●●●										O							
101 Ice Blue	TD, ZOx, IrOx, Ph	●●●●																	
83	N/S	●●●											OG						
91 Imitation Cerulean Blue	N/S	●●●●																	
89 Imitation Cobalt Blue	N/S	●●●●																	
70 Imitation Prussian Blue	N/S	●●●●																	
80 Indanthrene Blue	InP	●●●●																	
77 Indanthrene Blue 3R	InP																		
81 Indian Blue	InP	●●●●																OW	
87	Ph	●●●●																G	

Abbreviations used to signify composition correspond to recognized chemical abbreviations only in some cases. A detailed key is included on pp84-85.

LUKAS	MAIMERI	MARABU	MARCUS ART	MICHAEL HARDING	PEBEO	PELIKAN	PENTEL	PDQ	REEVES	RICH ART	ROBERSON	ROWNEY	SCHMINCKE	SENNELIER	SHIVA	SPECTRUM	J P STEPHENSON	TALENS	TITAN	UTRECHT	VALLEJO	WEBER	WINSOR & NEWTON
														OWPE									
											A												
											O			OGP									
	A																						
				G																			
	G																						
				W																			
																					A		
	O			G																			
		GS																					
		GS																					
				O																			
				G																			
			O													O							
OA																							
																						O	
					G										O								
				A																			
				A																			
				AW																			
	O																						
		O																					

KEY O oil A acrylic W watercolor G gouache P pigment S poster K alkyd E egg tempera   **Quality** O artists and students O artists O students O unspecified

#	COLOR	COMPOSITION	MANUFACTURERS' PERMANENCY RATING	BEROL	BLOCKX	BOCOUR	CALDER	CAL-WESTERN	CARAN D'ACHE	DANACOLORS	DURO	FERRARIO	GOLDEN	GRUMBACHER	HOLBEIN	HUNT SPEEDBALL	LAMBERTYE	LASCAUX	LEFRANC & BOURGEOIS	LIQUITEX
72	Indigo	SyIn	●●●●																	
72		SyIn, U	●●●●																	
72		Ph, IrOx	●●●●													O				
72		SyU, IrFc, IvBl	●●●																	
72		AaCs, LaBl, WiBl	●●●																	
72		TvBl, PrBl, U	●●●																	
72		LaBk, U, PrBl	●●●																	
72		Ph, CnBk, U	●●																	
82		N/S										OW		OW						
72	Indigo (Imit.)	IrFc, AaL	●●●●																G	
72	Indigo Extra	CcBo, SyU, Ph	●●●●																	
72	Indigo Modern	Ph, CcBo	●●●●																	
89	Katsura Blue	N/S	●●●											AG						
91	Lambertye Blue	Ph	●●●●														O			
73		N/S	●●●●														w			
77	Lascaux Blue	In																A		
91	Light Blue	Ph	●●●●																G	
90		N/S																G		S
92	Light Cerulean Hue	ClCpPhBl, TD, ZOx	●●●●																	O
70	Light Ultramarine	S-A-S-S	●●●●																G	
81	Lightproof Blue	Ph	●●●●																	
80		Ph, Ex	●●●																	
85	Manganese Azure Blue	**BaMg**	●●●●														OW			
92	Manganese Blue	**BaMg**	●●●●		O		O													
90		Ph	●●●●										A		O					
95		BaMg, BaSu	●●●●									**OW**								O
86		N/S				O								OAW	O	OW			w	
90	Manganese Cerulean Blue	BaMg	●●●●																	
87		BaMg, BaSu	●●●●																	
80	Marine Blue	N/S																		
82	Marine Blue Light	S-A-S-S, IvBk	●●●●																G	
72	Marine Blue Medium	S-A-S-S, IvBk	●●●●																G	
79	Medium Blue	BrU																		
81		N/S							O											
85	Mineral Blue	IrFc	●●																G	
89		N/S	●●●●																	
77	Monestial Blue (Phthalo)	Ph	●●●																	

Abbreviations used to signify composition correspond to recognized chemical abbreviations only in some cases. A detailed key is included on pp84-85.

LUKAS	MAIMERI	MARABU	MARCUS ART	MICHAEL HARDING	PEBEO	PELIKAN	PENTEL	PDQ	REEVES	RICH ART	ROBERSON	ROWNEY	SCHMINCKE	SENNELIER	SHIVA	SPECTRUM	J P STEPHENSON	TALENS	TITAN	UTRECHT	VALLEJO	WEBER	WINSOR & NEWTON
													OW										
													GS										
																							G
																							W
																							O
	W																						
												OW											
OW					OAW	G					O			OWG									S
																		O					
																		W					
													S										
		S			OG	G				S											A		
					O																		
													G										
													P										
	O																	O				O	
																							OW
															O	O					A		
					O																		
O													O										
													P										
							S																
		G																					
		S																					
													OW										
												OAW											

KEY O oil A acrylic W watercolor G gouache P pigment S poster K alkyd E egg tempera **Quality** O artists and students O artists O students O unspecified

COLOR	COMPOSITION	MANUFACTURERS' PERMANENCY RATING	BEROL	BLOCKX	BOCOUR	CALDER	CAL-WESTERN	CARAN D'ACHE	DANACOLORS	DURO	FERRARIO	GOLDEN	GRUMBACHER	HOLBEIN	HUNT SPEEDBALL	LAMBERTYE	LASCAUX	LEFRANC & BOURGEOIS	LIQUITEX
94 Monestial Turquoise (Phthalo)	Ph	●●●																	
79 Mountain Blue	U, Ph	●●●●																	
84 Myosotis Blue	TpL, CpFc	●																	
72 Navy Blue	N/S																		
76 New Blue	S-A-S-S	●●●																	
89 Orient Blue	Ph	●●●●															G		
84 Oriental Blue	N/S	●●●●											A						
91 Oriental Blue Lake	N/S	●●●●																	
Paris Blue	IrCyBl	●●●																	
	IrCyBl, Ph	●●●●																	
89	N/S									O									
80 Parrish Blue	N/S																		
89 Peacock Blue	TpL	●										G							
87	N/S												AWG						
75 Periwinkle Blue	S-A-S-S, IrFc	●●																	
91 Permanent Blue	Ph	●●●●												O					
72	S-A-S-S	●●●									O								
79	U	●●●			O														
72	N/S			O															
80 Permanent Blue Deep	PhC															A			
79 Permanent Blue Light	Ph/T															A			
87 Permanent Light Blue	ClCpPhBl+G, TD	●●●●																	A
96	ClCpPhBl+G, TD, ZOx	●●●●																	O
72 Permanent Indigo	AtBl	●●●															W		
89 Permasol Blue Deep	N/S																		
78 Permasol Blue Light	N/S																		
74 Persian Blue	Ph, S-A-S-S	●●●●															G		
76 Phthalo Blue	Ph	●●●●			OW	A		O	OA					OA					OAW
80 Phthalo Blue (Green Shade)	CpPh	●										A							
Phthalo Blue (Red Shade)	CpPh	●										A							
89 Phthalo Blue B2G	BtPh																		
94 Phthalo Greenish Blue	Ph	●●●●																	
89 Phthalo Cyanine Blue	CpPh	●●●●																	
82	ClCpPhBl	●●●●																	OA
80 Prussian Blue	IrFc	●●●			OWGS												OWG		
	Ph, U, IrOx	●●●●			O														
82	AkIrFc	●●●																	

Abbreviations used to signify composition correspond to recognized chemical abbreviations only in some cases. A detailed key is included on pp84-85.

LUKAS	MAIMERI	MARABU	MARCUS ART	MICHAEL HARDING	PEBEO	PELIKAN	PENTEL	PDQ	REEVES	RICH ART	ROBERSON	ROWNEY	SCHMINCKE	SENNELIER	SHIVA	SPECTRUM	JP STEPHENSON	TALENS	TITAN	UTRECHT	VALLEJO	WEBER	WINSOR & NEWTON
												O											
													WS										
																							G
										S													
																							O
					A								S										
					G																		
													OP										
													W										
OAW	G	G				G																	
								K															
																							G
																							G
																							OW
												OW											
											O												
	O																						
															O								
															O								
	A							K	AW				OAW					O			OA		OA
			O																				
				O																OA	A		
				O									OP					OW					
																							OWGK

KEY O oil A acrylic W watercolor G gouache P pigment S poster K alkyd E egg tempera   **Quality** O artists and students O artists O students O unspecified

	COLOR	COMPOSITION	MANUFACTURERS' PERMANENCY RATING	BEROL	BLOCKX	BOCOUR	CALDER	CAL-WESTERN	CARAN D'ACHE	DANACOLORS	DURO	FERRARIO	GOLDEN	GRUMBACHER	HOLBEIN	HUNT SPEEDBALL	LAMBERTYE	LASCAUX	LEFRANC & BOURGEOIS	LIQUITEX
72	Prussian Blue (contd)	IrMnFc	•••							O			OWG							
77		IrFc, Ph	•••																	
85		PolrFc	•••																	
72		FeAoFc	••••																OW	
82		N/S		S	OW			G	O		OW			OWG	O	OAW	G			
76	Prussian Blue (Phthalo)	Ph, OrP, CcB	••••																	
91	Pure Cerulean Blue	Co, Z	••••																	
79	Pure Cobalt Blue	CoOx, AlOx																		
	Purple Blue	Ph, Dx	••••															A		
85	Rembrandt Blue	Ph	••••																	
80	Rowney Indanthrene Blue	InBl	•••																	
88	Royal Blue	U, TD	••••																	
78		TD, CoAi, U	••••																	
88		CoAi, ZOx, TD																O		
88		N/S																		
78	Royal Blue Deep	TD, ZOx, U	•••																	
96	Royal Blue Light	TD, ZOx, U	•••																	
95	Sapphire Blue	Ph	•••															OA		
89		N/S	•••																	
86	Sevres Blue	Ph, ZOx	••••																	
89	Shiva Blue Deep	N/S																		
	Shiva Blue Light	N/S																		
	Sign Blue	N/S																		
75	Sky Blue	Ph, ZOx	••••																	
75		S-A-S-S	••••															G		
89		Ph	•••			OGP														
87		S-A-S-S, TmL	•																	
94	Space Blue	Ph, ZOx	••••															O		
87	Spectrum Blue	Ph	•••			G														
75		N/S																		
91	Spectrum Cerulean Blue	N/S																		
77	Spectrum Cobalt Blue	N/S																		
72	Speedball Blue (Phthalo)	Ph	•••												W					
81	Stephenson's Blue	Ph	•••																	
87	Thaline Blue	CpPh, ZOx	••••	O																
80	Thalo Blue	Ph	•••										OAW							
80	Titan Blue	Ph	••••																	

Abbreviations used to signify composition correspond to recognized chemical abbreviations only in some cases. A detailed key is included on pp84-85.

LUKAS	MAIMERI	MARABU	MARCUS ART	MICHAEL HARDING	PEBEO	PELIKAN	PENTEL	PDQ	REEVES	RICH ART	ROBERSON	ROWNEY	SCHMINCKE	SENNELIER	SHIVA	SPECTRUM	J P STEPHENSON	TALENS	TITAN	UTRECHT	VALLEJO	WEBER	WINSOR & NEWTON
												WG											
	OW										OW		OWGP	O							O		
OW	OWG			O	G	S	K	W	S	O						O					A		
																		O					
																				OA			
																				OA			
																		OAW					
											OA												
												G											
												A											
O						S																	
												O											
												O											
												S	G										
																		O					
														O									
														O									
									S														
																		O					
	OAG																						
												G											
																							G
																O							
																O							
																O							
																	O						
																			O				

KEY O oil A acrylic W watercolor G gouache P pigment S poster K alkyd E egg tempera **Quality** **O** artists and students O artists O students O unspecified

COLOR	COMPOSITION	MANUFACTURERS' PERMANENCY RATING	BEROL	BLOCKX	BOCOUR	CALDER	CAL-WESTERN	CARAN D'ACHE	DANACOLORS	DURO	FERRARIO	GOLDEN	GRUMBACHER	HOLBEIN	HUNT SPEEDBALL	LAMBERTYE	LASCAUX	LEFRANC & BOURGEOIS	LIQUITEX
82 Touareg Blue	Ph	••••															OW		
96 Transparent Blue	Ph	•••			O												O		
84	N/S	••											O						
92 Transparent Green Blue	Ph	•															G		
82 Transparent Vivid Primary Blue	BtPh	••••																	
90 Turquoise	TD, Ph	••••																	
93	OrP	•••																	
92	Ph, Ex	•••																	
91	Ac, Tm	•										W							
93	N/S						AG												S
92 Turquoise (Phthalo)	PhCp	•									A								
91 Turquoise Blue	BaMn	••••																	
91	Ph	••••																	
92	Ph, TD	••••														A	AG		
90	Ph, ZOx	••••															O		
93	U, Ph	••••													O				
93	Ph	••																	
86	N/S									OW			OWG		OAW	AG			
71 Turquoise Blue Deep	ATm, Ph	•										G							
75 Turquoise Blue Light	ATm	•										G							
72 Ultra Blue	Ph	•••												O					
80	N/S			A										W					
76 Ultramarine	SyU	••••																	
73	S-A-S-S	••••																	
73	N/S						AG			AW					OAW				
83 Ultramarine Ash Blue	LI	•••																	
75 Ultramarine Blue	U	••••																	
74	S-A-S-S	••••							OA			A	OAWG				A	OAW	
74	N/S			OAW		A		O		W	A		OA	A		AG			
73 Ultramarine Dark	U	••••																	
73	SyU	••••																	
73 Ultramarine Deep	U	••••																	
74	S-A-S-S	••••													O	WG			
76	SyU	••••																	
79	N/S									O									
78 Ultramarine Light	U	••••																	
73	S-A-S-S	••••													O	W			
75	SyU	••••																	

Abbreviations used to signify composition correspond to recognized chemical abbreviations only in some cases. A detailed key is included on pp84-85.

LUKAS	MAIMERI	MARABU	MARCUS ART	MICHAEL HARDING	PEBEO	PELIKAN	PENTEL	PDQ	REEVES	RICH ART	ROBERSON	ROWNEY	SCHMINCKE	SENNELIER	SHIVA	SPECTRUM	J P STEPHENSON	TALENS	TITAN	UTRECHT	VALLEJO	WEBER	WINSOR & NEWTON
			O																				
																						OA	
												A											
												G											
												A											
																				A			
															O								
																			O				
																	W						
																	A						
																	O						
																							G
					WG	G				S													
																	A						
	OAW											W	O										WG
	AWG					O	S																W
												AW										OA	
																			OA				
					OAWG				K	S		GS									**A**		A
												P											
												O											
																							O
	O																						
																			O				
																	OW						
OAG	OG					G							OWGP	O									S
												O											
																					O		
O																			O				
												GS	GS				OW						

KEY O oil A acrylic W watercolor G gouache P pigment S poster K alkyd E egg tempera   **Quality** **O** artists and students O artists *O* students ○ unspecified

COLOR	COMPOSITION	MANUFACTURERS' PERMANENCY RATING	BEROL	BLOCKX	BOCOUR	CALDER	CAL-WESTERN	CARAN D'ACHE	DANACOLORS	DURO	FERRARIO	GOLDEN	GRUMBACHER	HOLBEIN	HUNT SPEEDBALL	LAMBERTYE	LASCAUX	LEFRANC & BOURGEOIS	LIQUITEX
81 Ultramarine Light (contd)	N/S										O		OWG						
67 Ultramarine No 1 Deep	S-A-S-S	●●															O		
69 Ultramarine No 2 Light	S-A-S-S	●●															O		
73 Ultramarine Pale	N/S																		
75 Utrecht Blue	PhB, TW																		
91 Verditer Blue	N/S	●●●●											OW						
80 Winsor Blue	Ph	●●●																	

GREENS

COLOR	COMPOSITION	MANUFACTURERS' PERMANENCY RATING	BEROL	BLOCKX	BOCOUR	CALDER	CAL-WESTERN	CARAN D'ACHE	DANACOLORS	DURO	FERRARIO	GOLDEN	GRUMBACHER	HOLBEIN	HUNT SPEEDBALL	LAMBERTYE	LASCAUX	LEFRANC & BOURGEOIS	LIQUITEX
111 Acacia Green	Ph, LeCh	●●															G		
118 Acanthus Green	N/S	●●●●																	
105 Alizarin Green	Ph, TaL	●●											A						
104	N/S	●●●●																	
119 Antioche Green Deep	AzY, Ph	●●●															O		
118 Antioche Green Light	Ph, AzP																W		
108	AzY, Ph	●●															O		
125 Antique Green Earth	E	●●●●																	
Armor Green	Ph	●●●●															OAWG		
Astral Green	N/S												A						
122 Aubusson Green	Ph	●●●●											O				OW		
105 Baryte Green	N/S	●●●																	
100 Bellini Green	Ph				O														
102 Blockx Green	ClCpPh	●●●●		O															
103 Blue Green	CrOx																		
100	N/S															A			S
94 Blue Green (Spectrum)	N/S																		
108 Bocour Green	PH				WA														
126 Bohemian Green Earth	E	●●●●																	
125	Cr, Ir, Al Sis	●●●●																	
106 Bright Aqua Green	ClCpPhG+Bl, TD	●●●●																	A
105	ClCpPhG+BL, TD, ZOx																	O	
111 Bright Green	Ph, ArY	●●●																	
103	F, Ph	●●●●												OW					
119	N/S													OWA					
112 Brilliant Green	Ph, Qt	●●●●															A		
97	Ph, AzY	●●●										G					G		

Abbreviations used to signify composition correspond to recognized chemical abbreviations only in some cases. A detailed key is included on pp84-85.

LUKAS (OAG)	LUKAS (OG)	MAIMERI	MARABU	MARCUS ART	MICHAEL HARDING	PEBEO	PELIKAN	PENTEL	PDQ	REEVES	RICH ART	ROBERSON	ROWNEY	SCHMINCKE	SENNELIER	SHIVA	SPECTRUM	J P STEPHENSON	TALENS	TITAN	UTRECHT	VALLEJO	WEBER	WINSOR & NEWTON
														OWGP	O									S
							G																	
																				A				
																								OWG

LUKAS (OAG)	LUKAS (OG)	MAIMERI	MARABU	MARCUS ART	MICHAEL HARDING	PEBEO	PELIKAN	PENTEL	PDQ	REEVES	RICH ART	ROBERSON	ROWNEY	SCHMINCKE	SENNELIER	SHIVA	SPECTRUM	J P STEPHENSON	TALENS	TITAN	UTRECHT	VALLEJO	WEBER	WINSOR & NEWTON
														O										
														W	O									
O																								
											O													
														OP										
G																								
	S													W										
									S															
GP														O										
														P										
														A										

KEY O oil A acrylic W watercolor G gouache P pigment S poster K alkyd E egg tempera **Quality** O artists and students ◑ artists ◔ students ○ unspecified

COLOR	COMPOSITION	MANUFACTURERS' PERMANENCY RATING	BEROL	BLOCKX	BOCOUR	CALDER	CAL-WESTERN	CARAN D'ACHE	DANACOLORS	DURO	FERRARIO	GOLDEN	GRUMBACHER	HOLBEIN	HUNT SPEEDBALL	LAMBERTYE	LASCAUX	LEFRANC & BOURGEOIS	LIQUITEX
118 Brilliant Green (contd)	Ph					S													
115	ArY, Ph, ZOx	•••																	
111	ClCpPhG, AyY, TD, ZOx																		O
103	N/S		S						W								G		O
111 Brilliant Green (Anil)	An	•																	
114 Brilliant Yellow Green	PhAzY																		
128 Bronze Green	N/S	••••																	OA
97 Brunswick Green	N/S	••••																	
108 Cadmium Green	CaS	••••											G						
108	CS, Ph	••••										O							
105	CaS, CrOx	••••																	
119	CaS, V	•••															O		
121	CaS, Ph, OrP	•••																	
111	CaS, CrOx	•••																	
103	N/S	•••																	
102 Cadmium Green Deep	CaS, CrOx	••••																	
103	CaS, Ph																		
122	N/S	•••														A			
102 Cadmium Green Deep (Hue)	Ph, AzP, ZOx	•••											OAW						
111 Cadmium Green Light	CaS, CrOx	••••															O		
112	CaS, Ph															A			
117	N/S	•••																	
111 Cadmium Green Light (Hue)	Ph, AzP, ZOx	•••											A						
118 Cadmium Green Medium	CaS, Ph															A			
108 Cadmium Green Middle	N/S	•••											OA						
110 Cadmium Green Pale	CaS, V	•••																	
111	N/S	••••											OWG						
112 Cadmium Green-Yellow	CaS, Ph															A			
119 Celadon Green	Ph, AzY	•••															A		
100	N/S	•••											O				G		
China Vermilion	N/S								W										
125 Chartreuse	N/S	••••																	
99 Chinese Green	BtNN	••																	
119 Chrome Green	LeCh, IrFc	•••																	O
114	LeCh-PrBlC	•••																	

Abbreviations used to signify composition correspond to recognized chemical abbreviations only in some cases. A detailed key is included on pp84-85.

LUKAS	MAIMERI	MARABU	MARCUS ART	MICHAEL HARDING	PEBEO	PELIKAN	PENTEL	PDQ	REEVES	RICH ART	ROBERSON	ROWNEY	SCHMINCKE	SENNELIER	SHIVA	SPECTRUM	JP STEPHENSON	TALENS	TITAN	UTRECHT	VALLEJO	WEBER	WINSOR & NEWTON
																							G
	O					G																	
														G									
													W										
					G																		
					G								W										
													A										
	O																						
												O											
													O										
											O												O
					OAG										O								
																		O					
														O									
																		O	.				
													O					O					
														O									
													S					O					
													O										O
						G																	
																							O
												O											

KEY O oil A acrylic W watercolor G gouache P pigment S poster K alkyd E egg tempera   **Quality** O artists and students O artists O students O unspecified

	COLOR	COMPOSITION	MANUFACTURERS' PERMANENCY RATING	BEROL	BLOCKX	BOCOUR	CALDER	CAL-WESTERN	CARAN D'ACHE	DANACOLORS	DURO	FERRARIO	GOLDEN	GRUMBACHER	HOLBEIN	HUNT SPEEDBALL	LAMBERTYE	LASCAUX	LEFRANC & BOURGEOIS	LIQUITEX
117	Chrome Green (contd)	CrY, ClCpPh	••••		O															
95	Chrome Green (Imit.)	AzNk, Ph	••••															W		
	Chrome Green Dark	N/S	••••																	
101	Chrome Green Deep	LeCh, Ph	•••															G		
99		N/S	••															G		
119	Chrome Green Light	LeCh, Ph	•••																	
122		N/S	•••															G		
107	Chrome Green No 1.	AzY, IrFc	••															O		
99	Chrome Green No 2.	AzY, Ph	•••															O		
113	Chrome Green No 3.	AzY, Ph	•••															O		
117	Chrome Green No 4.	AzY, Ph	•••															O		
112	Chrome Green No 5.	AzY, Ph	•••															O		
124	Chrome Oxide Green	CrOx	••••														A			
120	Chromium Oxide Green	CrOx	••••			OAG				A		A	OAW					A		
121		CrOx, TD, Ans, Ars	••••										G							
124		AhCuSx	••••																	
124		N/S	••••			O									OA					
10	Cinnabar Green	CrY, PrBl, RwSi	••																	
116		LeCh, IrOx, Ph	••																	
		N/S									AW									
95	Cinnabar Green Deep	Ph, OrP	••••																	
121		AzP, Ph	•••																	
120		IrOx, OrP	•••																	
100		CrY, PrBl, Rw Si	••																	
127		N/S	•••									OW		O						
99	Cinnabar Green Deep (Imit.)	N/S	•••																	
119	Cinnabar Green Deep Ex.	CaS, CrOx	••••																	
111	Cinnabar Green Light	Ph, OrP	••••																	
114		IrOx, OrP	•••																	
125		LeCh, IrOx, Ph	••																	
10		N/S	•••									OW								
109	Cinnabar Green Light Ex.	CaS, SyU	••••																	
116	Cinnabar Green Pale	LeCr, IrOx, Ph	••																	
113		N/S																		
113	Cinnabar Green Yellow	N/S	•••																	
10	Cinnabar Green Yellowish	AzP, Ph	•••																	
105	Cobalt Green	Co, ZOx	••••			O												O		

Abbreviations used to signify composition correspond to recognized chemical abbreviations only in some cases. A detailed key is included on pp84-85.

LUKAS	MAIMERI	MARABU	MARCUS ART	MICHAEL HARDING	PEBEO	PELIKAN	PENTEL	PDQ	REEVES	RICH ART	ROBERSON	ROWNEY	SCHMINCKE	SENNELIER	SHIVA	SPECTRUM	JP STEPHENSON	TALENS	TITAN	UTRECHT	VALLEJO	WEBER	WINSOR & NEWTON
												O											
												O			O								O
													OWGP										
												O			O								
												O	OWGP										O
																						OA	
																		OAW		OA			
									A				OWP								A		
																							O
													O										
													S										
													OG										
	O																						
																		O					
																							O
	G					G							O										
G																							
																		O					
	O												G										
																		O					
													O										
													O										
																		O					
													O										
						G																	
													OG										
	O																						
											O							W					OW

KEY O oil A acrylic W watercolor G gouache P pigment S poster K alkyd E egg tempera   **Quality** O artists and students O artists O students O unspecified

COLOR	COMPOSITION	MANUFACTURERS' PERMANENCY RATING	BEROL	BLOCKX	BOCOUR	CALDER	CAL-WESTERN	CARAN D'ACHE	DANACOLORS	DURO	FERRARIO	GOLDEN	GRUMBACHER	HOLBEIN	HUNT SPEEDBALL	LAMBERTYE	LASCAUX	LEFRANC & BOURGEOIS	LIQUITEX
105 Cobalt Green (contd)	Co-ZC, CaSv	●●●●																	
98	Co-ZC, OrP	●●●																	
105	N/S	●●●													W				
123 Cobalt Green Deep	Co, ZOx	●●●●																	
94	IrCh, Co	●●●														O			
122	N/S	●●●●								O									
105 Cobalt Green Light	Co, ZOx	●●●●														O	O		
105	N/S	●●●●								O									
105 Cobalt Green Pale	Co, ZOx	●●●●														O			
94 Cobalt Turquoise	Al, Co, CrOx	●●●																	
105 Compound Green	OrPs, CaY	●●●●																	
108 Corot Green	Ph, IvBl	●●●●															G		
94 Cyanin Green	Ph	●●●●																	
99 Cypress Green	NNG	●●●●																	
94 Cyprus Green	Tm, AL	●															G		
98 Cyprus Green I	N/S																		
111 Cyprus Green II	N/S																		
102 Cyprus Green 1 Permanent	AzNk, CrOx	●●●●															W		
111 Cyprus Green 2 Permanent	Ph, AzP	●●●●															W		
108 Dark Bright Green	N/S	●●●●																	
94 Dark English Green	N/S	●●●																	
102 Dark Green	N/S																		
122 Dark Hooker Green	N/S	●●●●														A		S	
104 Deep English Green	N/S	●●●●																	
116 Dirty Green	AyYG, SyHyIrOx, BoApCn	●●●																	O
108 Emerald Green	Ph	●●●●			OAW GS														
111	Ph, TD	●●●●							O										
108	Ph, OrP	●●●●																	
123	Ph, ZOx	●●●●																	
111	CaSB, TD, Ph	●●●●																	
106	Ph, AzP	●●●																	
118	AzP, Ph, ZOx	●●●																	
103	Ph, Ans, Ars	●●●										W							
105	ClCpPhG, AyY, TD	●●●●																AS	
108	ClCpPhG, AyY, TD, ZOx	●●●●																	O

Abbreviations used to signify composition correspond to recognized chemical abbreviations only in some cases. A detailed key is included on pp84-85.

LUKAS	MAIMERI	MARABU	MARCUS ART	MICHAEL HARDING	PEBEO	PELIKAN	PENTEL	PDQ	REEVES	RICH ART	ROBERSON	ROWNEY	SCHMINCKE	SENNELIER	SHIVA	SPECTRUM	JP STEPHENSON	TALENS	TITAN	UTRECHT	VALLEJO	WEBER	WINSOR & NEWTON
												G											
												O											
				O		S							W		O								
	O											W						O	O				O
													OP										
	O											WP						O					
													OP										
												O											
																							OW
																			O				
				W																			
																							G
					G																		
					G																		
				G																			
				O																			
					O					S											A		S
				W																			
				O																			
																		A					
																		W					
																		O					
																						O	
OW																							
																		O					

KEY O oil A acrylic W watercolor G gouache P pigment S poster K alkyd E egg tempera **Quality** O artists and students O artists O students O unspecified

COLOR	COMPOSITION	MANUFACTURERS' PERMANENCY RATING	BEROL	BLOCKX	BOCOUR	CALDER	CAL-WESTERN	CARAN D'ACHE	DANACOLORS	DURO	FERRARIO	GOLDEN	GRUMBACHER	HOLBEIN	HUNT SPEEDBALL	LAMBERTYE	LASCAUX	LEFRANC & BOURGEOIS	LIQUITEX
108 Emerald Green (contd)	ClCpPhG, AyY, 10G, ZOx																	W	
108	N/S	•••			W		GA			OW						G			
108 Emerald Green (Imit.)	Ph, Z, Mn	•••															W		
115 Emerald Green (Subst.)	N/S	•••																	O
98 Emerald Green Extra	Ph, ZOx	••••																	
117 Emerald Tint	N/S																		
102 Emerald Green Viridian	CuHx	••••		O															
122 English Green	N/S	••••												OW					
97 English Green Deep	F, Ph	••••												O					
112 English Green Light	F, Ph	••••												O					
122 English Green Medium	IrFc, LeCh	••															G		
110 Extra Light English Green	N/S	•••																	
101 Fir Green	E, Ph, CcBo	••••																	
102 Forest Green	BaS of A3, NaY, Ph, Tm, Ans, Ars	•••										G							
104 French Green	N/S																		
116 Geniune Golden Green	OrP	•••																	
115 Green	N/S																		
117 Green (Spectrum)	N/S																S		
103 Green Deep	Ph, Ans, Ars	•••										G							
	N/S													O					
124 Green Earth	**E**	••••												W					
125	E, OrP	••••																	
99	IrOx, Ph	••••							O										
120	ChOx, IrOx, Mn	••••									W								
122	IrOx + ChOx	••••									O								
125	ChOx, E	••••																	
122	HyCuSx, CcNIIrOx Mn, BoApCn	••••																W	
125	E, Ph	•••																	
122	N/S	••••			OAW					W			O						
125 Green Earth Ancient	N/S	••••								O									
125 Green Earth Hue	NIEP, PhB	••••																	
126	HsCuSx, NIIrOxMn, BoApCn	••••																O	
112 Green Field	Ph, LeCh	•••																G	
104 Green G	Co-Al-NK-TC																		
116 Green Gold	**NKAzP**	••••																	
116	N/S				A			O		A	A								

Abbreviations used to signify composition correspond to recognized chemical abbreviations only in some cases. A detailed key is included on pp84-85.

	LUKAS	MAIMERI	MARABU	MARCUS ART	MICHAEL HARDING	PEBEO	PELIKAN	PENTEL	PDQ	REEVES	RICH ART	ROBERSON	ROWNEY	SCHMINCKE	SENNELIER	SHIVA	SPECTRUM	JP STEPHENSON	TALENS	TITAN	UTRECHT	VALLEJO	WEBER	WINSOR & NEWTON
	OWG				**O**AWG		S			S				OWG								A		O
															PE									
																			O					
																								S
					O														O					
		S																						
														O										
																S						A		
								S																
	OW																							
														G										
														W										
														OAG										
	OW				**O**W				K					O	**O**WP									
																						O		
			G																					
		A																						
					WG				K															

KEY O oil A acrylic W watercolor G gouache P pigment S poster K alkyd E egg tempera **Quality** **O** artists and students O artists *O* students ◯ unspecified

COLOR		COMPOSITION	MANUFACTURERS' PERMANENCY RATING	BEROL	BLOCKX	BOCOUR	CALDER	CAL-WESTERN	CARAN D'ACHE	DANACOLORS	DURO	FERRARIO	GOLDEN	GRUMBACHER	HOLBEIN	HUNT SPEEDBALL	LAMBERTYE	LASCAUX	LEFRANC & BOURGEOIS	LIQUITEX
103	Green Lake	P-M-T	•••																	
117		Ph, Ar	•••																	
101		N/S									O									
97	Green Lake Deep	Ph	••••																	
101		OrP	•••																	
		N/S																		
120	Green Lake Light	OrP	••••																	
127		OrP	•																	
124	Green Lake Permanent	Ph, An	••••																	
117	Green Light	Pm, Ans, Ars, TD	••															W		
111		N/S											G							
	Green Light (Anil.)	An	•					A									O			
111	Green Medium	Pm, Ph, Ans, TD	•••										G							
122	Green Oxide	N/S						A												
122	Green Oxide of Chromium	CrOx	••••															OW		
		N/S																		
108	Green Paul Veronese	OrP	••••																	
	Green-Yellow	N/S																		
102	Grumbacher Permanent Bright Green	Ans, Ars, Ph	•••										O							
112		Ph, Ans, Ca, ZOx	•••										O							
114	Grumbacher Yellow Green	Pm, Ans, Ars, TD	••										G							
118	Holly Green	N/S																		
117	Hooker's Green	Ph, AzP	••••																	
99		Fe-Ni-Bt-Na	••										O					W		
		IrBtNN	•••																A	
124		ClCpPhG, AyY, BoApCn	••••																W	
		NiG			W															
114		N/S	•••										A		A	W				
122 / 103	Hooker's Green 1 + 2	Ph, OrP	••••																	
103	Hooker's Green Dark	Ph, IrNa	••																	
103	Hooker's Green Deep	Ph, AzP, CcE	••••																	
101		Ph, Ans, Ars	••										W							
99		Ans, Ars, NP	••											W						
99		N/S	••		A															
108	Hooker's Green Light	Ph, CcE	••••																	
121		Ph, IrNa	••																	

Abbreviations used to signify composition correspond to recognized chemical abbreviations only in some cases. A detailed key is included on pp84-85.

	LUKAS	MAIMERI	MARABU	MARCUS ART	MICHAEL HARDING	PEBEO	PELIKAN	PENTEL	PDQ	REEVES	RICH ART	ROBERSON	ROWNEY	SCHMINCKE	SENNELIER	SHIVA	SPECTRUM	JP STEPHENSON	TALENS	TITAN	UTRECHT	VALLEJO	WEBER	WINSOR & NEWTON
		O																						
																	O							
		G																						
														W										
														OS										
					G																			
														W										
														O										
															G									
					G																			
														OS										
														W										
										S														
																				A				
																						A		
										O	A		W									A		
													W											
																								W
																		W						
						W																		
																		W						
																								W

KEY O oil A acrylic W watercolor G gouache P pigment S poster K alkyd E egg tempera   **Quality** O artists and students O artists O students O unspecified

COLOR	COMPOSITION	MANUFACTURERS' PERMANENCY RATING	BEROL	BLOCKX	BOCOUR	CALDER	CAL-WESTERN	CARAN D'ACHE	DANACOLORS	DURO	FERRARIO	GOLDEN	GRUMBACHER	HOLBEIN	HUNT SPEEDBALL	LAMBERTYE	LASCAUX	LEFRANC & BOURGEOIS	LIQUITEX
102 Hooker's Green Light (contd)	Ph, Ars, Ans	••										W							
	Ans, Ars, NiP	••										W							
122	ClCpPhG, AyY, BaApCn	••••																W	
115 Hooker's Green Pale	N/S	••																	
104 Imitation Veronese Green	N/S	••••																	
97 Japanese Green Deep	Ph, AzY	•••																	OG
112 Japanese Green Light	Ph, AzY	•••																	OG
Jenkins Green	ApCn, NkAz	•									A								
102 Lambertye Green	Ph	••••													O				
122 Lamoriniere Green	ChOx	••••	O																
102 Lascaux Green Deep	PhC																A		
97	Ph-TC																A		
124 Leaf Green	CaSBA, IrOx, CaS-S	••••																	
113	Ph				WGS														
110	N/S		S																
125 Leaf Green Dark	CaSB, IrOx	••••																	
110 Leaf Green Light	CaSB, IrOx	••••																	
112 Light Bright Green	N/S	••••																	
119 Light Cadmium Green	N/S	••••																	
7 Light Chinese Green	N/S	••••																	
104 Light Emerald Green	N/S	••••																	
108	ClCpPhG, AyY, TD, ZOx	••••																O	
114 Light English Green	N/S	•••																	
111 Light Green	F, Ph	••••													O				
117	V																		
110	N/S	••••													AW				
106 Light Green Bluish	N/S																		
103 Light Green Deep	Ph, AzY	••••															G		
112 Light Green Oxide	VtNk, Z, TOx	••••																	
112	NkCoTOx	••••																A	
111	NkTi, CoZOx													A			A		
123 Light Hooker Green	N/S	••••								W									
Lime Green	Qt, Ph	••••															A		
111 May Green	Ph, OrP	••••																	
115	BrGPt																		
116	N/S																		

Abbreviations used to signify composition correspond to recognized chemical abbreviations only in some cases. A detailed key is included on pp84–85.

LUKAS	MAIMERI	MARABU	MARCUS ART	MICHAEL HARDING	PEBEO	PELIKAN	PENTEL	PDQ	REEVES	RICH ART	ROBERSON	ROWNEY	SCHMINCKE	SENNELIER	SHIVA	SPECTRUM	JP STEPHENSON	TALENS	TITAN	UTRECHT	VALLEJO	WEBER	WINSOR & NEWTON
									W														
				A																		W	
																					O		
												S											
														O									
																					O		
																					O		
				G																			
				W																			
				G																			
				G																			
				O																			
												S											
				G									W										S
					G																		
																					A		
				W																			
												W											
												O											
	G																						
					G																		

KEY O oil A acrylic W watercolor G gouache P pigment S poster K alkyd E egg tempera   **Quality** O artists and students o artists O students O unspecified

COLOR	COMPOSITION	MANUFACTURERS' PERMANENCY RATING	BEROL	BLOCKX	BOCOUR	CALDER	CAL-WESTERN	CARAN D'ACHE	DANACOLORS	DURO	FERRARIO	GOLDEN	GRUMBACHER	HOLBEIN	HUNT SPEEDBALL	LAMBERTYE	LASCAUX	LEFRANC & BOURGEOIS	LIQUITEX
107 Medium Green	BrVrG																		
108 Middle Bright Green	N/S	••••																	
108 Middle English Green	N/S	•••																	
125 Middle Olive	N/S						G												
117 Mistletoe Green	ArY, Ph	•••																	
99 Mixed Green Deep	ChOx, CoY	••••		O															
124 Mixed Green Light	ChOx, ZoX	••••		O															
122 Moss Green	OrP	•••																	
99	NN, Ph	•••																	
	LeCh																G		
125 Olive Green	GOx	••••														W			
125	YOx											G							
125	NIlrOxMn, ClCpPhG	••••																	O
107	NN	••••																	
116	Ph, At	••••															G		
125	E, BtNN	••••															W		
125	Rs Wi, WiG	•••													OW				
125	Ph, Al	•••																	
120	OrP	•••																	
120	Ph, OrP, SyM	•••																	
125	AzP, CcE	•••																	
125	Bl, Ph, IrOx	•••																	
125	AlL, S-A-S-S	••																	
125	Ph				G														
119	CrAzY																		
102	EG															A			
116	N/S	•••		W										W					O
Olive Green Deep	Ph, OrP	••••																	
Olive Lake	N/S																		
122 Opaque Green	AzP, CrOx	•••																	
103 Opaque Green Light	Ph, ZS	••••																	
120	OrP	••••																	
122 Opaque Chromium Oxide	**CrOx**	••																	
118 Oriental Green	N/S	••••								OA									
94 Oriental Green Lake	N/S	••••																	
Oxide of Chrome	N/S																		

Abbreviations used to signify composition correspond to recognized chemical abbreviations only in some cases. A detailed key is included on pp84-85.

LUKAS	MAIMERI	MARABU	MARCUS ART	MICHAEL HARDING	PEBEO	PELIKAN	PENTEL	PDQ	REEVES	RICH ART	ROBERSON	ROWNEY	SCHMINCKE	SENNELIER	SHIVA	SPECTRUM	JP STEPHENSON	TALENS	TITAN	UTRECHT	VALLEJO	WEBER	WINSOR & NEWTON
		G																					
				G																			
				O																			
																							G
													G										
													W										
																							W
																							G
																		O					
																		O					
																		W					
											O												
																						O	O
	G																						
G					O				S		O	OWGS		O				O			A		S
					G																		
											A												
											W	OAW											
											O												
OA											O				O								
				O																			
				G																			
						O																	

KEY O oil A acrylic W watercolor G gouache P pigment S poster K alkyd E egg tempera **Quality** O artists and students O artists O students O unspecified

	COLOR	COMPOSITION	MANUFACTURERS' PERMANENCY RATING	BEROL	BLOCKX	BOCOUR	CALDER	CAL-WESTERN	CARAN D'ACHE	DANACOLORS	DURO	FERRARIO	GOLDEN	GRUMBACHER	HOLBEIN	HUNT SPEEDBALL	LAMBERTYE	LASCAUX	LEFRANC & BOURGEOIS	LIQUITEX
122	Oxide of Chromium	**CrOx**	••••		A															
122	Oxide of Chromium Opaque	CrOx			O															
123	Permanent Green	AzP, Ph	••••															O		
99		CaS, Ph	••••																	
117		CaS, CrOx	••••																	
98		Ph, OrP	•••																	
122		Ph	•••			OAWG														
		PhG, ZW																		
		HnY, PhG																		
		CaY, ClCpPh																		
112		N/S	••						O		O		O				A			
100	Permanent Green Deep	CrOx	••••																	
101		ClCpPhG, AyY, TD	••••																	
102		Ph, IrOx	••••																A	
105		V,I OrP	••••																	
123		Ph, OrP	••••																	
102		Az, Ph	•••																	
103		ArY, P-MC	••																	
104		V	••••																	
100		ClCpPhG, AyY5GX TD, ZOx	••••																O	
101		Ph, NkT															A			
101		N/S			O															
111	Permanent Green Light	CaZSu, ClCpPhG	••••							O									**A**	
111		ClCpPhG, AyY5GX TD, ZOx	••••																O	
112		Ph, OrP	••••																	
111		Ph AzP	••••																	
111		Ca Su, AzP	••••																	
111		Ca Su, CrOx	••••																	
105		Ca Su Ba, Ph	••••										A							
107		Ans, Ars, Ph	•••										W							
105		CrOx, Ans, Ars	•••										O							

Abbreviations used to signify composition correspond to recognized chemical abbreviations only in some cases. A detailed key is included on pp84-85.

LUKAS	MAIMERI	MARABU	MARCUS ART	MICHAEL HARDING	PEBEO	PELIKAN	PENTEL	PDQ	REEVES	RICH ART	ROBERSON	ROWNEY	SCHMINCKE	SENNELIER	SHIVA	SPECTRUM	JP STEPHENSON	TALENS	TITAN	UTRECHT	VALLEJO	WEBER	WINSOR & NEWTON
			O								0					O							OWG
				OA																			
	A																						
	W											O											
																				O			
																				A			
																				A			
	W																	O			A		
																		A					
	O																						
												O											
												G											
	O																						G
												WP											
																							S
												OAWG											
																		W					
																		A					
	O																						

KEY O oil A acrylic W watercolor G gouache P pigment S poster K alkyd E egg tempera **Quality** O artists and students O artists O students O unspecified

COLOR		COMPOSITION	MANUFACTURERS' PERMANENCY RATING	BEROL	BLOCKX	BOCOUR	CALDER	CAL-WESTERN	CARAN D'ACHE	DANACOLORS	DURO	FERRARIO	GOLDEN	GRUMBACHER	HOLBEIN	HUNT SPEEDBALL	LAMBERTYE	LASCAUX	LEFRANC & BOURGEOIS	LIQUITEX
111	Permanent Green Light (contd)	CrOx, AzP	•••																	
111		CrOx, ZCh	•••																	
112		ArY, P-MC	••																	
112		ClCpPhG, CaZSu	••••																	
106		Ph/T																		W
108		N/S	•		OA													A		
102	Permanent Green Medium	Ph, CaZSu, BaSl ZOx	••••							O	W	A			O					
118	Permanent Green Mid	ArY, P-MCd	••																	
118	Permanent Green Middle	N/S																		
	Permanent Hooker's Green	N/S								W										
	Permanent Light Green	N/S																		
99	Permanent Olive Green	Ph, OrP	••••																	
121		OrP	•••																	
122	Permanent Sap Green	NkAz, SyHylrOx, ClCpPhG	••••																O	
	Permanent Yellow Green	AzP, Ph	•••																	
115	Permasol Green	N/S																		
122	Persian Green Deep	Ph, AzY	•••																	
119	Persian Green Light	Ph, AzY	•••										O					G		
111	Phthalo Emerald	Ph													A			G		
122	Phthalo Green	Ph	•••			OAW		A	O	O										
102	Phthalo Green (Blue Shade)	PyClCpPh	••									A			OA					
107	Phthalo Green (Yellow Shade)	Py, CpPh	•									A								
102	Phthalo Green GG	Ph	•••																	
108	Phthalo Green Light	Ph	•••																	
115	Phthalo Yellow Green	Ph	•••																	
110		Hn Y10G, Ph	•••																	
107	Phthalocyanine Green	Ph, ClCp	••••																	
103	Pinaster Green	Ph, AzY	••••																OAW	
122	Pine Green	N/S																G		
99	Prussian Green	Ph, OrP	••••																	
99		IrBtNa, Ph	•••																	
		N/S																		
	Rembrandt Blue Green	Ph	••••																	
	Rembrandt Bluish Green	Ph	••••																	

Abbreviations used to signify composition correspond to recognized chemical abbreviations only in some cases. A detailed key is included on pp84-85.

LUKAS	MAIMERI	MARABU	MARCUS ART	MICHAEL HARDING	PEBEO	PELIKAN	PENTEL	PDQ	REEVES	RICH ART	ROBERSON	ROWNEY	SCHMINCKE	SENNELIER	SHIVA	SPECTRUM	JP STEPHENSON	TALENS	TITAN	UTRECHT	VALLEJO	WEBER	WINSOR & NEWTON
																		O					
																							O
																							G
																							S
																							G
																							S
								K															
													W										
													O										
																		O					
															O								
									OW														
								K	A				OAW									OA	K
			G																				
									A												OA		
																					O		
								K															
	A	S		O																OA	A		
	G																						S
													W										O
																							W
						G												W					
																		O					

KEY O oil A acrylic W watercolor G gouache P pigment S poster K alkyd E egg tempera **Quality** O artists and students O artists O students O unspecified

#	COLOR	COMPOSITION	MANUFACTURERS' PERMANENCY RATING	BEROL	BLOCKX	BOCOUR	CALDER	CAL-WESTERN	CARAN D'ACHE	DANACOLORS	DURO	FERRARIO	GOLDEN	GRUMBACHER	HOLBEIN	HUNT SPEEDBALL	LAMBERTYE	LASCAUX	LEFRANC & BOURGEOIS	LIQUITEX
102	Rembrandt Green	Ph	●●●●																	
103	Rich Green Deep	Ph	●●●●																G	
108	Roberson's Green	N/S																		
126	Saint Michel Green	IrFc, LeCr	●●																G	
	Sap Green	Ph, CcG	●●●●																	
99		BtNN	●●●●														O			
120		Ph, At	●●●																W	
99		NiBtNaP	●●●																	
120		Ph	●●●				OWA													
107		OrP	●●●																	
113		Ph, Q	●●●										OWA							
103		NNG	●●															OA		
119		TzY, Ph	●●				G													
		IrNiBt, HnY																		
125		N/S									OW			OA	OA					
119 126	Sap Green 1 + 2	OrP	●●●●																	
	Sap Green Bluish	N/S																		
	Sap Green Yellowish	N/S																		
91	Sea Green	Pm, Ph, An, Ar, TD	●●●													W				
105		Ph	●●●				S													
99		N/S										G						OW		
	Sevres Green	Ph, ZOx	●●●●																	
107	Shiva Green	N/S																		
105	Spectrum Cobalt Green (Syn.)	N/S	●●																	
108	Spectrum Emerald Green	N/S	●●																	
	Spectrum Green	Ph	●●●		G															
112		CrOx	●●																	
97	Spectrum Viridian Green	N/S	●●																	
107	Speedball Green (Phthalo)	Ph	●●●												W					
	Stephenson's Green	Ph	●●●																	
118	Sunproof Green	Ph	●●●●																	
	Talens Green Deep	Ph, OrP	●●●																	
	Talens Green Light	Ph, AzP	●●●																	
124	Terre Verte	E	●●●●				O				O									
125		Al, CrOx	●●●●															W		

Abbreviations used to signify composition correspond to recognized chemical abbreviations only in some cases. A detailed key is included on pp84-85.

LUKAS	MAIMERI	MARABU	MARCUS ART	MICHAEL HARDING	PEBEO	PELIKAN	PENTEL	PDQ	REEVES	RICH ART	ROBERSON	ROWNEY	SCHMINCKE	SENNELIER	SHIVA	SPECTRUM	JP STEPHENSON	TALENS	TITAN	UTRECHT	VALLEJO	WEBER	WINSOR & NEWTON
																	OAW						
										O													
																W							
OW																							OWK
												OS						OA	O				
																						O	
																				O			
OWG	S			OAW			S		OAW		O			OW	O								
													W										
	G																						
													W										
		G																					
															O			O					
															O								
																O							
																O							
																O							
																O							
																O							
																O							
													G										
																		O					
																		O					
									O		O							OW					OAW
			O																				

KEY O oil A acrylic W watercolor G gouache P pigment S poster K alkyd E egg tempera   **Quality** O artists and students O artists *O* students ○ unspecified

No.	COLOR	COMPOSITION	MANUFACTURERS' PERMANENCY RATING	BEROL	BLOCKX	BOCOUR	CALDER	CAL-WESTERN	CARAN D'ACHE	DANACOLORS	DURO	FERRARIO	GOLDEN	GRUMBACHER	HOLBEIN	HUNT SPEEDBALL	LAMBERTYE	LASCAUX	LEFRANC & BOURGEOIS	LIQUITEX
105	Terre Verte (contd)	IrOx, Sl	••••																	
129		Oc, Ph, Iv	•••															O		
		N/S																		
97	Thaline Green	ClCpPh, ZOx	••••		O															
104	Thalo Green	Ph	•••										OAW							
114	Thalo Yellow Green	Ans, Ars, Ph	•••										**W**							
110		CaS, BaSu, Ph	•••										A							
112		Phs, Ans, Ars, ZOx	•••										O							
108	Titan Green Deep	Ph	••••																	
105	Titan Green Light	OrPs, CaY	•••																	
105	Transparent Green	Ph	•••																	
97	Transparent Vivid Green	Ph	••••															O		
112	True Green	N/S																		
	Turquoise Green	Ph	•••				WAS											A		
94		ClCpPhBl, G, TD	••••																	A
98		ClCpPhBl, G, TD, ZOx																		O
97	Ultramarine Green	S-A-S-S	••••																	
115	Utrecht Green	PhG, HnYR																		
	Venetian Green	N/S														G				
100	Vermilion Green Deep	OrP, IrOx, Ph	••••																	
124	Vermilion Green Light	OrP, IrOx, Ph	••••																	
122	Verona Green Earth	**E**	••••																	
105	Veronese Green	F, Ph, T	••••									O				O				
104		N/S										W				OA				
108	Veronese Green (Imit.)	Ph, BaCh	••••																G	
123	Veronese Green Shade	Ph, AzNk	••••															O		
104	Viridian	**CrOx**	••••			G					O		OW					OW		
		Ph	••••			WS														
99		E, Ph	••••																	
100		CrOx, Ph	•••										W							
102		HsCuSx	••••																	OW
104		N/S		S		OAW			O		WA				O	OW	OAW			
105	Viridian Hue	N/S	••																	
108	Viridian (Imit.)	Ph, AzY	••••																G	
107		Ph	•••															O		
	Viridian (Subst.)	N/S																		

Abbreviations used to signify composition correspond to recognized chemical abbreviations only in some cases. A detailed key is included on pp84-85.

LUKAS	MAIMERI	MARABU	MARCUS ART	MICHAEL HARDING	PEBEO	PELIKAN	PENTEL	PDQ	REEVES	RICH ART	ROBERSON	ROWNEY	SCHMINCKE	SENNELIER	SHIVA	SPECTRUM	JP STEPHENSON	TALENS	TITAN	UTRECHT	VALLEJO	WEBER	WINSOR & NEWTON
																						W	
														O									
																			O				
																			O				
		O																					
G													G										S
	O																						
																				A	A		
													W										
													W										
													O										
				OWG																			
				O																			
OW											O		OG				O	OW	O				OWGK
																		O					
																					O		
W			O				S		K				WGPE	O			O			O			S
								OW													A		
OG							G						S										
													P										

KEY O oil A acrylic W watercolor G gouache P pigment S poster K alkyd E egg tempera **Quality** O artists and students O artists O students O unspecified

COLOR	COMPOSITION	MANUFACTURERS' PERMANENCY RATING	BEROL	BLOCKX	BOCOUR	CALDER	CAL-WESTERN	CARAN D'ACHE	DANACOLORS	DURO	FERRARIO	GOLDEN	GRUMBACHER	HOLBEIN	HUNT SPEEDBALL	LAMBERTYE	LASCAUX	LEFRANC & BOURGEOIS	LIQUITEX
99 Viridian (Tint)	N/S												o						
104 Viridian Glowing	CrOx	••••																	
104 Viridian Lake	TpL	•																	
122 Viridian Matt	CrOx	••••																	
110 Vivid Lime Green	ClCpPhG, AyY, TD	••••																A	
110	AyY, ClCpPhG, TD, ZOx	••••																	o
119 Warm Green	Ph	••••															WA		
108 Water Green	Ph, AzY	••••															G		
108 Winsor Emerald	ArY, Ph	•••																	
108	ArY, Ph, ZOx	•••																	
111 Winsor Fast Green	AzMeP	•••																	
102 Winsor Green	Ph	•••																	
102	ArY, Ph	•••																	
119 Winton Green	N/S																		
110 Yellow Green	N/S						G							o					S
110 Yellow Green (Spectrum)	N/S																		
111 Yellow Green Deep	N/S																		
113 Yellowish Green	CaSu, Ph	••••																	
110	AzP, Ph	•••																	
110	OrP	•••																	
111 Zinc Green Deep	N/S										o								
110 Zinc Green Light	N/S										o								

BROWNS

COLOR	COMPOSITION	MANUFACTURERS' PERMANENCY RATING	BEROL	BLOCKX	BOCOUR	CALDER	CAL-WESTERN	CARAN D'ACHE	DANACOLORS	DURO	FERRARIO	GOLDEN	GRUMBACHER	HOLBEIN	HUNT SPEEDBALL	LAMBERTYE	LASCAUX	LEFRANC & BOURGEOIS	LIQUITEX
152 Asphaltum	BoBk, TaY, NaR, IrOx	••																	
	As																		
128 Asphaltum Extra	OrP	••																	
151 Bister	CcE, IvBn	•••															G		
153 Bistre	E, IrOx	••••												o					
148 Bitume	N/S	•																	
150 Bitumen	**Ns As**	•																	
152 Bitumen Lake Vibert	IrOx, Cn	••••															o		
138 Brown	Bs	••••																	
134	N/S																	S	
135 Brown (Spectrum)	N/S																		

Abbreviations used to signify composition correspond to recognized chemical abbreviations only in some cases. A detailed key is included on pp84-85.

LUKAS	MAIMERI	MARABU	MARCUS ART	MICHAEL HARDING	PEBEO	PELIKAN	PENTEL	PDQ	REEVES	RICH ART	ROBERSON	ROWNEY	SCHMINCKE	SENNELIER	SHIVA	SPECTRUM	JP STEPHENSON	TALENS	TITAN	UTRECHT	VALLEJO	WEBER	WINSOR & NEWTON
												WP											
												OAW GP											
																							G
												OAW GP											
																							OW
																							G
																							K
																							G
																							OW
																							S
			O																				
	GS				O								W										
							S																
								S															
																		A					
																		W					
																		O					
																						O	
													O										
																		O					
													OW										
O																							
	G																						
															S								
							S																

KEY O oil A acrylic W watercolor G gouache P pigment S poster K alkyd E egg tempera **Quality** O artists and students O artists O students O unspecified

No.	COLOR	COMPOSITION	MANUFACTURERS' PERMANENCY RATING	BEROL	BLOCKX	BOCOUR	CALDER	CAL-WESTERN	CARAN D'ACHE	DANACOLORS	DURO	FERRARIO	GOLDEN	GRUMBACHER	HOLBEIN	HUNT SPEEDBALL	LAMBERTYE	LASCAUX	LEFRANC & BOURGEOIS	LIQUITEX
148	Brown Light	IrOx, BiH, An, AB	●●●●										G							
147	Brown Madder	Aa, OrP	●●●																	
143		AaLVr, AzP	●●●																	
60		At, IrOx, Cn	●●										OW							
146		N/S																		
145	Brown Madder (Alizarin)	IrOx, Aa	●●●																	
145		SyM, OrP	●●●																	
60	Brown Madder Lake	N/S	●●●																	
136	Brown Ochre	E	●●●●		O															
135		IrOx	●●●●															O		
135		N/S	●●●●																	
153	Brown Ochre Deep	E, CcE, Cn	●●●●																	
128	Brown Ochre Light	E, CcE, Cn	●●●●																	
		E	●●●●		O															
138	Brown Pink	IrOx, AzY	●●●●															G		
134		IrOx	●●●●																	
128		E, IrOx	●●●●																	
139	Transparent Brown	AaL, TaL, BoBl	●●																	
149		N/S	●●●●												O					
149	Brownish Madder	CcNIIrOxMn, DhAtAu, SyHyIrOx	●●																	O
149	Burnt Carmine	Sym, SyU	●●●																	
144	Burnt Green Earth	E, CcE	●●●●															W		
141	Burnt Orange	Ans, Ars, IrOx, BiH	●●●										G							
139	Burnt Sienna	CcE	●●●●										OAW					OWG		
149		CclrOx	●●●●			OWG				O							O	A	A	
148		CcNIIrOx	●●●●									A							OW	
138		E, IrOx	●●●●							A										
141		N/S	●●●●	S	OAW			A	G	O	O	O				OAW	OAW			O
138	Burnt Sienna (Hue)	IrOx	●●●●										G	OAWG						
139	Burnt Sienna Deep	E	●●●●		O															
	Burnt Sienna Light	E	●●●●		O															
151	Burnt Umber	CcE	●●●●														O	OWG		
153		IrOx	●●●●			OW	OWG													
151		CclrOx	●●●●							O				W						
152		NlCclrOx, Mn	●●●●							A			A	OAW				A	OAW	
150		E, IrOx	●●●●																	
		CcNIIrOx	●●●●																	
153		N/S	●●●●	S				A			O	O		OAWG	OAW	OAW				

Abbreviations used to signify composition correspond to recognized chemical abbreviations only in some cases. A detailed key is included on pp84-85.

LUKAS	MAIMERI	MARABU	MARCUS ART	MICHAEL HARDING	PEBEO	PELIKAN	PENTEL	PDQ	REEVES	RICH ART	ROBERSON	ROWNEY	SCHMINCKE	SENNELIER	SHIVA	SPECTRUM	JP STEPHENSON	TALENS	TITAN	UTRECHT	VALLEJO	WEBER	WINSOR & NEWTON
													W										
	O																						
											O			OWP									
												OW											O
																		O					
				G																			
													OW	P									
											O												
OG											O			O									
																		O					
																		O					
													O										
													W										
												OW											
											O			OW									
																		O					
OWG													OGP					O					
																		OAWK				OA	OAW
	OW											OAW	WGPS										G
P																				OA			
													OA										
AWP	A		O	OAWG	OG	S	K	OAW	S	O	O			OWG PE	O				O		A		S
P	OW		O										OAWG					OWAS			OA		K
												OAW											
																							G
																				OA			
OWG	OAW			OAWG	G		K	OAW	S	O			OWGP	O		O			O		A		S

KEY O oil A acrylic W watercolor G gouache P pigment S poster K alkyd E egg tempera   **Quality** O artists and students O artists O students O unspecified

#	COLOR	COMPOSITION	MANUFACTURERS' PERMANENCY RATING	BEROL	BLOCKX	BOCOUR	CALDER	CAL-WESTERN	CARAN D'ACHE	DANACOLORS	DURO	FERRARIO	GOLDEN	GRUMBACHER	HOLBEIN	HUNT SPEEDBALL	LAMBERTYE	LASCAUX	LEFRANC & BOURGEOIS	LIQUITEX
153	Burnt Umber Light	CcNllrOx, Mn	•									A								
137	Burnt Yellow Ochre	N/S	••••																	
151	Cassel Brown/Vandyck Brown	N/S	•••																	
154	Cassel Earth	E	••••	O														OG		
153		E, IrOx	••••																	
152		N/S			O						O									
151	Cassel Earth (Imit)	N/S	••••																	
153	Cassel Earth Mineral	IrOx, BoBk	••••													O				
	Chocolate	N/S																		
149	Chocolate Brown	N/S																		
153	Cocoa Brown	IrOx, BiH, Mn	••••											G						
	Coloured Sepia	CcEOrP	••••																	
152	Dark Brown	BuUm	••••																	
151		N/S												A						S
151	Dark Burnt Sienna	N/S																		
131	Dark Ochre	N/S																		
149	Deep Brown	N/S																		
148	Deep Ochre	E, CcE, Cn	••••														AG			
148		N/S									W									
153	Deep Umber	CclrOx, Mn, IrOx	••••											G						
135	Gold Ochre	IrOx, Au	•••																O	
132		ElrOx		O																
	Golden Burnt Ochre	CcE	••••								P									
125	Green Umber	N/S	••••																	
128	Greenish Umber	E	••••																	
125		ClCpPhG, NllrOxMn	••••																O	
151	Grumbacher Transparent Brown	CclrOx, Mn, CclrOx	••••											O						
149	Havanah Lake	ToR, E, IrL	•••																	
		BoBk, PeB	••••															G		
128	Italian Earth	E	••••	O																
154	Kassel Earth	E	••••																	
143	Light Brown	N/S												A			AG			S
148	Light Ochre	E									W									
131		IrOx, E																		
131		IrOx																		
154	Madder Brown	CclrOx, Ag	•••																	
144	Mars Brown	IrOx	••••	O									O	O						

Abbreviations used to signify composition correspond to recognized chemical abbreviations only in some cases. A detailed key is included on pp84-85.

LUKAS	MAIMERI	MARABU	MARCUS ART	MICHAEL HARDING	PEBEO	PELIKAN	PENTEL	PDQ	REEVES	RICH ART	ROBERSON	ROWNEY	SCHMINCKE	SENNELIER	SHIVA	SPECTRUM	JP STEPHENSON	TALENS	TITAN	UTRECHT	VALLEJO	WEBER	WINSOR & NEWTON
O	G																						
P																							
	O																						
													O										
						G								O									
O																							
							S														W		
													W	W									
		G																					
		S																					
		G																					
																		O					
													O AW PS										
O G													O PS					O					
																							G
	O																						
													O GP W AS										
								O															
																							O
	O																						

COLOR	COMPOSITION	MANUFACTURERS' PERMANENCY RATING	BEROL	BLOCKX	BOCOUR	CALDER	CAL-WESTERN	CARAN D'ACHE	DANACOLORS	DURO	FERRARIO	GOLDEN	GRUMBACHER	HOLBEIN	HUNT SPEEDBALL	LAMBERTYE	LASCAUX	LEFRANC & BOURGEOIS	LIQUITEX
152 Mars Brown (contd)	CclrOx, IrOx	••••																	
135	Cn, IrOx	••••																	
145	Cn, Al, IrOx	••••																O	
128	E	••••																O	
147	N/S																	W	
144 Mars Deep Brown	**IrOx**																		
139 Mars Light Brown	**IrOx**																		
134 Medium Brown	CcE																		
135	N/S																		
132 Natural Sepia	E	••••																	
152 Natural Umber	N/S						AG												
137 Ochre	N/S						AG												
128 Olive Brown	IrOx																		
137 Orient Earth	IrOx, F	••••															A		
128 Oriental Brown	N/S	••••										O							
145 Oxide Brown Deep	IrOx																		
144 Oxide Brown Light	IrOx																A		
135 Permanent Brown	AzC																A		
153 Permanent Asphaltum	SyHyIrOx, CcNIIrOxMn	••••															A		
151 Permasol Brown	N/S																	O	
146 Pozzouli Earth	**E**	••••																	
143	IrOx	••••																	
140	N/S																		
150 Raw Sepia	**Sp**	•••															W		
153	E	••••															G		
152	CcE, Cn																OWG		
132 Raw Sienna	E																OWG		
131	IrOx																A		
	NIEP	••••																	
131	N/S																		
153 Raw Umber	**E**	••••				OWG			OA						O		OWG		
153	IrOx	••••		OAW															
152	NIIrOx, Mn	••••									A	OAWG					A	OAW	
	NIEP	••••																	
139	N/S						A	O			OW			OAWG	OAW	OW	GA		
142 Red Brown	IrOx	••••															GO		

Abbreviations used to signify composition correspond to recognized chemical abbreviations only in some cases. A detailed key is included on pp84-85.

	LUKAS	MAIMERI	MARABU	MARCUS ART	MICHAEL HARDING	PEBEO	PELIKAN	PENTEL	PDQ	REEVES	RICH ART	ROBERSON	ROWNEY	SCHMINCKE	SENNELIER	SHIVA	SPECTRUM	JP STEPHENSON	TALENS	TITAN	UTRECHT	VALLEJO	WEBER	WINSOR & NEWTON
												O												
						O						O			O							A		
				G																				
				G																				
			G																					
			S																					
			G			G																		
							O															A		
						A																		
																O								
														W										
														P										
														O										
															WG				OW					
														OGP										
														AWS										
																					OA			
		OAWG			O																			
	P	OW	O		O										OAW GPS				OA					OAWK
													OWA									OA		G
															OWG									
															PE	O	O			O		A		
																					OA			
	OWG	OAW				OAW	G		K	OAW	P	O												
															WGPE									

KEY O oil A acrylic W watercolor G gouache P pigment S poster K alkyd E egg tempera **Quality** **O** artists and students O artists *O* students ○ unspecified

#	COLOR	COMPOSITION	MANUFACTURERS' PERMANENCY RATING	BEROL	BLOCKX	BOCOUR	CALDER	CAL-WESTERN	CARAN D'ACHE	DANACOLORS	DURO	FERRARIO	GOLDEN	GRUMBACHER	HOLBEIN	HUNT SPEEDBALL	LAMBERTYE	LASCAUX	LEFRANC & BOURGEOIS	LIQUITEX
148	Red Ochre	IrOx, BoN Ar	●●●																	
152	Rembrandt Brown	CcE, SyU, Cn	●●●●																	
148	Roman Ochre	N/S									O									
152	Rowney Transparent Brown Q		●●●																	
135	Rust Brown	EnR																		
152	Sennelier Brown	N/S	●●●																	
152	Sepia	CclrOx, Mn	●●●●											G						
153		CclrOx, IrOx, Cn	●●●●											W						
154		CnBk, E, CclrOx, HcBk	●●●●																	
153		Bs, LaBk	●●●●																	
153		E	●●●●															G		
153		ArR, IrOx, HcBk	●●●																	
152		IrOx					G													
152		N/S			W						OW			O	W	W				
154	Sepia (Imit.)	N/S	●●●●																	
153	Sepia (Modern)	CcE, BoCn	●●●●																	
152	Sepia Brown	N/S									W									
152	Sepia Brown Tone	E, OrP	●●●●																	
151	Sepia Deep	N/S	●●●●													W				
153	Sepia Extra	CcE, BoCn																		
153	Sepia Natural (Mineral)	CclrOx, Mn, Cn	●●●●									W								
151	Sepia Umber	N/S																	O	
152	Sepia Warm (Mineral)	CclrOx, Mn, Cn	●●●●									W								
129	Stil De Grain Brown	IrOx	●●●●												O					
142		AaL, AzP, Ph	●●●																	
148		OrP	●●●																	
140		N/S									W									
131	Stil De Grain Vert	IrOx, OrP																		
130	Stone Gall	N/S	●●●●																	
149	Talens Brown	SyU, E, OrP	●●●																	
152	Titan Brown	IrOx	●●●●																	
42	Titan-Buff	TDRu	●									A								
129	Toledo Brown	E	●●●●															G		
135	Translucent Brown Oxide	IrOx	●●●●																	
152	Transparent Brown	E	●●●●																	
135		AzP, Cn	●●●●																O	
129		At	●●●																W	
151		IrOx	●●●	O																

Abbreviations used to signify composition correspond to recognized chemical abbreviations only in some cases. A detailed key is included on pp84-85.

LUKAS	MAIMERI	MARABU	MARCUS ART	MICHAEL HARDING	PEBEO	PELIKAN	PENTEL	PDQ	REEVES	RICH ART	ROBERSON	ROWNEY	SCHMINCKE	SENNELIER	SHIVA	*SPECTRUM	JP STEPHENSON	TALENS	TITAN	UTRECHT	VALLEJO	WEBER	WINSOR & NEWTON
																							G
																		O					
O																							
		G										O											
														O									
	W																						
																							W
																							W
												W											
W	WG				**W**		P				O			O									
O																							
																		W					
													W										
																		O					
																					A		
	O																	O					
	W																						
													W	W									
																		O	O				
													O										
	O																						

KEY O oil A acrylic W watercolor G gouache P pigment S poster K alkyd E egg tempera   **Quality** O artists and students O artists O students O unspecified

COLOR	COMPOSITION	MANUFACTURERS' PERMANENCY RATING	BEROL	BLOCKX	BOCOUR	CALDER	CAL-WESTERN	CARAN D'ACHE	DANACOLORS	DURO	FERRARIO	GOLDEN	GRUMBACHER	HOLBEIN	HUNT SPEEDBALL	LAMBERTYE	LASCAUX	LEFRANC & BOURGEOIS	LIQUITEX
145 Transparent Oxide Brown	IrOx	●●●●																	
129 Unbleached Titanium	N/S				A														
152 Vandyck Brown	E	●●●●																OW	
153	IrOx	●●●●														O		OW	
148	BoBk, IrOx, At	●●●●																	
129	CcE, BoBk																	OG	
148	CcE, BoCn	●●●●																	
128	CcNIIrOxMn	●●●●																	O
153	LbE	●●										OW							
128	N/S										W			OW					
151 Vandyck Brown Umber	ApCn,NIHyIrOx, CcNIIrOxMn	●●●●																	W
148 Velvet Brown	N/S	●●●●																	
128 Warm Sepia	CnBk, E	●●●●																W	
152	CcE	●●●																G	
128 Yellow Brown	N/S																		
133 Yellow Brown Brilliant	IrOx																		

BLACKS/GRAYS

COLOR	COMPOSITION	MANUFACTURERS' PERMANENCY RATING	BEROL	BLOCKX	BOCOUR	CALDER	CAL-WESTERN	CARAN D'ACHE	DANACOLORS	DURO	FERRARIO	GOLDEN	GRUMBACHER	HOLBEIN	HUNT SPEEDBALL	LAMBERTYE	LASCAUX	LEFRANC & BOURGEOIS	LIQUITEX
154 Anthracite	N/S				O												A		
154 Bellini Grey	N/S				O														
Black	ApBkCn	●●●●											G						
	IrOxBk	●●●●																	
	LaBk																		
	CnBk					S													
	N/S		S				A	AG								A	AG		S
Black (Spectrum)	N/S																		
Black for Fresco	N/S																		
Black Iron Oxide	IrOx	●●●●																	
Black Ivory	N/S																		
Black Lake	N/S	●●●●																	
Black Oxide	IrOx					O													
Black Oxide of Iron	IrOx	●●●●																	
Blue Black	BoBk, VgBk	●●●●																	
	IvBk, U	●●●●																	
	N/S									O									
161 Blue Grey	S-A-S-S, IvBk	●●●																	
161 Bluish Grey 1	TD, E	●●●																G	
164 Bluish Grey 2	TD, Cn	●●●																	

Abbreviations used to signify composition correspond to recognized chemical abbreviations only in some cases. A detailed key is included on pp84-85.

Lukas	Maimeri	Marabu	Marcus Art	Michael Harding	Pebeo	Pelikan	Pentel	PDQ	Reeves	Rich Art	Roberson	Rowney	Schmincke	Sennelier	Shiva	Spectrum	JP Stephenson	Talens	Titan	Utrecht	Vallejo	Weber	Winsor & Newton
																		OW					
													WO										
																		A					
													GP									O	
																		W					
W	OWG			OAW	G								OWG PE								A		
				G																			
																							W
					G																		
													O										
												A	A										
																					A		
	G																						
	W	S			O	S								S								G	
										A													
													P										
									A														
	G																						
													GP										
				G																			
													P										
												O											O
											O												OW
													OS										
													OS										

KEY O oil A acrylic W watercolor G gouache P pigment S poster K alkyd E egg tempera   **Quality** O artists and students O artists O students O unspecified

Page	COLOR	COMPOSITION	MANUFACTURERS' PERMANENCY RATING	BEROL	BLOCKX	BOCOUR	CALDER	CAL-WESTERN	CARAN D'ACHE	DANACOLORS	DURO	FERRARIO	GOLDEN	GRUMBACHER	HOLBEIN	HUNT SPEEDBALL	LAMBERTYE	LASCAUX	LEFRANC & BOURGEOIS	LIQUITEX
	Bone Black	ApCn	●									A								
130	Brownish Grey 1	TD, E	●●●																	
129	Brownish Grey 2	TD, E	●●●●																	
	Candle Black	LaBk	●●●●																	
	Carbon Black	ApCnBk	●●●●						O			A				W				
154	Charcoal Grey	CrCg	●●●●																	
154		ApCn	●●●●										W							
154		CcBo	●●●●																	
154		N/S			W															
	Cold Black	CnSuSi, SoAi	●●●●															O		
165	Cold Grey	ZOx, CcBo	●●●●																	
	Cool Black	N/S													A					
164	Dark Grey	N/S																		
156	Davy's Grey	Sz	●●●●																	
155		IrOx, Ph, ApBoCn	●●●●										W							
154		N/S	●●●											OW						
	Deep Black	BkAeL	●●●															G		
	Ferrous Black	N/S																		
159	French Grey	N/S																		
	Graphic Black	N/S																		
157	Graphite Grey	CtCn	●									A								
154	Grey	ApBoCn, IrOx, TD	●●●●										G							
		Cn Bk				S														
157		Vg Bk																		
154		N/S				G		AG												S
164	Grey (Spectrum)	N/S																		
	Grey Deep	IvBk, RwUm, TW																		
	Grey Light	IvBk, RwUm, TW																		
164	Grey Medium	IvBk, RwUm, TW																		
158 162	Grey Nos 1-5	CnBk, E, TD	●●●											G						
161	Grey of Grey	N/S												OW						
161	Grey Pale	N/S																		
157	Grey V-5	N/S	●●●											A						
83	Grumbacher Grey	S-A-S-S, BoCn	●●●●										A							
156 159 160 165	Grumbacher Grey Nos 1-4	ZOx, BoCn, IrOx	●●●●										O							

Abbreviations used to signify composition correspond to recognized chemical abbreviations only in some cases. A detailed key is included on pp.84-85.

LUKAS	MAIMERI	MARABU	MARCUS ART	MICHAEL HARDING	PEBEO	PELIKAN	PENTEL	PDQ	REEVES	RICH ART	ROBERSON	ROWNEY	SCHMINCKE	SENNELIER	SHIVA	SPECTRUM	JP STEPHENSON	TALENS	TITAN	UTRECHT	VALLEJO	WEBER	WINSOR & NEWTON
													OS										
													OS										
				W																		W	
																							OW
																	W						
																	O						
	S																						
																							OW
															O								
							S																
	G																						
													A										
			G											G									S
								A															
																			A	A			
																			A	A			
																				A			
																							G
			G																				

KEY O oil A acrylic W watercolor G gouache P pigment S poster K alkyd E egg tempera **Quality** O artists and students O artists O students O unspecified

COLOR	COMPOSITION	MANUFACTURERS' PERMANENCY RATING	BEROL	BLOCKX	BOCOUR	CALDER	CAL-WESTERN	CARAN D'ACHE	DANACOLORS	DURO	FERRARIO	GOLDEN	GRUMBACHER	HOLBEIN	HUNT SPEEDBALL	LAMBERTYE	LASCAUX	LEFRANC & BOURGEOIS	LIQUITEX
Iron Oxide Black	IrOx																		
Ivory	N/S	••••																	
Ivory Black	ApBoCn	••••	O		OWG				O			**OW**		O			OAWG	AO	
	CcBo	••••																	
	CcBoCn, Ps																		
	N/S			OAW						OAW			OWG	OW	OW				
Jet Black	AeL	•••											G						
Lamp Black	**Ba Hc**	••••			OWG														
	ApCn	••••							O			OW							W
	CcBo	••••																	
	HcBk, VgBk	••••																	
	HcBk															W			
	N/S			OW									OAW						W
164 Lascaux Grey	TCBk															A			
161 Light Grey	N/S															G			
Mars Black	IrOx	••••							A			OA					OA		
	SylrOx	••••								A									A
	N/S			OA				O											
Mixing Black	N/S																		
154 Monochrome Cool	N/S	•••											O						
161 Mouse Grey	ZSu, IvBk	•••															G		
165 Neutral Colour	CnBk, U	••••																	
165	N/S	••																	
Neutral Grey Value 3-8	BoApCn, NIIrOxMn, TD	••••																	A
	BoApCn, NIIrOxMn, TD, ZOx	••••																	O
159 Neutral Shade	N/S	••••																	
155 Neutral Tint	CzCn	••••															W		
158	AaC, LaBk, WiBl	••																	
165	CcBo, DxP																		
156	N/S														W				
Opaque Mars Black	IrOx	••••																	
Oxide Black	IrOx	••••														A			
Payne's Black	N/S														W				
154 Payne's Grey	U, VgBk	••••																	
159	BoBk, CoAlSi, SuSi	••••																	
155	IrFc, IvBk																G		

Abbreviations used to signify composition correspond to recognized chemical abbreviations only in some cases. A detailed key is included on pp84-85.

LUKAS	MAIMERI	MARABU	MARCUS ART	MICHAEL HARDING	PEBEO	PELIKAN	PENTEL	PDQ	REEVES	RICH ART	ROBERSON	ROWNEY	SCHMINCKE	SENNELIER	SHIVA	SPECTRUM	JP STEPHENSON	TALENS	TITAN	UTRECHT	VALLEJO	WEBER	WINSOR & NEWTON
O																					A		
																				OA			G
			O																				
OW											O	OW	OGP					OW				OAW	OWG
																			O				
				OAW		G	K		OAW				OWG / PS	OWG / PE	O	O							AS
																							G
											O	W					P						OWK
																			O			O	G
																OW							
						G					O												
													OW										
			O			G			W							O					A		S
A		G																			A		
																				OA			
											O		OP	O							A		A
						G																	
W																							
W																							
			W																				
													W										
																							W
															OW			W					
																						W	
	O																						
													P					A					
											OW												
																						OA	
											OW												

KEY O oil A acrylic W watercolor G gouache P pigment S poster K alkyd E egg tempera **Quality** O artists and students O artists O students O unspecified

	COLOR	COMPOSITION	MANUFACTURERS' PERMANENCY RATING	BEROL	BLOCKX	BOCOUR	CALDER	CAL-WESTERN	CARAN D'ACHE	DANACOLORS	DURO	FERRARIO	GOLDEN	GRUMBACHER	HOLBEIN	HUNT SPEEDBALL	LAMBERTYE	LASCAUX	LEFRANC & BOURGEOIS	LIQUITEX
155	Payne's Grey (contd)	Da, LaBk, MsR, U	●●●●																	
154		AtCn																W		
154		IrOx,Ph, QP	●●●●																	
		IrOx, Ph																A		
155		CcBo, Ph	●●●●																	
155		BoHpCn, S-A-S-S	●●●●										O						OA	
		IvBk, UBI	●●●●																	
155		Cn, Ph	●●●										W							
155		Cn, TD, Ph, Q	●●●										G							
155		PySu, S-A-S-S, ApCn	●									A								
155		Cn, Ph, Pm											W							
154		S-A-S-S, BoApCn																	W	
155		CcBo, Ph	●●●●																	
165		U				OW														
155		N/S										W		O		OW			OAW	
	Peach Black	VgCn	●●●●															OW		
		N/S	●●●											OW						
163	Pearl Grey	N/S																		
	Permanent Black	CnBk	●															A		
	Poster Black	N/S																		
159	Steel Grey	N/S																		
	Texture Black	N/S																		
	Titanium Black	N/S																	A	
	Transparent Black	Cn	●●●															O		
		N/S	●●●											O						
	Trichromatic Black	N/S	●●●●																	
	Velvet Black	AeL	●●●													O		G		
	Vine Black	CcVgCn	●●●●													O				
		ApWoCn	●●●●		O															
	Warm Black	N/S													A					
159	Warm Grey	ZOx, BuE, CcBo	●●●●																	
164		N/S	●●●●																	
161	Yellow Grey	ZSu, IvBk	●●●															G		

Abbreviations used to signify composition correspond to recognized chemical abbreviations only in some cases. A detailed key is included on pp84-85.

	LUKAS	MAIMERI	MARABU	MARCUS ART	MICHAEL HARDING	PEBEO	PELIKAN	PENTEL	PDQ	REEVES	RICH ART	ROBERSON	ROWNEY	SCHMINCKE	SENNELIER	SHIVA	SPECTRUM	JP STEPHENSON	TALENS	TITAN	UTRECHT	VALLEJO	WEBER	WINSOR & NEWTON
					O						O													OWK
																			A					
																			W					
																					A			
																			W					
																						A		
				W	G					AW				OW	O								W	K
														OW										
																						A		
										A														S
																						A		
															O									
				G																				
	O																							
														W										
														P										
																			O					
				G																				

COLOR **WHITES**	COMPOSITION	MANUFACTURERS' PERMANENCY RATING	BEROL	BLOCKX	BOCOUR	CALDER	CAL-WESTERN	CARAN D'ACHE	DANACOLORS	DURO	FERRARIO	GOLDEN	GRUMBACHER	HOLBEIN	HUNT SPEEDBALL	LAMBERTYE	LASCAUX	LEFRANC & BOURGEOIS	LIQUITEX
Blackout White	N/S						A												
China White	N/S	••••																	
China White (Zinc)	ZOx	•••																	
Chinese White	**ZOx**	••••															W		
	TD	••••				W							W						
	N/S	•••			W									W	W				
Covering White	N/S	••••																	
Cremnitz White	**LeCa**	•••																	
Dolomie (Cream)	N/S																		
Effect White	N/S																		
Flake Everwhite	BcLeCe	••••																O	
Flake White	BcLeCe		O															O	
	BcLeCe, ZOx	•••										O	O						
	RuTOx	••••														O			
	ZSu, BaSl					O													
Flake White Nos 1+2	N/S	•••																	
	N/S																O		
Foundation White	LeCe	•••																	
Graphic White	N/S																		
Iridescent White	T, Mi	••••																	
Isolating White	TOx	••••															G		
Ivory	N/S										W								
Lithopone	**ZOx, BaSl**	••••																	
Lithopone White	N/S																		
Magna White	N/S				A														
Meudon White	N/S																		
Mixed White	ZOx, TD	••••														O			
	BcCeLe, ZOx	••••	O																
Mixed White (Titanium/Zinc)	TD, ZOx	••••																	
Neo-Zinc White	N/S												O						
Neo-Zinc White N.	N/S												O						
Neo-Zinc White Soft	N/S												O						
Opaque Titanium—Zinc White	TOx, ZSl	••••																	
Opaque White	ZSu	•••																	
Pearl White	T-Mi	••••																	
Permalba White (Original)	ZOx, TD	••••																	
Permanent Chinese White	ZOx	••••																	
Permanent White	TD, ZOx	••••																G	

Abbreviations used to signify composition correspond to recognized chemical abbreviations only in some cases. A detailed key is included on pp84-85.

	LUKAS	MAIMERI	MARABU	MARCUS ART	MICHAEL HARDING	PEBEO	PELIKAN	PENTEL	PDQ	REEVES	RICH ART	ROBERSON	ROWNEY	SCHMINCKE	SENNELIER	SHIVA	SPECTRUM	JP STEPHENSON	TALENS	TITAN	UTRECHT	VALLEJO	WEBER	WINSOR & NEWTON
					W																			
													W		W									
																			W					**W**
					G																			
														O										S
															P									
		G																						
	OW																							
															P				O	O				
												O	O											**O**K
																								O
				O											**OW**E		O							O
																								O
		G																					A	
														P										
															P									
															P									
																		O						
																		O						
			O																					
														OW										
		A																						
																								O
														W										
															G			*O*						

COLOR	COMPOSITION	MANUFACTURERS' PERMANENCY RATING	BEROL	BLOCKX	BOCOUR	CALDER	CAL-WESTERN	CARAN D'ACHE	DANACOLORS	DURO	FERRARIO	GOLDEN	GRUMBACHER	HOLBEIN	HUNT SPEEDBALL	LAMBERTYE	LASCAUX	LEFRANC & BOURGEOIS	LIQUITEX
Permanent White (contd)	TD	●●●				GP													
	N/S													G					
Permasol White	N/S																		
Poster White	N/S																		
Powdered Marble	NlCaCe	●●●●																	
Priming White	TW, ZOx, BaSl	●●●												O					
Purified Chalk	**CaCb**	●●●●																	
Silver White	N/S									O									
Silver White (Imit.)	ZSl	●●●																	
Special Titan White	N/S	●●●●															W		
Structure White	ZSu, Ex	●●●																	
Super Hiding White	ZOx, TOx	●●●●															G		
Superba White	TD, ZOx	●●●●									O								
Supra Rapid White	ZOx, TD	●●●●																	
Supra White	ZOx, TD	●●●●																	
Texture White	TD	●●●●				A													
Titan White	TD, ZOx	●●●●																O	
Titan Zinc White	N/S												O						
Titanium + Zinc White	N/S	●●●●																	
Titanium Everwhite	TD, ZOx	●●●●																O	
Titanium White	**TD**	●●●●			O				A	W	A	A			O	A	OAG	A	
	TD, ZOx	●●●●							O		O								
	TOx	●●●●	O																
	N/S			OA				O		OA			OA	OA	OAW				
Titanium Zinc Everwhite	TD, ZOx	●●●●																O	
Titanium Zinc White	N/S				O												O		
Underpainting White	TD, ZOx	●●●●																	
Utrecht White	TD, ZOx	●●●●																	
White	TD	●●●●			S							G							
	OpW																		
	TD, ZSu																		
	N/S		S				GA									AG		S	
White (Spectrum)	N/S																		
Zinc Everwhite	ZOx	●●●●																O	
Zinc (Chinese) White	ZOx	●●●●																W	
Zinc White	**ZOx**	●●●●	O		OG				O		A	O	O		O		O		
	ZOx, TD	●●●●																	

Abbreviations used to signify composition correspond to recognized chemical abbreviations only in some cases. A detailed key is included on pp84-85.

LUKAS	MAIMERI	MARABU	MARCUS ART	MICHAEL HARDING	PEBEO	PELIKAN	PENTEL	PDQ	REEVES	RICH ART	ROBERSON	ROWNEY	SCHMINCKE	SENNELIER	SHIVA	SPECTRUM	JP STEPHENSON	TALENS	TITAN	UTRECHT	VALLEJO	WEBER	WINSOR & NEWTON
									S														G
			G																				
														O									
																							S
												P											
																				O			
												P											
				O																			
				G																			
												A											
O																							
O																							
												GA							O				
				O																			
				O																			
OAW			O									O					P	OA		A			O
												OP							O		•O		O
				OA			K		OA		O		OGP	O	O						A	W	OAW
																							O
																			O				
												A											
	G																						
		G																					
																					A	G	
W	S				OG	S																	
							S																
OW			O	O								OGP		P				O	O	O			O
																					O		

KEY O oil A acrylic W watercolor G gouache P pigment S poster K alkyd E egg tempera   **Quality** O artists and students O artists O students O unspecified

COLOR	COMPOSITION	MANUFACTURERS' PERMANENCY RATING	BEROL	BLOCKX	BOCOUR	CALDER	CAL-WESTERN	CARAN D'ACHE	DANACOLORS	DURO	FERRARIO	GOLDEN	GRUMBACHER	HOLBEIN	HUNT SPEEDBALL	LAMBERTYE	LASCAUX	LEFRANC & BOURGEOIS	LIQUITEX
Zinc White (contd)	ZSu, BaSl	•••								W					O				
	N/S			O						O			AG						
Zinc-Titanium White	ZOx, TD	••••											O						
MISCELLANEOUS																			
Aluminium	BnPw, Dg																		
Beige	N/S																		
Copper	IrOx, TD, Mi	••••										O							
	WeBn																		
	Bg																		
	N/S																		
Cream	N/S																		
Florentine Gold	N/S																		
Fluorescent Blue	N/S				S														
Fluorescent Cerise Red	N/S																		
Fluorescent Deep Magenta	N/S																		
Fluorescent Green	N/S				S														
Fluorescent Lemon	N/S																		
Fluorescent Lemon Yellow	N/S																		
Fluorescent Light Magenta (Pink)	N/S																		
Fluorescent Orange	N/S				S														
Fluorescent Pink	N/S				S														
Fluorescent Red	N/S				S														
Fluorescent Red-Orange	N/S																		
Fluorescent Violet	N/S				S														
Fluorescent White	N/S																		
Fluorescent Yellow	N/S				S														
Fluorescent Yellow-Orange	N/S																		
Gold	N/S				S								O						
Gold (Imit.)	N/S	••																	
Gold (Metallic)	McBn																		
Green Gold	N/S																		
Interference Blue	T, Mi											A							
Interference Gold	T, Mi											A							
Interference Green	T, Mi											A							
Interference Red	T, Mi											A							
Interference Violet	T, Mi											A							
Iridescent Blue	N/S			A															

Abbreviations used to signify composition correspond to recognized chemical abbreviations only in some cases. A detailed key is included on pp84-85.

LUKAS	MAIMERI	MARABU	MARCUS ART	MICHAEL HARDING	PEBEO	PELIKAN	PENTEL	PDQ	REEVES	RICH ART	ROBERSON	ROWNEY	SCHMINCKE	SENNELIER	SHIVA	SPECTRUM	JP STEPHENSON	TALENS	TITAN	UTRECHT	VALLEJO	WEBER	WINSOR & NEWTON
																							G
				O				OW					OE	O	O	P							
												0	O										
												P											
																				A			
												P											
												P											
	S					G																	
															O					A			
																							S
	S								S			S											
									S														
									S														
	S								S			S											
	S																						
							S		S														
									S														
	S						S		S			S											
	S						S					S											
	S						S		S			S											
									S														
									S														
	S								S														
	S						S					S											
									S														
							S																
																						G	
												S									OA		
														O									

COLOR	COMPOSITION	MANUFACTURERS' PERMANENCY RATING	BEROL	BLOCKX	BOCOUR	CALDER	CAL-WESTERN	CARAN D'ACHE	DANACOLORS	DURO	FERRARIO	GOLDEN	GRUMBACHER	HOLBEIN	HUNT SPEEDBALL	LAMBERTYE	LASCAUX	LEFRANC & BOURGEOIS	LIQUITEX
Iridescent Bronze	T, Mi	••••																A	
Iridescent Copper	T, Mi	••••									A							A	
Iridescent Dark Green	N/S				A														
Iridescent Gold	T, Mi	••••			A						A							A	
Iridescent Light Green	N/S				A														
Iridescent Orange	N/S				A														
Iridescent Pearl	T, Mi										A								
Iridescent Pewter	T, Mi	••••																A	
Iridescent Pink	N/S				A														
Iridescent Red	N/S				A														
Iridescent Red Gold	N/S				A														
Iridescent Silver	T, Mi	••••									A							A	
Iridescent Stainless Steel	IrCrNk										A								
Iridescent Violet	N/S				A														
Iridescent White	TD, Mi	••••											A					**A**	
	N/S				A													A	
Iridescent Yellow	N/S				A														
Luminous Blue Violet	N/S												G						
Luminous Green	N/S												P						
Luminous Lemon	N/S												A						
Luminous Magenta	N/S												G						
Luminous Opera	N/S												AG						
Luminous Orange	N/S												A						
Luminous Red	N/S												A						
Luminous Rose	N/S												AG						
Luminous Violet	N/S												A						
Luminous Yellow	N/S												A						
Metallic Copper	PwCp	••••																O	
Metallic Gold	PwCp-Z	••••		O														O	
Metallic Silver	PwAl	••••		O														O	
Old Gold	N/S																		
Pale Gold	Ne																		
	Bg																		
	N/S																		
Pearl Blue	N/S	••••											A						
Pearl Copper	N/S	••••											AG						
Pearl Gold	N/S	••••											**AG**						

Abbreviations used to signify composition correspond to recognized chemical abbreviations only in some cases. A detailed key is included on pp84-85.

LUKAS	MAIMERI	MARABU	MARCUS ART	MICHAEL HARDING	PEBEO	PELIKAN	PENTEL	PDQ	REEVES	RICH ART	ROBERSON	ROWNEY	SCHMINCKE	SENNELIER	SHIVA	SPECTRUM	JP STEPHENSON	TALENS	TITAN	UTRECHT	VALLEJO	WEBER	WINSOR & NEWTON
															O								
															O								
															O								
																							S
													P										
													P										
		S			G	G								G									
													S										

KEY O oil A acrylic W watercolor G gouache P pigment S poster K alkyd E egg tempera **Quality** O artists and students O artists O students O unspecified

COLOR	COMPOSITION	MANUFACTURERS' PERMANENCY RATING	BEROL	BLOCKX	BOCOUR	CALDER	CAL-WESTERN	CARAN D'ACHE	DANACOLORS	DURO	FERRARIO	GOLDEN	GRUMBACHER	HOLBEIN	HUNT SPEEDBALL	LAMBERTYE	LASCAUX	LEFRANC & BOURGEOIS	LIQUITEX
Pearl Green	N/S	●●●●												A					
Pearl Pink	N/S	●●●●												A					
Pearl Red	N/S	●●●●												A					
Pearl Sparkle	N/S	●●●●												A					
Pearl White	N/S	●●●●												AG					
Pearl Yellow	N/S	●●●●												A					
Permanent Bronze	Mi, TROx, YOx	●●●●																	
Permanent Gold	Mi, TROx, YOx	●●●●																	
Permanent Silver	Mi, TROx, YOx	●●●●																	
Rich Gold	We																		
	Bg																		
Rich Gold Bronze	N/S																		
Rich Pale Gold	We																		
	Bg																		
Silver	We																		
	Gb																		
	Ti, Mi																		
	N/S					S								O					
Silver (Imit.)	N/S	●●																	
Silver (Metallic)	McAl																		
Silver Bronze	N/S	●●																	
Thalo Bronze	TD, IrOx, Mi	●●●●											A						
Thalo Copper	TD, IrOx, Mi	●●●●											A						
Thalo Gold	TD, IrOx, Mi	●●●●											A						
Thalo Silver	TD, ApCn, Mi												A						
White (Fluorescent)	N/S																		

Abbreviations used to signify composition correspond to recognized chemical abbreviations only in some cases. A detailed key is included on pp84-85.

LUKAS	MAIMERI	MARABU	MARCUS ART	MICHAEL HARDING	PEBEO	PELIKAN	PENTEL	PDQ	REEVES	RICH ART	ROBERSON	ROWNEY	SCHMINCKE	SENNELIER	SHIVA	SPECTRUM	JP STEPHENSON	TALENS	TITAN	UTRECHT	VALLEJO	WEBER	WINSOR & NEWTON
												S											
												S											
												S											
																				A			
												W								A			
												P								A			
					G	G						P											
												W											
												P											
												P											
												P											
												P											
												S									A		
		S					S																S
						G	G																G
																						O	
												W											
		S															G						

KEY **O** oil **A** acrylic **W** watercolor **G** gouache **P** pigment **S** poster **K** alkyd **E** egg tempera   **Quality** **O** artists and students **O** artists **O** students **O** unspecified

HOW TO USE THE INKS CHART

1 2 4 3 5 6

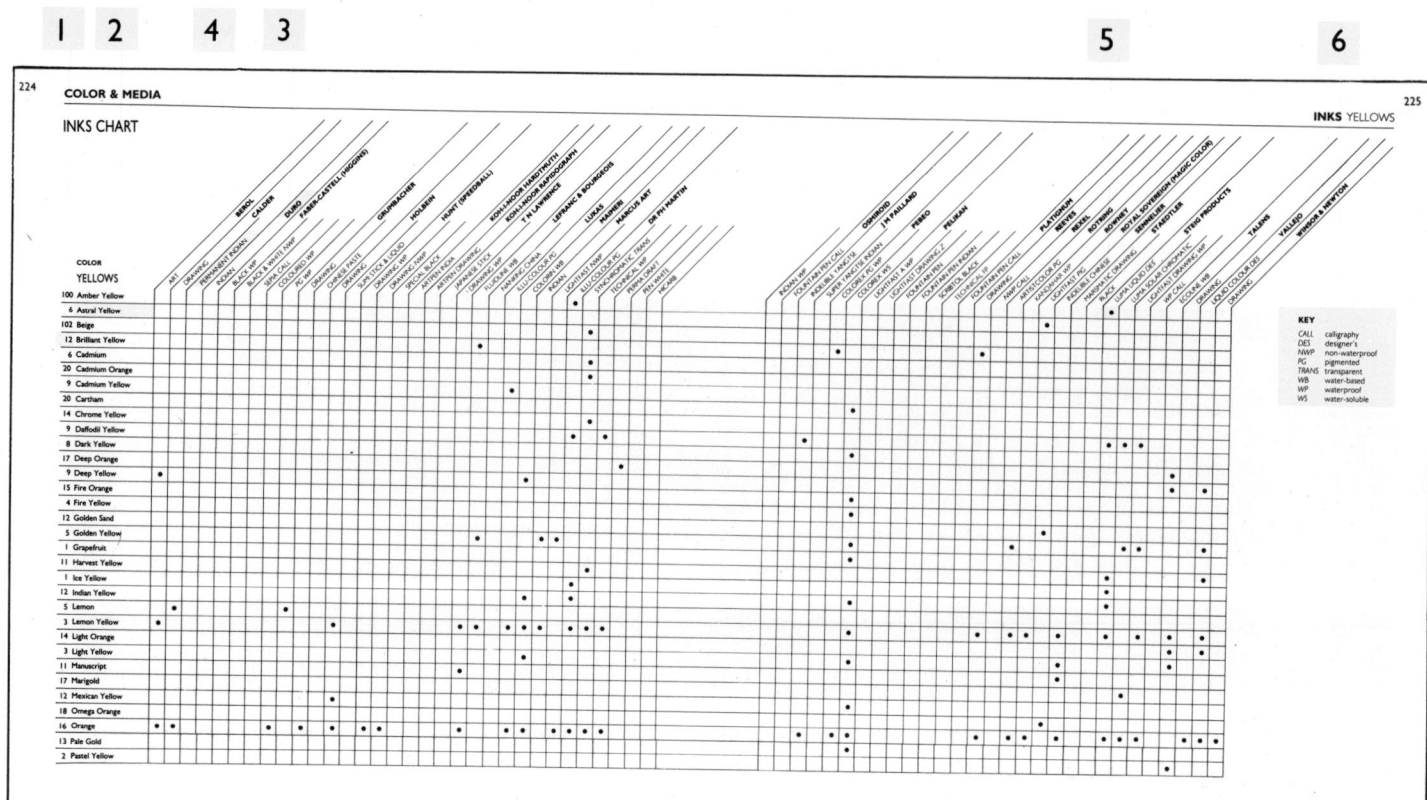

INKS CHART

COLOR YELLOWS

100 Amber Yellow
6 Astral Yellow
102 Beige
12 Brilliant Yellow
6 Cadmium
20 Cadmium Orange
9 Cadmium Yellow
20 Cartham
14 Chrome Yellow
9 Daffodil Yellow
8 Dark Yellow
17 Deep Orange
9 Deep Yellow
15 Fire Orange
4 Fire Yellow
12 Golden Sand
5 Golden Yellow
1 Grapefruit
11 Harvest Yellow
1 Ice Yellow
12 Indian Yellow
5 Lemon
3 Lemon Yellow
14 Light Orange
3 Light Yellow
11 Manuscript
17 Marigold
12 Mexican Yellow
18 Omega Orange
16 Orange
13 Pale Gold
2 Pastel Yellow

KEY

CALL — calligraphy
DES — designer's
NWP — non-waterproof
PG — pigmented
TRANS — transparent
WB — water-based
WP — waterproof
WS — water-soluble

1 The number beside each ink color relates to a numbered color sample (see pp 80-81). This sample will show you what the color of the ink looks like.

2 Ink colors are listed alphabetically down the page. They are divided up into eight groups consisting of yellows, red, violets, blues, greens, browns, blacks, grays and miscellaneous colors. To establish which manufacturer produces a particular color, follow the relevant column horizontally across the chart.

3 Manufacturers are listed alphabetically across the top of the chart. To establish which colors are produced by a manufacturer, follow the relevant column vertically down the chart.

4 Ranges of inks are listed under the manufacturer. The name of each range corresponds to the name used by the manufacturer. Codes indicate suitability and permanence.

CALL calligraphy
DES designer's
NWP non-waterproof
PG pigmented
TRANS transparent
WB water-based
WP waterproof
WS water-soluble

5 ● in the chart indicates that the range of ink at the top of the vertical column includes the color at the far left of the horizontal column.

6 A key to the codes is included on every spread.

INKS CHART

YELLOWS

COLOR	BEROL		CALDER		DURO		FABER-CASTELL (HIGGINS)				GRUMBACHER		HOLBEIN			HUNT (SPEEDBALL)				KOH-I-NOOR HARDTMUTH			KOH-I-NOOR RAPIDOGRAPH	T N LAWRENCE		LEFRANC & BOURGEOIS	LUKAS	MAIMERI	MARCUS ART		DR PH MARTIN	
	ART	DRAWING	PERMANENT INDIAN	INDIAN	BLACK WP	BLACK & WHITE NWP	SEPIA CALL	COLOURED WP	PG WP	DRAWING	CHINESE PASTE	DRAWING	SUMI STICK & LIQUID	DRAWING WP	DRAWING NWP	SPECIAL BLACK	ARTPEN INDIA	ARTPEN DRAWING	JAPANESE STICK	DRAWING WP	FLUIDLINE WB	NANKING CHINA	ILLU-COLOUR PG	COLORIN WB	INDIAN	LIGHTFAST NWP	ILLU-COLOUR PG	SYNCHROMATIC TRANS	TECHNICAL WP	PERMA DRAFT	PEN WHITE	HICARB
100 Amber Yellow																											•					
6 Astral Yellow																																
102 Beige																												•				
12 Brilliant Yellow																					•											
6 Cadmium																												•				
20 Cadmium Orange																												•				
9 Cadmium Yellow																							•									
20 Cartham																																
14 Chrome Yellow																												•				
9 Daffodil Yellow																											•		•			
8 Dark Yellow																																
17 Deep Orange																														•		
9 Deep Yellow	•																							•								
15 Fire Orange																																
4 Fire Yellow																																
12 Golden Sand																																
5 Golden Yellow																					•			•	•							
1 Grapefruit																																
11 Harvest Yellow																												•				
1 Ice Yellow																											•					
12 Indian Yellow																								•			•					
5 Lemon		•							•																							
3 Lemon Yellow	•											•								•	•		•	•	•		•	•	•			
14 Light Orange																																
3 Light Yellow																								•								
11 Manuscript																				•												
17 Marigold																																
12 Mexican Yellow												•																				
18 Omega Orange																																
16 Orange	•	•						•		•		•		•	•					•			•	•		•	•	•	•			
13 Pale Gold																																
2 Pastel Yellow																																

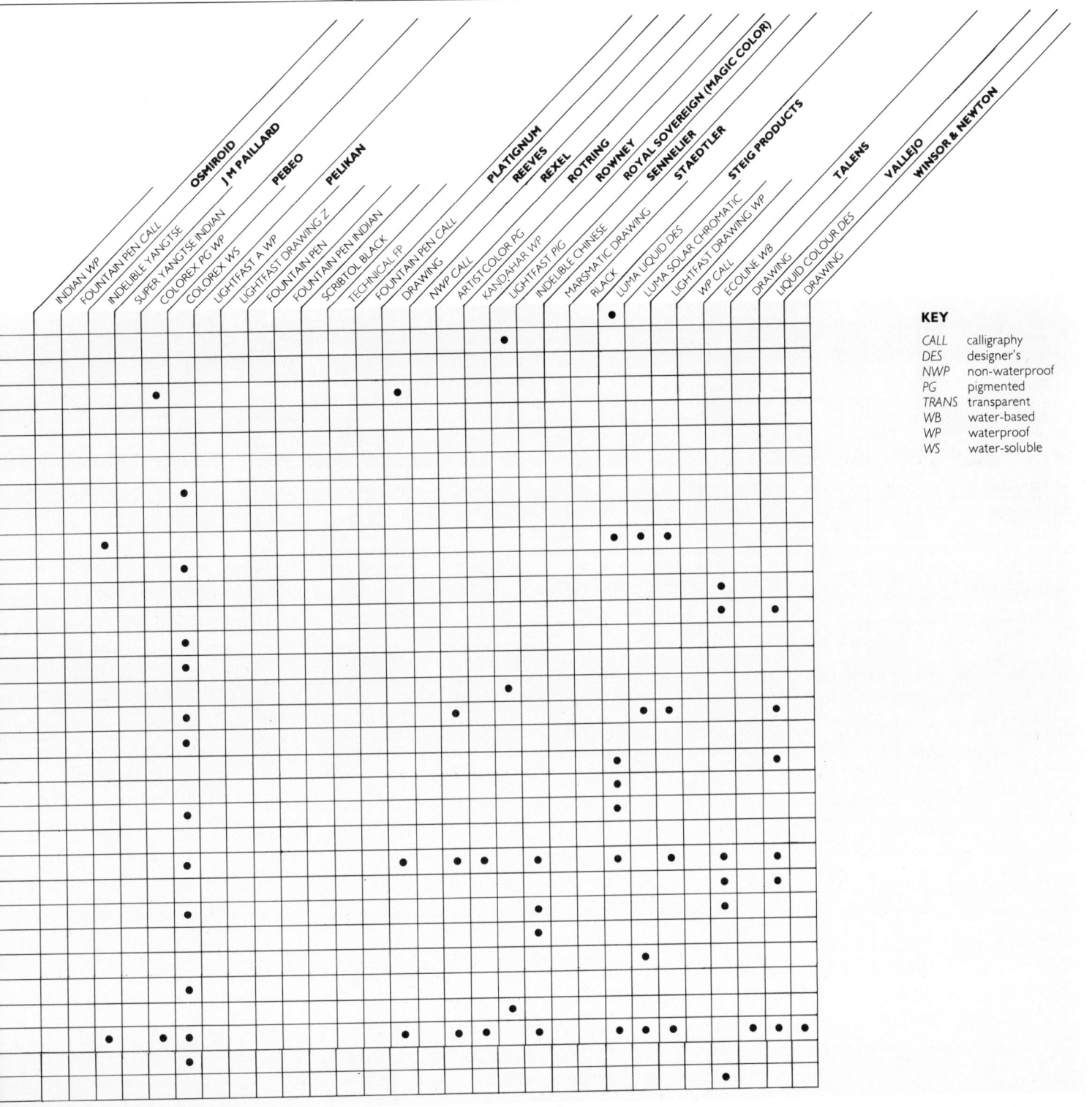

KEY

CALL	calligraphy
DES	designer's
NWP	non-waterproof
PG	pigmented
TRANS	transparent
WB	water-based
WP	waterproof
WS	water-soluble

Brands (left to right): BEROL · CALDER · DURO · FABER-CASTELL (HIGGINS) · GRUMBACHER · HOLBEIN · HUNT (SPEEDBALL) · KOH-I-NOOR HARDTMUTH · KOH-I-NOOR RAPIDOGRAPH · T N LAWRENCE · LEFRANC & BOURGEOIS · LUKAS · MAIMERI · MARCUS ART · DR PH MARTIN

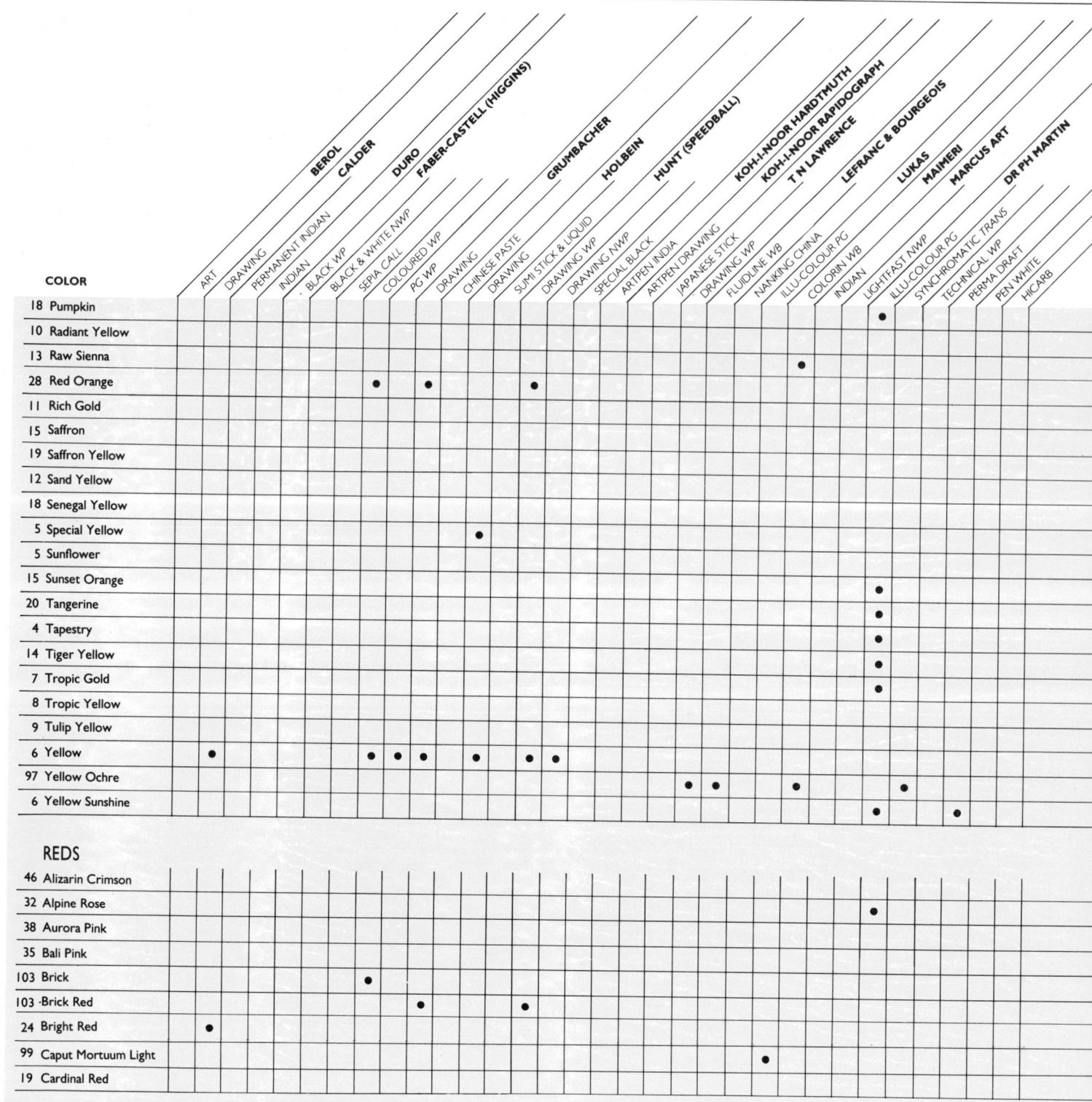

COLOR	ART	DRAWING	PERMANENT INDIAN	INDIAN	BLACK WP	BLACK & WHITE NWP	SEPIA CALL	COLOURED WP	PG WP	DRAWING	CHINESE PASTE	DRAWING	SUMI STICK & LIQUID	DRAWING WP	DRAWING NWP	SPECIAL BLACK	ARTPEN INDIA	ARTPEN DRAWING	JAPANESE STICK	DRAWING WB	FLUIDLINE WB	NANKING CHINA	ILLU-COLOUR PG	COLORIN WB	INDIAN	LIGHTFAST NWP	ILLU-COLOUR PG	SYNCHROMATIC TRANS	TECHNICAL WP	PERMA DRAFT	PEN WHITE	HICARB
18 Pumpkin																									●							
10 Radiant Yellow																																
13 Raw Sienna																						●										
28 Red Orange								●		●			●																			
11 Rich Gold																																
15 Saffron																																
19 Saffron Yellow																																
12 Sand Yellow																																
18 Senegal Yellow																																
5 Special Yellow											●																					
5 Sunflower																																
15 Sunset Orange																									●							
20 Tangerine																									●							
4 Tapestry																									●							
14 Tiger Yellow																									●							
7 Tropic Gold																									●							
8 Tropic Yellow																																
9 Tulip Yellow																																
6 Yellow		●						●	●	●	●		●	●																		
97 Yellow Ochre																	●	●			●					●						
6 Yellow Sunshine																									●			●				

REDS

COLOR	ART	DRAWING	PERMANENT INDIAN	INDIAN	BLACK WP	BLACK & WHITE NWP	SEPIA CALL	COLOURED WP	PG WP	DRAWING	CHINESE PASTE	DRAWING	SUMI STICK & LIQUID	DRAWING WP	DRAWING NWP	SPECIAL BLACK	ARTPEN INDIA	ARTPEN DRAWING	JAPANESE STICK	DRAWING WB	FLUIDLINE WB	NANKING CHINA	ILLU-COLOUR PG	COLORIN WB	INDIAN	LIGHTFAST NWP	ILLU-COLOUR PG	SYNCHROMATIC TRANS	TECHNICAL WP	PERMA DRAFT	PEN WHITE	HICARB
46 Alizarin Crimson																																
32 Alpine Rose																									●							
38 Aurora Pink																																
35 Bali Pink																																
103 Brick								●																								
103 Brick Red										●			●																			
24 Bright Red		●																														
99 Caput Mortuum Light																				●												
19 Cardinal Red																																

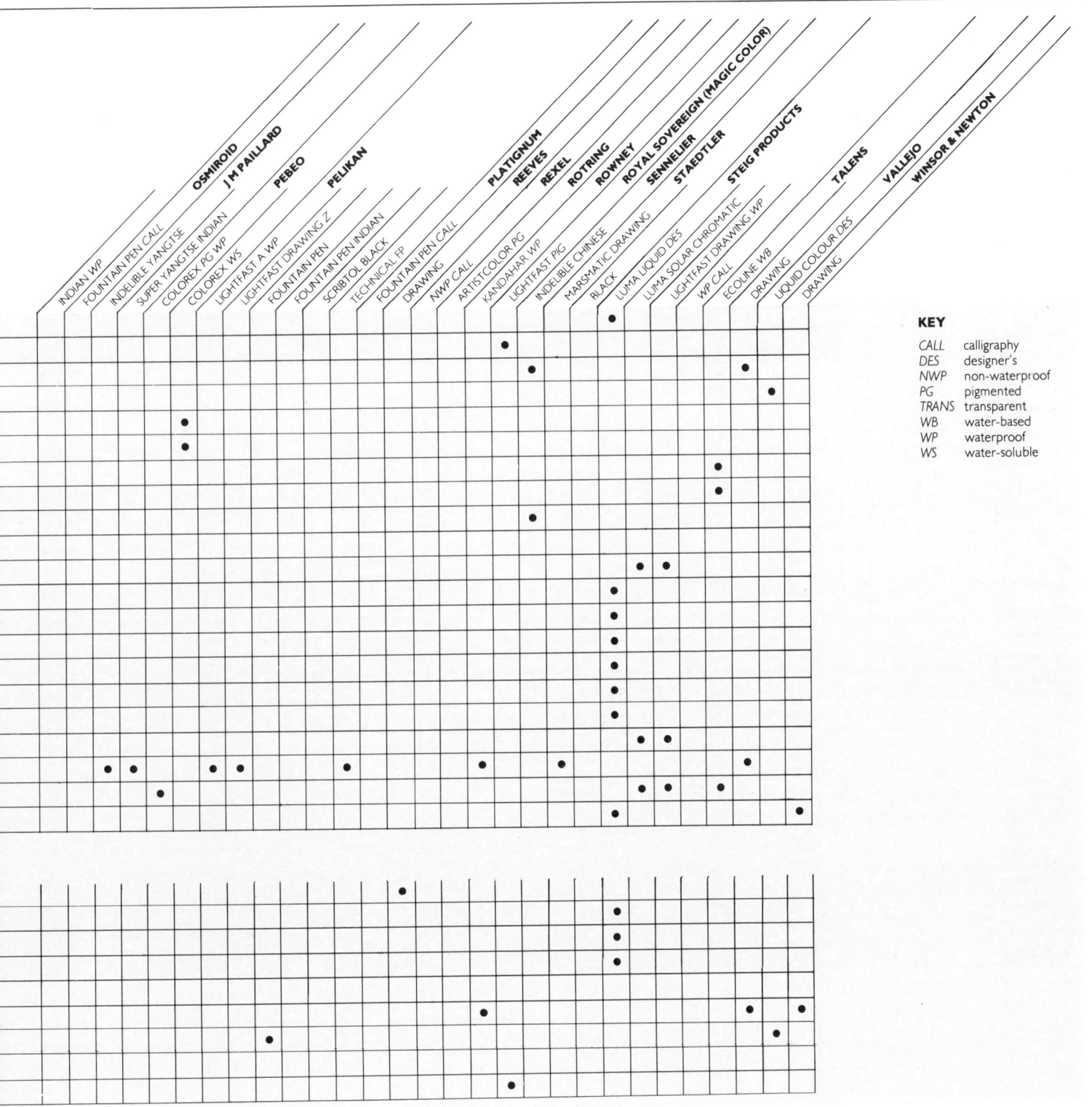

KEY

CALL	calligraphy
DES	designer's
NWP	non-waterproof
PG	pigmented
TRANS	transparent
WB	water-based
WP	waterproof
WS	water-soluble

COLOR	BEROL		CALDER	DURO		FABER-CASTELL (HIGGINS)					GRUMBACHER		HOLBEIN				HUNT (SPEEDBALL)		KOH-I-NOOR HARDTMUTH			KOH-I-NOOR RAPIDOGRAPH	T N LAWRENCE			LEFRANC & BOURGEOIS	LUKAS	MAIMERI	MARCUS ART	DR PH MARTIN		
	ART	DRAWING	PERMANENT INDIAN	INDIAN	BLACK WP	BLACK & WHITE NWP	SEPIA CALL	COLOURED WP	PG WP	DRAWING	CHINESE PASTE	DRAWING	SUMI STICK & LIQUID	DRAWING WP	DRAWING NWP	SPECIAL BLACK	ARTPEN INDIA	ARTPEN DRAWING	JAPANESE STICK	DRAWING WP	FLUIDLINE WB	NANKING CHINA	ILLU-COLOUR PG	COLORIN WB	INDIAN	LIGHTFAST NWP	ILLU-COLOUR PG	SYNCHROMATIC TRANS	TECHNICAL WP	PERMA DRAFT	PEN WHITE	HICARB
48 Carmine	●							●			●							●				●										
46 Carmine Red							●		●				●						●													
20 Cartham																						●										
49 Cerise																										●						
46 Cherry Red											●																●					
31 Coral Red																																
46 Crimson		●																									●					
49 Cyclamen																						●					●					
48 Deep Red																																
29 Fire Red																												●				
26 Flame Red																																
39 Fuchsia																											●					
40 Hot Pink																	●															
43 Ice Pink																											●					
35 Indian Pink																																
25 Jewel Red																																
41 Lake																										●						
37 Light Rose																						●										
45 Magenta							●	●										●	●		●	●	●	●			●					
45 Mars Red																																
29 Ming Red																																
47 Moss Rose													●														●					
44 Orchid Pink																																
39 Panther Pink																																
38 Paradise Pink																																
49 Parma Rose																						●										
33 Pastel Red																																
34 Pastel Rose																																
23 Pepper Red																																
24 Persimmon																			●								●					
45 Pink																		●	●													
20 Poppy																																

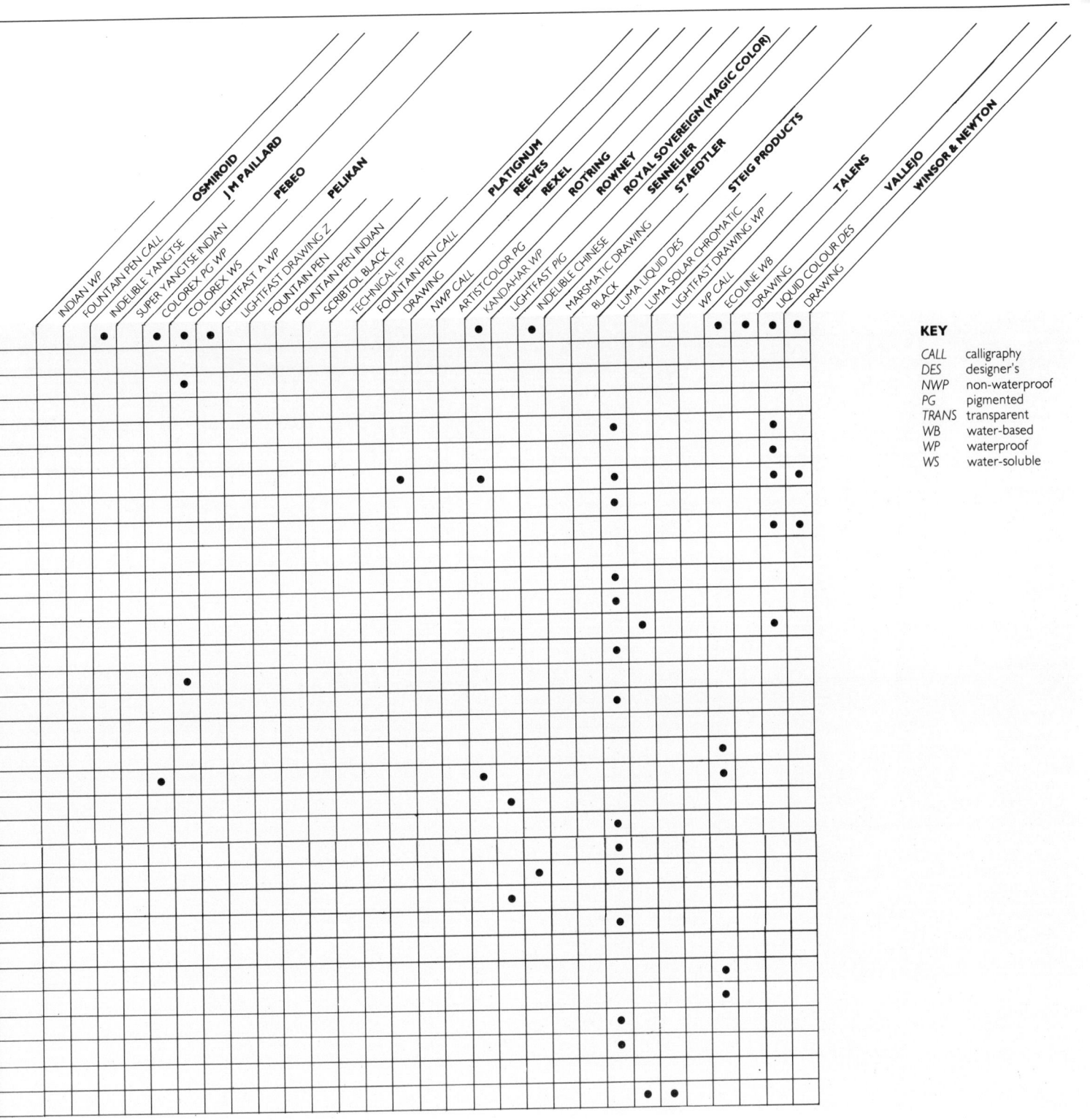

KEY

CALL	calligraphy
DES	designer's
NWP	non-waterproof
PG	pigmented
TRANS	transparent
WB	water-based
WP	waterproof
WS	water-soluble

COLOR	BEROL		CALDER		DURO			FABER-CASTELL (HIGGINS)				GRUMBACHER		HOLBEIN			HUNT (SPEEDBALL)		KOH-I-NOOR HARDTMUTH		KOH-I-NOOR RAPIDOGRAPH	T N LAWRENCE		LEFRANC & BOURGEOIS		LUKAS		MAIMERI	MARCUS ART		DR PH MARTIN	
	ART	DRAWING	PERMANENT INDIAN	INDIAN	BLACK WP	BLACK & WHITE NWP	SEPIA CALL	COLOURED WP	PG WP	DRAWING	CHINESE PASTE	DRAWING	SUMI STICK & LIQUID	DRAWING WP	DRAWING NWP	SPECIAL BLACK	ARTPEN INDIA	ARTPEN DRAWING	JAPANESE STICK	DRAWING WP	FLUIDLINE WB	NANKING CHINA	ILLU-COLOUR PG	COLORIN WB	INDIAN	LIGHTFAST NWP	ILLU-COLOUR PG	SYNCHROMATIC TRANS	TECHNICAL WP	PERMA DRAFT	PEN WHITE	HICARB
42 Raspberry																										●						
30 Red	●	●							●					●	●	●	●	●								●						
29 Red (Scarlet)										●																						
46 Rhodamine																													●			
41 Rose																			●	●												
21 Rose Carthame																												●				
48 Rose Madder																											●					
37 Rose Pink																					●											
34 Rose Tyrian																																
46 Rubine																							●									
99 Russet								●					●																			
100 Rust																																
100 Sanguine																																
30 Scarlet												●							●				●		●	●						
27 Scarlet Red								●																								
20 Special Red												●																				
36 Sunrise Pink																										●						
22 Sunset Red																										●						
37 Tahiti Red																										●						
40 Tropic Pink																										●						
41 Tulip Red																										●						
25 Turkish Red																																
42 Tyrian Pink																				●												
46 Velvet Red																																
28 Vermilion	●	●										●	●							●		●	●				●					
26 Vermilion Light Red																						●										
47 Violet Red																																
95 Wild Rose																										●						
103 Wine Red												●																●				

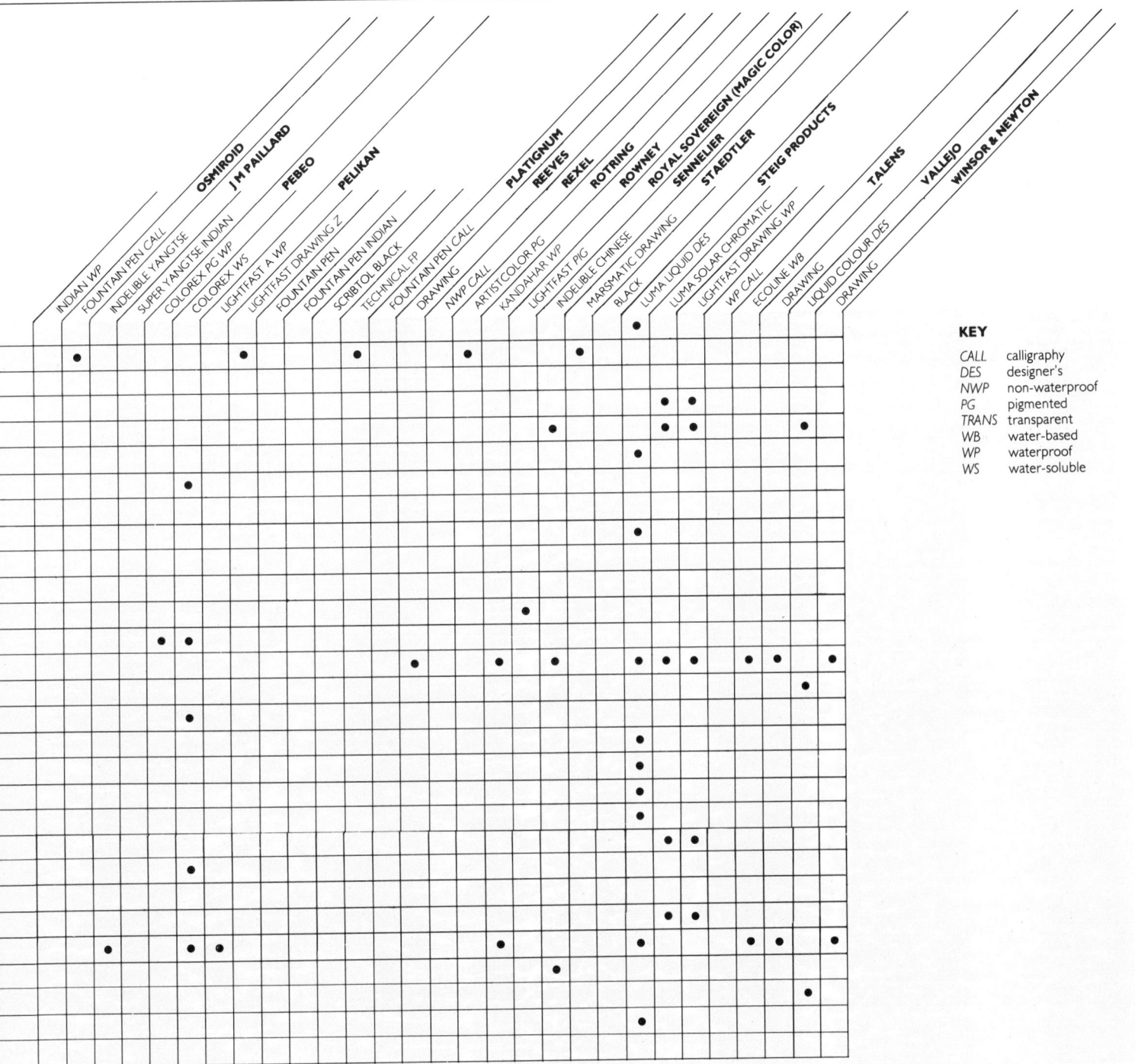

KEY

CALL	calligraphy
DES	designer's
NWP	non-waterproof
PG	pigmented
TRANS	transparent
WB	water-based
WP	waterproof
WS	water-soluble

COLOR

COLOR	BEROL		CALDER		DURO		FABER-CASTELL (HIGGINS)						GRUMBACHER			HOLBEIN	HUNT (SPEEDBALL)		KOH-I-NOOR HARDTMUTH		KOH-I-NOOR RAPIDOGRAPH	T N LAWRENCE	LEFRANC & BOURGEOIS			LUKAS	MAIMERI	MARCUS ART	DR PH MARTIN			
	ART	DRAWING	PERMANENT INDIAN	INDIAN	BLACK WP	BLACK & WHITE NWP	SEPIA CALL	COLOURED WP	PG WP	DRAWING	CHINESE PASTE	DRAWING	SUMI STICK & LIQUID	DRAWING WP	DRAWING NWP	SPECIAL BLACK	ARTPEN INDIA	ARTPEN DRAWING	JAPANESE STICK	DRAWING WP	FLUIDLINE WB	NANKING CHINA	ILLU-COLOUR PG	COLORIN WB	INDIAN	LIGHTFAST NWP	ILLU-COLOUR PG	SYNCHROMATIC TRANS	TECHNICAL WP	PERMA DRAFT	PEN WHITE	HICARB
VIOLETS																																
54 Blue Violet											●									●												
50 Delta Violet																																
51 French Lilac																																
55 Indigo Violet																																
53 Mineral Violet																				●												
50 Pansy																																
49 Parma																																
52 Pastel Violet																																
48 Plum																																
50 Purple	●	●																●								●						
49 Red Violet							●							●	●					●												
50 Reddish Violet							●		●		●	●											●									
49 Rose Violet																																
50 Royal Purple																																
53 Special Violet											●																					
51 Sweet Violet																																
53 Ultramarine Violet																				●	●											
54 Violet	●	●					●		●		●		●					●		●				●	●	●	●					
54 Violet Lake																						●										
BLUES																																
67 Adriatic Blue																																
72 Aqua Blue																																
74 Aquamarine																																
63 Aster Blue																																
62 Blue	●		●				●	●					●	●		●		●														
64 Blue (Ultramarine)										●																						
59 Brilliant Blue		●	●																													
65 Cerulean Blue																										●						
66 Chinese Blue																																
63 Cobalt																																
63 Cobalt Blue		●									●											●		●	●							

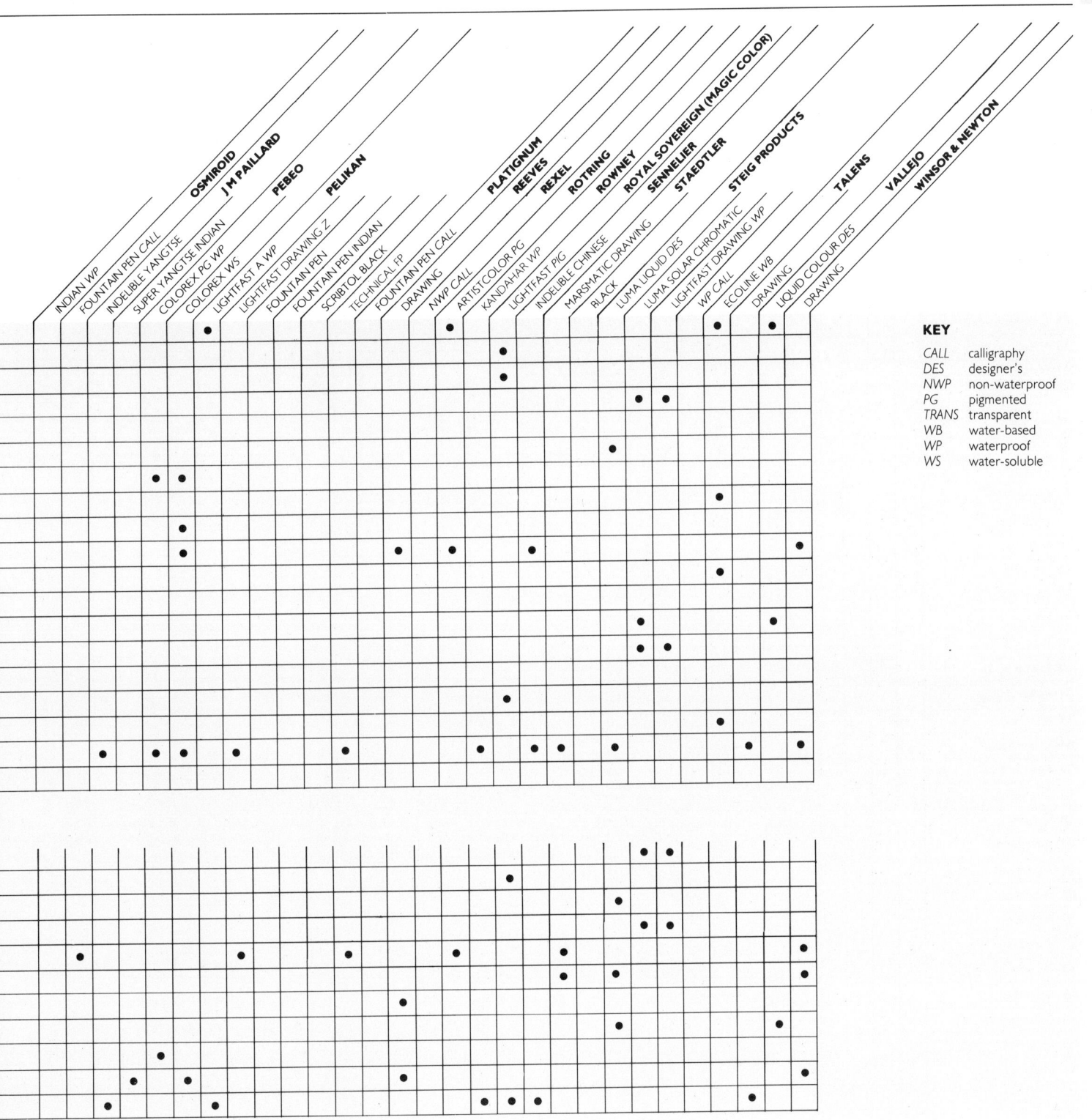

KEY

CALL	calligraphy
DES	designer's
NWP	non-waterproof
PG	pigmented
TRANS	transparent
WB	water-based
WP	waterproof
WS	water-soluble

Code	Color	BEROL		CALDER	DURO	FABER-CASTELL (HIGGINS)						GRUMBACHER		HOLBEIN				HUNT (SPEEDBALL)		KOH-I-NOOR HARDTMUTH		KOH-I-NOOR RAPIDOGRAPH	T N LAWRENCE	LEFRANC & BOURGEOIS			LUKAS		MAIMERI	MARCUS ART	DR PH MARTIN		
		ART	DRAWING	PERMANENT INDIAN	INDIAN	BLACK WP	BLACK & WHITE NWP	SEPIA CALL	COLOURED WP	PG WP	DRAWING	CHINESE PASTE	DRAWING	SUMI STICK & LIQUID	DRAWING WP	DRAWING NWP	SPECIAL BLACK	ARTPEN INDIA	ARTPEN DRAWING	JAPANESE STICK	DRAWING WP	FLUIDLINE WB	NANKING CHINA	ILLU-COLOUR PG	COLORIN WB	INDIAN	LIGHTFAST NWP	ILLU-COLOUR PG	SYNCHROMATIC TRANS	TECHNICAL WP	PERMA DRAFT	PEN WHITE	HICARB
64	Cornflower Blue																																
65	Cyan																		●		●		●	●									
65	Harvest Blue																																
55	Hyacinth Blue																										●						
69	Ice Blue																										●						
61	Indigo								●		●				●						●								●				
57	Iris Blue																										●						
66	Lagoon Blue																																
56	Light Blue																																
50	Magenta									●												●											
63	Monastral Blue																																
68	Navy Blue																																
61	Nòrway Blue																										●						
59	Ocean Blue																													●			
63	Orchid Blue																																
73	Oriental Blue																																
73	Pastel Blue																																
64	Peacock Blue																																
56	Prussian Blue		●										●								●			●			●	●					
56	Purple Blue																																
58	Royal Blue																																
58	Sapphire Blue																							●									
66	Sky Blue																							●									
60	Slate Blue																										●						
60	Special Blue												●																				
68	Turquoise	●							●		●		●		●						●			●			●	●	●				
62	Twilight Blue																																
59	Ultra Blue																										●						
59	Ultramarine	●							●		●				●						●			●		●	●	●	●				
57	Ultramarine Deep																					●											
66	Ultramarine Light																					●											

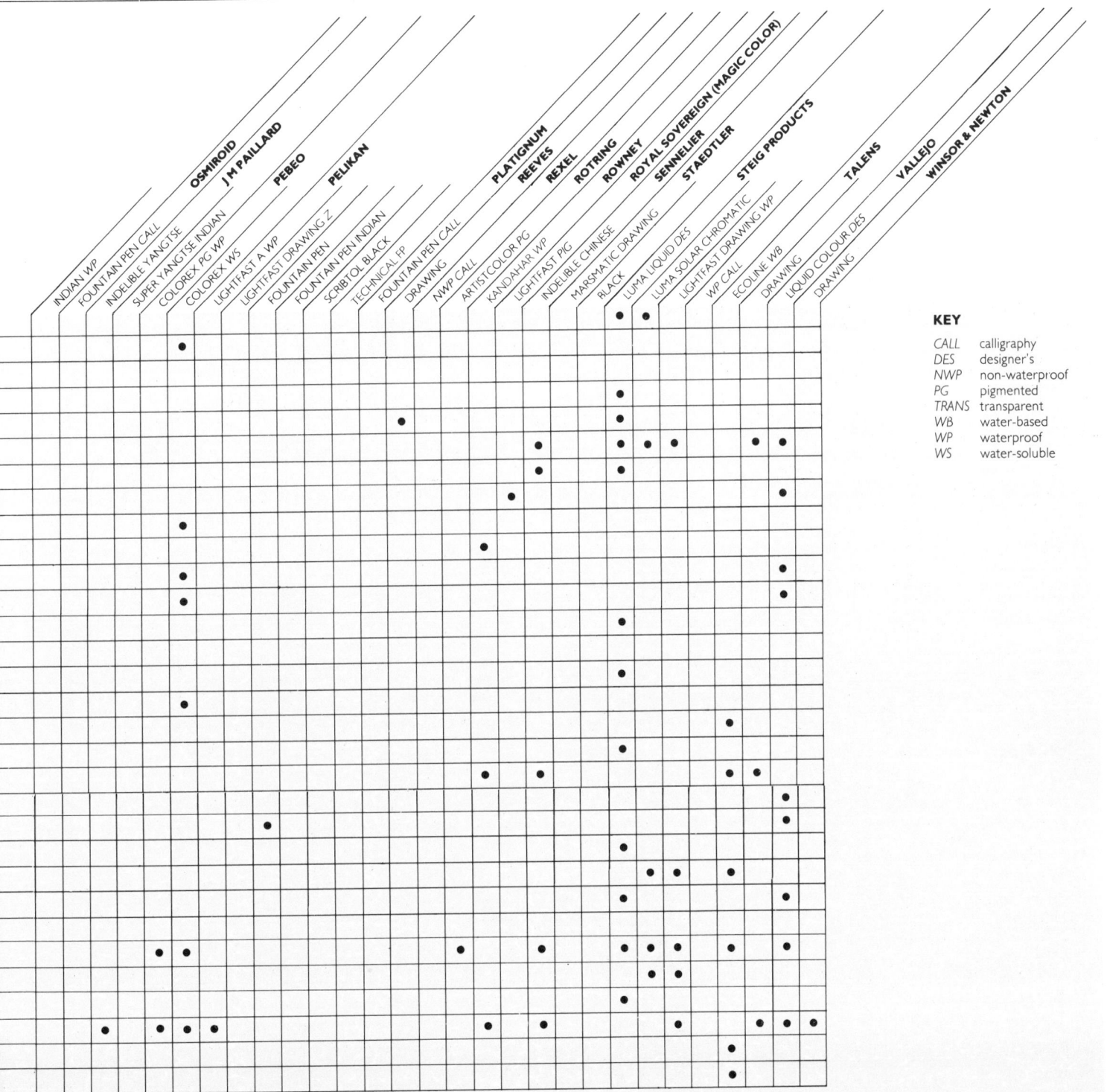

KEY

CALL	calligraphy
DES	designer's
NWP	non-waterproof
PG	pigmented
TRANS	transparent
WB	water-based
WP	waterproof
WS	water-soluble

COLOR	BEROL ART	BEROL DRAWING	CALDER PERMANENT INDIAN	CALDER INDIAN	DURO BLACK WP	DURO BLACK & WHITE NWP	DURO SEPIA CALL	FABER-CASTELL (HIGGINS) COLOURED WP	FABER-CASTELL PG WP	FABER-CASTELL DRAWING	FABER-CASTELL CHINESE PASTE	GRUMBACHER DRAWING	GRUMBACHER SUMI STICK & LIQUID	GRUMBACHER DRAWING WP	HOLBEIN DRAWING NWP	HOLBEIN SPECIAL BLACK	HUNT (SPEEDBALL) ARTPEN INDIA	HUNT ARTPEN DRAWING	HUNT JAPANESE STICK	KOH-I-NOOR HARDTMUTH DRAWING WP	KOH-I-NOOR HARDTMUTH FLUIDLINE WB	KOH-I-NOOR RAPIDOGRAPH NANKING CHINA	KOH-I-NOOR RAPIDOGRAPH ILLU-COLOUR PG	T N LAWRENCE COLORIN WB	T N LAWRENCE INDIAN	LEFRANC & BOURGEOIS LIGHTFAST NWP	LUKAS ILLU-COLOUR PG	LUKAS SYNCHROMATIC TRANS	MAIMERI TECHNICAL WP	MARCUS ART PERMA DRAFT	DR PH MARTIN PEN WHITE	DR PH MARTIN HICARB
57 Victoria Blue																																
59 Washable Royal Blue																																

GREENS

COLOR	ART	DRAWING	PERMANENT INDIAN	INDIAN	BLACK WP	BLACK & WHITE NWP	SEPIA CALL	COLOURED WP	PG WP	DRAWING	CHINESE PASTE	DRAWING	SUMI STICK & LIQUID	DRAWING WP	DRAWING NWP	SPECIAL BLACK	ARTPEN INDIA	ARTPEN DRAWING	JAPANESE STICK	DRAWING WP	FLUIDLINE WB	NANKING CHINA	ILLU-COLOUR PG	COLORIN WB	INDIAN	LIGHTFAST NWP	ILLU-COLOUR PG	SYNCHROMATIC TRANS	TECHNICAL WP	PERMA DRAFT	PEN WHITE	HICARB
83 Apple Green																																
82 April Green																											•		•			
75 Avocado Green																														•		
78 Bamboo Green											•																					
74 Blue Green																																
74 Bluish Green																																
61 Bottle Green																																
80 Brilliant Green		•															•	•			•											
84 Bronze Green																																
81 Calypso Green																											•					
85 Chartreuse																					•						•					
65 Cyan																		•														
71 Cypress Green																																
76 Deep Green																				•			•									
80 Emerald		•										•			•													•				
89 Fern Green																																
78 Fir Green																																
83 Fire Green																																
73 Firefly Green																																
78 Forest Green																																
77 Gamma Green																																
89 Gold Green																		•														
95 Golden Olive																																
83 Grass Green	•																										•					
78 Green	•	•						•	•					•	•					•			•	•	•							
71 Green Deep										•												•	•									
77 Green Field																					•											
88 Green Gold																						•	•									

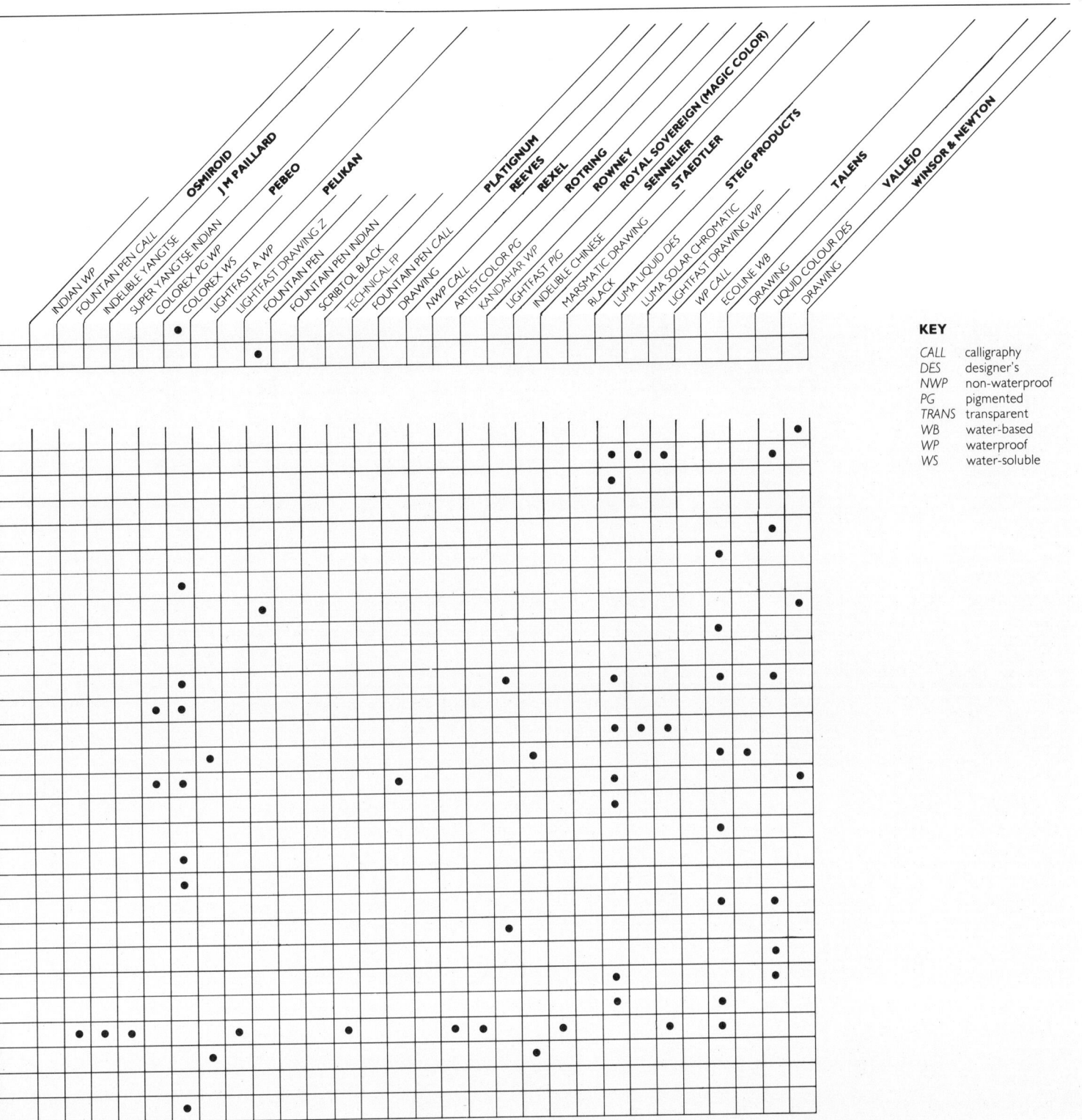

KEY

CALL	calligraphy
DES	designer's
NWP	non-waterproof
PG	pigmented
TRANS	transparent
WB	water-based
WP	waterproof
WS	water-soluble

COLOR

Manufacturer / media column order (left to right):

- **BEROL:** ART, DRAWING
- **CALDER:** PERMANENT INDIAN, INDIAN
- **DURO:** BLACK WP, BLACK & WHITE NWP
- **FABER-CASTELL (HIGGINS):** SEPIA CALL, COLOURED WP, PG WP, DRAWING
- **GRUMBACHER:** CHINESE PASTE, DRAWING
- **HOLBEIN:** SUMI STICK & LIQUID, DRAWING WP, DRAWING NWP
- **HUNT (SPEEDBALL):** SPECIAL BLACK, ARTPEN INDIA, ARTPEN DRAWING
- **KOH-I-NOOR HARDTMUTH:** JAPANESE STICK
- **KOH-I-NOOR RAPIDOGRAPH:** DRAWING WP
- **T N LAWRENCE:** FLUIDLINE WB, NANKING CHINA, ILLU-COLOUR PG
- **LEFRANC & BOURGEOIS:** COLORIN WB, INDIAN
- **LUKAS:** LIGHTFAST NWP, ILLU-COLOUR PG
- **MAIMERI:** SYNCHROMATIC TRANS
- **MARCUS ART:** TECHNICAL WP, PERMA DRAFT
- **DR PH MARTIN:** PEN WHITE, HICARB

COLOR	ART	DRAWING	PERMANENT INDIAN	INDIAN	BLACK WP	BLACK & WHITE NWP	SEPIA CALL	COLOURED WP	PG WP	DRAWING	CHINESE PASTE	DRAWING	SUMI STICK & LIQUID	DRAWING WP	DRAWING NWP	SPECIAL BLACK	ARTPEN INDIA	ARTPEN DRAWING	JAPANESE STICK	DRAWING WP	FLUIDLINE WB	NANKING CHINA	ILLU-COLOUR PG	COLORIN WB	INDIAN	LIGHTFAST NWP	ILLU-COLOUR PG	SYNCHROMATIC TRANS	TECHNICAL WP	PERMA DRAFT	PEN WHITE	HICARB
80 Green Light (Leaf)									•																							
84 Hooker's Green																											•					
86 Ice Green																										•						
75 Jungle Green																										•						
70 Juniper Green																										•						
81 Leaf Green								•					•																			
86 Light Green									•									•	•		•	•										
87 Lime Green																																
83 Linden Green											•																					
81 May Green											•																					
83 Meadow Green																																
92 Moss Green											•													•								
80 Nile Green																										•						
90 Olive Green																				•				•		•	•	•				
82 Oriental Green																																
85 Pale Green																																
77 Pastel Green																																
93 Payne's Green																																
85 Pea Green																																
93 Sap Green																					•											
92 Special Green											•																					
88 Spring Green																																
71 Spruce Green																												•				
70 Thalo Green																																
70 Turquoise Green														•																		
71 Viridian	•	•																	•			•					•					
85 Yellow Green																																

BROWNS

COLOR	ART	DRAWING	PERMANENT INDIAN	INDIAN	BLACK WP	BLACK & WHITE NWP	SEPIA CALL	COLOURED WP	PG WP	DRAWING	CHINESE PASTE	DRAWING	SUMI STICK & LIQUID	DRAWING WP	DRAWING NWP	SPECIAL BLACK	ARTPEN INDIA	ARTPEN DRAWING	JAPANESE STICK	DRAWING WP	FLUIDLINE WB	NANKING CHINA	ILLU-COLOUR PG	COLORIN WB	INDIAN	LIGHTFAST NWP	ILLU-COLOUR PG	SYNCHROMATIC TRANS	TECHNICAL WP	PERMA DRAFT	PEN WHITE	HICARB
98 Acorn Brown																																
102 Antelope Brown																										•		•				
96 Brou De Noix (Walnut)																																

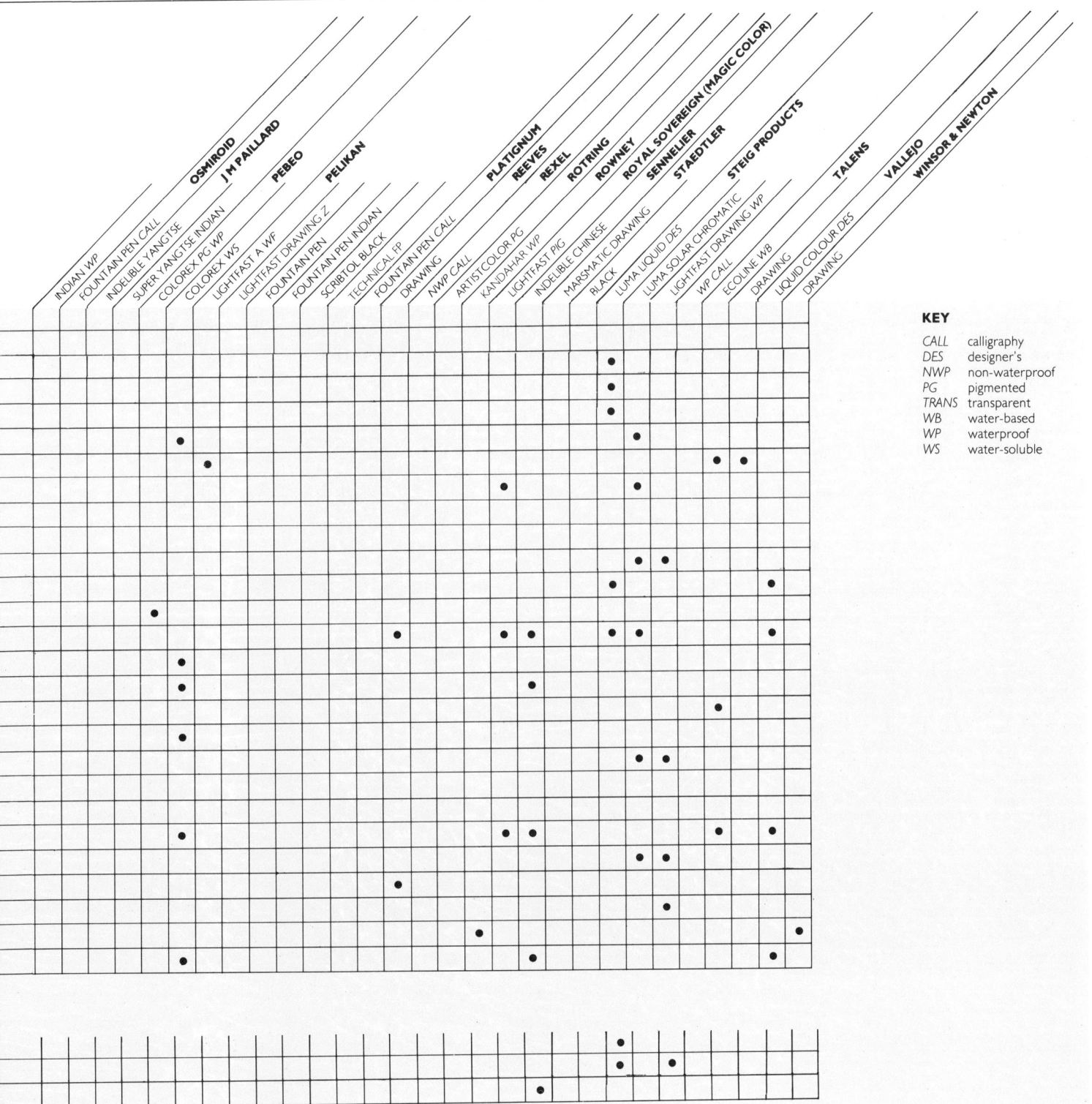

KEY

CALL	calligraphy
DES	designer's
NWP	non-waterproof
PG	pigmented
TRANS	transparent
WB	water-based
WP	waterproof
WS	water-soluble

COLOR	BEROL		CALDER	DURO	FABER-CASTELL (HIGGINS)							GRUMBACHER	HOLBEIN				HUNT (SPEEDBALL)		KOH-I-NOOR HARDTMUTH		KOH-I-NOOR RAPIDOGRAPH	T N LAWRENCE		LEFRANC & BOURGEOIS		LUKAS		MAIMERI	MARCUS ART		DR PH MARTIN	
	ART	DRAWING	PERMANENT INDIAN	INDIAN	BLACK WP	BLACK & WHITE NWP	SEPIA CALL	COLOURED WP	PG WP	DRAWING	CHINESE PASTE	DRAWING	SUMI STICK & LIQUID	DRAWING WP	DRAWING NWP	SPECIAL BLACK	ARTPEN DRAWING	ARTPEN INDIA	JAPANESE STICK	DRAWING WP	FLUIDLINE WB	NANKING CHINA	ILLU-COLOUR PG	COLORIN WB	INDIAN	LIGHTFAST NWP	ILLU-COLOUR PG	SYNCHROMATIC TRANS	TECHNICAL WP	PERMA DRAFT	PEN WHITE	HICARB
86 Brown	•	•					•	•					•	•		•			•													
106 Brown (Sepia)									•																							
19 Burnt Orange																										•						
99 Burnt Sienna		•									•									•			•				•					
98 Burnt Sienna (Russet)	•								•																							
105 Burnt Umber		•																		•												
105 Chocolate Mousse																													•			
101 Coffee Brown																										•						
106 Deep Brown																																
98 Deep Ochre																																
18 Gold Ochre																												•				
97 Golden Brown																						•				•						
98 Light Brown																											•					
98 Loam Brown																																
104 Mahogany																										•						
98 Natural Sienna																										•						
99 Navajo Brown																																
101 Nut Brown																																
94 Ochre (Gold)																																
100 Orange Brown																																
107 Peat Brown																																
103 Red Brown																																
99 Red Ochre																			•			•										
103 Reddish Brown																											•					
105 Saddle Brown																											•					
102 Seal Brown																											•					
106 Sepia							•				•								•			•	•			•	•					
98 Sienna											•																					
99 Special Brown											•																					
97 Tawny																																
19 Terra Cotta											•																					
96 Tobacco																						•				•						

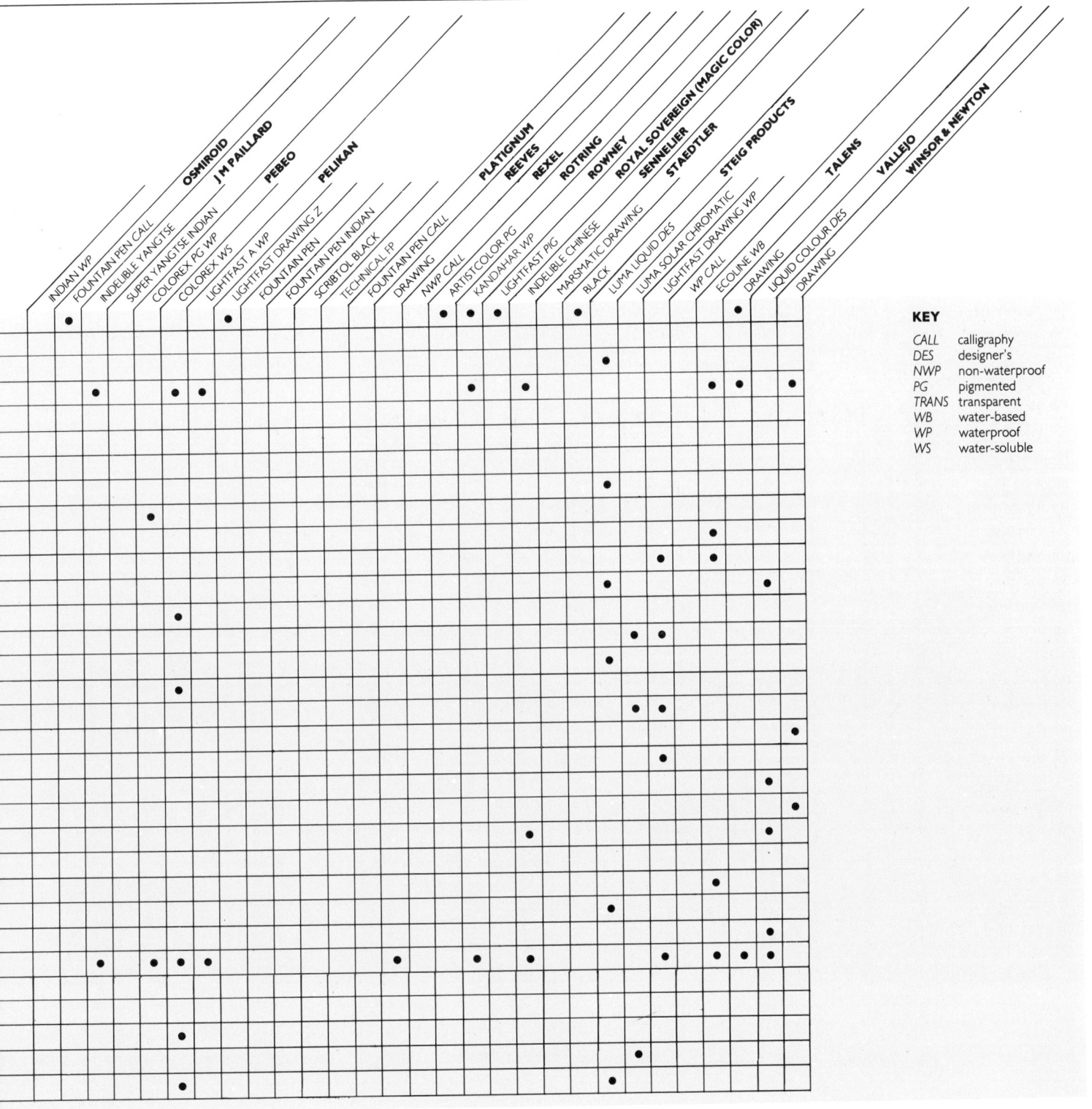

OSMIROID
J M PAILLARD
PEBEO
PELIKAN
PLATIGNUM
REEVES
REXEL
ROTRING
ROWNEY
ROYAL SOVEREIGN (MAGIC COLOR)
SENNELIER
STAEDTLER
STEIG PRODUCTS
TALENS
VALLEJO
WINSOR & NEWTON

INDIAN WP
FOUNTAIN PEN CALL
INDELIBLE YANGTSE
SUPER YANGTSE INDIAN
COLOREX PG WP
COLOREX WS
LIGHTFAST A WP
LIGHTFAST DRAWING Z
FOUNTAIN PEN
FOUNTAIN PEN INDIAN
SCRIBTOL BLACK
TECHNICAL FP
FOUNTAIN PEN CALL
DRAWING
NWP CALL
ARTISTCOLOR PG
KANDAHAR WP
LIGHTFAST PIG
INDELIBLE CHINESE
MARSMATIC DRAWING
BLACK
LUMA LIQUID DES
LUMA SOLAR CHROMATIC
LIGHTFAST DRAWING WP
WP CALL
ECOLINE WB
DRAWING
LIQUID COLOUR DES
DRAWING

KEY

CALL	calligraphy
DES	designer's
NWP	non-waterproof
PG	pigmented
TRANS	transparent
WB	water-based
WP	waterproof
WS	water-soluble

The following chart maps colors against manufacturers' products. A bullet (•) indicates the color is available in that product.

COLOR	BEROL ART	BEROL DRAWING	CALDER PERMANENT INDIAN	DURO INDIAN	DURO BLACK WP	FABER-CASTELL (HIGGINS) BLACK & WHITE NWP	HIGGINS SEPIA CALL	HIGGINS COLOURED WP	HIGGINS PG WP	GRUMBACHER DRAWING	GRUMBACHER CHINESE PASTE	HOLBEIN DRAWING	HOLBEIN SUMI STICK & LIQUID	HOLBEIN DRAWING WP	HUNT (SPEEDBALL) DRAWING NWP	HUNT SPECIAL BLACK	HUNT ARTPEN INDIA	HUNT ARTPEN DRAWING	KOH-I-NOOR HARDTMUTH JAPANESE STICK	KOH-I-NOOR HARDTMUTH DRAWING WP	KOH-I-NOOR RAPIDOGRAPH FLUIDLINE WB	T N LAWRENCE NANKING CHINA	T N LAWRENCE ILLU-COLOUR PG	T N LAWRENCE COLORIN WB	LEFRANC & BOURGEOIS INDIAN	LUKAS LIGHTFAST NWP	LUKAS ILLU-COLOUR PG	MAIMERI SYNCHROMATIC TRANS	MARCUS ART TECHNICAL WP	DR PH MARTIN PERMA DRAFT	DR PH MARTIN PEN WHITE	DR PH MARTIN HICARB
105 Vandyck Brown																										•						
99 Violet Brown																																
BLACKS/GRAYS																																
107 Black	•		•	•	•	•				•	•	•			•	•	•		•	•	•	•		•	•	•	•	•	•			•
107 Black (Indian)																			•													
107 Blue-Black																																
107 Bluish Black																											•					
107 Brilliant Black																																
108 Cold Grey																																
112 Cool Grey																							•									
108 Dark Grey																											•					
108 Deep Grey																											•					
108 Grey											•																					
111 Light Grey																											•					
110 Medium Grey																											•					
108 Mink Grey																																
109 Neutral Grey																				•												
112 Neutral Tint								•		•			•																			
112 Payne's Grey																											•					
107 Special Black												•																				
112 Stone Grey																											•					
107 Trichrom Black																											•					
108 Turtle Dove Grey																																
91 Turtle Grey																																
109 Warm Grey																							•									
MISCELLANEOUS																																
White	•	•				•						•	•	•					•	•	•	•							•			
Gold		•																		•												
Silver		•																		•												

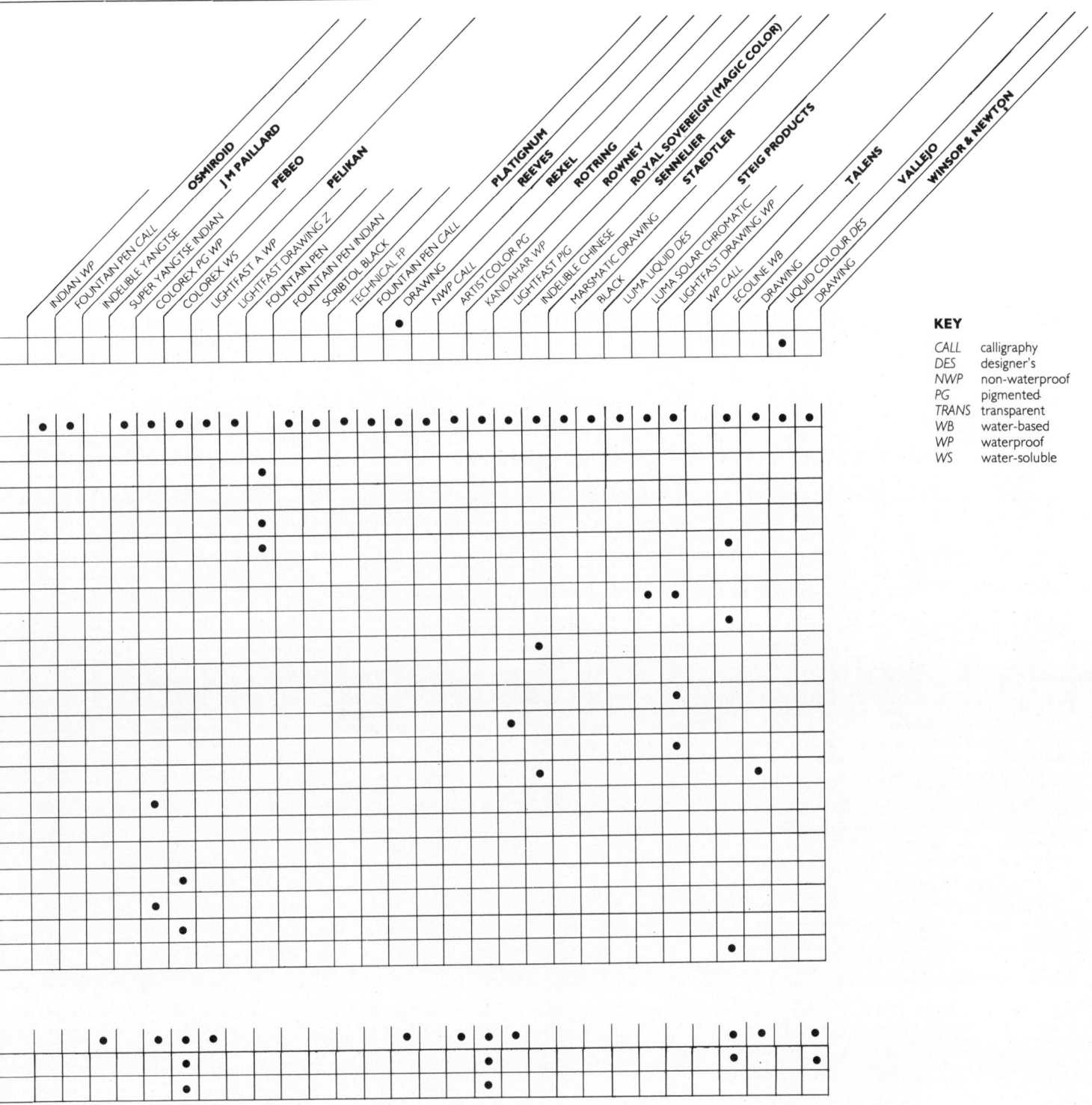

KEY

CALL	calligraphy
DES	designer's
NWP	non-waterproof
PG	pigmented
TRANS	transparent
WB	water-based
WP	waterproof
WS	water-soluble

HOW TO USE THE PASTELS AND CRAYONS CHART

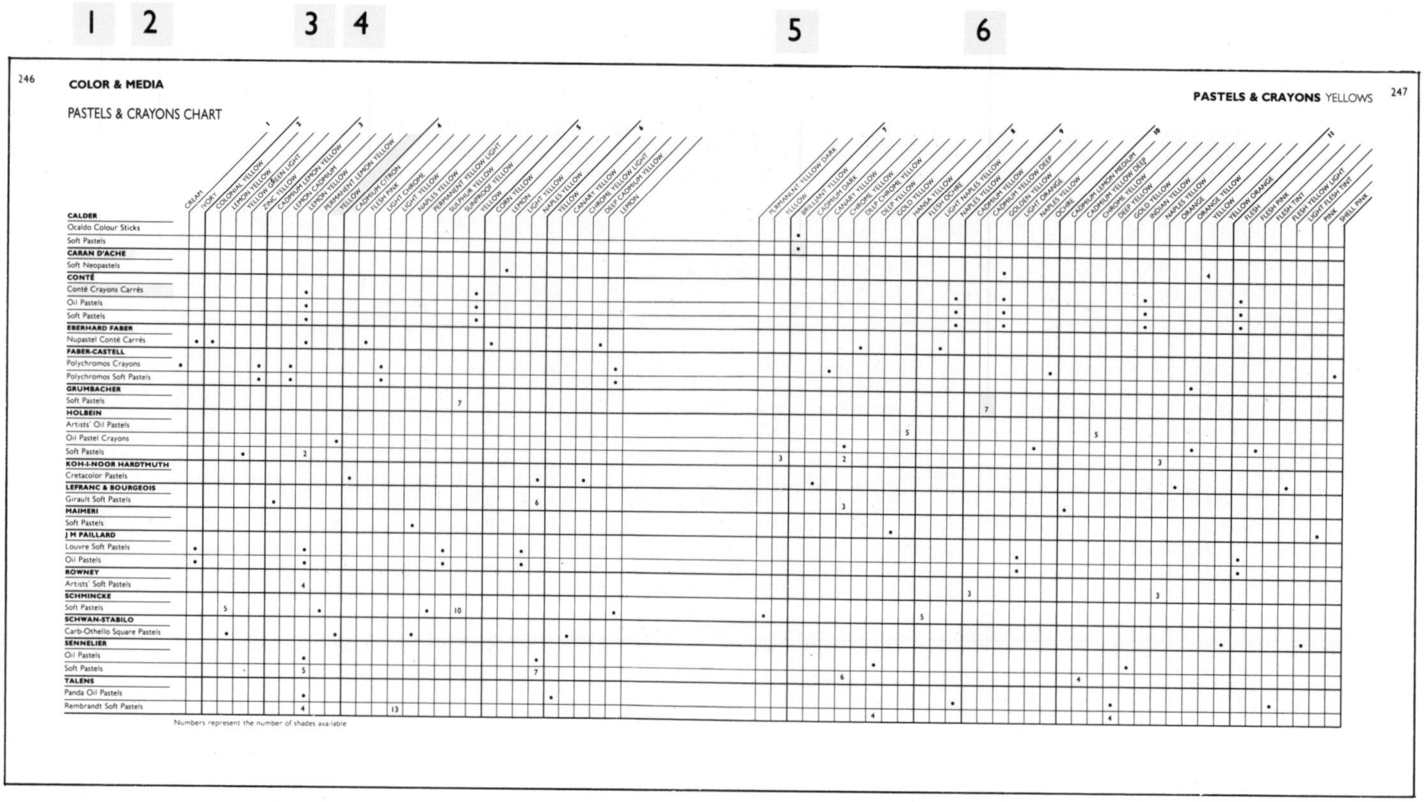

1 2   3 4   5   6

246

COLOR & MEDIA

PASTELS & CRAYONS CHART

PASTELS & CRAYONS YELLOWS   247

CALDER
Ocaldo Colour Sticks
Soft Pastels
CARAN D'ACHE
Soft Neopastels
CONTÉ
Conté Crayons Carrés
Oil Pastels
Soft Pastels
EBERHARD FABER
Nupastel Conté Carrés
FABER-CASTELL
Polychromos Crayons
Polychromos Soft Pastels
GRUMBACHER
Soft Pastels
HOLBEIN
Artists' Oil Pastels
Oil Pastel Crayons
Soft Pastels
KOH-I-NOOR HARDTMUTH
Cretacolor Pastels
LEFRANC & BOURGEOIS
Girault Soft Pastels
MAIMERI
Soft Pastels
J M PAILLARD
Louvre Soft Pastels
Oil Pastels
ROWNEY
Artists' Soft Pastels
SCHMINCKE
Soft Pastels
SCHWAN-STABILO
Carb-Othello Square Pastels
SENNELIER
Oil Pastels
Soft Pastels
TALENS
Panda Oil Pastels
Rembrandt Soft Pastels

Numbers represent the number of shades available

---

1 Manufacturers are listed alphabetically down the page. To establish which colors a particular manufacturer produces, follow the relevant column horizontally across the page.

2 Ranges of pastels and crayons are listed beneath the name of the manufacturer. Carré pastels are square.

3 The numbers running along the top of the chart relate to numbered color samples (see p82). Several different color names may be listed alphabetically under one number.

4 Colors are listed across the top of the chart, using the manufacturer's name. They are arranged in a color spectrum, starting with yellows and ending with blacks, grays and whites. The colors within each numbered group are arranged in alphabetical order.

5 • in the chart indicates that the range of pastels or crayons at the far left of the horizontal column includes the color at the top of the vertical column.

6 A number in the chart indicates the number of shades available in a particular color.

HOW TO USE THE COLORED PENCILS, LEADS AND WATER-SOLUBLE CRAYONS CHART

1   2   3   4   5

COLORED PENCILS, LEADS AND
WATER-SOLUBLE CRAYONS CHART

MANUFACTURER	RANGE
BEROL	Verithin Crayon Pencils
	Colour Craft/Prismacolor (US) Pencils
CARAN D'ACHE	Prismalo I Thin Watercolour Pencils
	Prismalo II Thick Watercolour Pencils
	Neocolor II Aquarelle Crayons
CONTE	Aquarelle Pencils
	Pastel Pencils
	Coloured Drawing Pencils
EBERHARD FABER	Design Crayon Pencils
FABER-CASTELL	Polychromos Coloured Pencils
	Durer Water-Soluble Pencils
	Durer Coloured Leads
	Coloured Drawing Pencils
KOH-I-NOOR HARDTMUTH	Mona Lisa Watercolour Crayons
	Thin-lead Colour Pencils
	Mona Lisa Crayon Pencils
	Mona Lisa Watercolour Pencils
	Coloured Drawing Pencils
	Coloured Leads
	Coloured Drawing Leads
REXEL CUMBERLAND	Derwent Watercolour Pencils
	Derwent Colourthin Pencils
	Derwent Studio Pencils
	Derwent Artists' Pencils
ROWNEY	Victoria Colour Pencils
SCHWAN-STABILO	Carb-Othello Pencils
	Stabilotone Watercolour Pencils
	Thin-lead Pencils
STAEDTLER	Karat Watercolour Pencils
	Mars Lumochrom Pencils
	Noris Unipoint Pencils

1 Manufacturers are listed alphabetically down the page. To establish which colors a particular manufacturer produces, follow the relevant column horizontally across the page.

2 Ranges of colored pencils and leads are listed beneath the name of the manufacturer. Where a range goes under different names in different countries, both names are included. Aquarelle pencils are water-soluble.

3 The numbers running along the top of the chart relate to numbered color samples (see p 83). Several different color names may be listed alphabetically under one number.

4 Colors are listed across the top of the chart using the manufacturer's name. They are arranged in a color spectrum, starting with yellows and ending with blacks, grays and whites. To establish which manufacturer produces a particular color, follow the relevant column vertically down the page.

5 • in the chart indicates that the range of pencils and leads at the far left of the horizontal column includes the color at the top of the vertical column.

PASTELS & CRAYONS CHART

	CREAM	IVORY	COLONIAL YELLOW	LEMON YELLOW	YELLOW GREEN LIGHT	ZINC YELLOW	CADMIUM LEMON YELLOW	LEMON CADMIUM	LEMON YELLOW	PERMANENT LEMON YELLOW	YELLOW	CADMIUM CITRON	FLESH PINK	LIGHT CHROME	LIGHT YELLOW	NAPLES YELLOW	PERMANENT YELLOW LIGHT	SULPHUR YELLOW	SUNPROOF YELLOW LIGHT	SUNPROOF YELLOW	YELLOW	CORN YELLOW	LEMON	LIGHT YELLOW	NAPLES YELLOW	YELLOW	CANARY YELLOW	CHROME YELLOW LIGHT	DEEP CADMIUM YELLOW	LEMON
CALDER																														
Ocaldo Color Sticks																				•										
Soft Pastels																														
CARAN D'ACHE																														
Soft Neopastels																				•										
CONTÉ																														
Conté Crayons Carrés								•										•												
Oil Pastels								•										•												
Soft Pastels								•										•												
EBERHARD FABER																														
Nupastel Conté Carrés	•	•						•				•						•									•			
FABER-CASTELL																														
Polychromos Crayons	•					•	•						•																	
Polychromos Soft Pastels						•	•						•																•	
GRUMBACHER																														
Soft Pastels																	7												•	
HOLBEIN																														
Artists' Oil Pastels																														
Oil Pastel Crayons										•																				
Soft Pastels				•				2																						
KOH-I-NOOR HARDTMUTH																														
Cretacolor Pastels											•											•			•					
LEFRANC & BOURGEOIS																														
Girault Soft Pastels						•																								
MAIMERI																						6								
Soft Pastels																														
J M PAILLARD																														
Louvre Soft Pastels	•							•								•				•										
Oil Pastels	•							•								•				•										
ROWNEY																														
Artists' Soft Pastels								4																						
SCHMINCKE																														
Soft Pastels			5						•						•		10										•			
SCHWAN-STABILO																														
Carb-Othello Square Pastels			•							•				•										•						
SENNELIER																														
Oil Pastels								•																						
Soft Pastels								5														•								
TALENS																														
Panda Oil Pastels								•														7								
Rembrandt Soft Pastels								4					13										•							

Numbers represent the number of shades available

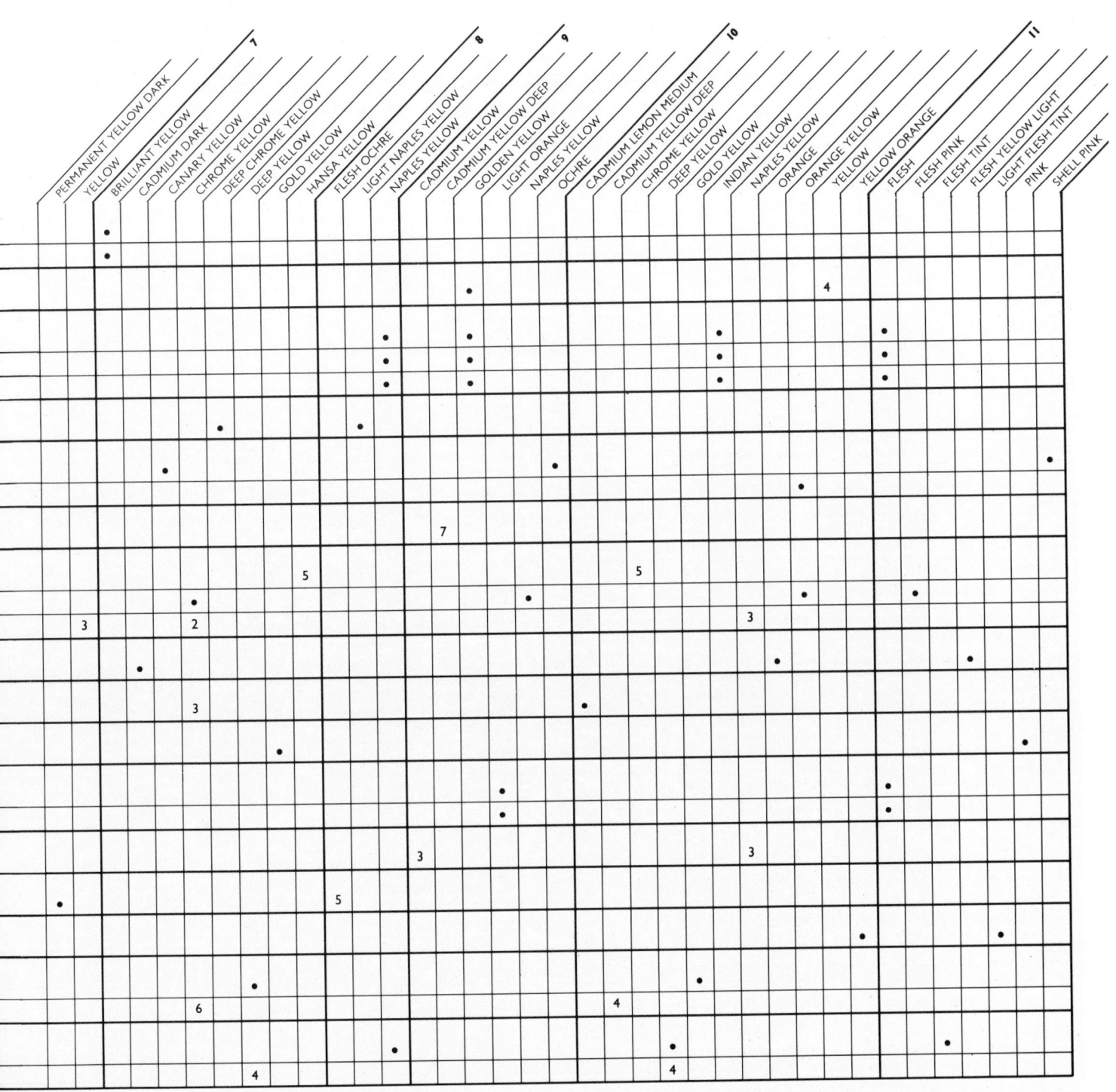

	12 CADMIUM ORANGE	DEEP ORANGE	LIGHT ORANGE	ORANGE	13 SUNPROOF ORANGE	BRIGHT YELLOW	BRILLIANT YELLOW	BURNT ORANGE	CADMIUM YELLOW	LEMON YELLOW	PERMANENT RED LIGHT	SALMON PINK	ORANGE	VERMILION LIGHT	YELLOW ORANGE	14 CADMIUM ORANGE YELLOW	CADMIUM ORANGE YELLOW	PALE TANGERINE	PALE VERMILION	ORANGE	YELLOW ORANGE	CADMIUM RED ORANGE	15 FLESH COLOUR DARK	DARK FLESH TINT	LIGHT ORANGE	MEDIUM FLESH	PALE ORANGE	PEACH
CALDER																												
Ocaldo Color Sticks			•																									
Soft Pastels											•																	
CARAN D'ACHE																												
Soft Neopastels									•							•												
CONTE																												
Conté Crayons Carrés			•																					•				
Oil Pastels			•																					•				
Soft Pastels			•																					•				
EBERHARD FABER																												
Nupastel Conté Carrés	•						•									•											•	
FABER-CASTELL																												
Polychromos Crayons																								2				
Polychromos Soft Pastels																								2				
GRUMBACHER																												
Soft Pastels	7								7																			
HOLBEIN																												
Artists' Oil Pastels								5																				
Oil Pastel Crayons																		•									•	
Soft Pastels													3					2										
KOH-I-NOOR HARDTMUTH																												
Cretacolor Pastels												•										2						
LEFRANC & BOURGEOIS																												
Girault Soft Pastels						5								•														
MAIMERI																												
Soft Pastels												•																
J M PAILLARD																												
Louvre Soft Pastels		•																										
Oil Pastels		•																										
ROWNEY																												
Artists' Soft Pastels	3															•				•								
SCHMINCKE																												
Soft Pastels					5				5																			
SCHWAN-STABILO																												
Carb-Othello Square Pastels												•										•						
SENNELIER																												
Oil Pastels						•										•												
Soft Pastels						8								3														
TALENS																												
Panda Oil Pastels		•																										
Rembrandt Soft Pastels									5							5												

Numbers represent the number of shades available

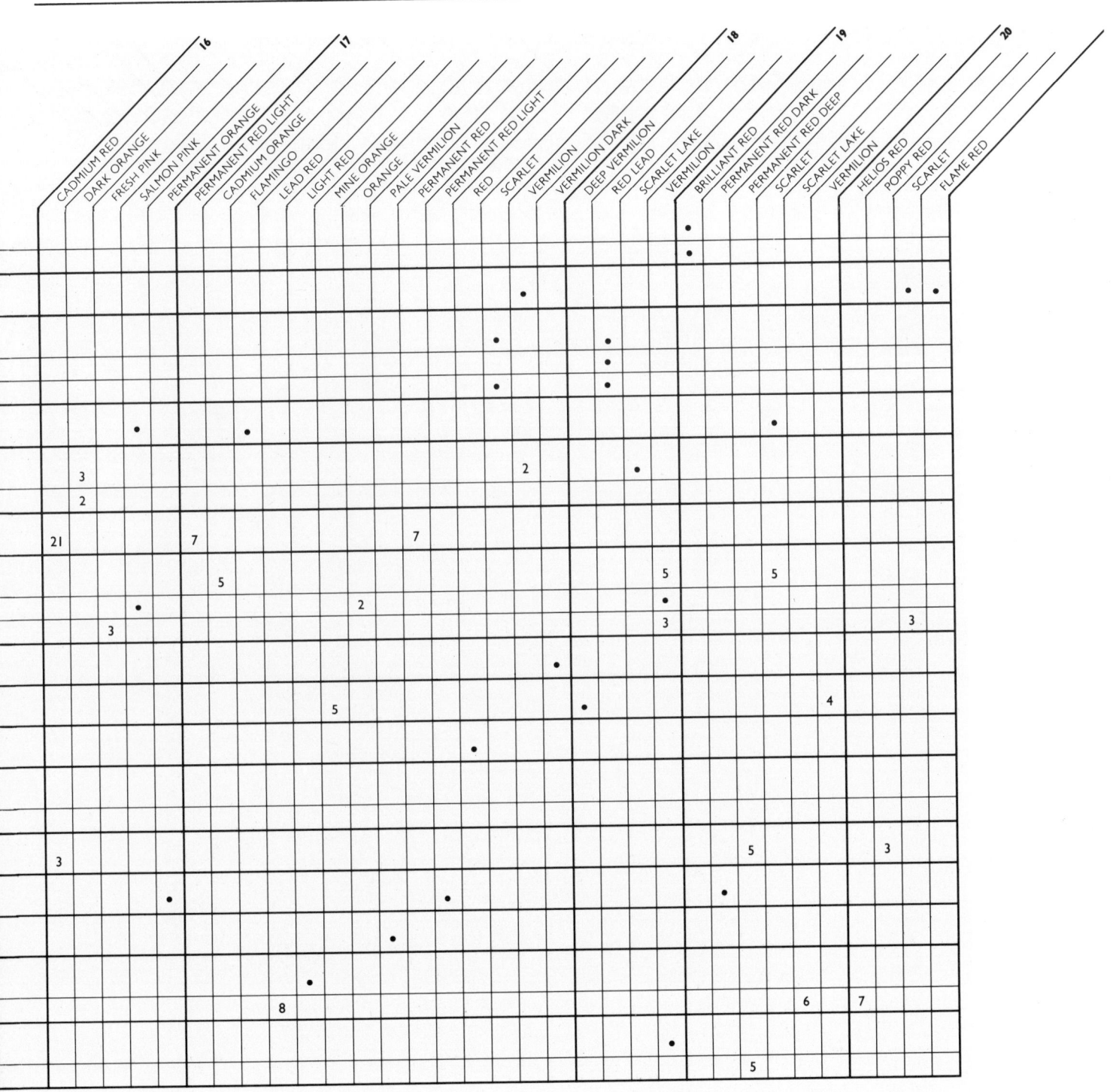

				21					22				23				24				25				26		
	BRIGHT RED	CARMINE RED	LIGHT GERANIUM RED	POMPEIAN RED	RED	VERMILION	DARK CARMINE	ROSE	ROSE LAKE	CARMINE LAKE	CRIMSON	DARK ROSE	DEEP RED	PERMANENT RED	CRIMSON	PERMANENT RED	RUBY RED	SCARLET	CARMINE	CARMINE EXTRA FINE	CARMINE RED	CRIMSON	CRIMSON LAKE	CARMINE	CARMINE MADDER	CARMINE RED	MADDER LAKE DEEP	RUSSET
CALDER																												
Ocaldo Color Sticks										•																		
Soft Pastels										•																		
CARAN D'ACHE																												
Soft Neopastels																			•							•		
CONTE																												
Conté Crayons Carrés					•																							
Oil Pastels					•																	•						
Soft Pastels					•																	•						
EBERHARD FABER																												
Nupastel Conté Carrés											•																	
FABER-CASTELL																												
Polychromos Crayons			•			•																						
Polychromos Soft Pastels						•																						
GRUMBACHER																												
Soft Pastels																				7								
HOLBEIN																												
Artists' Oil Pastels																					5		5					
Oil Pastel Crayons													5				•											
Soft Pastels															3								3					
KOH-I-NOOR HARDTMUTH																												
Cretacolor Pastels				•															•				•					
LEFRANC & BOURGEOIS																												
Girault Soft Pastels						5		3	•									6										
MAIMERI																												
Soft Pastels																												
J M PAILLARD																												
Louvre Soft Pastels	•																											
Oil Pastels	•																											
ROWNEY																												
Artists' Soft Pastels						4																						
SCHMINCKE																												
Soft Pastels																									5	5		
SCHWAN-STABILO																												
Carb-Othello Square Pastels	•													•														
SENNELIER																												
Oil Pastels						•	•					•				•												
Soft Pastels						9									7	9							10					
TALENS																												
Panda Oil Pastels																												
Rembrandt Soft Pastels																										5		

Numbers represent the number of shades available

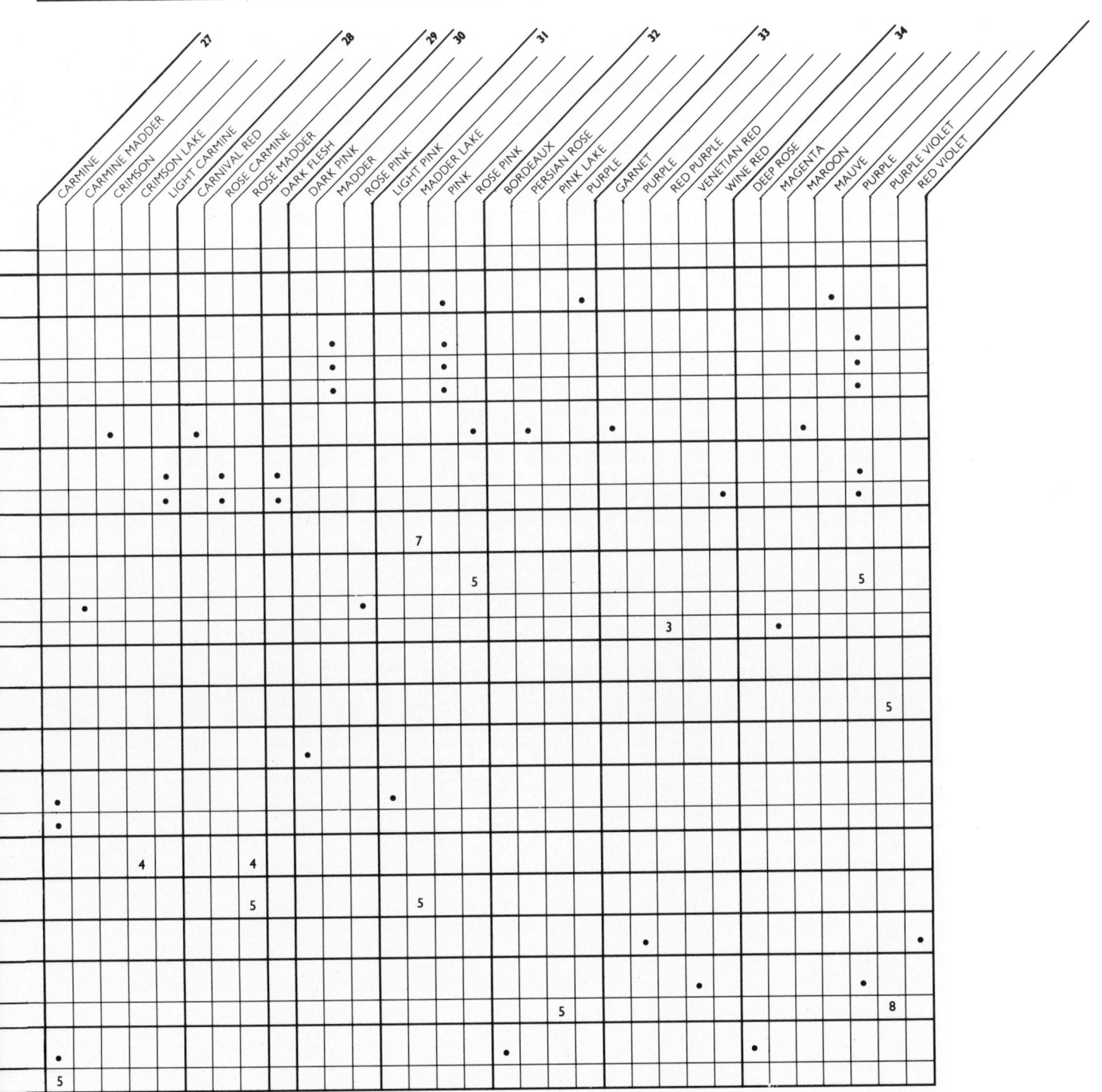

	35					36		37			38								39						40				41		
	CORAL	LIGHT ROSE	ROSE MADDER	ROSE MADDER LAKE	PERMANENT ROSE	CYCLAMEN	PINK	HELIOTROPE	LAVENDER	LILAC	PURPLE I	HYACINTH VIOLET	MAGENTA	PANSY VIOLET	PERSIAN VIOLET	PURPLE 2	REDDISH PURPLE	RED VIOLET LIGHT	BORDEAUX	GREY ROSE	OLD ROSE	OLD VIOLET	PINK MADDER LAKE	PLUM	REDDISH PURPLE	RED VIOLET	DEEP VIOLET	MADDER VIOLET	RED VIOLET	SUNFAST THIO VIOLET	VIOLET LIGHT
CALDER																															
Ocaldo Color Sticks																															
Soft Pastels																															
CARAN D'ACHE																															
Soft Neopastels								•	•																					•	
CONTE																															
Conté Crayons Carrés						•			•				•																		
Oil Pastels						•			•				•																		
Soft Pastels						•			•				•																		
EBERHARD FABER																															
Nupastel Conté Carrés	•										•									•		•					•				
FABER-CASTELL																															
Polychromos Crayons				•								•										•			•						
Polychromos Soft Pastels				•								•										•			•						
GRUMBACHER																	7											7			
Soft Pastels																	7											7			
HOLBEIN																															
Artists' Oil Pastels																															
Oil Pastel Crayons																			•												
Soft Pastels						3													3												
KOH-I-NOOR HARDTMUTH																															
Cretacolor Pastels		•													•														•		
LEFRANC & BOURGEOIS																															
Girault Soft Pastels																															
MAIMERI																															
Soft Pastels								•																		3					
J M PAILLARD																															
Louvre Soft Pastels																															
Oil Pastels																															
ROWNEY														3										3								
Artists' Soft Pastels														3										3								
SCHMINCKE																															
Soft Pastels		5								5					5										5						
SCHWAN-STABILO																															
Carb-Othello Square Pastels		•					•																								
SENNELIER																								•							
Oil Pastels																								•							
Soft Pastels																									7						
TALENS																															
Panda Oil Pastels	•								•															•	•						
Rembrandt Soft Pastels				5												4															

Numbers represent the number of shades available

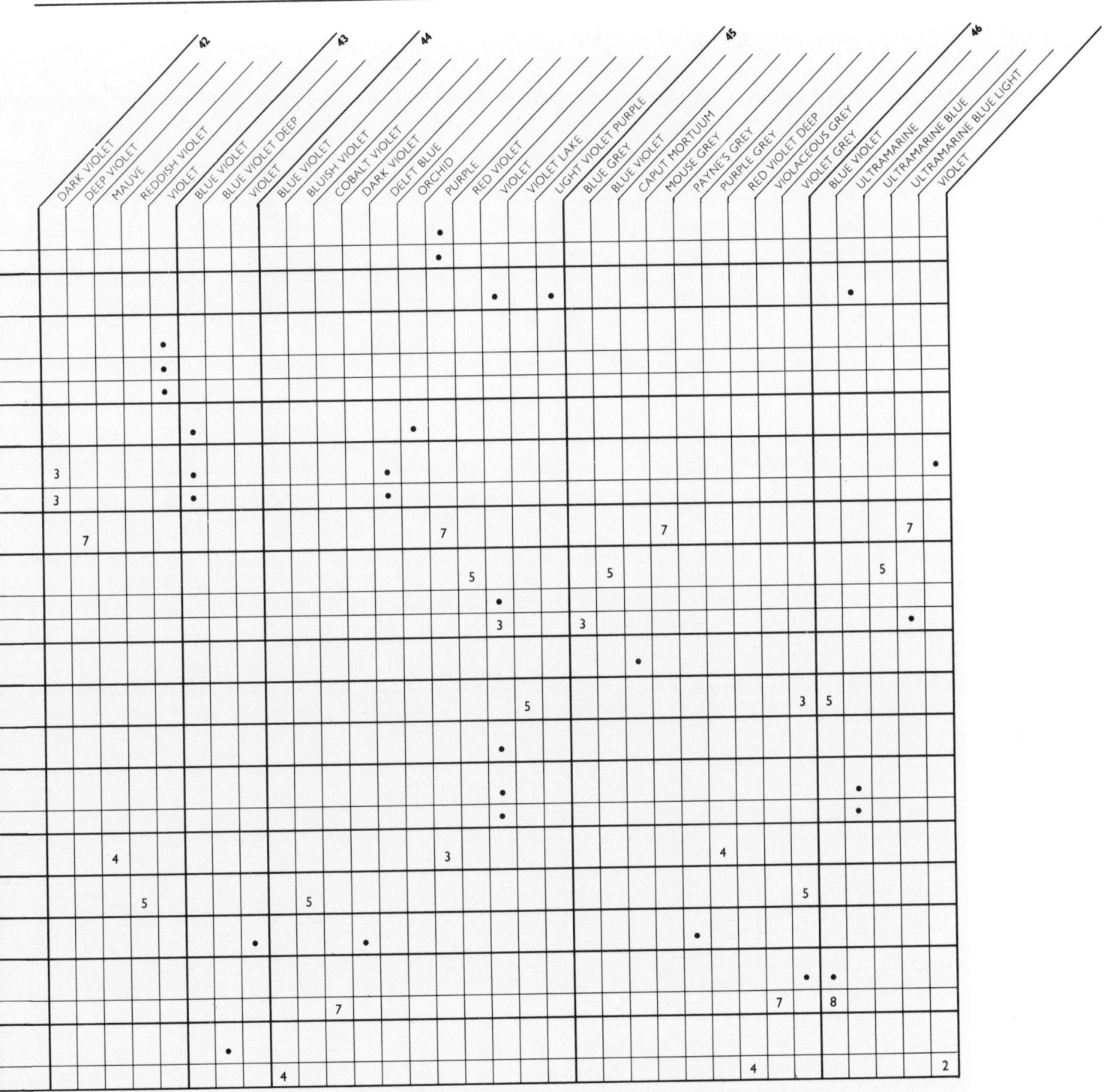

	47 BLUE PURPLE	BLUISH PURPLE	BLUISH VIOLET	COBALT	PRUSSIAN BLUE	ULTRAMARINE BLUE	DARK ULTRAMARINE	DEEP COBALT	48 FRENCH ULTRAMARINE	LIGHT BLUE	PRUSSIAN BLUE	SAPPHIRE BLUE	ULTRAMARINE	ULTRAMARINE BLUE DEEP	ULTRAMARINE BLUE LIGHT	BRILLIANT BLUE	LIGHT COBALT BLUE	ULTRAMARINE DARK	49 ULTRAMARINE DEEP	COBALT BLUE	DELFT BLUE	PALE ULTRAMARINE	ULTRAMARINE	ULTRAMARINE BLUE	50 ULTRAMARINE LIGHT	COBALT BLUE	LIGHT BLUE	SKY BLUE	51 SKY TURQUOISE
CALDER																													
Ocaldo Color Sticks														•															
Soft Pastels														•															
CARAN D'ACHE																													
Soft Neopastels			•							•																			
CONTE																													
Conté Crayons Carrés				•		•																							
Oil Pastels				•		•															•								
Soft Pastels				•		•															•								
EBERHARD FABER																													
Nupastel Conté Carrés																						•			•				
FABER-CASTELL																													
Polychromos Crayons							•								•											•			
Polychromos Soft Pastels							•								•											•			
GRUMBACHER																													
Soft Pastels		7											7																
HOLBEIN																													
Artists' Oil Pastels													5					5											
Oil Pastel Crayons																													
Soft Pastels					•						3																		
KOH-I-NOOR HARDTMUTH																													
Cretacolor Pastels	•								•							•			•										
LEFRANC & BOURGEOIS																													
Girault Soft Pastels	3																•						3						
MAIMERI																													
Soft Pastels																													
J M PAILLARD																													
Louvre Soft Pastels																		2										•	
Oil Pastels																		2										•	
ROWNEY																													
Artists' Soft Pastels								3																3					
SCHMINCKE																													
Soft Pastels																5							5						
SCHWAN-STABILO																													
Carb-Othello Square Pastels											•									•									
SENNELIER																													
Oil Pastels									•																				
Soft Pastels	6									3							9												
TALENS																													
Panda Oil Pastels											•																		
Rembrandt Soft Pastels																													

Numbers represent the number of shades available

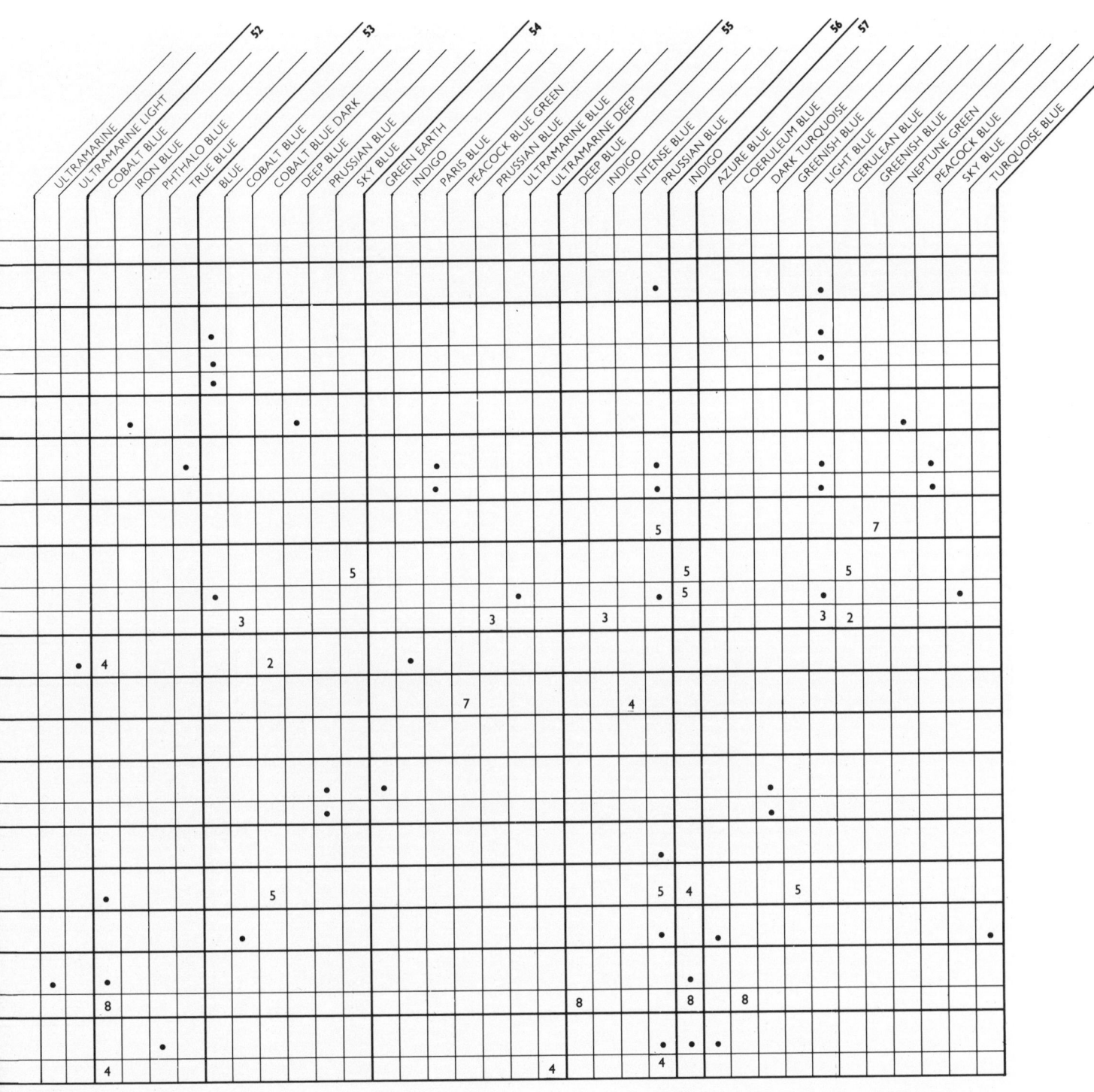

	BLUE HAZE	COERULEUM	GREY BLUE	ICE BLUE	PAYNE'S GREY	BREMEN BLUE	PHTHALO BLUE	PRUSSIAN BLUE	TURQUOISE BLUE	LIGHT BLUE	LIGHT TURQUOISE	SKYE BLUE	AQUAMARINE	BLUE GREEN	CERULEAN BLUE	EMERALD GREEN	GREEN BLUE	PALE BLUE	TURQUOISE	BLUISH GREEN	COBALT GREEN	COBALT GREEN LIGHT	COMPOSE GREEN LIGHT	SMOKE GREEN	TURQUOISE
CALDER																									
Ocaldo Color Sticks														•											
Soft Pastels						•																			
CARAN D'ACHE																									
Soft Neopastels																								•	
CONTE																									
Conté Crayons Carrés				•						•					•										
Oil Pastels				•						•					•										
Soft Pastels				•						•					•										
EBERHARD FABER																									
Nupastel Conté Carrés	•							•			•													•	
FABER-CASTELL																									
Polychromos Crayons						•					•														
Polychromos Soft Pastels						•					•														
GRUMBACHER																									
Soft Pastels		7																							
HOLBEIN																									
Artists' Oil Pastels													5												
Oil Pastel Crayons															•				•						
Soft Pastels						2							2									3			
KOH-I-NOOR HARDTMUTH																									
Cretacolor Pastels					•																				
LEFRANC & BOURGEOIS																									
Girault Soft Pastels							4													4					
MAIMERI																									
Soft Pastels																•									
J M PAILLARD																									
Louvre Soft Pastels																									
Oil Pastels																									
ROWNEY																									
Artists' Soft Pastels	4										3														
SCHMINCKE																									
Soft Pastels																			5						
SCHWAN-STABILO																									
Carb-Othello Square Pastels			•																						
SENNELIER																									
Oil Pastels							•															•			
Soft Pastels					10															7					
TALENS																									
Panda Oil Pastels								•						•											
Rembrandt Soft Pastels						5													5						

Numbers represent the number of shades available

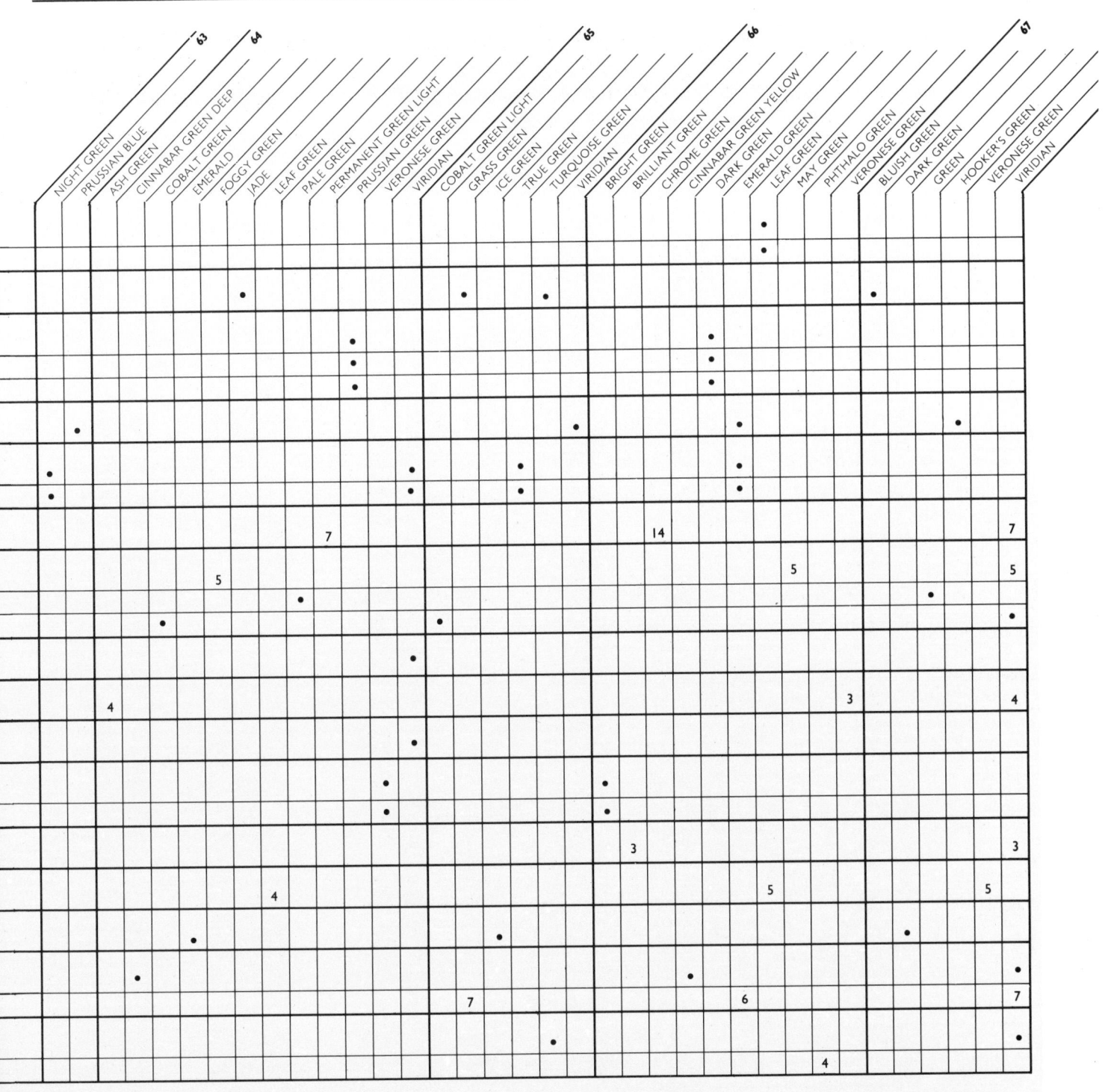

Column group markers across the top: 68, 69, 70, 71, 72

Manufacturer / Product	Blue Green	Dark Green	Deep Green	Emerald Green	Sea Green	Turquoise Green	Focus Green	Forest Green	Hooker's Green	Mineral Green	Permanent Green	Permanent Green Deep	Barite Green	Chrome Green	Chrome Green Light	Cinnabar Green	English Green	Fern Green	Leaf Green	Moss Green	Cold Green	Erin Green	Olive Green Light	Sap Green	Deep Green	Chrome Green Deep	Fir Green	Grass Green	Green Earth	Juniper Green
CALDER																														
Ocaldo Color Sticks																														
Soft Pastels																														
CARAN D'ACHE																														
Soft Neopastels																			•											
CONTE																														
Conté Crayons Carrés			•						•																					
Oil Pastels			•						•																					
Soft Pastels			•																											
EBERHARD FABER																														
Nupastel Conté Carrés	•																•				•									
FABER-CASTELL																														
Polychromos Crayons				•				•											•			•						•		
Polychromos Soft Pastels				•				•											•			•						•		
GRUMBACHER																														
Soft Pastels											7																			
HOLBEIN																														
Artists' Oil Pastels			5						5																					
Oil Pastel Crayons			•																								•			
Soft Pastels	•					•													•					3						
KOH-I-NOOR HARDTMUTH																														
Cretacolor Pastels														•							•									
LEFRANC & BOURGEOIS																														
Girault Soft Pastels																4														
MAIMERI															•															
Soft Pastels															•															
J M PAILLARD																														
Louvre Soft Pastels		•																												
Oil Pastels		•																												
ROWNEY																														
Artists' Soft Pastels								4																						
SCHMINCKE																														
Soft Pastels																			5	5										
SCHWAN-STABILO																														
Carb-Othello Square Pastels						•		•					•					•					•					•		
SENNELIER																														
Oil Pastels												•																		
Soft Pastels													8																	
TALENS																														
Panda Oil Pastels																										•				
Rembrandt Soft Pastels											3			4											5					

Numbers represent the number of shades available

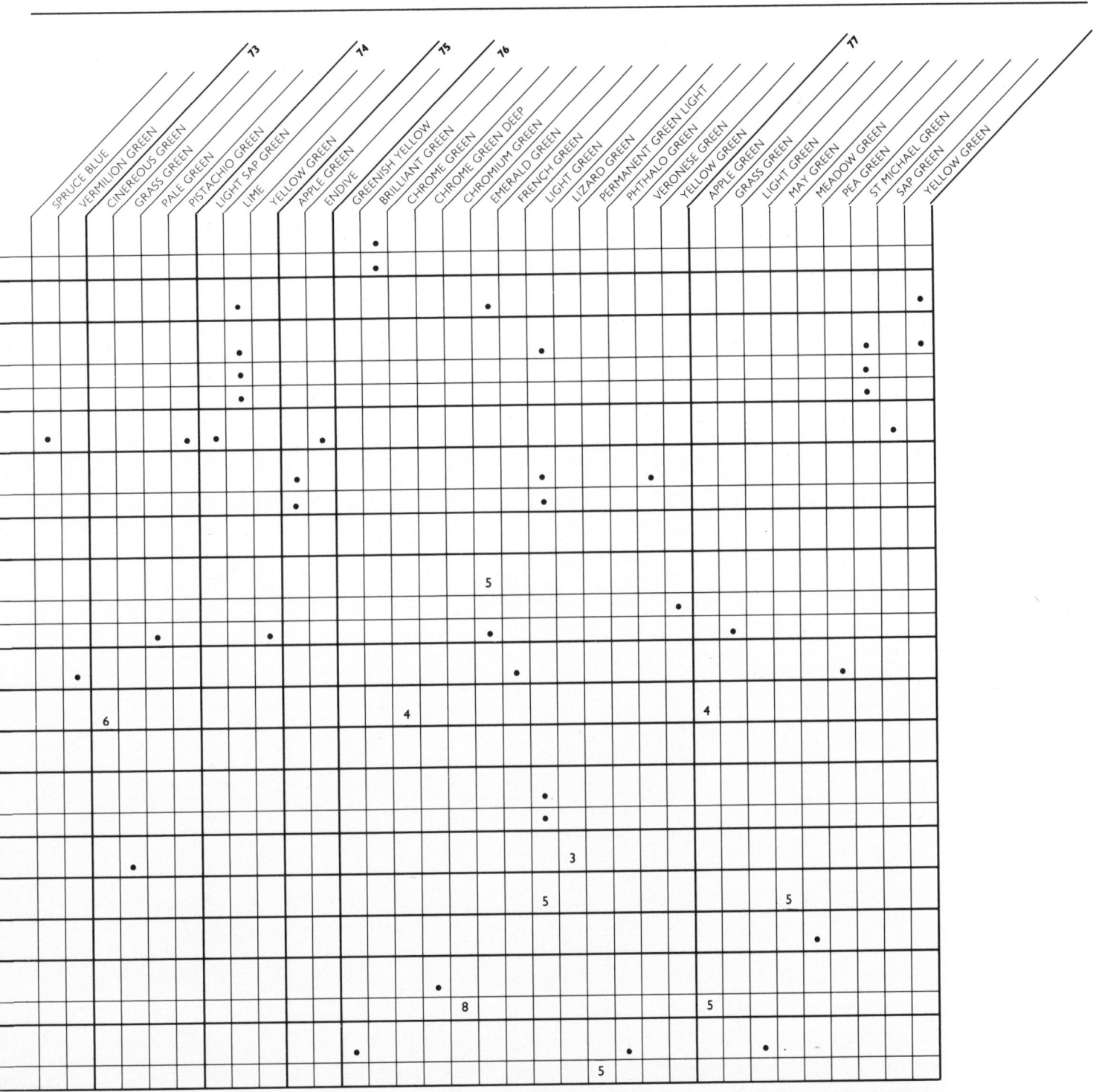

Column group markers across the top: **78** · **79** · **80** · **81** · **82**

	Eden Green	Green Grey	Grey Green	Olive Green	Chromium Oxide Green	Citrine Green	Green Earth	Grey Green	Light Emerald	Medium Green	Olive Green	Olive Ochre Dark	Sap Green	Terre Verte	Beach Green	Light Olive	Olive Green Light	Olive Ochre Light	Reseda Green	Bottle Green	Cedar Green	Moss Green	Sap Green	Bohemian Green	Foggy Green	Olive	Olive Green	Olive Green Dark
CALDER																												
Ocaldo Color Sticks																												
Soft Pastels																												
CARAN D'ACHE																												
Soft Neopastels														•											•			
CONTE																												
Conté Crayons Carrés		•																										
Oil Pastels		•																										
Soft Pastels		•																										
EBERHARD FABER																												
Nupastel Conté Carrés	•				•							•					•											
FABER-CASTELL																												
Polychromos Crayons		•																•					•					
Polychromos Soft Pastels		•																•					•					
GRUMBACHER																												
Soft Pastels	7								7									7										
HOLBEIN																												
Artists' Oil Pastels									5										5									
Oil Pastel Crayons							•															•						
Soft Pastels	•								•									•					3					
KOH-I-NOOR HARDTMUTH																												
Cretacolor Pastels						•																						•
LEFRANC & BOURGEOIS																												
Girault Soft Pastels												2				•												
MAIMERI																												
Soft Pastels																												
J M PAILLARD																												
Louvre Soft Pastels		•																										
Oil Pastels		•																										
ROWNEY																												
Artists' Soft Pastels											3												4					
SCHMINCKE																												
Soft Pastels	10			5						5					5			5		5								
SCHWAN-STABILO																												
Carb-Othello Square Pastels							•																•					
SENNELIER																												
Oil Pastels								•																				
Soft Pastels						6										7												
TALENS																												
Panda Oil Pastels				•										•														
Rembrandt Soft Pastels																							4					

Numbers represent the number of shades available

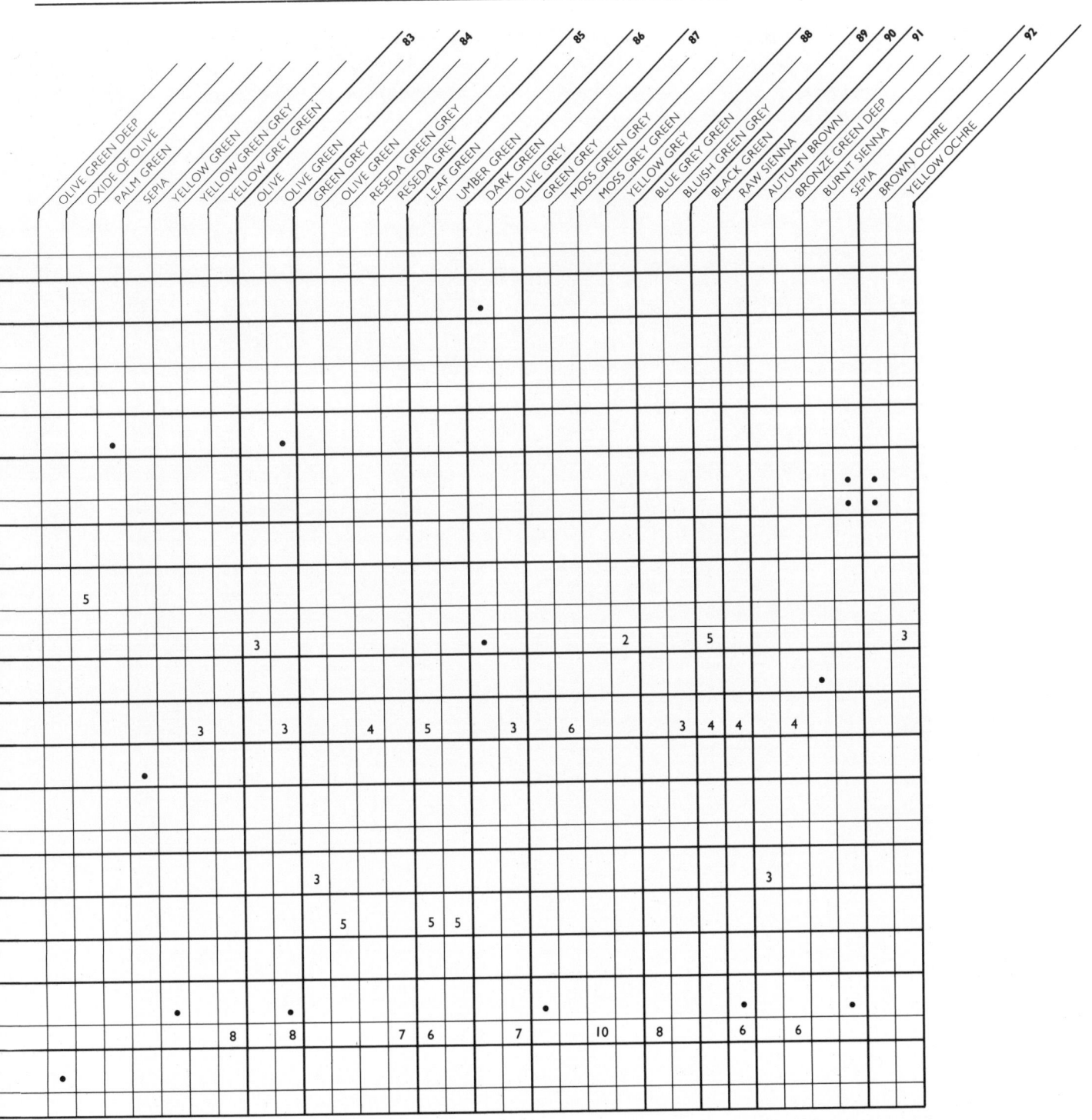

Column groups: 93, 94, 95, 96, 97

	BRONZE GREEN LIGHT	OLIVE BROWN	RAW UMBER	RED GREY	SEPIA	BEIGE GREY	BROWN OCHRE	NUT BROWN	OCHRE	OLIVE BROWN DARK	RAW UMBER	LIGHT OCHRE	OCHRE	RAW SIENNA	SANDALWOOD	YELLOW OCHRE	BURNT LIGHT OCHRE	GAMBOGE	GOLD OCHRE	LIGHT OCHRE	PALE OCHRE	RAW SIENNA	YELLOW OCHRE	GOLD OCHRE	ORANGE OCHRE	OXIDE YELLOW	SIENA NATURAL	YELLOW OCHRE
CALDER																												
Ocaldo Color Sticks																												
Soft Pastels																												
CARAN D'ACHE																												
Soft Neopastels	•																											
CONTE																												
Conté Crayons Carrés																												
Oil Pastels																												
Soft Pastels																												
EBERHARD FABER																												
Nupastel Conté Carrés							•							•					•									
FABER-CASTELL																												
Polychromos Crayons		•									•											•						
Polychromos Soft Pastels		•									•											•						
GRUMBACHER																												
Soft Pastels							7	7								7												
HOLBEIN																												
Artists' Oil Pastels																												
Oil Pastel Crayons								•												•					5			
Soft Pastels	3				3					•																		
KOH-I-NOOR HARDTMUTH																												
Cretacolor Pastels																				•						•		
LEFRANC & BOURGEOIS																												
Girault Soft Pastels	4				3											4												3
MAIMERI																												
Soft Pastels																						•						
J M PAILLARD																												
Louvre Soft Pastels																												
Oil Pastels																												
ROWNEY																												
Artists' Soft Pastels				4						3				3						3								
SCHMINCKE																												
Soft Pastels						•				5	5				5								5					
SCHWAN-STABILO																												
Carb-Othello Square Pastels				•							•											•						
SENNELIER																												
Oil Pastels																										•		
Soft Pastels	6				7											7												7
TALENS																												
Panda Oil Pastels																					•	•						
Rembrandt Soft Pastels			4										5									5	5					

Numbers represent the number of shades available

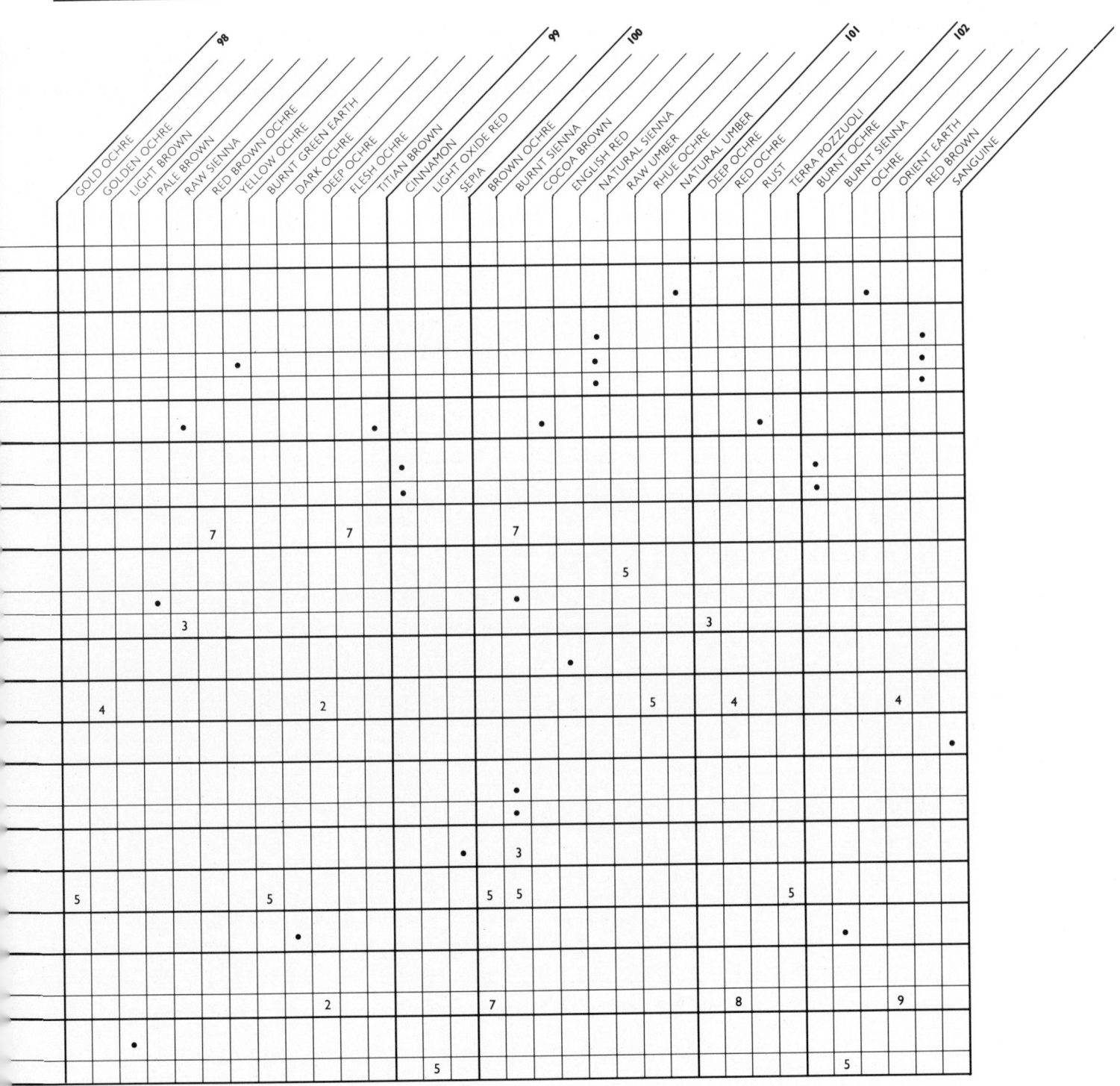

Section markers across the top: **103**, **104**, **105**, **106**

	BURNT SIENNA	INDIAN RED	LIGHT OXIDE RED	POMPEIAN RED	SANGUINE	SANGUINE RED	VENETIAN RED	ENGLISH RED	PALE BROWN	RED BROWN	RED OCHRE	SANGUINE	VENETIAN RED	BURNT SIENNA	CAPUT MORTUUM RED	DEAD LEAF	DEAD LEAF GREEN	INDIAN RED	POMPEIAN RED	SANGUINE ORANGE	TUSCAN RED	BROWN	BURNT CARMINE	ENGLISH RED	LACQUERED BROWN	MADDER BROWN	MARS VIOLET	RAW SIENNA	RED EARTH
CALDER																													
Ocaldo Color Sticks												•																	
Soft Pastels																													
CARAN D'ACHE																													
Soft Neopastels																													
CONTE																													
Conté Crayons Carrés																											•		
Oil Pastels																											•		
Soft Pastels																											•		
EBERHARD FABER																													
Nupastel Conté Carrés	•									•									•										
FABER-CASTELL																													
Polychromos Crayons			•									•				•													
Polychromos Soft Pastels												•																	
GRUMBACHER																													
Soft Pastels																						7							
HOLBEIN																													
Artists' Oil Pastels	5								5			5														5			
Oil Pastel Crayons																					•								
Soft Pastels								3				3										2							
KOH-I-NOOR HARDTMUTH																													
Cretacolor Pastels																													
LEFRANC & BOURGEOIS																													
Girault Soft Pastels						4			4								5						3						
MAIMERI																													
Soft Pastels																													
J M PAILLARD																													
Louvre Soft Pastels					•														3										
Oil Pastels					•														3										
ROWNEY																								4					
Artists' Soft Pastels																								4					
SCHMINCKE																													
Soft Pastels						5																							
SCHWAN-STABILO																													
Carb-Othello Square Pastels				•													•				•								
SENNELIER																													
Oil Pastels																													
Soft Pastels						8		7						7															
TALENS																													
Panda Oil Pastels	•	•																											
Rembrandt Soft Pastels	4													5											5				

Numbers represent the number of shades available

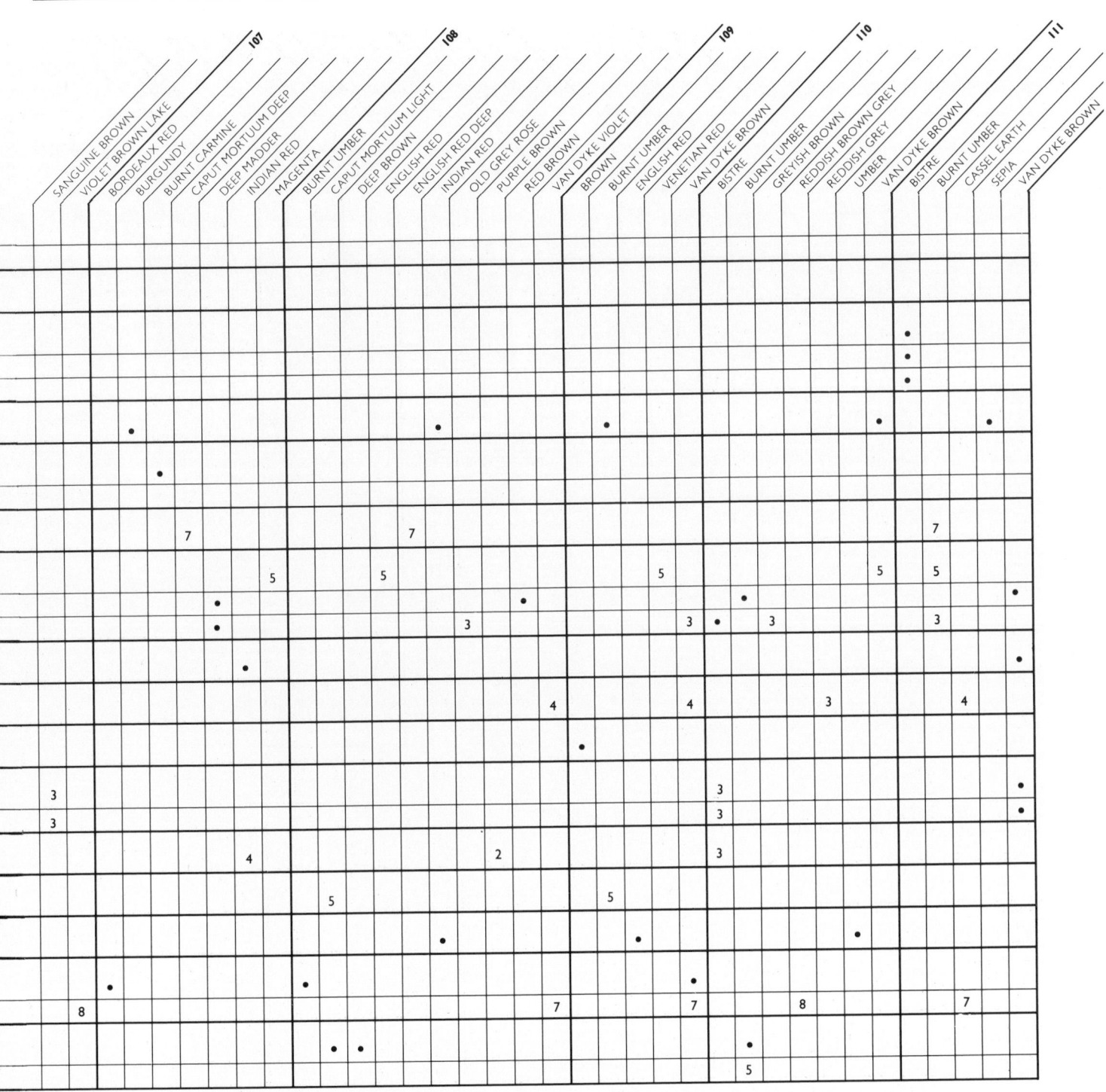

Brand / Product						112		113						114	115		116			117	118	119		120	121	122
	CAPUT MORTUUM DARK	CORDOVAN	HOT BROWN	BURNT UMBER	DARK GREY	LEAD BROWN	NATURAL UMBER	SATURNE BROWN	VAN DYKE BROWN	MUMMY	SEPIA BROWN	BROWN GREY	UMBER	BLACK BROWN	BROWN	BURNT UMBER	VAN DYKE BROWN	MOUSE GREY	FLESH OCHRE	BISTRE	VAN DYKE BROWN	REDDISH BROWN GREY	VERMILION BROWN	BURNT SIENNA	DARK BROWN	LAKE BROWN
CALDER																										
Ocaldo Color Sticks																										
Soft Pastels																										
CARAN D'ACHE																										
Soft Neopastels														●												
CONTE																										
Conté Crayons Carrés						●					●															
Oil Pastels						●					●															
Soft Pastels						●					●															
EBERHARD FABER																										
Nupastel Conté Carrés	●																									
FABER-CASTELL																										
Polychromos Crayons								●																		
Polychromos Soft Pastels								●																		
GRUMBACHER																										
Soft Pastels																										
HOLBEIN																										
Artists' Oil Pastels																										
Oil Pastel Crayons																						●				
Soft Pastels				3																						
KOH-I-NOOR HARDTMUTH																										
Cretacolor Pastels														●												
LEFRANC & BOURGEOIS																										
Girault Soft Pastels							3		3		3			2		4	4	4				3	4		3	
MAIMERI																										
Soft Pastels																										
J M PAILLARD																										
Louvre Soft Pastels																										
Oil Pastels																										
ROWNEY																										
Artists' Soft Pastels																			4							
SCHMINCKE																										
Soft Pastels	5		5						5	5						5	5									
SCHWAN-STABILO																										
Carb-Othello Square Pastels																										
SENNELIER																										
Oil Pastels																●			●	●						
Soft Pastels		5			4				7		6		5			8	10	10			5	7		5		
TALENS																										
Panda Oil Pastels																										
Rembrandt Soft Pastels																										

Numbers represent the number of shades available

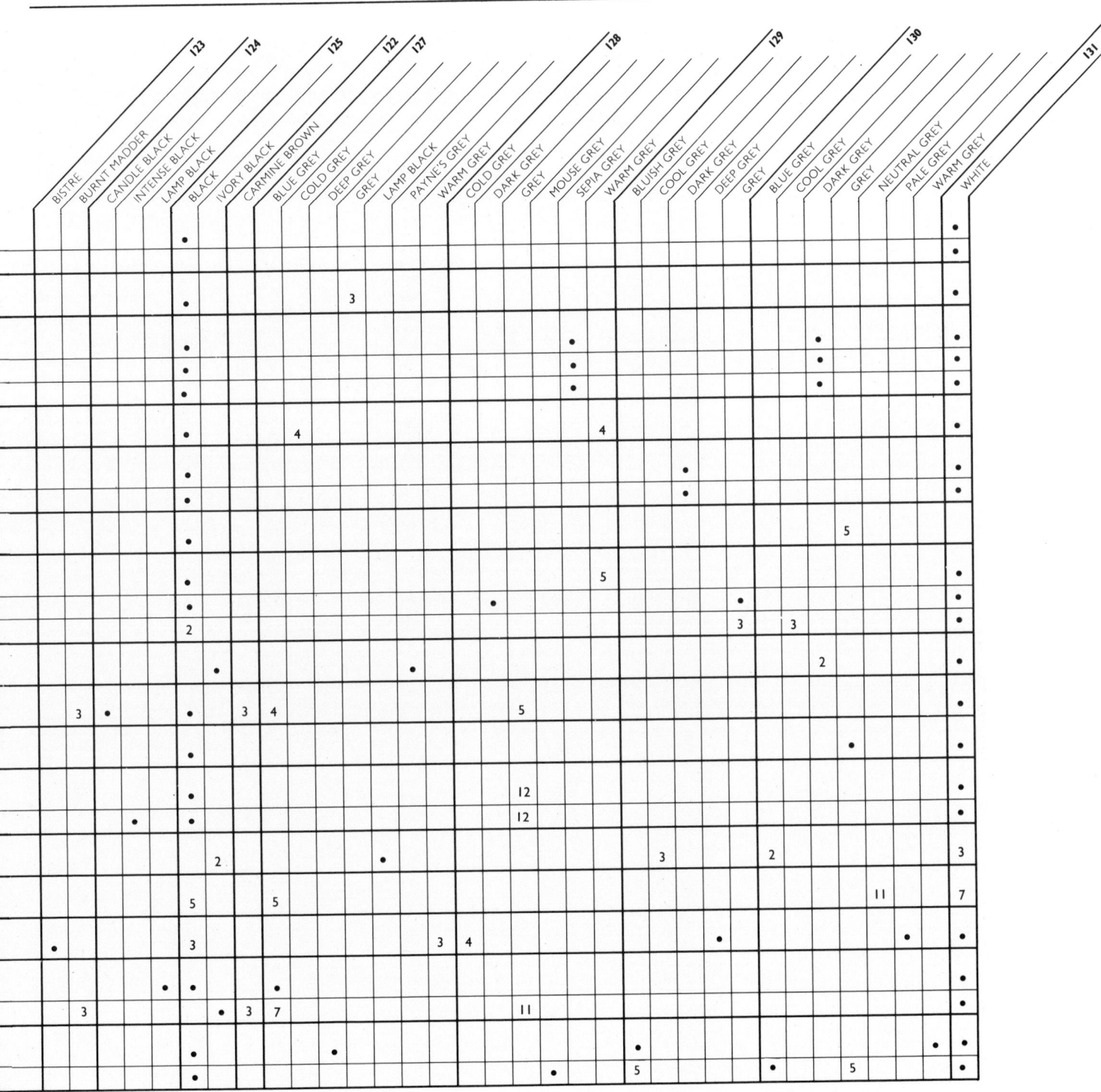

COLORED PENCILS, LEADS AND WATER-SOLUBLE CRAYONS CHART

MANUFACTURER	RANGE	LEMON YELLOW	LIGHT YELLOW	ZINC YELLOW	CANARY YELLOW	LEMON	YELLOW	LEMON CADMIUM	LEMON	LEMON YELLOW	PRIMROSE	LEMON CADMIUM	NAPLES YELLOW	CHROME YELLOW	DARK YELLOW	GOLD	YELLOW	CREAM	PRIMROSE YELLOW	STRAW YELLOW	YELLOW	CANARY YELLOW	GOLDEN YELLOW	LIGHT CHROME	YELLOW
BEROL	Verithin Crayon Pencils	●													●							●			
	Colour Craft/Prismacolor (US) Pencils									●															●
CARAN D'ACHE	Prismalo I Thin Watercolour Pencils					●															●				
	Prismalo II Thick Watercolour Pencils					●															●				
	Neocolor II Aquarelle Crayons								●												●				
CONTE	Aquarelle Pencils																●								
	Pastel Pencils						●																		
	Coloured Drawing Pencils																						●		
EBERHARD FABER	Design Crayon Pencils	●					●							●				●							
FABER-CASTELL	Polychromos Coloured Pencils			●								●													
	Dürer Water-Soluble Pencils											●						●						●	
	Dürer Coloured Leads											●													
	Coloured Drawing Pencils																								
KOH-I-NOOR HARDTMUTH	Mona Lisa Watercolour Crayons									●															
	Thin-lead Colour Pencils									●															
	Mona Lisa Crayon Pencils									●															
	Mona Lisa Watercolour Pencils									●															
	Coloured Drawing Pencils																								
	Coloured Leads									●															
	Coloured Drawing Leads																								
REXEL CUMBERLAND	Derwent Watercolour Pencils			●																					
	Derwent Colourthin Pencils														●										
	Derwent Studio Pencils			●				●																	
	Derwent Artists' Pencils			●				●																	
ROWNEY	Victoria Colour Pencils							●							●				●	●					
SCHWAN-STABILO	Carb-Othello Pencils	●							●								●		●	●					
	Stabilotone Watercolour Pencils						●						●												
	Thin-lead Pencils	●					●			●			●												
STAEDTLER	Karat Watercolour Pencils		●				●															●			
	Mars Lumochrom Pencils		●												●										
	Noris Unipoint Pencils		●		●																				

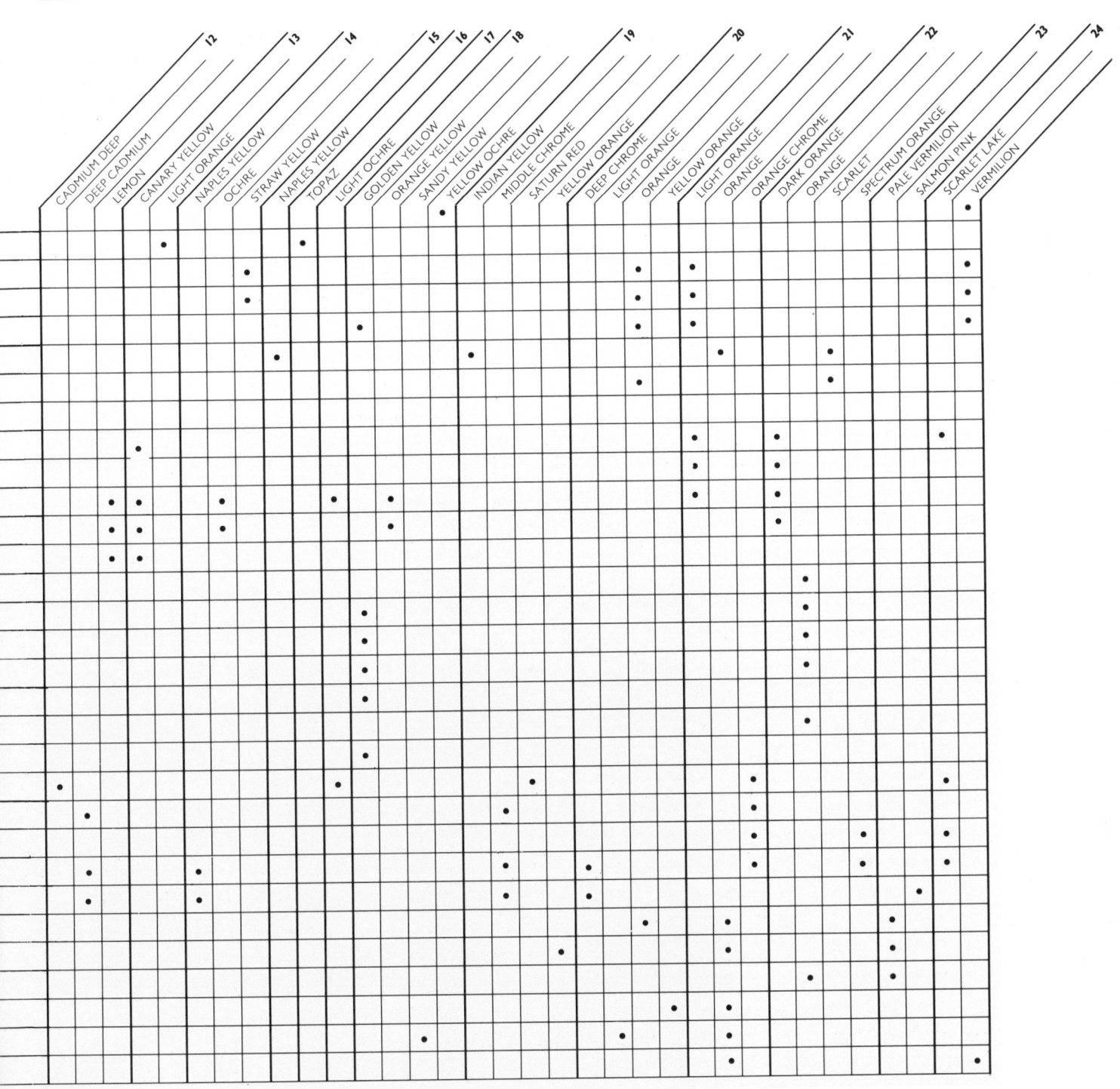

MANUFACTURER	RANGE	SCARLET	SCARLET RED	RED	RED LEAD	VERMILION	SCARLET	SCARLET LAKE	VERMILION	DARK RED	LIGHT GERANIUM RED	RED	GERANIUM LAKE	FLAME RED	RED	CARMINE RED	POMPEIAN RED	RED	FLESH PINK	FLESH	LIGHT FLESH TINT	LIGHT FLESH
BEROL	Verithin Crayon Pencils	●																				
	Colour Craft/Prismacolor (US) Pencils	●									●											
CARAN D'ACHE	Prismalo I Thin Watercolour Pencils					●							●									
	Prismalo II Thick Watercolour Pencils					●							●									
	Neocolor II Aquarelle Crayons					●							●									
CONTE	Aquarelle Pencils																●					
	Pastel Pencils			●							●								●			
	Coloured Drawing Pencils																					
EBERHARD FABER	Design Crayon Pencils				●	●															●	
FABER-CASTELL	Polychromos Coloured Pencils						●			●											●	
	Dürer Water-Soluble Pencils				●					●												
	Dürer Coloured Leads									●												
	Coloured Drawing Pencils																					
KOH-I-NOOR HARDTMUTH	Mona Lisa Watercolour Crayons							●														
	Thin-lead Colour Pencils							●														
	Mona Lisa Crayon Pencils							●														
	Mona Lisa Watercolour Pencils							●														
	Coloured Drawing Pencils																					
	Coloured Leads							●														
	Coloured Drawing Leads																					
REXEL CUMBERLAND	Derwent Watercolour Pencils																					
	Derwent Colourthin Pencils																	●				
	Derwent Studio Pencils											●						●				
	Derwent Artists' Pencils											●						●				
ROWNEY	Victoria Colour Pencils		●			●																
SCHWAN-STABILO	Carb-Othello Pencils				●											●				●		
	Stabilotone Watercolour Pencils								●					●								
	Thin-lead Pencils				●										●							
STAEDTLER	Karat Watercolour Pencils	●															●					
	Mars Lumochrom Pencils																●					
	Noris Unipoint Pencils	●																				

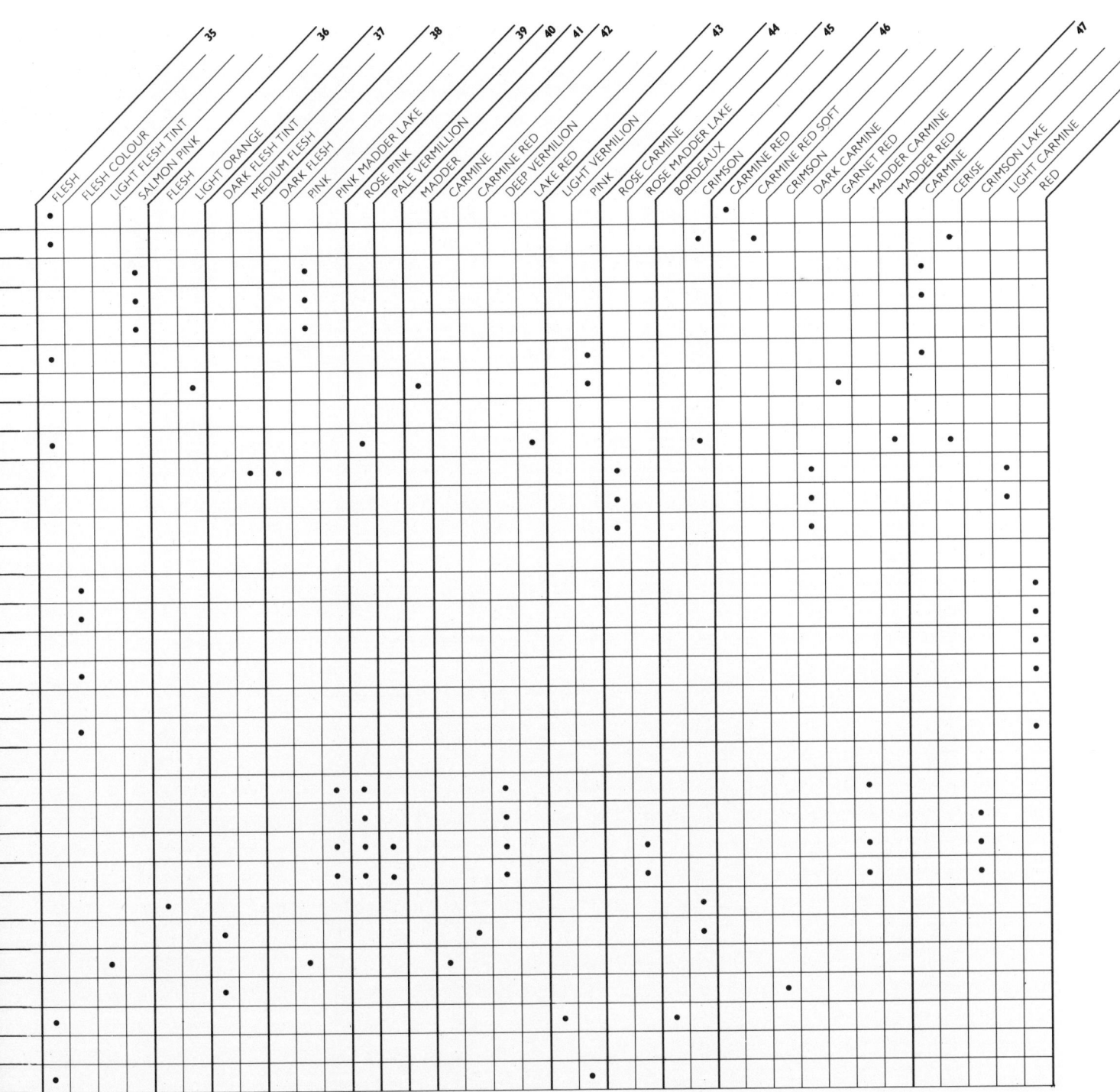

MANUFACTURER	RANGE	PINK	ROSE MADDER LAKE	PURPLE	RUBY COLOURED	48 WINE RED	49 PURPLE	RED VIOLET	CYCLAMEN	50 MAGENTA	ROSE	51 LILAC	ROSE MADDER	CYCLAMEN	52 PURPLE	ROSE	53 HELIOTROPE	VIOLET	MAGENTA	54 CYCLAMEN	LAVENDER	55 MAGENTA	56
BEROL	Verithin Crayon Pencils					•			•											•			
	Colour Craft/Prismacolor (US) Pencils																						
CARAN D'ACHE	Prismalo I Thin Watercolour Pencils												•										
	Prismalo II Thick Watercolour Pencils												•										
	Neocolor II Aquarelle Crayons												•										
CONTE	Aquarelle Pencils							•															
	Pastel Pencils											•											
	Coloured Drawing Pencils																						
EBERHARD FABER	Design Crayon Pencils																						
FABER-CASTELL	Polychromos Coloured Pencils	•		•																•			
	Dürer Water-Soluble Pencils																						
	Dürer Coloured Leads																						
	Coloured Drawing Pencils																						
KOH-I-NOOR HARDTMUTH	Mona Lisa Watercolour Crayons		•																				
	Thin-lead Colour Pencils		•																•				
	Mona Lisa Crayon Pencils		•																•				
	Mona Lisa Watercolour Pencils		•																•				
	Coloured Drawing Pencils																						
	Coloured Leads		•																•				
	Coloured Drawing Leads																						
REXEL CUMBERLAND	Derwent Watercolour Pencils																	•					
	Derwent Colourthin Pencils																						
	Derwent Studio Pencils																	•					
	Derwent Artists' Pencils																	•					
ROWNEY	Victoria Colour Pencils																•						
SCHWAN-STABILO	Carb-Othello Pencils		•		•					•			•										
	Stabilotone Watercolour Pencils									•						•							
	Thin-lead Pencils	•														•							
STAEDTLER	Karat Watercolour Pencils							•												•			
	Mars Lumochrom Pencils			•																			
	Noris Unipoint Pencils							•															

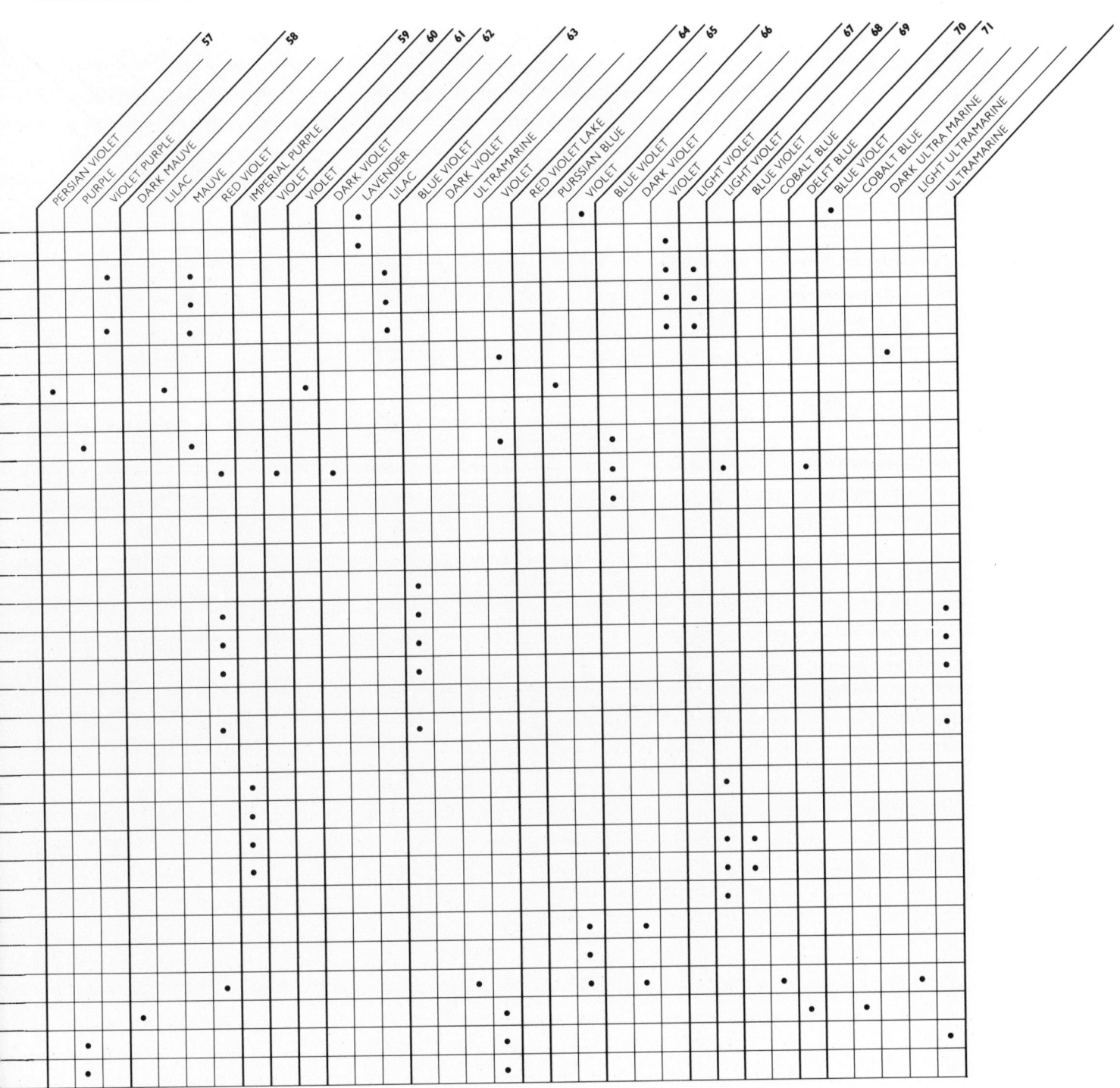

MANUFACTURER	RANGE	DARK ULTRA MARINE	DEEP COBALT	ULTRAMARINE	ULTRAMARINE BLUE	DELFT BLUE	PARIS BLUE	ULTRA BLUE	ULTRAMARINE	CYAN	LIGHT COBALT BLUE	ULTRAMARINE	PALE ULTRAMARINE	SKY BLUE	SMALT BLUE	BLUE	COBALT	DARK BLUE	ULTRAMARINE	ULTRAMARINE BLUE	VICTORIA BLUE	LAVENDER	TRUE BLUE
BEROL	Verithin Crayon Pencils																	•					
	Colour Craft/Prismacolor (US) Pencils					•																	
CARAN D'ACHE	Prismalo I Thin Watercolour Pencils		•												•						•		
	Prismalo II Thick Watercolour Pencils		•												•						•		
	Neocolor II Aquarelle Crayons		•												•								
CONTE	Aquarelle Pencils																						
	Pastel Pencils						•							•									
	Coloured Drawing Pencils																						
EBERHARD FABER	Design Crayon Pencils			•															•				
FABER-CASTELL	Polychromos Coloured Pencils	•			•					•		•									•		
	Dürer Water-Soluble Pencils									•											•		
	Dürer Coloured Leads									•											•		
	Coloured Drawing Pencils																						
KOH-I-NOOR HARDTMUTH	Mona Lisa Watercolour Crayons																						
	Thin-lead Colour Pencils																						
	Mona Lisa Crayon Pencils																						
	Mona Lisa Watercolour Pencils																						
	Coloured Drawing Pencils																						
	Coloured Leads																						
	Coloured Drawing Leads																						
REXEL CUMBERLAND	Derwent Watercolour Pencils			•						•													
	Derwent Colourthin Pencils									•													
	Derwent Studio Pencils			•						•			•										
	Derwent Artists' Pencils			•						•			•										
ROWNEY	Victoria Colour Pencils																						
SCHWAN-STABILO	Carb-Othello Pencils		•								•												
	Stabilotone Watercolour Pencils		•																				
	Thin-lead Pencils							•										•					
STAEDTLER	Karat Watercolour Pencils							•							•								
	Mars Lumochrom Pencils														•								
	Noris Unipoint Pencils																			•			

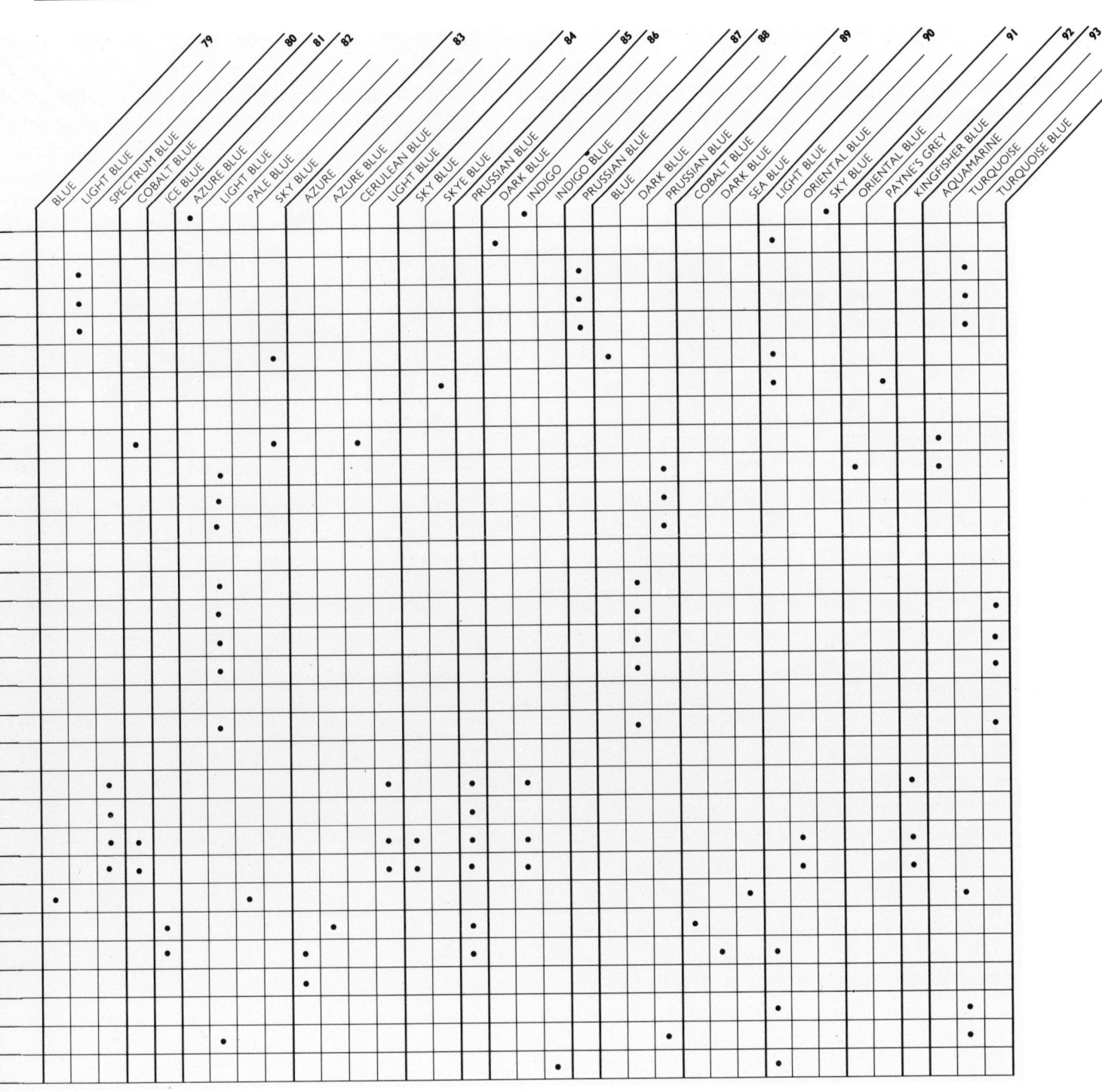

MANUFACTURER	RANGE	LIGHT AQUAMARINE	SEA GREEN	TURQUOISE BLUE	TURQUOISE GREEN	GREEN BLUE	94 JADE GREEN	PRUSSIAN GREEN	95 BLUISH GREEN	96 TURQUOISE BLUE	SEA GREEN	97 TURQUOISE GREEN	98 EMERALD GREEN	PARIS GREEN	99 GREY GREEN	JUNIPER GREEN	100 EARTH GREEN	JUNIPER GREEN	101 DARK GREEN	GREEN	102 NIGHT GREEN	103 DARK GREEN	104 GRASS GREEN
BEROL	Verithin Crayon Pencils	•																•			•		
	Colour Craft/Prismacolor (US) Pencils																			•			
CARAN D'ACHE	Prismalo I Thin Watercolour Pencils							•												•			
	Prismalo II Thick Watercolour Pencils							•												•			
	Neocolor II Aquarelle Crayons							•												•			
CONTE	Aquarelle Pencils											•											
	Pastel Pencils				•		•					•											
	Coloured Drawing Pencils																						
EBERHARD FABER	Design Crayon Pencils	•											•										
FABER-CASTELL	Polychromos Coloured Pencils								•				•			•			•				
	Dürer Water-Soluble Pencils																		•				
	Dürer Coloured Leads																		•				
	Coloured Drawing Pencils																						
KOH-I-NOOR HARDTMUTH	Mona Lisa Watercolour Crayons																						
	Thin-lead Colour Pencils																						
	Mona Lisa Crayon Pencils																						
	Mona Lisa Watercolour Pencils																						
	Coloured Drawing Pencils																						
	Coloured Leads																						
	Coloured Drawing Leads																						
REXEL CUMBERLAND	Derwent Watercolour Pencils		•			•																	
	Derwent Colourthin Pencils																						
	Derwent Studio Pencils		•	•		•								•									
	Derwent Artists' Pencils		•	•		•								•									
ROWNEY	Victoria Colour Pencils																						
SCHWAN-STABILO	Carb-Othello Pencils								•	•					•		•						
	Stabilotone Watercolour Pencils								•	•					•		•						
	Thin-lead Pencils								•	•													
STAEDTLER	Karat Watercolour Pencils																						
	Mars Lumochrom Pencils																						
	Noris Unipoint Pencils																						

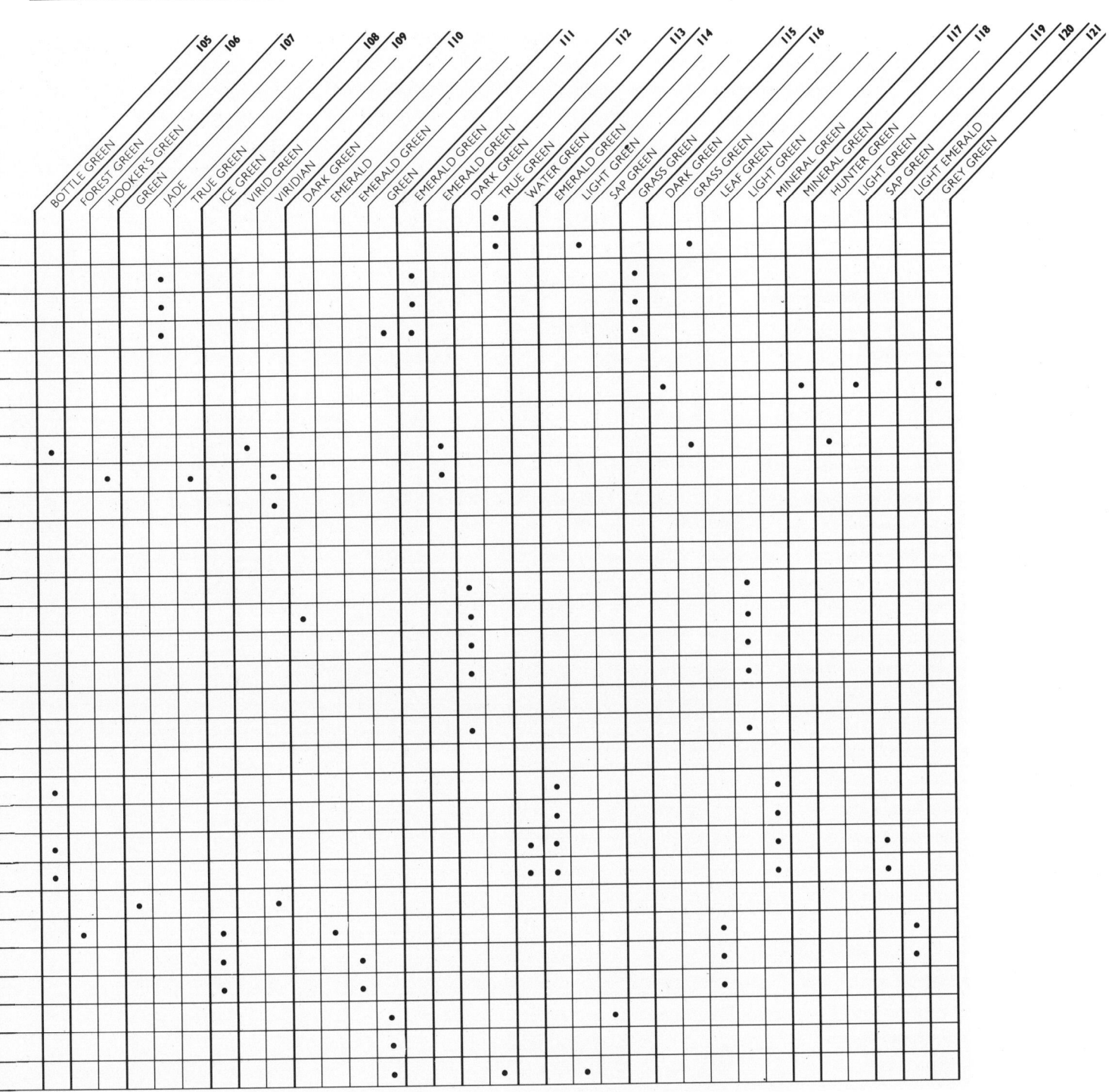

MANUFACTURER	RANGE	122 LIGHT GREEN	GRASS GREEN	123 LIGHT GREEN	PEA GREEN	YELLOW GREEN	LIGHT GREEN	WILLOW GREEN	124 LIME	APPLE GREEN	EVE GREEN	125 MAY GREEN	PALE GREEN	126 SAINT-MICHAEL GREEN	YELLOW GREEN	LIGHT GREEN	MEADOW GREEN	MOSS GREEN	127 SAP GREEN	LIGHT OLIVE	128 CEDAR GREEN	129/130 OLIVE GREEN
BEROL	Verithin Crayon Pencils	•																				
	Colour Craft/Prismacolor (US) Pencils			•																		
CARAN D'ACHE	Prismalo I Thin Watercolour Pencils				•		•												•			
	Prismalo II Thick Watercolour Pencils				•		•												•			
	Neocolor II Aquarelle Crayons				•		•												•			
CONTE	Aquarelle Pencils												•									
	Pastel Pencils						•						•								•	
	Coloured Drawing Pencils																					
EBERHARD FABER	Design Crayon Pencils									•												
FABER-CASTELL	Polychromos Coloured Pencils					•		•									•	•		•		
	Dürer Water-Soluble Pencils							•									•	•				
	Dürer Coloured Leads							•									•	•				
	Coloured Drawing Pencils																					
KOH-I-NOOR HARDTMUTH	Mona Lisa Watercolour Crayons																					
	Thin-lead Colour Pencils													•								
	Mona Lisa Crayon Pencils													•								
	Mona Lisa Watercolour Pencils													•								
	Coloured Drawing Pencils																					
	Coloured Leads													•								
	Coloured Drawing Leads																					
REXEL CUMBERLAND	Derwent Watercolour Pencils									•												
	Derwent Colourthin Pencils	•																				
	Derwent Studio Pencils	•								•												
	Derwent Artists' Pencils	•								•												
ROWNEY	Victoria Colour Pencils										•											
SCHWAN-STABILO	Carb-Othello Pencils																•	•				
	Stabilotone Watercolour Pencils														•							
	Thin-lead Pencils															•						
STAEDTLER	Karat Watercolour Pencils						•													•		
	Mars Lumochrom Pencils		•																			
	Noris Unipoint Pencils	•																				

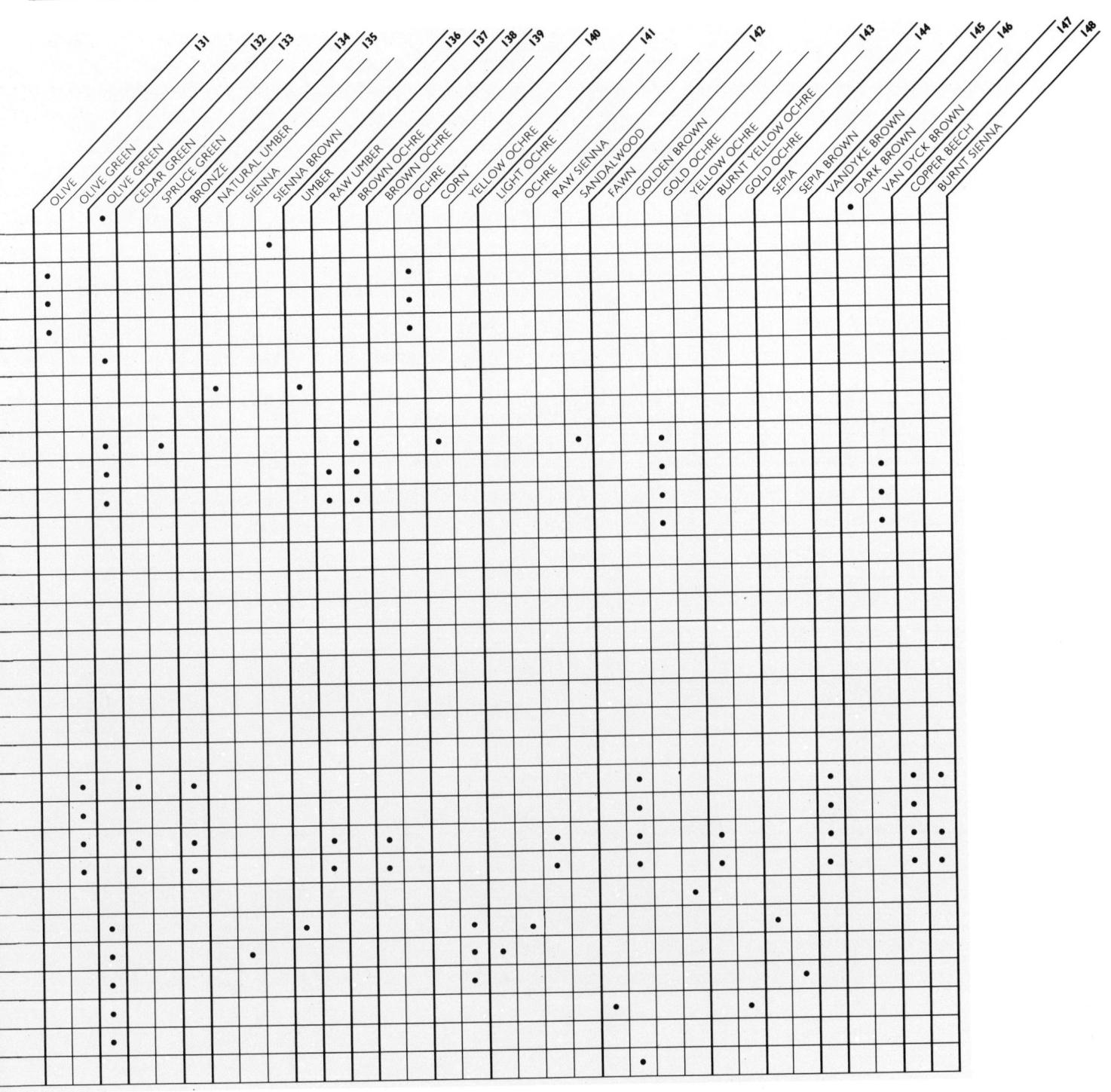

Reference numbers across the top: 149, 150, 151, 152, 153, 154, 155, 156, 157

MANUFACTURER	RANGE	YELLOW OCHRE	BURNT OCHRE	DARK OCHRE	GOLDEN BROWN	OCHRE	YELLOW OCHRE (149)	BISTRE (150)	BROWN	VANDYKE BROWN	BISTRE	LIGHT BROWN (151)	VENETIAN RED	CINNAMON (152)	TERRACOTTA	BROWN	DARK BROWN (153)	ENGLISH RED (154)	TUSCAN RED (155)	INDIAN RED (156)	ORANGE OCHRE	RED EARTH (157)
BEROL	Verithin Crayon Pencils			•										•						•		
	Colour Craft/Prismacolor (US) Pencils										•											
CARAN D'ACHE	Prismalo I Thin Watercolour Pencils							•														
	Prismalo II Thick Watercolour Pencils							•														
	Neocolor II Aquarelle Crayons							•														
CONTE	Aquarelle Pencils	•					•															
	Pastel Pencils	•								•												
	Coloured Drawing Pencils																					
EBERHARD FABER	Design Crayon Pencils													•								
FABER-CASTELL	Polychromos Coloured Pencils		•										•									
	Dürer Water-Soluble Pencils		•																			
	Dürer Coloured Leads		•																			
	Coloured Drawing Pencils																					
KOH-I-NOOR HARDTMUTH	Mona Lisa Watercolour Crayons					•																
	Thin-lead Colour Pencils					•																
	Mona Lisa Crayon Pencils																					
	Mona Lisa Watercolour Pencils																					
	Coloured Drawing Pencils																					
	Coloured Leads					•																
	Coloured Drawing Leads																					
REXEL CUMBERLAND	Derwent Watercolour Pencils																					
	Derwent Colourthin Pencils																					
	Derwent Studio Pencils											•										
	Derwent Artists' Pencils											•										
ROWNEY	Victoria Colour Pencils																					
SCHWAN-STABILO	Carb-Othello Pencils		•						•									•		•		
	Stabilotone Watercolour Pencils		•						•								•					
	Thin-lead Pencils								•											•		
STAEDTLER	Karat Watercolour Pencils																					
	Mars Lumochrom Pencils			•											•							
	Noris Unipoint Pencils				•								•									

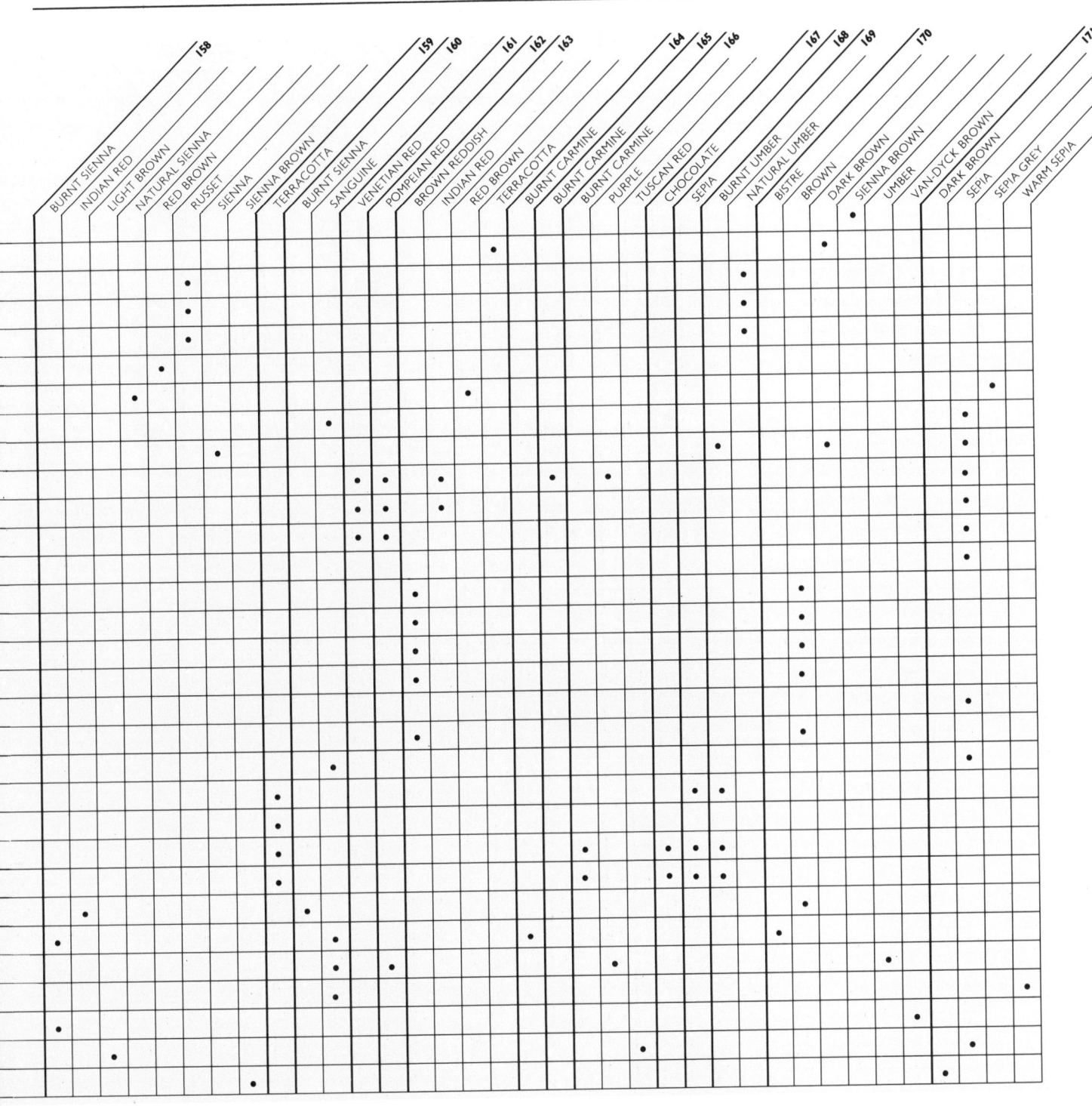

MANUFACTURER	RANGE	DARK GREY	DEEP WARM GREY	BLACK	IVORY BLACK	DEEP COLD GREY	BLUE GREY	SLATE GREY	COLD DEEP GREY	DARK GREY	GREY	LIGHT GREY	MEDIUM COLD GREY	COLD MEDIUM GREY	GREY	COLD LIGHT GREY	LIGHT COLD GREY	SILVER GREY	DARK GREY	LIGHT GREY	PALE COLD GREY
								172		173	174	175	176				177		178		179
BEROL	Verithin Crayon Pencils		●																		
	Colour Craft/Prismacolor (US) Pencils		●																		
CARAN D'ACHE	Prismalo I Thin Watercolour Pencils		●										●								
	Prismalo II Thick Watercolour Pencils		●										●								
	Neocolor II Aquarelle Crayons		●										●								
CONTE	Aquarelle Pencils		●																		
	Pastel Pencils		●																●		
	Coloured Drawing Pencils		●																		
EBERHARD FABER	Design Crayon Pencils		●				●	●					●		●						
FABER-CASTELL	Polychromos Coloured Pencils	●	●														●				
	Dürer Water-Soluble Pencils		●						●												
	Dürer Coloured Leads		●																		
	Coloured Drawing Pencils		●																		
KOH-I-NOOR HARDTMUTH	Mona Lisa Watercolour Crayons		●																		
	Thin-lead Colour Pencils		●																		
	Mona Lisa Crayon Pencils		●																		
	Mona Lisa Watercolour Pencils		●																		
	Coloured Drawing Pencils			●																	
	Coloured Leads		●																		
	Coloured Drawing Leads			●																	
REXEL CUMBERLAND	Derwent Watercolour Pencils				●																
	Derwent Colourthin Pencils			●	●																
	Derwent Studio Pencils			●	●																
	Derwent Artists' Pencils			●	●																
ROWNEY	Victoria Colour Pencils		●																		
SCHWAN-STABILO	Carb-Othello Pencils	●			●							●			●				●		
	Stabilotone Watercolour Pencils	●	●		●							●			●				●		
	Thin-lead Pencils		●													●	●				
STAEDTLER	Karat Watercolour Pencils		●								●										
	Mars Lumochrom Pencils		●							●											
	Noris Unipoint Pencils		●																		

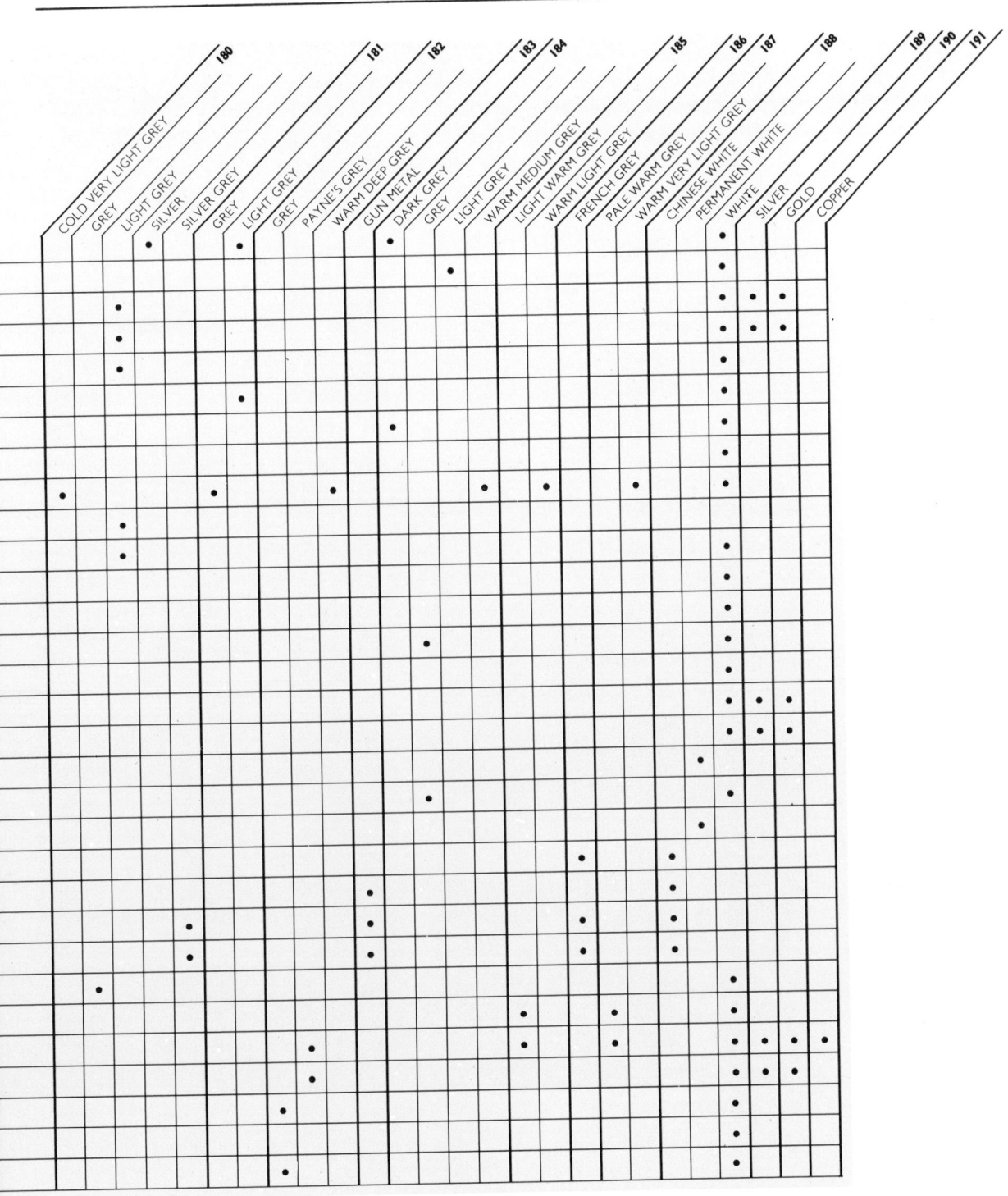

PAPER SIZES

The 'A' series system of sizing paper is calculated so that each size is made by dividing the size immediately above into two equal parts. A0 is the basic size and is one square metre in area. This system has now been officially adopted in more than 25 countries, and it is probable that this system will gradually replace the wide range of paper sizes used in Great Britain and the US.

The last measurement given for any paper size follows the direction of the grain.

BRITISH PAPER SIZES

	in	mm
Foolscap	17×13.5	432×343
Double Foolscap	27×17	686×432
Crown	20×15	508×381
Double Crown	30×20	762×508
Quad Crown	40×30	1016×762
Double Quad Crown	60×40	1524×1016
Post	19.25×15.5	489×394
Double Post	31.5×19.5	800×495
Double Large Post	33×21	838×533
Sheet and ½ Post	23.5×19.5	597×495
Demy	22.5×17.5	572×445
Double Demy	35×22.5	889×572
Quad Demy	45×35	1143×889
Music Demy	20×15.5	508×394
Medium	23×18	584×457
Royal	25×20	635×508
Super Royal	27.5×20.5	699×521
Elephant	28×23	711×584
Imperial	30×22	762×559

AMERICAN PAPER SIZES

in	mm
17×22	431.8×558.8
17×28	431.8×711.2
19×24	482.6×609.6
22×24	558.8×609.6
24×38	609.6×965.2
25×38	635×965.2
26×29	660.4×736.6
28×34	711.2×863.6
28×42	711.2×1066.8
28×44	711.2×1117.6
29×52	736.6×1320.8
32×44	812.8×1117.6
34×44	863.6×1117.6
35×45	889×1143
36×48	914.4×1219.2
38×50	965.2×1270
41×54	1041.4×1371.6

ISO 'A' SERIES

	in	mm
A0	33.11×46.81	841×1189
A1	23.39×33.11	594×841
A2	16.54×23.39	420×594
A3	11.69×16.54	297×420
A4	8.27×11.69	210×297
A5	5.83×8.27	148×210
A6	4.13×5.83	105×148
A7	2.91×4.13	74×105
A8	2.05×2.91	52×74
A9	1.46×2.05	37×52
A10	1.02×1.46	26×37

CONVERSION TABLES

IMPERIAL/METRIC

in	cm
1	2.54
2	5.08
3	7.62
4	10.16
5	12.70
6	15.24
7	17.78
8	20.32
9	22.86
10	25.40
12 (1ft)	30.48
20	50.80
30	76.20
36 (1yd)	91.44
40	101.60
50	127.00
60	152.40
70	177.80
80	203.20
90	228.60
100	254.00

METRIC/IMPERIAL

cm	in
1	0.394
2	0.787
3	1.181
4	1.575
5	1.969
6	2.362
7	2.756
8	3.150
9	3.543
10	3.937
20	7.874
30	11.811
40	15.748
50	19.685
60	23.622
70	27.559
80	31.496
90	35.433
100 (1m)	39.370

ADDRESSES OF MANUFACTURERS AND DISTRIBUTORS

ABLESCOT MARCHANT
Unit 10
Rangemor Road
Rangemor Industrial Area
London N15 4NG
UK

ADIT
Via Segrino 8
20098 Sesto Ulteriano
Milan
ITALY

ALVIN (General)
PO Box 188
Windsor
CT 06095
US

ANCO WOOD SPECIALTIES INC
71-08 80th Street
Glendale
NY 11385
US

APT
Unit 6
Blackwell Industrial Estate
Lanrick Road
London E14
UK

ARCHES
see **PAPETERIE ARJOMARI PRIOUX**

ARTBIN
see **FLAMBEAU PRODUCTS**

ATLANTIS PAPER CO LTD
Gulliver's Wharf
105 Wapping Lane
London E1 9RW
UK

B&J INDUSTRIES INC
23961 Craftsman Road
Calabasas
CA 91302
US

BARCHAM GREEN & CO LTD
Hayle Mill
Maidstone
Kent ME15 6XQ
UK

BEMBOKA
see **J & R WALKER**

BEMISS-JASON
1625 Lemoine Avenue
Fort Lee
NJ 07024
US

BEROL LTD (UK)
Oldmedow Road
King's Lynn
Norfolk PE30 4JR
UK

BEROL USA
Eagle Road
Danbury
CT 06810
US

BIENFANG
see **HUNT MANUFACTURING CO**

BINNEY & SMITH INC (Liquitex)
1100 Church Lane
PO Box 431
Easton
PA 18042
US

BLAIR ART PRODUCTS INC
8282 Boyle Parkway
PO Box 286
Twinsburg
OH 44087
US

BLOCKX
Rue de Liège 39
Clavier 5291
BELGIUM

BLUNDELL HARLING
Regulus Works
Lynch Lane
Weymouth
Dorset DT4 9DW
UK

BOCOUR ARTIST COLORS INC
100 Fencl Lane
Hillside
IL 60162
US

R K BURT & CO LTD
57 Union Street
London SE1 1SD
UK

BURTON HOLT LTD
PO Box 3
Cranbrook
Kent TN17 2LR
UK

CALDER COLOURS LTD (Ocaldo)
Nottingham Road
Ashby-de-la-Zouch
Leics LE6 5DR
UK

CAL-WESTERN PAINTS INC
11748 Slanson Avenue
Santa Fe Springs
CA 90670
US

PAPETERIES DE CANSON ET MONTGOLFIER SA
BP 139
07104 Annany
FRANCE

CARAN D'ACHE SA
19 Chemin du Foron
Case Postale 169
1226 Thônex-Genève
SWITZERLAND

CARTIERE MILIANI FABRIANO
PO Box 82
60044 Fabriano
ITALY

CHARTWELL
Long Drive
Greenford
Middx UB6 8NX
UK

CLAESSENS PVDA
Molenstraat 47
B 8790 Waregem
BELGIUM

P H COATE & CO
Meare Green Court
Stoke St Gregory
Taunton
Somerset TA3 6HY
UK

COIT CALLIGRAPHICS INC
Old Mill Road
Box 209
Georgetown
CT 06829
US

COLUMBIA
Artists Supplies Division
Chatham
NY 12037
US

COMPTON MARBLING
Tisbury
Salisbury
Wilts SP3 6SG
UK

CONTE (US)
see **HUNT INTERNATIONAL CO INC**

CONTE (UK) LTD
Park Farm Industrial Estate
Park Farm Road
Folkstone
Kent CT19 5EY
UK

L CORNELISSEN & SON
22 Great Queen Street
Covent Garden
London WC2B 5BH
UK

WILLIAM COWLEY
Parchment & Vellum Works
97 Caldecote Street
Newport Pagnell
Buckinghamshire
UK

CRESCENT CARDBOARD CO
PO Box XD
100 West Willow Road
Wheeling
IL 60090
US

CRESTWOOD PAPER CO INC
315 Hudson Street
New York
NY 10013
US

CUMBERLAND
see **REXEL**

DAHLE (UK) LTD
37 Camford Way
Luton
Beds LU3 3AN
UK

DAHLE (USA)
6 Benson Road
Oxford
CT 06483
US

DALER-ROWNEY LTD
PO Box 10
Bracknell
Berks RG12 4ST
UK

DANACOLORS INC
1833 Egbert Avenue
San Francisco
CA 94124
US

DA VINCI
Gustav-Adolf-Strasse 33
8500 Nürnberg 70
WEST GERMANY

DEKA TEXTILFARBEN GMBH
Kapellen Strasse 18
8025 Unterhaching
WEST GERMANY

ALOIS K DIETHELM AG (Lascaux)
Lascaux Farbenfabrik
CH-8306 Brüttisellen
WEST GERMANY

DURO ART INDUSTRIES INC
1832 Juneway Terrace
Chicago
Il 60626
US

DUX GMBH
Postfach 1480
D8520 Erlangen
WEST GERMANY

EBERHARD FABER INC
Crestwood
Wilkes-Barre
PA 18773
US

C W EDDING (UK) LTD
North Orbital Trading Estate
St Albans
Herts AL1 1XQ
UK

C W EDDING & CO
Kornkamp 40
Ahrensburg 2070
WEST GERMANY

ESBE (Xavier de Langlais)
4/6 Impasse Milord
75018 Paris
FRANCE

ETS ROGER JULLIAN
70-74 Rue du Mal de Lattre
de Tassigny
94700 Maisons-Alfort
FRANCE

FABER-CASTELL CORPORATION
41 Dickerson Street
Newark
NJ 07107
US

FABER-CASTELL (UK) LTD
Crompton Road
Stevenage
Herts SG1 2EF
UK

FABRIANO AMERICA INC
PO Box 10210
Lansing
MI 48901
US

FALKINER FINE PAPERS LTD
4 Mart Street
London WC2E 9PA
UK

TESSA FANTONI
3 Franconia Road
London SW4 9NB
UK

FERRARIO BELLE ARTI
29 Via Marzocchi
40012 Calderara di Remo
ITALY

FISCO PRODUCTS LTD
Brook Road
Rayleigh
Essex SS6 7XD
UK

FLAMBEAU PRODUCTS (ArtBin)
PO Box 97
15981 Val-Plast Road
Middlefield
OH 44062
US

FREDRIX
see **TARA MATERIALS INC**

FRISK PRODUCTS LTD
4 Franthorne Way
Randlesdown Road
London SE6 3BT
UK

GAEBEL ENTERPRISES INC
100 Ball Street
PO Box 276
East Syracuse
NY 13057
US

GENERAL
see **ALVIN**

GILLETTE (UK) LTD
Great West Road
Isleworth
Middlesex
UK

GOLDEN ARTIST COLORS INC
Bell Road
Box 91
New Berlin
NY 13411
US

GOOD FLY CO
54-3 Tateh Road
Section 1
Taipei
TAIWAN

GRIFFIN MANUFACTURING CO INC (Grifhold)
PO Box 308
Webster
NY 14580
US

GRIFHOLD
see **GRIFFIN MANUFACTURING CO INC**

M GRUMBACHER INC
460 West 34th Street
New York
NY 10001
US

GUANGHWA CO LTD
7-9 Newport Place
London WC2 7JR
UK

GUARRO CASAS SA
Via Layetana 37
Barcelona 3
SPAIN

HABICO
Postfach 1161
8802 Bechhofen adH
WEST GERMANY

HAHNERMUHLE
Buttenpapierfabrik
Postfach 4
D 3354 Dassel
WEST GERMANY

HAMILTON BRUSHES
Bush House
Rosslyn Crescent
Harrow
Middlesex
UK

A S HANDOVER LTD
Angel Yard
Highgate High Street
London N6 5JU
UK

MICHAEL HARDING'S
ARTISTS MATERIALS
Unit B
114 High Street
Southborough
Tunbridge Wells
Kent
UK

HELIX INTERNATIONAL LTD
PO Box 15
Lye
Stourbridge
West Midlands
UK

ESMOND HELLERMAN LTD
Hellerman House
Harris Way
Windmill Road
Sunbury-on-Thames
Middx TW16 7EW
UK

HERGA
see SMITH ANDERSON & CO
LTD

HOLBEIN ART MATERIALS
INC
2-2-5 Ueshio
Minami-ku
Osaka-542
JAPAN

HOLLINGWORTH
see WIGGINS TEAPE PAPER
LTD

HUNT INTERNATIONAL CO
INC (Conté US)
1405 Locust Street
Philadelphia
PA 19102
US

HUNT MANUFACTURING
CO (Bienfang and Hunt
Speedball)
230 South Broad Street
Philadelphia
Penn 19102
US

HUNT SPEEDBALL
see HUNT
MANUFACTURING CO

INVERESK PAPER CO LTD
4575 Eastern Avenue
Cincinnati
OH 45236
US

ISABEY
12 Rue Léon-Jost
75017 Paris
FRANCE

ITALPLASTIC SPA
22077 Olgiate Comasco
Via Vitt. Emanuele 7
Como
ITALY

JAKAR INTERNATIONAL
LTD
Hillside House
2-6 Friern Park
London N12 9BX
UK

KAICUT
Kai-Cutlery Co Ltd
International Division
3-9-7 Iwamote-Cho
Chiyoda-ku
Tokyo 101
JAPAN

KDS HI
24 Matsuda-cho
Higashi-Kujo
Minami-ku
Kyoto 601
JAPAN

KEUFFEL & ESSER CO
900 Lanidex Plaza
Parsippany
NJ 07054
US

KIU FONG ENTERPRISE CO
LTD
PO Box 3219
Taipei
TAIWAN

KOH-I-HOOR HARDTMUTH
1091 Vienna
Liechtensteinstrasse 155
AUSTRIA

KOH-I-NOOR
RAPIDOGRAPH INC (Pelikan)
100 North Street
Bloomsbury
NJ 08804
US

KUM-ONIT
A Klebes GmbH & Co KG
Essenbacher Strasse 2
PO Box 2160
D 8520 Erlangen
WEST GERMANY

LAMBERTYE
see J M PAILLARD

LANGFORD & HILL
10 Warwick Street
London W1R 6LS
UK

XAVIER DE LANGLAIS
see ESBE

LANGNICKEL
229 West 28th Street
New York
NY 10001
US

LASCAUX
see ALOIS K DIETHELM AG

T N LAWRENCE
2-4 Bleeding Heart Yard
Greville Street
Hatton Garden
London EC1N 8SL
UK

LEFRANC & BOURGEOIS
Zone Industrielle Nord
BP337
72007 Le Mans Cedex
FRANCE

LECHERTIER BARBE
see E PLOTON LTD

LERCHE BÜROSTAHLWAREN
Postfach 18 01 64
5650 Solingen
WEST GREMANY

LION BRUSH WORKS LTD
Planet Place
Killingworth
Newcastle-upon-Tyne
NE12 0RZ
UK

LIQUITEX
see BINNEY & SMITH INC

L P BRUSH CO
32 Graystone Road
Whitstable
Kent
CT5 2JX
UK

A LUDWIG & SONS LTD
71 Parkway
Camden Town
London NW1 7QJ
UK

LUKAS
see DR FRIEDRICH
SCHOENFELD & CO

LUMA
see STEIG PRODUCTS

MAGIC COLOUR
see ROYAL SOVEREIGN

MAIMERI ARTISTS
MATERIALS LTD
Hartlebury Trading Estate
Hartlebury
Nr Kidderminster
Worcs DY10 4YB
UK

MARABU
Ermin Martz GmbH & Co
D-7146 Tamm
WEST GERMANY

MARCUS ART (AUSTRALIA)
PTY LTD
218 Hoddle Street
Abbotsford
Victoria 3067
AUSTRALIA

MARCUS ART PTY LTD
2654 South La Cienega
  Avenue
Los Angeles
CA 90034
US

MARTIN/F WEBER
COMPANY (Weber)
Wayne & Windrim Avenues
Philadelphia
PENN 19144
US

DR PH MARTINS
see SALIS INTERNATIONAL
INC

MARTOR — ARGENTAX
EH Beermann Kg
Katternberger Strasse 24A
100378
D 5650 Solingen 1
WEST GERMANY

MASTRI CARTAI EDITORI
Casella Postale 4
06074 Ellera Umbra
ITALY

MEAD PAPER
CORPORATION
PO Box 100812
Atlanta GA 30348
US

MICRON
2080 Caselle Lurani
Milano
ITALY

MITCHELL & MALIK LTD
Duchy Manor Mill
Hazzards Hill
Mere
Wilts BA12 6ER
UK

MOBIUS & RUPPERT
Wöhrmuhle 2
D-8520 Erlangen
WEST GERMANY

MYERS
PO Box 16
Oldbury
W Mids B68 8HF
UK

NIPPON TRANSFER PAPER
CO LTD
3-29 Nakano 4-chome
Higashisumiyoshi-ku
Osaka 546
JAPAN

ROBAN NOAKES
Space Studios
16 Belsham Street
London E9
UK

OCALDO
see CALDER COLOURS LTD

OLFA CORPORATION
Higashi Nakamota 2-11-8
Higashinari-ku
Osaka 537
JAPAN

OLFA PRODUCTS
CORPORATION
7 Woodland Avenue
Larchmont
NY 10538
US

ORAM & ROBINSON LTD
Cadmore Lane
Cheshunt
Waltham Cross
Herts EN8 9SG
UK

OSMIROID
see E S PERRY LTD

J M PAILLARD (Lambertye)
43 Rue Jean Corroyer
60250 Mouy
FRANCE

PAPETERIES ARJOMARI
PRIOUX (Arches)
3 Rue du Pont de Lodi
BP 2306
75261 Paris Cedex 06
FRANCE

PARAGON RAZOR CO LTD
Little London Road
Norton Hammer
Sheffield 8
UK

PDQ ARTISTS OIL PAINTS
6059 Larchmont Ct
San José
CA 95123
US

PEBEO
St-Marcel BP 12
13367 Marseille Cedex 11
FRANCE

PEBEO OF AMERICA INC
PO Box 373
Williston
VT 05495
US

PELIKAN (US)
see KOH-I-NOOR
RAPIDOGRAPH

PELIKAN (UK)
see G H SMITH & PARTNERS
LTD

PENOL
A/S Chr Olsen
Emdempvej 28A
2100 Kobenhaun ø
Copenhagen
DENMARK

PENNELLI CINGHIALE
46015 Cicognaria
Mantova
ITALY

PENTEL OF AMERICA
2715 Columbia Street
Torrance
CA 90503
US

E S PERRY LTD (Osmiroid)
Gosport
Hants PO13 0AL
UK

PLASTIFORM INC
3341 Towerwood
Suite 201
Dallas
TX 75234
US

PLATIGNUM PLC
Platignum House
Six Hills Way
Stevenage
Herts SG1 2AY
UK

PLATIGNUM PEN OF
AMERICA
3210 Bettline Road
Suite 114
Dallas
TX 75234
US

E PLOTON LTD (Lechertier
Barbe)
273 Archway Road
London N6 5AA
UK

PHILIP POOLE & CO LTD
182 Drury Lane
London WC2B 5QL
UK

PREMIER BRUSH CO
3 Eastbourne Avenue
Acton
London W3 6JR
UK

PRO ARTE
Wychwood
Sutton in Craven
West Yorkshire
UK

PROFESSIONAL ARTS
GROUP/3M (Scotch)
3M House
PO Box I
Bracknell
Berks BG12 IJU
UK

QUILLCRAFT
61 Bayford Road
Littlehampton
BN17 5NW
UK

RABONE CHESTERMAN LTD
Bow Works
Pomona Street
Sheffield S11 8JP
UK

RAPHAEL
Souer Zi
Rue Lamarck
2203 Saint-Brienc
FRANCE

REEVES
PO Box 91
Wealdstone
Harrow
Middx HA3 5RH
UK

REMBRANDT
see ROYAL TALENS BV

REXEL LTD (Cumberland and
William Mitchell)
Gatehouse Road
Aylesbury
Buckinghamshire
UK

RICH ART COLOR CO INC
109 Graham Lane-Lodi
NJ 07644
US

RISING PAPER CO
Housatonic
MASS 01236
US

ROBERSON & CO LTD
77 Parkway
London NW1
UK

ROTRING (UK)
Building One
GEC Estate
East Lane
Wembley
Middx HA9 7PY
UK

GEORGE ROWNEY & CO
LTD
PO Box 10
Bracknell
Berks RG12 4ST
UK

ROYAL SOVEREIGN
GRAPHICS (Magic Colour)
Brittania House
100 Drayton Park
London N5 1NA
UK

RUSSELL & CHAPPLE LTD
23 Monmouth Street
London WC2H 9DE
UK

SALIS INTERNATIONAL INC
(Dr PH Martin's)
4093 North 28th Way
Hollywood
Florida 33020
US

SANFORD CORPORATION
Bellwood
IL 60104
US

H SCHMINCKE & CO
PO Box 3120
D-4006 Erkrath
WEST GERMANY

SCHOELLERSHAMMER
Schoeller Sohne GmbH &
Co KG
Postfach 147
D 5160 Duren
WEST GERMANY

DR FRIEDRICH
SCHOENFELD & CO (Lukas)
Postfach 7427
4000 Düsseldorf I
WEST GERMANY

A SCHUTZMANN KG
Carl-Benz Strasse 10-12
8031 Gilching bei München
WEST GERMANY

SCHWAN-STABILO
Schwanhäusser GmbH & Co
8500 Nürberg
WEST GERMANY

SCHWAN-STABILO (US)
see SWAN PENCIL CO INC

SCOLAQUIP INDUSTRIES
LTD (Scolart)
Holmes Chapel
Cheshire CW4 8AG
UK

SCOTCH
see PROFESSIONAL ARTS
GROUP/3M

SELLOTAPE PRODUCTS
Elstree Way
Boreham Wood
Herts WD6 1RU
UK

SENNELIER
Rue du Moulin-A-Cailloux
Orly
Senia 408
94567 Rungis Cedex
FRANCE

SHAEFFER
see TEXTRON

SHIVA INC
4320 West 190th Street
Torrance
CA 90509
US

SIMON ART
see D & J SIMONS & SONS
LTD

D & J SIMONS & SONS LTD
(Simonart)
124-128 Hackney Road
London E2 7QL
UK

ROBERT SIMMONS INC
45 West 18th Street
New York
NY 10011
US

SMITH ANDERSON & CO
LTD (Herga)
Fettykil Mill
Leslie
Fyfe
SCOTLAND

G H SMITH & PARTNERS
(Pelikan)
Berechurch Road
Colchester
CO2 7QH
UK

SPECTRUM OIL COLOURS
259 Queens Road
South Wimbledon
London SW19 8NY
UK

STAEDTLER (US) INC
PO Box 787
Chatsworth
CA 91311
US

STAEDTLER (UK) LTD
Ponyclun
Mid Glamorgan
CF7 8YJ
UK

STANLEY TOOL CO
Woodside Lane
Sheffield S3 9PV
UK

STEIG PRODUCTS (Luma)
Lakewood
NJ 08701
US

J P STEPHENSON
33 Station Road
Bawtry
S Yorks DN10 6PU
UK

STRATHMORE PAPER CO
Westfield
MASS 01085
US

SWAN PENCIL CO INC
(Schwan-Stabilo)
221 Park Avenue South
New York
NY 10003
US

SWANN-MORTON LTD
Penn Works
Owlerton Green
Sheffield 6
UK

ROYAL TALENS BV
(Rembrandt)
PO Box 4
7300 AA Apeldoorn
HOLLAND

TESTRITE INSTRUMENT CO
INC
135 Monroe Street
Newark
NJ 07105
US

TARA MATERIALS INC
(Fredrix)
111 Fredrix Alley
Lawrenceville
GA 30246
US

TITAN INDUSTRIES
Av. Bogatell 29-47
Barcelona 5
SPAIN

TUMBA BRUK AB
S-147 00 Tumba
Stockholm
SWEDEN

TWO RIVERS PAPER CO
Rosebank Mill
Stubbins
Nr Bury
Lancashire
UK

TEXTRON (Shaeffer)
Marylands Avenue
Hemel Hempstead
Herts HP2 7ER
UK

UCHIDA OF AMERICA
CORPORATION
69-34 51st Avenue
Woodside
NY 11377
US

F UCHIYAMA & CO LTD
No 188 1-Chome
Honmoku-Machi Nakaka
Yokohama
JAPAN

UNIQUE INSTRUMENTS LTD
Buckhurst Road
Telscombe Cliffs
New Haven BN9 7AH
UK

UTRECHT
MANUFACTURING
CORPORATION
33 35th Street
Brooklyn
NY 11232
US

PRODUCTOS VALLEJO
Vilanova I La Geltru
Barcelona
Apartado Postal 53
SPAIN

VAN GELDER
PO Box 210
7300 AE Apeldoorn
HOLLAND

J & R WALKER (Bemboka)
Bemboka Paper Mill
Bemboka NSW
AUSTRALIA

L WARD & CO (Whistler)
128 Fortune Green Road
London NW6 1DN
UK

WEBER
see MARTIN/F WEBER

WHATMAN LTD
Springfield Mill
Sandling Road
Maidstone ME14 2LE
UK

WHISTLER
see L WARD & CO

WIGGINS TEAPE PAPER LTD
(Hollingworth)
Gateway House
34 Marshgate Lane
Stratford
London E15 2NT
UK

WILKINSON SWORD
Liscartan House.
127 Sloane Street
London SW1X 9BA
UK

WINSOR & NEWTON
PO Box 91
Wealdstone
Harrow
Middx HA3 5QN
UK

WINSOR & NEWTON (US)
555 Winsor Drive
Secaucus
NJ 07094
US

X-ACTO
45-35 Van Dam Street
Long Island City
NY 11101
US

ZEBRA CO LTD
2-9 Higashi-gokencho
Shinjuku-ku
Tokyo 162
JAPAN

INDEX

Page numbers in *italic* refer to illustrations

CREDITS

All photographs were taken by Paul Forrester (except p.35, Clive Boden).
Artwork on pp.26-30 Mick Hill; pp.47-61 Andrew Popkiewicz.
Colour swatches on pp.74-79 painted by Ian Sidaway.